1986-1987: Introduction to Macroeconomics

Readings on Contemporary Issues

edited by

Peter D. McClelland
Cornell University

McGraw-Hill Book Company

New York   St. Louis   San Francisco   Auckland   Bogotá   Hamburg   Johannesburg   London
Madrid   Milan   Mexico   Montreal   New Delhi   Panama   Paris   São Paulo
Singapore   Sydney   Tokyo   Toronto

FOREWORD

To the student

When you signed up for a course entitled Macroeconomics, you probably had two expectations. The first was that you were about to study many of the problems featured in the national news media. Inflation, unemployment, federal deficits, the inadequacies of our present welfare system—these are but a few of the macroeconomic issues encountered almost daily as you read the newspaper or watch the evening news on television. Probably your second expectation, fostered by the same sources, was that your studies would help you to understand why economists have sharply differing opinions on how these problems should be attacked. If your course reading were confined to a textbook—any textbook—you would be in for a disappointment. These books invariably include little about contemporary problems, and even less about the national debate on how to solve them. The reasons are rather simple. Each author has his or her own opinion on the ideal solutions, and each text, not surprisingly, tends to emphasize that point of view. As for contemporary issues, no textbook that appears today (never mind last year) can possibly deal with them, because the lag between finished manuscript and appearance in the bookstore is usually twelve to eighteen months, or even longer.

This reader's main objective is to remedy these two defects. Assembled in early June, it attempts to give empirical flesh to those theoretical skeletons you will be learning about in lectures and from the textbook. It also emphasizes, wherever possible, different points of view on how to solve some of our most pressing macroeconomic problems. It cannot promise you a definitive resolution of those problems. But it should give you a sense of why they matter and why macroeconomic theory is relevant in attempting to solve them. The ultimate hope is that you will emerge from this reader and your course with a sense of how crucial these issues are to the future well-being of our nation and its citizens.

To the instructor

Teaching macroeconomics to undergraduates is a demanding assignment. The lecturer who strives to integrate textbook theory with national problems is constantly bedeviled by the speed with which the leading contemporary issues change—from unemployment to energy to inflation and then back to unemployment again, to mention but one of several recent sequences. Also in a constant state of flux are the mechanisms that dominate current analysis of these problems. The unabashed Keynesian approach tempered by a belief in the Phillips Curve has given way to such disparate topics as rational expectations, supply-side economics, and the merits of monetary targets. In the popular press, there is no shortage of commentary on both problems and associated causal mechanisms. The difficulty is that several dozen articles from different sources cannot be incorporated easily (or at all) into the reading list of a course in which enrollment may run to hundreds—at least not without creating pandemonium in the library. This book attempts to resolve this impasse. Readings were culled from a range of material in May, assembled in early June, and made available in bound form by mid-August. The result is viewed by both the editor and McGraw - Hill as part of an ongoing project. We update this volume annually, in terms of both topics covered and articles included. We hope that you will help us with that updating process. If you have any suggestions, I would appreciate hearing from you (Economics Department, Cornell University, Ithaca, N.Y. 14853). Such interaction with those who study and teach the subject will be a crucial ingredient if this annual reader is to satisfy the instructor while achieving that most important of objectives: fostering the student's interest in, and understanding of, contemporary American macroeconomic issues.

Peter D. McClelland

Ithaca, New York

INTRODUCTION TO MACROECONOMICS: READINGS ON CONTEMPORARY ISSUES—1986–1987 EDITION

1 2 3 4 5 6 7 8 9 0   SEMSEM   8 9 8 7 6

The editors were Paul V. Short and Linda A. Mittiga; the cover was designed by Caliber Design Planning, Inc.; the production supervisor was Diane Renda. Semline, Inc., was printer and binder.

Library of Congress Catalog Card Number: 86–061466

CONTENTS

Foreword

IV MONETARY AND FISCAL POLICY

V INSTITUTIONAL CHANGES IN MONEY AND BANKING

CHARTS

"Inflation, Disinflation, and the State of the Macroeconomy": Some Second Opinions

Herbert Stein

Economics is like medicine. If a patient receives a diagnosis on an important matter from any physician, he should seek a second opinion—even though he has a lot of confidence in the first doctor. So it is with advice about economics.

The 1986 Annual Report of the Council of Economic Advisers presents the diagnosis of the economy that matches the policy of the Reagan administration. This policy is, of course, well known and the subject of much controversy. The economic diagnosis that goes with the policy has, however, received less attention. My intention here is to present second opinions on some elements of that diagnosis. Presenting second opinions does not necessarily imply that the first opinions are wrong. It means only that economics, like medicine, is an uncertain science. The patient who receives a second opinion different from the first is aware of being in a difficult position. The patient must make his choice and in so doing becomes in a sense his own physician. But, of course, the patient was his own physician when he chose the first one, although he may have been less aware of that implication. The purpose of presenting second opinions about the economy is to inform the patients—ultimately the American people—of the choices before them.

This essay concentrates on chapter 1 of the economic report, entitled "Inflation, Disinflation, and the State of the Macroeconomy." It will deal with six major points that appear in the chapter.

Evaluation of the Recovery

The economic report is, by comparison with other statements of the administration, rather modest in describing the recovery that has occurred in the Reagan years. The report begins with the following sentences:

> The American economy is now in the fourth year of a robust expansion that has increased employment by more than nine million, sustained the greatest advance in business fixed investment of any comparable period in the postwar era, while inflation has remained at less than a third of the rate prevailing when the administration took office. Interest rates are at the lowest level of the decade. Long-term interest rates, in particular, have declined five percentage points from their peak in 1981, and home mortgage rates are down by seven percentage points.

The main problem with such a statement is selecting the relevant period of comparison. In the three years of the current expansion, from the fourth quarter of 1982 to the fourth quarter of 1985, real gross national product rose at

Herbert Stein is a Senior Fellow of the American Enterprise Institute.

an annual rate of 4.5 percent. This was exactly the average rate of increase in the first three years of the previous expansion of the postwar period.[1] By this measurement the current expansion has been about as robust as usual. But the 1981–1982 recession was unusually deep, and after an unusually deep recession we ordinarily have an unusually sharp rise. In the first three years of expansion after the 1974–1975 recession, real GNP rose at an annual rate of 5.5 percent. Perhaps we should say that the current recovery has been on the weak side, in view of the depth of the recession from which it began.

One way to evaluate the recent performance of the economy would be to look at a period longer than the recovery. We might, for example, look at the rise of economic activity in 1980–1985, the Reagan years. In

---

"The council seems to accept the common prejudice that high interest rates are a bad thing and low interest rates are a good thing. . . . This common prejudice is a relic of days when borrowers were many and poor and lenders were few and rich."

---

that period real GNP rose at an annual rate of 2.3 percent. This compares with an average annual rate of 3.4 percent for 1948–1980. It is also less than the 3.0 percent of the Carter years.

A similar statement can be made about employment. Employment did rise rapidly for three years from the bottom of the recession, but not as rapidly as from 1975 to 1978. In the whole Reagan period, employment rose by 1.5 percent per annum. This rate was just about the same as that in the postwar period (1948–1980) and distinctly less than that during the Carter administration.

This second opinion has to be considered:

> The recent performance of the economy with respect to output and employment does not appear extraordinary. In fact, it looks a little below par.

Some more persuasive ground for congratulations, and for believing that the administration has a superior brand of macroeconomic policy, may be found in the combination of output and inflation performance. One might say that the rise of output from 1980 to 1985, even though below our historical average, was good for a period in which the inflation rate was falling radically. But that takes us far from a simple declarative statement that there has been a robust recovery. It raises the questions of what would have been a reasonable expectation for output and

employment in an economy with a sharply declining inflation rate and whether the 1980–1985 performance was better or worse than the reasonable expectation. Some aspects of these questions will be taken up below in the discussion of monetary policy.

Certainly interest rates are at the lowest level of this decade, which means the lowest level of the Reagan administration. But they are higher than at any time before this decade since the Civil War. And in real terms, they are higher even than earlier in this decade or were when the report was written.

The council seems to accept the common prejudice that high interest rates are a bad thing and low interest rates are a good thing. At least they include the alleged decline of interest rates in the good news part of the report. This common prejudice is a relic of days when borrowers were many and poor and lenders were few and rich. That situation is much less true today, if it is still true at all. In any case, that prejudice is peculiar for a council that believes fervently in free markets and in the prices that such markets yield. Interest rates are prices determined in markets as free as any we know. There is no reason to be happier about low interest rates than about high ones.

My guess is that the council's concern with the lowness of interest rates is related to one of the dominant themes of this chapter—defensiveness about deficits. Critics of the administration's policy focus heavily on the alleged evils of deficits, including high interest rates. One defense against this charge is to point out that interest rates have declined. More will be said on this subject later.

Criticism of Monetary Policy

The council's discussion of monetary policy is paradoxical. The council believes that monetary policy is very important, and it has strong views of what good monetary policy is. It finds the monetary policy of the past five years to have been bad by its standards. Yet it finds the economic performance of the period to have been commendable on the whole.

Perhaps the reconciliation of these ideas is in the phrase "on the whole." The council believes that the disinflation of 1981–1982 was accompanied by an unnecessarily sharp recession, and it blames that recession mainly on monetary policy. The council's preferred monetary policy would have been a gradual reduction, beginning in 1981, in the rate of monetary growth, followed by stabilization of the rate of monetary growth at a low level. Instead monetary growth slowed sharply in 1981–1982, accelerated after mid-1982 until mid-1983, slowed again until late 1984, and then speeded up again. The monetary slowdown of 1981–1982 is held largely responsible for the depth of the recession.

Whether another, more gradual monetary policy would have decreased the inflation rate without so deep a recession is debatable. The basic question is revealed in the council's report:

> The extent of the economic disturbance associated with reducing inflation depends on the responsiveness of inflation expectations. . . . A disinflationary policy that assures the public of the government's commitment to controlling inflation and thereby fosters the adjustment of inflation expectations is therefore also likely to minimize the associated economic dislocation. (p. 35)

The question is which policy will best assure the public of the government's commitment. This question was much discussed by economists before the Reagan administration came into office. Some economists thought this assurance could be provided only by shock treatment—a short, deep cut in monetary growth intended to get the inflation down substantially and quickly. The willingness of the government to take such a step would show its seriousness of purpose and determination to risk the transitional consequences for employment. Also, the quick shock might get the disinflation over before political forces could gather to stop it. The main alternative policy was what was called at the time (1980) "committed gradualism." This would involve, as I said then, the following ingredients:

• a combination of measures that will be effective in reducing the inflation durably if there is general belief in the persistence of the measures

• cooperation between the president and the Federal Reserve

• a high degree of bipartisan support

• quantitative specification of intermediate-term goals and measures, so that deviation of the government from the program will be immediately visible

• rejection of any commitment about the unemployment rate

• rejection of measures that might seem to be substitutes for the steps necessary to stop inflation—specifically, "incomes policy" must be rejected.[2]

Economists were not certain which course would be most effective and disagreed in their estimates of the probabilities. The Reagan administration in 1981 chose gradualism. It did not, however, take the other steps that would constitute a commitment to gradualism. *Possibly*

their chosen course would have reduced the inflation with less recession than we had in 1982. But it is at least plausible that this gradualism, especially without more commitment than it had, would not have inspired confidence but would have been regarded as a replay of the failed gradualism of the 1970s. In that case we would have had an extended period of recession with little payoff in reduced inflation, and the policy might have been reversed before the goal was reached. In fact the policy, although possibly not premeditated, turned out to

"Evaluation of the Federal Reserve's policy of 1982–1985 is a puzzle from the standpoint of the council. The Federal Reserve did everything wrong, by the council's standards. Still the results do not look bad."

be a shock that reduced the inflation rate sharply by mid-1982, before political pressures to reflate became strong. The president supported the restrictive monetary policy or did not try to prevent it—as far as is publicly known. To say now that the administration's gradualist policy of 1981 would have yielded superior results is at least highly speculative.

Evaluation of the Federal Reserve's policy of 1982–1985 is a puzzle from the standpoint of the council. The Federal Reserve did everything wrong, by the council's standards. Still the results do not look bad. Several interpretations of this experience are possible:

• The results have not been bad yet, but they will be. Specifically, the big increase of the money supply of the past eighteen months will yet generate a surge of inflation.

• The presumption that finely tuned, discretionary monetary policy will generally yield inferior results to a policy of stable monetary growth is invalid—although it may possibly have been valid heretofore.

• The presumption is correct, but it refers to the average results over a very long period. It is not inconsistent with some period, even five years, of superior results from fine-tuning as a result of good luck or extraordinarily able management. The law that the odds against rolling five sevens in a row are 7775 to 1 are not inconsistent with the experience of having just rolled five sevens in a row.

Thus, instead of the unreservedly critical view of recent monetary policy taken in the council's report, a second opinion might say the following:

The period 1981 to 1985 was an extraordinarily

difficult one for monetary policy. The reduction of the inflation rate, which was a main object of policy, had an unpredictable effect on the demand for money. Changes in financial regulations and institutions also introduced great uncertainty into predictions of the demand for money. Following a flexible pragmatic policy, the Federal Reserve negotiated this difficult period with considerable success. This experience does not reject the earlier lesson that over a longer period a policy of stable monetary growth would be superior. It does, however, at least raise a question about that lesson.

Success in Promoting Investment

The promotion of investment is one of the main arenas in which the council finds success in the administration's program. This arena is, I believe, especially important for two reasons. First, the administration is a great champion of "pro-growth" policy, and stimulating investment is generally considered a prime method of promoting growth. Second, one of the main criticisms of the economic policy of the past five years is that the big deficits crowd out private investment and so depress growth. So the demonstration that investment has not been retarded but has actually increased by an unusual amount is key for defending the deficit policy.

As already quoted, the first sentence of the council's report says that the American economy has now "sustained the greatest advance in business fixed investment of any comparable period in the postwar era." In fact, as a table on page 39 of the report shows, not only gross business fixed investment but also total gross private domestic investment including residential fixed investment and inventory accumulation increased much faster in the first three years of the current expansion than in the first three years of the average postwar expansion.

Four qualifications must be noted about this picture:
• The 1982 trough was lower than that in the average of past recessions. In fact, the whole investment experience of the 1970s and 1980s was so erratic that finding a good base of reference is hard. Still, it is worth noting that between 1979 and 1985 real gross private investment rose by 2.1 percent per annum, whereas from 1948 to 1979 it rose by 3.3 percent per annum. Another way to look at this experience is to measure the behavior of investment from the previous peak of the economy to the quarter three years after the trough, which is where we were in the fourth quarter of 1985. On this basis, the rise of real total gross investment was less in the current cycle than in the average of the earlier postwar cycles. The rise in gross business fixed investment was, however, larger in this cycle than in the earlier ones.

• The rise in gross investment (domestic plus foreign) has been much less in this cycle than in the earlier cycles because foreign investment (the increase in assets abroad owned by Americans) has turned sharply negative during the current cycle. That is, the increase in total private assets owned by Americans has been much smaller in this cycle than in the earlier ones.

• The rise in net investment (gross investment, domestic and foreign, less allowances for depreciation) has also been less in this cycle than in earlier ones.

• In 1985 gross private domestic investment, net private domestic investment, and net private investment (domestic and foreign) were all below the ratios to GNP that they averaged in the postwar period before 1981. The ratio of gross private domestic investment to GNP was a little higher in 1985 than in 1972–1980, but the other ratios were lower.

One can debate whether gross investment is more important than net, or domestic investment more important than the sum of domestic plus foreign investment. But on the whole the investment performance does not seem to be a subject for congratulations but rather the reverse.

A recent ingenious editorial in the *Wall Street Journal* suggested that the prevailing emphasis on private investment as we conventionally measure it is wrong. It pointed out that some of what we call consumption is really investment and promotes growth or at least increases output. Personal expenditures for education are the leading example, but health expenditures might also qualify. Therefore, personal tax reductions that increase consumption may actually increase investment even though they have a negative effect on investment as usually defined, either because they increase the deficit or because they are balanced by an increase in business taxation.

Once this is said, however, it is difficult to avoid the next step, which is to say that some government expenditures are also investments. These expenditures include education; roads, bridges, and other infrastructures; health; and defense. The inclusion of defense may be a surprise; but if the country is not defended, growth may be abruptly terminated, no matter how much investment of the conventional kind has occurred.

We do not have good measures of all of these kinds of investment; especially we have no sensible way to add them together. Probably expenditure for investment as usually defined, plus education and public infrastructures, as a fraction of GNP has been low by postwar standards. Expenditures for health have been high, although their productivity is open to question. Defense expenditures have been higher than in most of the 1970s but lower than earlier in the postwar period.

A second opinion about investment might run like this:

By most measures the devotion of the national output to enhancing the future growth of income has not been large in recent years. But if the rebuilding of the national defenses was critical for survival, the change of policy in 1981 was absolutely vital to economic growth. Even in this case the question remains whether the rebuilding of the defenses could have been achieved without repressing other pro-growth investment. That is a question about deficits, expenditures, and taxes, to which we now turn.

Do Deficits Matter?

The council report treats deficits skittishly. It does not deny the possibility that deficits might be harmful but does not want to accept the idea that they have actually been harmful in the past five years. Thus the report says, "Evidence linking the fiscal deficit to interest rates, the value of the dollar, or even the trade balance is tenuous." It then explains why large *persistent* deficits are nevertheless a cause for concern, even though "the level of government spending should be the primary focus of policy." The reasons for concern it gives are these:
• Deficits may absorb saving and thereby adversely affect capital formation.
• Deficits may shift tax burdens into the future.
• Continuing deficits increase the interest cost burden.
• Persistent deficits contribute to the fear that the Federal Reserve will monetize the debt, thereby causing higher inflation and higher interest rates.

Such caution in interpreting the evidence and in appraising the consequences of possible developments is admirable with respect to most economic propositions, including propositions about deficits. But the policy question is not thereby avoided. The question is whether or not, recognizing our uncertainties, we should judge that the adverse consequences of the deficits is so large as to require corrective action. The judgment that seems implicit in the report is that the consequences of deficits are an additional reason for restraining government expenditures but not a sufficient reason for raising taxes.

The statement about the "tenuous" link between fiscal deficits on the one hand and interest rates, the value of the dollar, and the trade balance on the other is interesting. A plausible theory is that, other things being equal, a fiscal deficit makes interest rates, exchange rates, and the trade deficit higher. Empirical evidence prior to 1981 neither confirms nor denies this theory, either because the theory is wrong or because we have too few cases in which other things were equal. Since 1981 the economy has behaved as the theory predicts—there are large deficits, and there are high real interest rates, high exchange rates, and high trade deficits. The link may still be tenuous, but it is less tenuous than it was five years ago.

In any case, the link between fiscal deficits and interest rates and exchange rates is not what we are really interested in. We are interested in interest rates and exchange rates because of their effect on investment, domestic and

"This administration obviously does not believe that reducing federal expenditures and transferring them to private allocation would in general serve the constitutional purposes better. It does not believe that about defense expenditures, social security expenditures, or interest payments. Undoubtedly there are also other expenditures about which it does not believe that, but these three alone total 60 percent of federal expenditures."

foreign. But we can understand and observe the link between deficits and investment directly, without reference to interest rates and exchange rates. As the council explains, there is an accounting identity that says

Private Saving + Government Saving =
Domestic Investment + Net Foreign Investment

Government saving is the government surplus; a government deficit is negative government saving. Therefore, unless private saving increases equally, an increase in the government deficit must reduce the sum of domestic investment plus net foreign investment.

Gross private saving has remained at the 1970s level relative to GNP, above the level of the 1950s and 1960s. But gross private saving has not risen enough to offset the rise of the deficit. Thus, gross total saving—private plus government—has drifted down as a percentage of GNP. In 1985 it was lower than in any postwar years except 1953 and 1954, when we were experiencing the end of the Korean War and a recession. Net private saving is now significantly lower than in the 1950s, 1960s, or 1970s.

In 1981 some people hoped that the increase of the federal deficit would be offset by an increase of private saving so that the funds available for investment would not be reduced. That hope has not been realized. There was little reason to think that it would be.

A second opinion about the deficit might run like this:

The deficit has depressed private investment, domestic plus foreign, in the past five years. This is not necessarily a disaster. The United States is a rich country, and getting richer faster may not be our highest priority. This generation might say that the burden we are bearing for defending the country is enough of a sacrifice for our successors. Also, if people in the present generation want their children and grandchildren to have more income they can save more, which they have not been doing. A certain aspect of our current deficit position cannot go on forever. On reasonable assumptions the government cannot continuously run a deficit that exceeds its interest charges because, if it does, the government debt, the interest charges, and the deficit will all rise continuously relative to the GNP. This would lead in time to negative private investment and exhaustion of the capital stock. But, as I have said elsewhere, if something cannot go on forever it will stop. Stopping it now is not imperative.

What Caused the Deficit?

I usually walk home from my office in the afternoon. Last Friday it was raining, and my clothes were wet when I got home.

"Look at you," my wife said. "You're soaking wet. That's because you didn't use your umbrella."

"Whether it is better to spend $10 billion for nuclear submarines or $10 billion for private consumption is not a question of efficiency in anything but a metaphysical sense."

"But," I replied, "I didn't use my umbrella on Monday or Tuesday or Wednesday or Thursday. I didn't get wet then."

"Of course," she replied, with apparent logic. "It didn't rain on Monday or Tuesday or Wednesday or Thursday."

"So, you see," I declared triumphantly, "the reason I got wet was not that I failed to use my umbrella but because it rained."

I am reminded of this little soap opera by the discussion in the council's report and elsewhere of what caused the deficit. The report says that, of course, the deficit was caused by the increase of expenditures, not by deficiency of revenues, and it "demonstrates" this by pointing to a chart that shows that revenues as a percentage of GNP have been fairly constant since 1960 while expenditures have been rising. But one could equally say that the deficit was caused by the failure of revenues to rise as expenditures increased or by the decline of revenues relative to expenditures.

There is nothing to choose among such statements as objective, arithmetical explanations of the deficit. But no one cares for objective, arithmetical explanations. They want explanations that assign blame for the past and prescribe policies for the future. When my wife said that I got wet because I did not carry my umbrella, she was blaming me for that and recommending that I carry it on rainy days in the future. When the administration and the council say that the deficit was caused by rising expenditures, they are saying only that in their opinion the deficit should have been avoided by curbing expenditures and the deficit should be reduced in the future by curbing expenditures.

A second opinion statement about the causes of the deficit would be:

The deficit has been caused by failure to do whatever should have been done to prevent the deficit.

The Evil of Government Spending

A basic premise of the report, more assumed than argued, is that government spending is bad and taxing is bad. Reducing spending is a good thing and would presumably be a good thing even if there were no deficit.

With respect to the badness of taxes, the report only refers to "evidence that high and uneven marginal tax rates distort economic incentives and inhibit economic growth." No evidence is presented about the magnitude of these effects, and the report does not enter into the argument about whether the tax reforms now under consideration would inhibit or promote growth. I have always been puzzled by the proposition that there are revenue-neutral tax reforms that would promote growth but no revenue-raising tax reforms that would be neutral about growth.

The report's main statements about federal spending are the following: "Federal spending consumes an unprecedentedly large share of gross national product (GNP) for a peacetime period, diverting resources that could be more productively employed in the private sector" and "resources are generally used more efficiently in the private sector."

Terms like "more productively employed in the private sector" and "more efficiently in the private sector" are likely to be misunderstood. They suggest that a comparison is being made between the efficiencies of *production* in the public sector and in the private sector. That implication might be suitable in comparing the efficiency of producing a nuclear submarine at General Dynamics with the efficiency of producing the same submarine in a Navy shipyard. (Whichever is done, the cost will be a *government* expenditure, not a private expenditure.) But such comparisons are not relevant for most government expenditures. Whether it is better to spend $10 billion for nuclear submarines or $10 billion for private consumption is not a question of efficiency in anything but a metaphysical sense.

The federal government is very little in the business of production. It is very much in the business of allocating the output of the private sector, that is, of influencing for what purpose and for whose benefit the private sector output is used. The federal government produces about 3 percent of the GNP. It spends 25 percent of the GNP, and this expenditure affects the allocation of the GNP among uses and people. Other actions of government, such as taxes and regulation, also affect this allocation.

The federal government was established by the Constitution to serve certain objectives: "to form a more perfect Union, establish Justice, insure domestic Tranquility, provide for the common defence, promote the general Welfare, and secure the Blessings of Liberty to ourselves and our Posterity." The question that must be asked is whether the allocation of the national output that results from government expenditures is the best for serving these purposes.

This administration obviously does not believe that reducing federal expenditures and transferring them to private allocation would *in general* serve the constitutional purposes better. It does not believe that about defense expenditures, social security expenditures, or interest payments. Undoubtedly there are also other expenditures about which it does not believe that, but these three alone total 60 percent of federal expenditures. So at most it believes that the constitutional purposes would be better served by a reduction of 40 percent of federal expenditures. And the choice of that 40 percent must result from characteristics of particular expenditures and not from the inferiority of federal expenditures in general.

A second opinion about federal expenditures would be:

No general statement can be made about the superiority of federal expenditures over private expenditures. Specific statements could be made about specific expenditures; but they would depend on specific evidence, usually hard to get, and specific preferences, on which reasonable people will differ.

---

1. Revision of estimates after the report was published reduced the 1982–1985 rate of increase to 4.4 percent.
2. Herbert Stein, "Achieving Credibility," *Contemporary Economic Problems, 1980* (Washington, D.C.: American Enterprise Institute for Public Policy Research, 1980), p. 42.

2

Economic Choices 1987

Overview

AFTER four years of frustrating conflict over how to reduce huge federal deficits, in December 1985 Congress passed and the president signed the Balanced Budget and Emergency Deficit Control Act of 1985, better known as the Gramm-Rudman-Hollings act. This peculiar law specifies annual dollar targets that lower the federal deficit to zero by fiscal year 1991. It provides that if Congress and the president fail in any year to agree on a budget whose deficit meets the target, spending will be cut automatically by a formula whose effects, all agree, will damage the effectiveness of both defense and civilian government activities. This state of affairs reflects both the determination of Congress and the president to lower the deficits and their inability to agree how to do it. The law is a budgetary doomsday machine enacted to force the contending parties to come to an agreement in order to avoid the formula cuts that no one wants.

After enactment of the bill, the prospects for lower deficits seemed to brighten. In February the Congressional Budget Office projected annual deficits declining to about $100 billion by fiscal year 1991 without additional spending cuts or tax increases. The estimates contrasted sharply with earlier projections, which showed deficits remaining near $200 billion if policies were not changed. At the same time, interest rates and the value of the dollar were both falling. The press began to report that high deficits were a thing of the past, that they were curing themselves along with the associated symptoms of high interest rates and an overvalued dollar.

Is the Deficit Disappearing?

In February 1986, the Congressional Budget Office (CBO) issued another in its regular series of reports on what is called the baseline budget, showing estimates of what spending, revenues, and the deficit would be for the next five years if the economy grew at a moderately steady rate and no changes were made in current policy. The report was surprising because it projected baseline deficits declining from $208 billion in fiscal year 1986 to $104 billion in fiscal year 1991, instead of sticking near $200 billion as many observers had expected. At least superficially it looked as though half the battle had been won.

But this conclusion is too optimistic. The fact that the February 1986 baseline deficits were lower than previous estimates reflects a combination of actions already taken and assumptions about the future. First, the significant reductions made by Congress in fiscal year 1986 appropriations, plus the first round of automatic Gramm-Rudman-Hollings cuts that went into effect on March 1, 1986, reduced spending for fiscal year 1986 well below previous expectations. The February CBO baseline assumes that these cuts are not restored. Second, the baseline projections further assume that future defense appropriations grow only enough to compensate for inflation, not at the higher rates assumed in the recent past. Since some of the 1986 cuts will arouse sharp protests, and especially since the president is proposing continued growth in defense outlays after restoration of last year's cuts, it will take strong congressional determination and unity to hold to the CBO baseline. Deficit reduction of the magnitude projected in the baseline will not "just happen."

Why Deficits Should Be Reduced

In fiscal year 1986, federal government spending is likely to be just under $1 trillion, or about 24 percent of the gross national product. The federal government, however, is paying out five dollars for every four it takes in. Federal revenues are about 19 percent of GNP, leaving a deficit of about 5 percent of GNP.

If a deficit of this magnitude were caused by a deep recession, the deficit itself would not be reason for concern. It would serve to cushion the recession and would dwindle as the economy recovered. But the current deficits have persisted in an economy substantially recovered from recession. They are "structural," not temporary, and pose a serious threat to the future growth of the economy

If an economy is to grow, it must have a high level of investment in plant, equipment, and other forms of capital. To maintain a given level of investment, a nation must either save an equivalent amount from its current income or obtain capital from abroad. National saving is the sum of private and government saving. When the government runs a budget deficit, it "dissaves," and national saving goes down commensurately unless private businesses or individuals increase their saving to make up for the government dissaving. In 1972–81, net national saving in the United States was about 7 percent of gross national product. In 1982–85 it was only about 3 percent. The difference is attributable to the large rise in the budget deficit on top of a slight fall in private saving.

This dearth of national saving has put upward pressure on interest rates and would have cut U.S. investment drastically had it not been for a substantial inflow of capital from abroad. This inflow of foreign funds offers benefits—keeping U.S. interest rates from rising higher, thereby preventing a decline in investment levels—but it also exacts heavy costs. Capital inflow means high foreign demand for dollars and, hence, a high value for the dollar in foreign exchange markets. The expensive dollar, in turn, has impaired the competitiveness of U.S. firms in international markets. Both export industries, including agriculture, and industries competing with imports have found their markets shrinking. The result has been injury to both labor and capital in industries affected by international competition, as well as slower growth of the economy as a whole. If continued over the long run, large budget deficits would either reduce domestic investment or be financed by increasingly uncertain, and potentially reversible, capital inflow from abroad. In either case, living standards of U.S. citizens would fall: a reduced level of domestic investment would retard the growth of the economy, and continued heavy foreign investment would send a larger share of U.S. output abroad in payment of debt service or other returns to foreign investors.

The Road to Gramm-Rudman-Hollings

The structural deficits in the federal budget are the result of actions taken by the president and Congress in 1981, when Congress enacted the Reagan program of cutting taxes, increasing defense spending, and reducing domestic spending. Domestic spending cuts, however, were not large enough to offset increased defense spending and lower taxes, and most subsequent presidential proposals for additional domestic spending reductions have not been enacted. With the onset of the 1981–82 recession, precipitated by tight money and high interest rates, the actual deficit ballooned still more, and the national debt climbed rapidly. Servicing the larger debt at higher interest rates increased federal interest payments. Even after the economy recovered from the recession, the deficit persisted because federal spending, spurred by increases in defense and interest, was a higher share of GNP than before the recession, and revenues, because of the tax cuts, a lower share.

Although President Reagan won rapid congressional approval of his tax and spending proposals in 1981, the consensus disappeared as the huge deficits emerged. Thereafter, primarily under the leadership of the Senate, the contending parties hammered out painful yearly compromises that halted built-in growth in future deficits but left actual deficits above $200 billion.

The impasse over the budget for fiscal year 1986 dramatized the opposing views. The president's budget proposal, submitted to Congress in February 1985, called for continued defense growth and cuts of over $50 billion in nondefense spending—including wholesale elimination of several programs—aimed at reducing the 1986 deficit to $180 billion. Senate leaders made repeated attempts to work out a compromise plan to reduce the deficit more rapidly by slowing defense growth, broadening domestic cuts to include suspension of social security cost-of-living adjustments, and adding some revenue increases. But in the end they found both the president and the House leadership unwilling to accept such a plan. In late July Congress finally passed a budget resolution that slowed defense growth dramatically and called for smaller domestic cuts than the president had advocated. Congress hoped to reduce the fiscal 1986 deficit to $172 billion but failed to reach agreement on a reconciliation bill implementing many of the domestic spending reductions. That failure, together with unexpectedly slow growth in the economy, crushed all hopes for a fiscal 1986 deficit under $200 billion.

The Gramm-Rudman-Hollings bill passed Congress in the form of an amendment to a bill raising the public debt limit after a protracted struggle over which programs to protect from mandatory cuts. The legislation stipulates that the federal deficit be cut to $172 billion in fiscal year 1986 and $144 billion in 1987, and by $36 billion annually thereafter until it reaches zero in 1991. (For fiscal 1986, the cut was limited by the law to $11.7 billion, even though Congress realized that it was not nearly enough to reach that year's target.) The law instructs the directors of the Office of Management and Budget (OMB) and the Congressional Budget Office to determine, near the beginning of each fiscal year, whether the estimated deficit meets the target. If the deficit exceeds the target by $10 billion, half the excess spending must be cut from the defense budget and the other half from nondefense programs that are not protected. Protected programs include social security and a number of antipoverty programs. Within each category, sufficient reductions must be made in both defense and nondefense spending authority to cut outlays by a uniform percentage. The findings of the OMB and the CBO are transmitted to the comptroller general of the United States, who issues the final report on the cuts required to meet the deficit target. The president is instructed to "sequester" these amounts if an alternative plan has not been worked out with Congress.

Although the legislation had the support of the president and a bipartisan majority in both houses of Congress, the motives and expectations of the actors in this ongoing legislative drama differ widely. The president hopes to force Congress to accept his proposals to eliminate a number of nondefense programs and reduce outlays in others while continuing the defense buildup. Many members of Congress, including ranking Republicans, have already given notice that they will not support many of the nondefense outlay cuts sought by the president and will seek major cuts in his proposed defense outlays. Many lawmakers believe that the president must ultimately accept a tax increase in order to preserve his defense policy.

On February 7, 1986, a panel of three judges from the U.S. District Court for the District of Columbia ruled that because the Gramm-Rudman-Hollings bill grants executive powers to the comptroller general, who is an officer removable by Congress. it violates the principle of separation of powers in the U.S. Constitution. The ruling has been appealed to the Supreme Court. In anticipation of just such a ruling, the bill provides a fallback procedure under which the mandatory cuts would be implemented if the House and Senate passed a joint resolution approving the mandatory cuts, but the resolution must be signed by the president. Regardless of how the Supreme Court rules on procedure, both the president and Congress are under pressure to meet the deficit targets of the legislation.

Will Rapid Deficit Reduction Cause Recession?

The case for reducing the deficits is powerful, and the new budget law symbolizes the determination of Congress and the president to reduce them. It would, of course, be foolish to cut the deficit so rapidly that the economy plunges into recession, but several sources of economic strength make 1986 a good year to start deficit reduction. The stimulating effects of low interest rates and further declines in the value of the dollar are likely to offset the restrictive effects of following the targeted deficit reductions in the period 1987–89.

After slowing in 1985 and early 1986, growth in the economy seems likely to pick up later in 1986. Partly in response to the prospect of declining deficits, interest rates have come down and stock market prices have climbed rapidly in recent months. Lower interest rates and reduced costs of raising equity capital should stimulate both the housing market and investment. The substantial drop in the exchange value of the dollar from its peak in the first quarter of 1985 should stimulate net exports and increase output and employment in U.S. industries that compete in world markets. The rising cost of imports will add somewhat to inflation in the United States, but another favorable development—the rapid slide in oil prices—will have the opposite effect. Oil prices have fallen precipitously from their 1985 level of $27 a barrel. Even if they stabilize around $20 a barrel instead of a possible $10 to $15 a barrel, consumer prices will be reduced about 1 percent, real incomes will be up, and consumer demand strengthened. On the negative side, investment in the oil industry will be cut sharply, and the risk of defaults on loans to oil-exporting countries and to the domestic oil industry will grow. On balance, however, lower oil prices enhance the chances that the economy will grow strongly enough in 1986 to absorb deficit reduction without slowing.

Estimating the effect of reaching the deficit targets in 1987–89, of course, involves considerably more uncertainty. Reducing the structural deficit by 2.6 percent of GNP from 1986 through 1989, which is what the new budget law requires, would clearly have a major restrictive effect on the economy if not offset by some other stimulus. The most likely source of offsetting stimulus is a reduction in the current account deficit. Whether this stimulus is sufficiently large depends in turn on how much further the value of the dollar falls and how fast the economies of U.S. trading partners grow.

U.S. monetary authorities can be expected to try to keep the U.S. economy growing at about 3.5 percent a year as the budget deficit comes down. On the assumptions that the dollar falls 15 percent a year (from its level in January 1986) through 1988 and that foreign economies also grow at 3.5 percent a year, the U.S. current account deficit can be expected to shrink steadily, perhaps disappearing entirely by 1990. Under these conditions—which seem quite possible—the improved competitiveness of U.S. industry should stimulate the economy enough to offset the restrictive effect of budget deficit reduction. Slower growth abroad or smaller declines in the dollar would provide less offsetting stimulus. Much depends, therefore, on the willingness of foreign governments to expand their own economies and, especially, not to impede further readjustment of the dollar. If the dollar were to stay at its early 1986 levels, stimulus from net exports would be much smaller, even with strong growth abroad.

Avoiding Doomsday

The first practical consequence of Gramm-Rudman-Hollings was the sequestration of $11.7 billion in fiscal 1986 spending that took effect on March 1, 1986. Since the amount was relatively small and the fiscal year was nearly half over, Congress decided to let the automatic sequestration process take effect rather than try to reach agreement on alternative cuts. After exempt and specially treated programs were set aside, reducing outlays by $11.7 billion turned out to require cutting appropriations for defense by 4.9 percent and unprotected domestic programs by 4.3 percent. The difficulties of reducing ongoing programs by even such small percentages in midyear gave government agencies reason to hope that sequestration would not be repeated.

Indeed, almost everyone agrees that reaching the deficit targets by applying the sequestration formula in future years would introduce major distortions and inefficiencies into government activities. If, for example, the targets were reached by applying the sequestration formula to the CBO baseline projection for 1987–89, real defense spending would have to be $18 billion lower in 1989 than in 1986. Moreover, each line item would have to be cut by the same percentage, leaving no room for military judgment about whether certain items were more vital than others. Similarly, on the civilian side the automatic formula would be applied equally, and indiscriminately, to air traffic controllers, IRS auditors, and the national zoo. The sequestration results applied to 1987 and beyond clearly constitute, as intended, an alternative to be avoided. There must be a better way to reduce the deficits.

Three Alternative Budget Strategies

Reducing the budget deficit to meet the Gramm-Rudman-Hollings targets will require critical decisions about broad national priorities.

—How much of the deficit reduction should be realized through spending cuts and how much through tax increases?

—Of the spending cuts, how much should be in defense and how much in civilian programs?

—Should social security and related entitlement programs share in the cuts?

—In other programs, should the cuts be evenly distributed, or should they be highly selective?

Gramm-Rudman-Hollings Priorities

While everyone agrees that application of the sequestration formula in the new budget law would be devastating, the broad outlines of Gramm-Rudman-Hollings reflect the realities of the political environment in which it was shaped and therefore represent a feasible budget strategy. Such a strategy would avoid a tax increase, which many in Congress are certainly reluctant to support, especially over presidential opposition. It would also exempt social security and certain programs for the poor from mandatory cuts and give special treatment to other health and retirement programs. And it would divide the remaining cuts between defense and the unprotected domestic programs, a kind of rough justice reflecting a political compromise between those who give highest priority to national security and those who believe the defense buildup has gone far enough.

The Administration's Proposal

The budget proposal presented by the president in February 1986 reflects quite a different approach. The president would achieve some of the reduction in the deficit through the sale of public assets and several small tax increases. He would leave social security benefits untouched, but make substantial reductions in other programs that would be wholly or partially protected under Gramm-Rudman-Hollings, especially medicare, medicaid, and student aid. He requests restoration of most of the $14 billion cut from defense budget authority in 1986 and proposes increases of 3 percent a year over inflation in subsequent years. The bulk of deficit reduction is accomplished by deep but highly selective cuts in the unprotected civilian programs, including outright abolition of a number of programs.

The Recommended Alternative

Reaching the 1989 Gramm-Rudman-Hollings deficit target solely by cutting spending poses unnecessarily grim choices. Slashing defense spending as much as would be required under the package that preserves Gramm-Rudman-Hollings priorities would be risky to national security. After the recent rapid modernization of military equipment, reducing defense budgets substantially below current levels would lead to unbalanced forces with sophisticated equipment and insufficient funds to operate and maintain it effectively. Deep cuts in civilian programs would curtail important government services. Programs that hardly anyone regards as wasteful—scientific research, medical care for low-income people, job training, and maintenance of the nation's highways and bridges—would be cut. It would be preferable to raise taxes by about $50 billion, or about 1 percent of GNP, in 1989. We propose, therefore, an alternative budget that would hold the defense budget at fiscal year 1986 levels with allowance for inflation, accept some of the cuts proposed by the president, spread the burden of deficit reduction more broadly (to include, for example, social security beneficiaries), and restore some funds in programs cut too deeply already.

Our recommended alternative requires a tax increase of $50 billion in 1989 to help alleviate the unacceptable consequences of the other two options. Such a tax increase would keep the GNP share of general revenue—that is, revenue other than payroll taxes for social security and medicare—below the level in 1981. Yet it would be sufficient to avoid cuts that would weaken the nation's defense and undermine the ability of the federal government to perform essential public services and to provide support for the poor and disadvantaged. Real defense spending would be the same in fiscal 1989 as in 1986 and would support a strong defense posture. Real outlays of unprotected nondefense programs would decline 10 percent between 1986 and 1989, but the cuts would be concentrated in low-priority programs.

It should be emphasized that the outlay estimates under all three options assume that budget decisions for fiscal 1987 and beyond will begin with the spending levels mandated under the Gramm-Rudman-Hollings sequestration procedures that went into effect on March 1, 1986. These cuts reduced budget outlays by $18 billion in fiscal 1987, $21 billion in 1988, and $23 billion in 1989. Any spending above these levels would require equal

Table 1-3. *Alternative Revenue Sources, Fiscal Years 1987–91*
Billions of dollars

	Income tax[a]		Excise tax[b]			
Year	Rate increase (2 percentage points)	Surtax (9 percent)	Oil[c]	Gasoline[d]	Alcohol and tobacco[e]	Value-added tax (4 percent)[f]
1987	33.2	32.4	20.4	25.6	6.8	...
1988	47.7	46.3	21.8	25.6	9.5	33.9
1989	52.4	50.9	22.1	25.6	9.6	51.3
1990	57.0	55.6	22.5	25.2	9.6	55.2
1991	62.1	60.8	22.9	24.9	9.6	59.4

Sources: Congressional Budget Office; and authors' estimates.
a. Includes individual and corporation income taxes. Based on H.R. 3838 as enacted by the House of Representatives.
b. Assumes increases would be effective October 1, 1986.
c. Tax of $5 a barrel on domestic and imported oil.
d. Tax increase of 30 cents a gallon.
e. Increase cigarette tax to 32 cents a pack and double tax on alcohol. Assumes scheduled reduction of cigarette tax from 16 cents to 8 cents a pack on March 15, 1986.
f. Includes exemptions for food, housing, and medical care. Assumes effective date of January 1, 1988.

offsetting cuts in other programs or a larger tax increase than the $50 billion provided in our preferred option.

Tax Options

The question of which taxes to raise to help meet the Gramm-Rudman-Hollings deficit targets, and by how much, is complicated by still another policy debate—tax reform. With the strong support of the president, Congress is now considering an overhaul of the personal and corporation income taxes. The goal is to broaden the bases of these income taxes by eliminating tax preferences and to apply the extra revenue to reduction of marginal tax rates. The question is how the objective of tax reform—a fairer tax system—can be wedded to the goal of reducing the deficit.

Congress can address this issue in one of three ways, as shown in table 1-3. First, the tax reform bill already passed by the House of Representatives (H.R. 3838) could be modified to raise more income tax revenues than are produced under present law. Congressional leaders must decide whether to raise those revenues in the reform bill or in separate legislation. Second, selective excise taxes on consumer goods could be increased. Higher taxes on petroleum products, alcoholic beverages, and tobacco products, which enjoy lower tax rates in the United States than they do in most other countries, would not only raise revenues but advance other objectives as well. For example, increased taxes on oil or gasoline would encourage energy conservation, and higher taxes on distilled spirits, wine, beer, and cigarettes could reduce consumption of products that are injurious to health. Third, Congress could enact a new broad-based consumption tax. The two leading alternatives are a federal retail sales tax or a value-added tax. The major difference is administrative; the sales tax is collected only at the retail stage, while the value-added tax is collected at all stages of production. Such taxes are potentially large revenue producers and could be used to finance some of the rate reductions in the tax reform bill as well as to increase federal revenues.

We believe that the best instruments for raising the revenues necessary to reach the Gramm-Rudman-Hollings targets are the individual and corporation income taxes. These taxes are imposed at rates that reflect social judgments about ability to pay and are designed to take into account the economic circumstances of taxpaying units. Consumption taxes, whether levied on selected commodities or on a broad base, would impose heavier burdens on poor and low-income families than on those higher up in the income scale.

Income tax revenues can be raised by broadening the tax base further or by making smaller rate cuts than are now contemplated in the House bill. Additional potential base-broadening measures include limitations on the amount or types of employee fringe benefits that are excluded from tax, an increase in the proportion of social security benefits that is taxed, or limitation of the deductibility of state and local taxes on individual federal income tax returns.

Political opposition to these changes may mean that additional revenues will have to come mainly from rate increases. Income tax rates can be increased in two simple ways. All tax rates can be increased by the same number of percentage points, or all tax payments can be increased by the same percentage. A 2 percentage point increase in the individual and corporation tax rates or a 9 percent surtax would raise somewhat more than the $50 billion revenue increase proposed by our recommended alternative to reach the deficit target for 1989. If H.R. 3838 survives in anything like its present form, such rate increases should be more acceptable than they would have been without tax reform.

Among the excise taxes, the largest potential revenue producers are those on oil and gasoline. A tax of $5 a gallon on imported oil would raise about $7.5 billion in fiscal 1989; the same tax on domestic as well as imported oil would generate $22 billion. Both taxes would boost prices, but the entire price increase would go into the federal Treasury under the general oil tax, while the import tax would siphon off most of it to domestic producers. A gasoline tax of 30 cents a gallon would raise about $26 billion in 1989 and would prevent declines in gasoline prices that might undermine consumers' incentives for owning fuel-efficient cars.

Excise taxes on tobacco products and alcoholic beverages have declined in real terms in the last three decades because they have not kept up with inflation. Doubling liquor taxes by 1989 would restore these taxes to their real levels in 1973; increasing cigarette taxes to 32¢ a pack would restore them to their real levels in 1958. Together, these increases would boost revenues by almost $10 billion in 1989. The additional taxes would require heavy consumers of such products to pay an extra share of the costs they impose on society for health care. Reasonable increases in excise taxes could add from $15 billion to $30 billion to federal revenues in 1989.

Broad-based consumption taxes are capable of producing a great deal of revenue at low rates. A retail sales tax or value-added tax that exempts food, housing, and medical care would raise about $12.5 billion for each percentage point of tax in 1989. Thus a tax rate of 4 percent would meet the revenue target of $50 billion for that year. But because of the delays of introducing a new tax, it would be necessary to resort to other revenue increases to meet the 1987 and 1988 targets. In our view, Congress should turn to such a tax only if it becomes clear that the needed revenues cannot be raised from the income and excise taxes.

Improving the Budget Process

The impasse over the deficit has put great strains on the process by which the U.S. government makes budget decisions. Budget making is always difficult, particularly when power is divided, as it is under the Constitution, between the president and Congress. For the last several years the president and Congress have held divergent views about how to reduce the deficits and have displayed only limited willingness to compromise. Progress toward lower deficits has been slow and painful.

It seems unlikely that any changes in budget-making procedures could have ameliorated this political conflict. Unless the United States is willing to give up the constitutional separation of powers and move toward a parliamentary system—a move for which the authors have little enthusiasm—there will occasionally be times when Congress and the president disagree.

The enactment of Gramm-Rudman-Hollings reflected the mutual frustration of Congress and the president over their inability to agree on a plan to reduce deficits. They hoped that by agreeing in advance to cut spending in ways no one regarded as desirable, they would force themselves to compromise on a more sensible way to reduce the deficit.

While the new budget law may have the intended effect of forcing an agreement, it is still a bad way to make a budget and should be repealed. Aiming for any fixed dollar target for the deficit—such as zero in fiscal year 1991—without regard for the state of the economy could force the government to adopt fiscal policy that would undermine the economy's health. Moreover, cutting deficits by formula rather than by deliberate consideration of relative priorities is an abdication of responsible decision-making.

3

IS LOW INFLATION WORTH IT?

Casualties mount in the Federal Reserve's war on inflation

By the Center for Popular Economics

Each February, the Council of Economic Advisors publishes a document with a title meant to impress: Economic Report of the President. *The report is crammed with tables of data covering every segment of the economy. But it also has a political flavor because its economic analysis is written by the top economists of the administration in power. Recent reports cast the Reagan administration's conservative economic policies in a favorable light and optimistically evaluate the performance of the U.S. economy under Reaganomics.*

*In February, the progressive economists at the Center for Popular Economics released their own version of the ERP—*Economic Report of the People. *The CPE report analyzes the costs of conservative economics on the U.S. economy and on women, people of color, labor and rural populations. The authors also chart the rise of conservative economic policies begining with Paul Volcker's appointment as Federal Reserve Chairman and followed soon after by Ronald Reagan's election as president.*

The Volcker-Reagan strategy to restore vigor to the U.S. economy consisted of a tight monetary policy on the one hand, and supply side tax cuts and reductions in government social spending on the other. According to the authors, neither policy has been successful in stemming the long-term deterioration of the economy.

They argue that the one ostensible success of conservative economics — knocking down the rate of inflation — is illusory. Anti-inflation policies have generated growing indebtedness in the economy and a huge federal debt — for which a price will be paid in the future.

The following excerpt from Economic Report of the People *explores the Federal Reserve's war on inflation and estimates the economic casualties that resulted.*

MOVING RIGHT

Conservative economic policies have not improved the lives of most Americans. The fundamental problems of the U.S. economy, however, are structural and pre-date the Volcker-Reagan strategy. Since the mid 1960s signs of weakness in basic economic structure and performance have been accumulating. The after-tax rate of return on corporate capital — the capitalist's eye view of the economic health of the economy — peaked two decades ago and has languished since.

Beset by low productivity growth, spiraling oil prices and declining international competitiveness, Jimmy Carter had given up on his strategy for dealing with the problems of the American economy. With the help of G. William Miller, then Chairman of the Federal Reserve, Carter's approach was to run a loose monetary policy and a tight budget policy. The easy credit policies of the Fed resulted in generally lower interest rates in the U.S. and this encouraged people to desert the dollar in favor of currencies that carried higher interest rates. This caused the dollar to fall *vis-a-vis* U.S. competitors.

The problem with Carter's policy of low interest rates, economic expansion and dollar depreciation was that it generated inflation. As a result, it shifted

E*very important economic indicator except inflation reveals continuing economic deterioration under conservative economics.*

Growth rates of output have also been failing over the long term. While the U.S. and world economy have continued to endure the ups and downs of cyclical recession and recovery, the long downward secular trend has been the primary backdrop for domestic economic policies.

When Ronald Reagan kicked off his presidential election campaign in 1979, the U.S. economy was in serious trouble. Inflation was running at 13% a year. The unemployment rate was 5.8%.

the burdens of America's long-run economic problems onto U.S. banks and financial institutions. Bankers found that the interest they had to pay on deposits climbed faster than those they took in as charges on loans. Bond dealers found it difficult to sell long-term bonds in an inflationary environment because of the great uncertainty about their long-run value.

As the dollar's value sank with inflation, large banks and corporations holding dollars in 1978 and 1979 began to panic. By the summer of 1979, a major sell-off of the dollar occurred and a full-fledged currency crisis broke out. Miller resigned and Carter appointed Paul Volcker as chairman of the Fed.

Carter hoped that Volcker, a banker's banker, could restore the world's confidence in the dollar and the American banks. Almost immediately, Volcker's Federal Reserve System raised interest rates to break the inflationary spiral and dollar depreciation. In the process, the Fed sparked a sharp recession just prior to the 1980 election.

Volcker's appointment, in short, meant the abandonment of the Carter strategy, and soon thereafter, of Jimmy Carter. In combination — but not always in cooperation — Volcker and Reagan fashioned a new economic strategy which promised to find a non-inflationary solution to the U.S. economy's problems. It did not work. They beat inflation. But they did not reverse the long-run structural decline of the U.S. economy.

THE RIGHT STUFF?

The economy did not boom; it lapsed into a record setting recession. By raising real interest rates, monetarism succeeded in driving up the value of the dollar, putting workers and unions on the defensive. But the promised harvest of plenty failed to materialize.

High interest rates recess the economy by making it harder and more costly for business, home buyers, and others to borrow. Businesses and individuals cut back on spending for new plants and equipment and new consumer goods. This in turn reduces the demand for labor and thus increases unemployment. With unemployment high, labor's bargaining power erodes and workers lose the ability to fight for higher wages and better working conditions for fear of losing their jobs.

High interest rates also increase the value of the dollar by attracting investors around the world to buy up dollars to invest in high-yielding U.S. assets. This will lower the prices of many imported goods and domestic goods that compete with imports — thereby reducing the overall rate of inflation.

If fighting inflation were the only goal of economic policy, monetarism would be just what the doctor ordered. But economies cannot live on low inflation alone. A well working economy must make productive use of its resources — both human and material. Fighting inflation by putting people out of work and idling machines — even if successful — may leave the economy an inflation-free disaster area rather than a stable source of a plentiful livelihood for its members.

But capitalist economies run on profits and the U.S. economy is no exception. So the key to understanding why monetarism backfired is to analyze its effect on profits.

By increasing the cost and decreasing the availability of credit and recessing the economy, the Federal Reserve's high interest rate policy threatened rather than bolstered profits. Businesses welcomed their increased bargaining power with labor; but with high unemployment it became harder to sell products.

As a result, monetarism shifted the problems of the U.S. economy from banks and other financial institutions onto families trying to make ends meet and onto manufacturing corporations.

NEITHER NEW NOR IMPROVED

Every important economic indicator except inflation reveals continuing economic deterioration under conservative economics. Between 1980 and 1985 conservative economics produced the lowest average rate of growth of real GNP of any business cycle in the post-war period. It also generated record rates of unemployment. In 1985, unemployment was higher than it had been at any cycle peak since the Great Depression. However, inflation in 1985 fell to the lowest rate for a peak year since 1959. And in 1984, the economy grew at an overall rate of 6.8%

Do not the achievements — low inflation and a strong expansion from the depths of the 1980-1982 recession — indicate the success of conservative economics? To answer this question we may ask: how much did it cost to fight inflation the Volcker-Reagan way? And what did it cost to achieve one year (1984) of rapid economic growth?

The problem with fighting inflation with recessions is that recessions are costly. Workers are thrown out of work, factories are idled, and businesses lose profits. If conservative economics represented a new, improved method of inflation fighting, then it would have reduced the amount of unemployment required to reduce inflation.

But careful studies of the relationship between inflation and unemployment have found that conservative economics has not altered the trade-off between inflation and unemployment. Taking into account the effects of raw material prices (such as oil) on inflation, it takes as much unemployment to reduce inflation now as it did before 1980. What made conservative economics different was that the Federal Reserve was willing to generate more unemployment and keep it higher longer than previous monetary policy makers had been willing to do. And the cheap imports, made possible by the overvalued dollar, helped keep the lid on prices.

How many goods and services could the U.S. economy have produced if between 1980 and 1984 the government had put people back to work rather than throwing them out of jobs? In other words, how high would GNP have been if unemployment had been lower?

Lower unemployment increases the output of goods and services (GNP) in two ways: first, more people are working, producing goods and services. And many workers who had previously given up looking for jobs re-enter the labor force and get jobs. Second, when more people are working, productive capacity is more fully utilized, and productivity is higher because there is less waste of plant and equipment.

To estimate the effects of these two factors we first calculated how many people would have been working had the unemployment rate been lower, taking account of the fact that the lower unemployment would draw discouraged workers back into the labor force. We consider these discouraged workers to be truly unemployed, even though they are not officially counted that way. We estimate the true size of the labor force and the true level of unemployment by asking how many people would seek work and find it if a low (3%) unemployment rate were maintained over a period of years. Those who would have been working in this hypothetical high employment scenario would have produced more. By comparing how much would have been produced with how much was actually produced, we can calculate the costs of using unemployment to fight inflation.

At the hypothetical high unemployment level of 6%, the economy between

1980 and 1984 would have produced over $800 billion more than it did. If the economy had operated at full employment—around 3%—the lost output was a whopping $2 trillion.

What if those responsible for macroeconomic policy had tried gradually to bring the unemployment rate down, rather than trying to raise it? If unemployment had been 5% in 1980, 4% in 1981 and 1982, and 3% in 1983 and 1984 instead of the average of 8.4% over the period, real GNP would have grown at an annual rate of 4.1% between 1980 and 1984. By post-war standards, this is not an unusually high rate. In fact, it is about equal to the 4.2% growth rate between 1960 and 1969.

The bottom line is that the cost of fighting inflation compared with a gradual move towards a 3% unemployment rate was $1.7 trillion, an average of over 10% of GNP, between 1980 and 1984. That is more than $28,000 for every family and over $10,000 for every person in the country. As economists are fond of saying, you can buy just about anything for a price—even poverty.■

The CENTER FOR POPULAR ECONOMICS in Amherst, Massachusetts was founded in 1978 by a group of progressive economists to offer workshops on basic and alternative economics to activists. Information on the CPE Summer Institute can be obtained from CPE, Box 785, Amherst, MA 01004.

Economic Prospects for 1986

PRESENT TAX REFORM IS IRRELEVANT

By MURRAY L. WEIDENBAUM,

A CYNIC once said that economic forecasting is neither an art nor a science — it is a hazard. The present time is a good example of what he meant. Most forecasters are now lowering their predictions of real economic growth for 1985 and 1986. This shift comes soon after a period in which economists were raising their projections of growth for the American economy. Not too surprisingly, all this has not exactly inspired public confidence in the ability of economists to make reliable forecasts. The harsh reality is that economists are not good at estimating the economy's performance for very short time periods, such as the next month or quarter. However, the record for forecasts of year-to-year changes is much better.

For example, each month a group of 50 professional economic forecasters provides a consensus estimate for the year ahead. The result is called Blue Chip Economic Indicators. The forecasts made by the panel in October of each year is especially important, because that month is the typical starting point for the annual company planning cycle.

Over the past eight years, the Blue Chip panel's October estimates of real growth for the next year have turned out to be within 1.2 percentage points of the actual figure. The record on inflation is about the same, with the Blue Chip panel averaging within 1.1 percentage points. That record will not qualify for the Guinness Book of World Records, but it suggests why government and business executives continue to rely on economic forecasts.

When we step back from the details of econometric models, we can spot some basic trends. Virtually all forecasters are now singing a variation of the same song: 1985 and 1986 are not going to be nearly as good as 1984. But the economy will continue to grow, by between 2 and 3 percent. That compares to almost 7 percent last year.

The basic reason for the slowdown is that domestic production is much weaker than domestic consumption. The difference, of course, is due to the rising tide of imports. For a while, consumer credit can finance the gap between income earned and money spent. But most people's spending ultimately reflects their income. Thus, the more modest pace of domestic production and income generation is slowing down the purchases of American consumers.

As usual, there is a range of viewpoints among professional forecasters. The optimists see the GNP accelerating in 1986, as the economy gets its second wind. The pessimists expect the next recession to start some time in the coming 12 months. Personally, I am in the middle of the road.

I do not now see the seeds of the next recession. They may be there, but their sprouts are not yet visible to the naked eye. The usual factors that precede a recession are not present. Consumer sentiment, judged by the standard surveys, remains high. Significant excess capacity exists in American industry; in fact business investment continues at a high level. Inventories are balanced with sales. Interest rates are not rising; rather it is the money supply that is rising at a rapid clip. There is not much oomph in the economy, but there is nothing seriously pushing it down.

By 1986, however, the recovery will be four years old; that is rather mature when we consider past business cycles. It is not, however, an adequate reason for projecting the end of the expansion in the economy. It is an occasion for sounding a note of caution. The recovery is at the stage where it is susceptible to all sorts of negative influences that could lead to a downturn, but I do not now see the onset of recession.

HIGHLIGHTS OF ECONOMIC FORECAST

	1985	1986
Real GNP	+2.4%	+3.0%
Inflation	+3.7%	+4.2%
Unemployment	7.2%	7.0%

Inflationary Expectations

With the inflation rate hovering between 3 and 4 percent, it seems that the alarmists who have been forecasting an early return to escalating if not double digit inflation were wrong. Surely, the specific forecasts for high and rising inflation rates in 1984 and 1985 were off the board.

Nevertheless, I harbor a growing suspicion that the main error of some monetarists and other inflation alarmists was in timing. They forgot how long it took to build up the inflationary pressures of the late 1970s. On the other hand, perhaps too many of us have quickly forgotten how painful it was, as measured by high unemployment rates, to bring inflation down to current levels.

What concerns the monetarists is the extremely rapid rate of growth in the various monetary aggregates. M1 — the most widely watched monetary indicator — has been rising at a 13 percent annual rate since early this year. More specialized measures have also been expanding at a rapid rate. For example, the monetary base (a key ingredient in future money supply movements) has been expanding at a 9 percent rate since early in the year. More sanguine observers point to technical shifts, such as changes in the composition of deposits, to explain away the apparently excessive expansion of the money supply.

I believe that the monetarists are crying wolf again. What concerns me, however, is the way the fable ends. Eventually, the little boy was right. And some straws in the wind are worrisome.

What cannot be readily explained away is the rise in measured inflationary expectations. According to one recent survey, financial decision-makers anticipate that the inflation rate over the coming five years will be about 5½ percent a year. That is 170 basis points higher than the current inflation rate.

According to some observers, today's economic policy environment is reminiscent of 1967. 1972. and 1977. These were

Reprinted with permission of Murray L. Weidenbaum
and Vital Speeches of the Day, February 1, 1986.

the periods prior to the outbursts of rapid inflation in the fairly recent past. History does not have to repeat itself, but the current attitude toward inflation may be too sanguine.

The International Outlook

Let us take a few minutes to examine the foreign trade situation. The fact is that the United States is running a triple digit trade deficit. Meanwhile, Congress is searching for villains.

Let's face it. If Congress restricts imports, that raises the danger of retaliation against our exports. We do not have to guess about the consequences or remember as far back as the Smoot Hawley tariff of the 1930s. Recent experience with China provides a good example. When we imposed quotas on their textile exports to us, they promptly reduced their agricultural and chemical imports from us. The U.S. textile industry got the benefits, while our farmers and our chemical companies and their employees bore the costs.

A significant decline in the exchange rate of the dollar would be a far better solution to our international trade problems than any of the protectionist approaches. The 40 percent rise in the dollar since 1980 means a 40 percent price increase for U.S. firms competing against foreign goods. But that, in turn, gets us to our own budget deficit, which is at the heart of the superstrong dollar. And that has strictly a made-in-America label.

The Fiscal 1986 Budget

Looking at the Washington scene, the annual budget debate has become a sad spectacle. We all know what has to be done. It is not a question of bringing an outlandish $200 billion deficit down to merely an outrageous $180 billion or a bloated $150 billion annual level. It is a matter of restoring our country's finances to a semblance of balance.

To those who say that economic growth will cure our fiscal problems, I respond that the next recession — which we can neither pinpoint nor rule out — will push the budget deficit to a new peak. History argues for at least one more recession in the 1980s. It will only take an average downturn to accelerate government spending and slow down revenue sufficiently to produce a deficit of $250 billion a year or more.

Washington's favorite parlor game is still spin-the-budget. But it now has a new name, the Gramm-Rudman-Hollings amendment to the bill to raise the debt limit to $2 trillion. That amendment requires Congress and the President to reduce the deficit progressively until it is eliminated in fiscal 1991. This provision has been subjected to all sorts of criticism, some quite valid. But the fact remains that the Gramm approach is now the only legislative game in town to eliminate the deficit. The amendment reflects widespread exasperation with the status quo. It surely is a challenge to the Congress and the White House to do a better job of bringing spending into line with revenues.

At first blush, the Gramm-Rudman-Hollings bill seems to be an abdication of the Congressional budget function to the President. After all, if they don't cut enough, he has to do it. But, on reflection, the potential is more serious than that. The bill would let Congress do the popular thing — enact generous appropriations — while giving the President the onerous task of cutting spending or proposing tax increases.

In any event, we must remember that the meter is running. Interest payments are mounting steadily. Delay means choosing in the future between even larger spending cuts and more un-popular tax increases. The best way to reduce the deficit — and to lay the foundation for responsible tax reform in the years ahead — is to carry through that necessary pruning of federal spending programs. The key to reducing federal spending is simple but not easy. It is the ability to say no.

Tax Reform

Meanwhile, for most of 1985 politicians in both parties have been busy diverting attention from the difficult question of cutting the deficit by focusing on tax reform. It is discouraging to hear the representatives of both political parties on this subject. If you listen to Democratic spokesmen, you quickly learn that they are embracing tax reform in the hope that, in the voters' eyes, such action will return the party to the nation's mainstream.

But the Republicans are not any better on that score. They tell us that the beauty of their current tax reform plan is that it will help to attract blue collar families to the Republican party. The problems facing our nation deserve more serious responses than such exercises in cheap (or perhaps expensive) politics.

When we push aside the labels attached to any of the proposed "reforms" of the federal tax structure — be they Rostenkowski's approach, Kemp-Kasten, Bradley-Gephardt, the November Treasury proposal, or the current White House recommendations — we find that they are all variations of the same theme: reduce federal income taxes paid by American families and individuals and offset the revenue loss by raising taxes on business.

Most of those "loophole" closers boil down to increasing taxes on business, mainly by reducing incentives to investment. What this means is that the proposed tax reform will not really be economically neutral. By discouraging investment the proposed tax changes would depress the economy, preventing the achievement of revenue neutrality. It also means a higher budget deficit.

It is ironic that policymakers in Washington are seriously considering such tax changes just as the growth rate is slowing down. Moreover, many of the industries hard hit by imports would be precisely those faced with the largest tax increases. Why worry about the problems of meeting foreign competition? Businesses don't vote.

My sense of irony is further aroused by the fact that the investment incentives adopted in 1981, which were then hailed as tax reform, are now proposed for diminution also as part of tax reform. That sounds like the invention of a political perpetual motion machine.

When you think about the key economic challenges facing the U.S. in the 1980s — foreign competition, farm and foreign debts, and huge budget deficits — the tax reform now being discussed should be dismissed as irrelevant.

I will recap briefly. We are basically a strong and wealthy country that is not managing its economic affairs too well. We are consuming more than we are producing. We are spending more than we are earning. We are borrowing more than we are saving. As a result, the economic future is, in a phrase, so-so. I see no recession in sight, but economic growth is resuming at a very slow pace. Unemployment is leveling off at a high level. On the bright side, inflation is staying low for the time being. This is not a period that will go down in the economic history books, but it is not nearly as bad as the doom and gloom talk we continue to hear.

Year to Reach for Economic Stars

By Walter W. Heller

U.S. economic performance in 1986 bids fair to continue in a split-level mode, one characterized by a rate of expansion very close to White House projections and the other by abiding problems that have bedeviled the economy throughout the Reagan years. With a combination of good policy and good luck, this could be the year when brisk expansion is coupled with a turn for the better on the underlying problems that are corroding our economic future.

First, let's look at the bright side, the likelihood that 1986 will see something like the 4% expansion projected by the Reagan economists from fourth-quarter 1985 to fourth-quarter 1986, which they translate into a 3.4% year-over-year advance. I hasten to add that my forecast (made jointly with George Perry of the Brookings Institution) doesn't embrace the over-optimistic White House projection of 4% growth for the rest of the decade.

Stimulative Shift

What are the forces that will propel us into a comfortable orbit this year, and how will they affect particular sectors of the economy?

First is the drop of some 3½ percentage points in interest rates during the past 18 months, a stimulative shift that operates with a lag of perhaps nine to 12 months. That should give a nice boost to business plant and equipment spending. In contrast with the latest Commerce Deparment survey projecting a fairly good first half more than offset by a miserable second half, the prospect is for a continued expansion at about a 7½% pace (in current dollars) for the year as a whole.

As to housing, my expectation of 1.9 million starts in 1986 already looks a bit modest with starts coming out of the chute in January at an annualized pace of 2.1 million. Lower interest rates for auto purchases should enable auto sales to better the 11-million-unit level of 1985.

Whether interest rates ease further in 1986 depends on how the Federal Reserve deals with five unknowns: the size of the contractionary deficit cuts, the stimulative slide in oil prices, the strength of the economic expansion, the degree of weakness of the dollar, and the possible negative effects of tax reform on private investment. On balance, I would expect some modest easing of interest rates this year.

The second force is the delightful (for overall U.S. economic health) drop in oil prices. By releasing perhaps $50 billion of purchasing power for non-petroleum consumption and consumer saving, the lower prices will lubricate faster expansion while greasing the skids for inflation. Just when some analysts thought that consumers might head for the hills, this bonanza, added to a $400 billion jump in consumer net worth in 1985's fourth quarter alone (mostly due to soaring stock and bond prices)—not to mention rising employment and modest inflation—will keep consumer spending moving up almost as fast as the gross national product.

Third, with the help of a sliding dollar, the soaring trade deficit will turn downward before the year is out. Even if it simply leveled off, it would reduce the drag on U.S. output. And as it declines, the wedge that the huge import surplus drove between U.S. consumption and U.S. output will shrink. That boosts GNP.

Fourth, there is still some fiscal thrust left in the deficit engine, though one assumes that this will turn to a fiscal drag later in the year as deficit-cutting begins to take hold.

Apart from these boosters, the prosaic factor of inventory-building will play a significant role. What harpooned our bright forecasts for 1985 was an inventory shift from a huge buildup of more than $62 bil-

---

Board of Contributors

All told, unlike 1982, it looks as though "the luck of the Irish" will be working, overtime, in 1986.

---

lion in 1984 to a meager one of $7 billion in 1985. This year the buildup should be about $20 billion, a move of $13 billion in the right direction vs. a $55 billion slackening last year.

All this adds up to that 4% growth rate during the year, bringing GNP up to about $4.3 trillion for the year in current prices, or $3.7 trillion in 1982 prices. That performance, in turn, will pull unemployment down to 6½% or a little better by next November, a month I select more or less at random.

Meanwhile, inflation will be subdued. True, the welcome decline in the underlying rate of inflation (excluding mainly energy and food) seems to be coming to an end. But cheaper oil has come to the rescue for 1986, pulling prices down as much or more than the depreciating dollar pushes prices up. Inflation will chug along at about a 3½% rate for the year.

All told, unlike 1982, it looks as though "the luck of the Irish" will be working, overtime, in 1986.

That brings us to the darker side of the moon, to the persistent and pernicious problems that have been haunting our prosperity: a dismal productivity performance, the lowest national savings and investment rates in half a century, a serious slowdown in average growth of both actual and potential GNP, a reversal of our progress in overcoming poverty, and the saddling of future generations with enormous and growing IOUs, both at home and abroad.

Disappointing us all, productivity advances have slowed to a crawl so far in the 1980s. The short-lived spurt in 1983-84 was not even par for the course of rapid economic recovery. And 1985 was a washout: Productivity did not increase at all in the economy-wide non-farm business sector. Hobbled by the zero-growth in labor productivity, employers had to increase their hiring sharply in 1985.

If saving and investment were bounding merrily ahead, we could look forward to a better productivity performance. Instead, private savings and investment are being siphoned into the huge black hole of the federal deficit. New data for 1985 show that out of the net domestic savings flow of 8% of GNP, over half was sucked into that black hole. With net private domestic investment running at 5¾% of GNP (itself below normal), domestic savings fell $100 billion short of meeting the nation's financing needs. In the process of closing this record gap with foreign savings, we have become a debtor nation.

With productivity, savings and investment performing so poorly, and with a deep, double-dip recession ushering in the '80s, the country's average growth rate has dwindled to less than 2% a year thus far in the decade. Even with no recession and average 3% growth until 1990, the '80s

Reprinted with permission of Walter W. Heller, Regents' Professor of Economics, University of Minnesota.

would weigh in at less than 2.5% average growth, vs. 3.2% in the '70s and 4.2% in the '60s.

Malignant Effects

Accompanying these discouraging economic trends is the resurgence of poverty. The percentage of our population in poverty jumped by nearly one-third, from 11.7% in 1979 to 15.3% in 1983, before dropping a bit, to 14.4% in 1984. Aside from the Reagan years, that is still the highest rate since 1966. Even after allowing for food stamps and other non-cash transfers, poverty at 9% has risen by about two-fifths since the late 1970s. The malignant effects of deep recession coupled with tax and budget policies tilted against the lowest income groups have significantly outweighed the benign effect of economic recovery.

But 1986 could be the year in which we turn these trends around. If 4% growth materializes, if the president and Congress truly bite the deficit bullet, if the combined decline of the dollar and slide in oil prices turn the trade deficit around without touching off a new round of inflation, and if the Federal Reserve plays its rightful role as a balance wheel, warding off inflation while supporting expansion, we could indeed see a new economic beginning in 1986. Savings, investment, productivity and growth would pick up, and poverty would turn down.

An impossible dream? No. If the president, Congress and the Fed truly reach for it, it could well be within our grasp.

Mr. Heller is Regents' professor of economics at the University of Minnesota and former chairman of the Council of Economic Advisers under Presidents Kennedy and Johnson.

Price Pickup? After a Long Drop, Analysts See Inflation Intensifying

They Cite Bigger Pay Gains, Fed's Monetary Policy, Long Economic Rebound

A 50-Cent Dollar in 15 Years

By Alfred L. Malabre Jr.
And Lindley H. Clark Jr.
Staff Reporters of The Wall Street Journal

The remarkable, almost uninterrupted easing of inflation since 1979 seems about over, according to most economists who follow price movements. From now on, they add, the broad trend will be upward, though not so sharply as to set off a new wave of double-digit increases.

Such a consensus is apparent in the January issue of Blue Chip Economic Indicators, a Sedona, Ariz., newsletter that surveys 50 economists each month. On the average, they anticipate a progressive worsening of inflation. They believe that the consumer price index, which they see rising at an annual rate of 3.6% in the current quarter, will increase 3.7% annually in the second, 3.9% in the third and 4.2% in the fourth. Looking further ahead, they predict a continuing acceleration in 1987, with a 4.7% reading by year-end.

Although such numbers hardly foreshadow a new price spiral, they do mark a clear turn from the recent pattern. Since 1979, when consumer prices surged 13.4%, the yearly increases have consistently diminished. Beginning in 1983, they have been less than 4%, with last year's estimated gain of 3.6% the smallest in 15 years.

Impressive Evidence

The forecasters could be wrong, of course. Not long ago, they generally underestimated how much inflation would subside, and now they could be overestimating its revival. However, they cite impressive evidence that inflation may be stepping up: Various barometers of future price moves are rising again; the money supply is increasing rapidly and may accelerate further; the dollar's value against other currencies has dropped, and the business cycle has entered a period in which price pressures normally increase.

Although the forecasters emphasize that the pickup in inflation will be moderate, they don't dismiss its significance: If 4.7% annual price increases persist, they would halve the dollar's value in only 15 years.

One of the price barometers currently flashing warning signals is an index that reflects patterns in employment, industrial-material prices and debt and tends to foreshadow consumer price trends by about six months. Compiled by Columbia University economists, the index fell throughout much of 1984 and early last year, but now it has climbed to about 117 from a low of 113 last September (see chart).

In addition, wholesale prices, which also tend to foreshadow patterns at the consumer level, are turning around. For example, a Dow Jones commodity-price index, whose components range from coffee, copper and cotton to silver, soybeans and sugar, has risen to more than 133 from a late-September low of 112.

And the price of gold, which languished at about $325 an ounce during most of 1985, has suddenly shot sharply higher. Late yesterday, gold was quoted in the London market at $349.75 to $350.25 an ounce.

"The recent run-up in gold is very significant," says Lacy H. Hunt, an economist

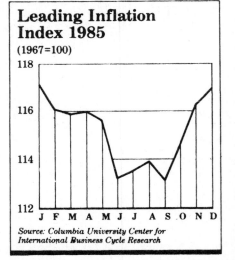

Leading Inflation Index 1985

(1967=100)

Source: Columbia University Center for International Business Cycle Research

at CM&M Group Inc., a New York securities firm, "Gold is the longtime barometer of inflation. . . . People say the Arabs are buying gold. Maybe so, but that doesn't explain why such metals as copper and aluminum are also on the rise. Aluminum prices are up about 30% just since November."

Money-Supply Growth

Recent Federal Reserve policy also is convincing many analysts that inflation will intensify. Last year, the M1 measure of the nation's money supply—currency plus checking accounts—expanded more than 12%, far above the 8% maximum set by the Fed in mid-1985. As a result, "there's too much liquidity sloshing around the banking system, and it will lead to higher inflation," says Lawrence A. Kudlow, the president of an economics consulting firm in Washington, D.C.

Looking ahead, most analysts expect the Fed to keep churning out money at a fast pace, to keep the dollar down and the economy growing despite any spending cuts or tax increases designed to pare the budget deficit. Rapid monetary growth hasn't sparked more severe inflation thus far, they say, because velocity—the rate at which money changes hands—has lagged. But a pickup in velocity is widely anticipated.

"The Fed is building up to a crisis," says Alan Greenspan, a New York economic consultant who headed President Ford's Council of Economic Advisers. "It has a record of success in curbing inflation and in getting the dollar's exchange rate down, but the time is coming when the Fed must choose between these successes."

His guess is that the Fed will focus on the dollar, holding it down through a continuing easy-money policy even at the risk of accelerating inflation. Moreover, the finance ministers of the U.S. and four major allies indicated, at a meeting last weekend in London, that they would like interest rates to decline further, and an attempt to achieve this would put more pressure on the Fed to keep monetary policy relatively easy or perhaps to ease it even more.

The dollar, of course, has fallen substantially since September, when the five nations agreed to work in concert to reduce its international value. As a result, many imported goods already are growing costlier for Americans. A weaker dollar in terms of the yen, for example, prompted Toyota Motor Corp. early this month to raise the suggested retail price of its cars and trucks an average of 3%. The move followed increases by Honda Motor Co., Nissan Motor Co. and Volkswagen of America Inc.

"A falling dollar reduces Americans' purchasing power and will cause higher inflation," says Mark Eaker, an economist at the University of North Carolina, adding that "it could also raise interest rates if foreigners demand higher returns on their investments." He cites a weakening dollar as a major reason for his forecast of "a resurgence of inflation to between 8% and 10%" by next year. To the extent that a weaker dollar reduces foreign competition, it is easier for U.S. companies to raise prices and for U.S. workers to demand more pay.

"Disinflation was hatched in an environment of a strengthening dollar," says Fred D. Kalkstein, an economist at the Philadelphia securities firm of Janney Montgomery Scott Inc., but now, he says, "inflation looms."

Business-Cycle Trends

Business-cycle trends also are beginning to rekindle inflation, analysts say. The current expansion passed the three-year mark in November; so it is nearly a half year longer than the average of previous economic upswings. As expansions lengthen, inflation normally picks up. Labor costs tend to accelerate as unemployment diminishes. Productivity gains, which serve to offset rising wages, become harder to achieve. Factory operations move closer to capacity, necessitating the use of less-efficient facilitise. Materials grow scarcer and production bottlenecks more frequent.

Such inflationary pressures have been unusually slow to build in this expansion, says Geoffrey H. Moore, the director of the Columbia Center for International Business Cycle Research. But he contends that they are beginning to do so now. "Almost unnoticed, labor costs have begun edging higher," he says, attributing the pattern to slowing productivity gains alongside relentlessly rising pay. In the expansion's first two years, he recalls, productivity rose briskly, but since then there has been little further advance. This partly indicates a tightening labor market, he says, adding that the share of working-age people not at work reached a record low of 39.2% last month.

CM&M's Mr. Hunt notes that the Labor Department's hourly wage index rose at an annual rate of 9.5% in December, up from a 6.5% gain in November. The speedup, he says, "suggests that the labor markets are tightening and business firms are being forced to bid up the prices that they pay in order to attract new employees." He regards the pattern as a sign that "inflationary pressures may begin to rebound faster than is generally expected."

Givebacks Wane

This, of course, is in sharp contrast to wage developments in the wake of the 1981-82 recession. Then, many employers were pressing for—and winning—so-called givebacks. Though no overall data are available, Michael Wachter, a labor economist at the University of Pennsylvania, believes that such concessions are becoming rarer.

Some yardsticks of inflationary pressure, of course, still militate against a new price speedup. At close to 80% of capacity, plant operating rates remain, on the average, well below levels that normally fuel inflation, economists say. Moreover, a survey by the National Association of Purchasing Management last month turned up no major delivery problems, much less any shortages of materials.

However, Mr. Moore believes that if the economy continues growing at a reasonable pace through this year and beyond, as most analysts expect, these "additional price pressures seem sure to arise."

Hardly anyone, it should be added, sees a resumption of the oil-price inflation that marked the 1970s. Now, in contrast, oil prices seem more likely to keep falling than to rise. Last year, the Organization of Petroleum Exporting Countries was unable to agree on production quotas, and the result was widespread price cutting. Many analysts anticipate further price reductions, though few look for deep cuts. And Mr. Hunt discounts the role of oil prices anyway.

"We're beginning to get a clear rise in inflation," he says, "and it will persist despite the weakness in oil prices. No individual commodity is capable of preventing the overall price level from moving up or down, as the case may be."

Slower Growth

Slower-than-expected economic growth also could forestall a price speedup, some analysts contend. Those at Wharton Econometric Forecasting Associates predict that the economy will grow only 2.8% this year. The Philadelphia consulting firm sees this relatively slow growth, along with antici-

pated spending reductions to trim the budget deficit, reducing inflation to 3.1% this year.

Even that rate appears high to a minority of analysts who expect a recession before year-end. Charles F. Eaton III, an economic consultant in Portsmouth, N.H., sees the economy already "overburdened" and facing increasing difficulties as the year unfolds. The upshot, he predicts, will be "falling prices by year-end." He concedes that in the interim "we may experience a reflation scare" but says it will be short-lived.

Whatever develops, inflation is unquestionably very much alive at present. Recent price increases range from an 11% New Year's Day jump in New York subway and bus fares to a $30-a-ton rise in certain steel-product prices to an 8.8% increase on various chewing tobaccos.

"Where do so many people get the idea that inflation has somehow faded away?" says Vincent Malanga, an economic consultant based in New York. "In reality, prices are increasing at rates that already are worrisome and threaten to become downright painful. I laugh when people talk about deflation. It's nonsense."

Yet the notion that inflation has faded away remains widespread. A recent University of Michigan survey of consumer attitudes finds that most people expect "low rates of inflation" to persist and adds that "gone are the days when consumers felt pressured to act by ever-escalating prices.

Mr. Kudlow suspects that such findings may simply reflect a lag in perception. "People tend to be slow to detect a major change in such trends," he says. "They were slow to realize that inflation was easing substantially in the early 1980s, after so many years of spiraling prices, and now there seems to be a delayed recognition that the trend has changed once again." He adds that "the political community seems to have dismissed inflation as a relic of the past, and this unfortunately has gotten a lot of play in the press." He expects that prices generally will soon be rising at annual rates of 6% or more, roughly double the early-1985 pace.

7

Unemployment

Four Brookings experts on unemployment and job training recently gathered for a discussion. The participants in the conversation were:

Martin Neil Baily, *a senior fellow in Economic Studies and editor of a recently published collection of essays entitled* Workers, Jobs, and Inflation.

Gary Burtless, *a senior fellow in Economic Studies and the assistant editor of the* Brookings Papers on Economic Activity.

Malcolm R. Lovell, Jr., *a guest scholar who was U.S. under secretary of labor from 1981 until this past spring and who is organizing a conference, to be held at Brookings in December of this year, on the problems of displaced workers.*

Roger D. Semerad, *the executive vice president of Brookings and chairman of the board of 70001 Ltd., a non-profit job training corporation; he was a staff assistant to Presidents Nixon and Ford, with responsibility for labor, education, and veterans affairs.*

What follows is an edited transcript of their remarks, beginning with an overview from Martin Neil Baily:

Baily: Most current forecasts predict that the unemployment rate will remain over 8 percent for the next two or three years, and that's under the assumption that there will be continued recovery. If those predictions are roughly accurate, then over the period 1980 to 1985 unemployment will have averaged about 8.5 percent. That compares with 6.2 percent for the 1970s and 4.8 percent for the 1960s. It's clear that the problem of unemployment in the U.S. is getting worse and worse, and an issue I've been looking at is to what extent the increase in unemployment is cyclical—that is to say, associated with fluctuations of demand in the economy—and to what extent it is structural.

It has been argued that the increase in unemployment between the '60s and the '70s could not have been a function of cyclical changes, because inflation was actually much worse in the '70s than it was in the '60s. I don't agree with that view. Aggregate demand was much too strong in the latter half of the 1960s. This gave the country the benefit of low unemployment, but it also resulted in accelerating inflation, which made for trouble in the 1970s. Moreover, in the 1970s the economy was also afflicted with a series of nasty shocks—the increase in the price of OPEC oil, for example—so that inflation was bad in that decade for reasons that weren't particularly associated either with the labor market or with any excess of aggregate demand in the economy, at least as a whole. In the '80s so far, high unemployment has been the side effect of curing inflation through demand restraint.

I'd like to introduce a concept that is a little controversial, but I think useful: the natural rate of unemployment. Basically, if unemployment fluctuates around the natural rate, we say this fluctuation is cyclical. If the natural rate itself changes—increases or decreases—this is because of some kind of structural change in the economy.

I've just been arguing in effect that unemployment was below its natural rate in the '60s, was about equal to its natural rate in the '70s, and so far in the '80s has been above its natural rate. But it's also true that the natural rate itself has risen. In other words, the shifts in the unemployment rate are not due entirely to cyclical differences; there have also been structural changes. It's hard to estimate exactly how much the natural rate has increased, but my best guess is that it's gone up from an unemployment rate of about 5 percent to one of about 6 percent over the course of the last twenty-five years.

The most important reason for this increase has been a change in the demographic composition of the labor force. It used to be that mature white males made up the bulk of the labor force—54 percent in 1955. By the late '70s, they accounted for only 40 percent of the labor force—and only 20 percent of the unemployed. Young people, women, and minorities have traditionally had higher unemployment rates than mature white males, and now these groups have become larger fractions of the labor force. Thus, in 1978, when the overall unemployment rate was 6 percent, persons 16 to 24 made up half of the unemployed.

The second reason, I find, for the rise in the natural rate of unemployment is that there has been some reduction in the financial necessity to accept employment. This is partly because of the increase in government transfer programs and partly because many families now have more than one earner. There's been a trend toward greater income security for families—a very desirable trend, for obvious reasons—and it's probably had the side effect of causing an increase in the natural rate of unemployment.

A lot of people have suggested that another reason for that increase has been a change in the mix of industries; some industries have risen and some have fallen. My own work has not found that to be a major cause.

From *The Brookings Review*, Fall, 1983. Copyright © 1983 by The Brookings Institution, Washington, D.C.

Lovell: If America is going to be as competitive as it can be in world markets, I think that one inevitable by-product of that effort will be an increase in the displacement of experienced workers. Let me explain.

I think that there is general agreement that the world economy will be better off with an open trading system, and that the United States, as a major economic force—not the economic force we used to be, but still a very major one —has an opportunity, perhaps even a responsibility, to promote and perpetuate open trading. This means, of course, that we'll have to work to be competitive within this system, and that in turn is going to require us to move rapidly into new technologies in both old and new industries. As these shifts take place, some people now working will lose their jobs—either because the plants that they currently work in will be shut down or because they are at the low end of the seniority list in declining firms. Now we don't really know precisely how many workers will be affected; that will depend to some extent on how vigorously we pursue a more competitive approach. But it is important that we as a society recognize that if we are going to be competitive, there will be some human costs involved—and that these costs should not be borne entirely by the individuals who are displaced. We need to put in place public and private mechanisms to help spread the costs of unemployment. Then we will be able to move rapidly to enhance the competitiveness of U.S. industry in both domestic and international markets.

Burtless: That raises a subject that has been getting a lot of attention recently: the decline—or alleged decline—of American competitiveness. There seems to be a notion that American workers and American capital don't compete very effectively in international markets, and that, consequently, they're being displaced by foreign companies. Well, one of our colleagues here at Brookings, Robert Lawrence, has assembled evidence that leads me to doubt that proposition. It turns out that between 1970 and 1979, international trade actually contributed towards growth in manufacturing jobs in the United States. In fact, the United States was somewhat unusual among Western industrial nations in that the number of manufacturing jobs in this country rose during that period.

Youth Unemployment

Baily: To some extent, recent increases in the natural rate of unemployment reflect patterns that are not necessarily unhealthy. For example, you'd expect to see more career experimentation among married women moving in and out of the labor force and among young people just starting up in their careers. In practice, however, unemployment—particularly among youths and most especially among minority youths—is much higher than these patterns would suggest. There clearly are some pathological problems.

I've always felt that these problems were on both the demand and supply sides of the labor market. With respect to demand, young people and women don't always have the same access to jobs that other workers have. That may be due in part to discrimination, in part to the effects of minimum wage laws. It may also be due to the fact that manufacturing jobs—paying fairly well, maybe with some prospects in them, but not requiring a lot of educational qualifications—do not account for as large a share of total jobs today as they did in the 1950s.

On the supply side of the market, I think there are problems with both motivation and skills. Young people are not being terribly well prepared in the schools. It's not just a matter of difficulties with literacy and numeracy, although those are obviously important problems; it's also a matter of inadequate vocational education. I'm not all that well-qualified to talk about the motivational aspect, but I think that when you have a history of unemployment, low job participation, and some discrimination, those factors tend to interact, and then people decide they don't want to look for jobs—they'll look for other ways of getting by.

Lovell: In addition to the problems you mentioned, Martin, there is at least one other. Many employers lack confidence in the skills of these young disadvantaged people. Whatever the precise mix of causation, employment among male minority youth has dropped precipitously since the middle 1950s, from approximately 55 percent to about 25 percent today. That's a very dramatic change—and a very serious problem. And this has taken place during a period in which we have had major efforts to deal with the disadvantaged youth population—the anti-poverty program, various manpower and employment and training programs—and they just haven't made a dent. The situation has just gotten worse, rather than better.

Semerad: I think we should point out that spending in the CETA program, which was supposed to encompass both employment and training, was very much skewed toward the employment side. Now, under the new Job Training Partnership Act, participants in training programs will not be paid stipends. That makes sense, because the motivation for taking part in these programs ought to be the chance to get ahead by acquiring job skills, not the chance to get subsidies.

As to the inadequacy of vocational education in high schools, a problem that Martin touched on, we need to find ways to reduce the stigma sometimes attached to being on a vocational education track. Also it's important not only that vocational education courses help students to develop marketable skills, but also that they convey some more general information about succeeding in the business world. Students coming out of these courses ought to understand the language of the workplace, how to find jobs, and how to keep them.

Lovell: That's a very important point. Forty-five percent of the students who finish high school do not go on to college. That proportion may be fine in terms of the needs of business for employees with additional education.

However, I think it's essential that we take a close look at just what skills are going to be needed over the next decade or two for those entry-level jobs not requiring college degrees. That way, the high schools can provide better-focused vocational education programs, and the young men and women themselves can more readily identify the skills that they will have to acquire in order to be competitive in the job market. I have no doubt but that the sort of analysis of skill requirements that I'm suggesting would reveal large gaps in what most high schools now offer in their vocational education curricula.

Burtless: Contrary to some of the views expressed earlier, I don't think that all of the government training programs for disadvantaged youth have been disasters. In the ones that have been less successful, we've attempted to invest small amounts per young person for training and employment, and this has had very little effect. It seems to take a very large investment to make a difference in someone who's had a disadvantaged background. For example, in the Job Corps program it costs about $10,000 to provide a year of help to a young person. But that's one of the federal programs that seems to be successful both in reducing crime and in raising later earnings among the people enrolled in it. The summer youth program, on the other hand, which just provides a little bit of money to people over the summer and probably very little useful work experience, seems to have no impact whatsoever on their later employability.

Baily: It's also worth mentioning that wage subsidy programs have not worked terribly well either. When, for example, the government gives subsidies to employers who hire people with criminal records, it is not surprising to find that these subsidies fail to produce a huge increase in the number of former felons that are hired. But it is surprising that even those employers who do hire former felons don't bother to collect the subsidy; it's just too much trouble. That kind of program is a favorite with economists—you subsidize the wage and increase employment—but it has not worked out well.

Burtless: Martin is right. In 1981, when I was examining experience under the Targeted Jobs Tax Credit, I found that disadvantaged youths—whose jobs could be covered by the subsidies—held about two million private-sector jobs a year. Yet only 115,000 of these jobs ended up being subsidized by the program in its first two years. Evidently, millions of employers either didn't know about the program or didn't bother to apply for the subsidies if they did. This kind of experience shows that targeted job subsidies might be wonderful in theory, but they don't have much impact in practice.

Semerad: Well, our experience with the targeted tax program was that it was a boon for large companies like the Marriott Corporation, which hired a lot of young people and apparently took the accounting time needed to take advantage of the tax credit. But for smaller companies, the paperwork just wasn't worth it; it was too complicated.

Lovell: There are two aspects to training. The first, of course, is that it provides skills. The second is that it identifies a group of people as being *qualified* for employment. For example, the people who go through an apprentice program may or may not be better qualified than those of their contemporaries who do not, but they have been designated as being more qualified.

Those who make hiring decisions need some rationale on which to base—and to defend—their judgments, and, particularly in connection with jobs that really require very little skill, completion of a training program can provide that rationale.

Semerad: You can dress these programs up with tax credits and subsidies, but basically what employers want is very simple: They want good hires. They don't expect or require that people already be trained in their businesses. What they want are people who are *ready* to be trained, who have the correct attitude and the necessary literacy and computation skills.

Baily: Subsidies can become a stigma, so that if there is going to be a subsidy, it should probably be a fairly general one. For example, a youth sub-minimum wage would apply to all young people and would, I think, facilitate apprenticeship programs. If you wanted to go further, you might put in place a training subsidy that was available for use by any teenager. You might end up giving it to more teenagers than you had to, but because of its general availability, the subsidy wouldn't carry with it a stigma. I doubt that even this type of subsidy would have a big effect, however.

Semerad: Your point about the stigma attached to subsidies is really important. Giving stipends to trainees can also undercut the effectiveness of programs. In 70001, Ltd.—the nation-wide job training organization that I chair.—we don't pay a stipend to kids in our programs. As a result, we find that we're working with youngsters who have decided that they're going to take care of themselves; we build on that sense of self-worth, that can-do attitude, and we reinforce it. We've worked primarily with disadvantaged kids, but now we're transferring the same combination of building skills and building self-esteem into programs for handicapped people, Vietnam veterans, and middle-aged women entering the workforce. Anything that government does that undermines self-esteem reduces potential success.

Displaced Workers

Baily: I'd like to get back to the comments that Mac made earlier about displaced workers. As Gary pointed out, Bob Lawrence has found that from 1970 to 1979 international trade created a lot of jobs in this country. While the United States has become somewhat less competitive in world markets since 1979, that's largely because the dollar has been overvalued—a trend that both Gary and I think will be reversed. My sense, Mac, is that your view is more pessimistic.

Lovell: No, I think that over time vigorous participation in the world market will yield an increase in the number of jobs and an increase in national wealth. My point is that in this process, there will be changes in the job mix in a number of industries—and those changes will force people to move from one kind of a job to another. They will obviously have less difficulty in a booming economy than in a static or declining one, but in any case there will be problems of adjustment—for example, middle-aged people whose skills are not responsive to the needs of the new technologies or workers who are displaced in geographic areas where there aren't many new jobs. So my point is that if, as I have suggested, a number of individuals are going to suffer so that the economy as a whole may prosper, then we as a society have some responsibility to share that cost and not place it entirely on those individuals.

Baily: How many people are we talking about?

Lovell: My estimate is that we're dealing with about two million people a year. The key issue is how many of those will have difficulty finding new jobs.

Burtless: I think that depends critically on how concentrated the unemployment is in a region. If there are a lot of declining industries in a region, then everyone in that region is going to have trouble finding jobs. But that's a regional economic problem; it's not a problem that a general displaced-worker program for the entire nation is going to help very much to solve.

Lovell: Well, it's a matter of what that program is. I think one would want to design a program that is flexible enough to deal with regional differences—and that makes it easier for displaced workers, wherever they are, to get back to work.

We have to recognize that the permanent loss of a job—even though it's through no fault of one's own—is a psychological shock of some magnitude. I think it probably ranges after death and divorce—it's on that order of magnitude—and I just don't think it's appropriate in a democratic society for us to say that people don't need any help just because there are other jobs. They don't need debilitating help, of course; what they need are options that will help them to move on their own into new employment more quickly.

Semerad: Is this tied in with the idea of a two-track unemployment insurance system?

Lovell: Yes, it is. Workers could be given a choice between the present unemployment insurance set-up, which provides benefits while requiring only that those drawing the benefits undertake a casual job search, and a program that would give displaced workers far more vigorous labor market exposure, training and educational options, testing, and counseling on job search techniques and problems of adjustment.

Semerad: I think that relocation will be a big problem. An older worker—even though he may have ten more productive years ahead of him—won't really want to move.

Lovell: Well, that's right. But in most areas of the country there will be jobs of one kind or another within a commuting radius of a displaced worker's residence; it's just that to be eligible for those jobs, a worker might well need some new training.

Semerad: It occurs to me that the high-tech phenomenon cuts both ways. On the one hand, we see opportunities; on the other hand, we worry about workers being displaced by robots. In my judgment, what needs to be made clear in public discussion is that what is on the horizon is not so much a total upheaval of existing industries as it is an introduction of new techniques.

Lovell: I think that's right. We're going to have an automobile industry and we're going to have a steel industry, but they probably will not employ the same percentage of the work force as they have historically.

Baily: To put all of this into perspective, I want to underscore one key point: the best program for employment that we could have right now—something that could take millions of workers off the unemployment rolls—would be a continued strong recovery. That would dwarf anything we could do with structural programs.

A 7% JOBLESS RATE IS JUST NOT GOOD ENOUGH

BY ALAN S. BLINDER

It is an era of complacency—of settling for a level of unemployment that's still cruelly high. The nation is in a period of prosperity. We should create more jobs

America seems to be the victim of the same revolution of falling expectations that afflicts Europe. Far too many people are far too complacent about high unemployment. December's civilian jobless rate of 6.9% marked the first time since early 1980 that unemployment has fallen below 7%. Is that something to crow about? Hardly. The unemployment rates that we now view as good news used to be associated with the bottoms of recessions.

I submit that we can and should do better than this. The average unemployment rate in 1985 was 7.2%. Of all the years between the Depression and 1980, only two—1975 and 1976—had an annual unemployment rate that high. To me, that says the economy deserves no better than a C in employment on its 1985 report card. I teach my children that they should not be content with receiving a gentleman's C. Neither should the nation.

The case for discontentment starts, but does not end, with abhorrence for waste. Suppose the civilian unemployment rate today were 5.8%, which was the average rate of 1979, instead of 6.9%. Roughly 2 million more Americans would be working. Fewer people who want full-time work would have to settle for part-time work. Productivity would be higher. And gross national product would be about 2.5% larger than it is now. That works out to more than $400 for every man, woman, and child in America—enough new goods and services to provide everyone with some decent clothing or a good television set or food for about two months.

PSYCHOLOGICAL HARM. This lost output is, in economist Arthur Okun's apt phrase, just the tip of the iceberg that forms in a cold economy. Psychological, as well as economic, harm is visited on unemployment's victims, many of whom lose their self-respect, even their hope, along with their job. No wonder crime, mental and physical illness, divorce, and suicide all rise when unemployment rises.

Nor is that all the harm that is done. In a booming economy, people move rapidly up the occupational ladder; in a sick economy, they fall down. Discrimination breaks down faster when companies are scrambling for workers, not when workers are queuing up for jobs. It is no accident that World War II turned "equality of opportunity" from a slogan into a reality while the Depression turned it into a farce. Upward mobility is part of the glue that holds a democratic capitalist society together. Economic slack weakens that glue.

And who doubts that a booming economy is more conducive to investment, innovation, and entrepreneurship than a stagnant one? As the cliché says, a rising tide raises all boats, and that includes especially those that have just been launched. From 1962 to 1973 the country's relatively healthy economy experienced only one mild recession, an average unemployment rate of 4.7%, and productivity growth of about 2.5% per annum. From 1973 to 1985 our sickly economy suffered through two long recessions and one short one, an average unemployment rate of 7.5%, and productivity growth of only about 1% per year. This association of low unemployment with high productivity growth was no coincidence.

The social costs of unemployment would be high even if they were borne evenly. But plainly they are not. Instead, those least able to cope with adversity are given the greatest share.

WOUNDING THE WOUNDED. When recessions draft men and women into the reserve army of the unemployed, the disadvantaged—especially the young and the black—go first. The privileged go last. Americans should think twice, and three times, about the social implications of imposing such high costs on the young and on a disadvantaged racial minority. For this and other reasons, the poverty rolls ebb and flow with the unemployment rolls, and high unemployment leads to a more unequal distribution of income.

A weak economy strikes yet another blow against equality, I believe, by undermining public generosity. Charity, as they say, begins at home. And it may also end at home when personal economic circumstances turn sour.

It was no accident that the government's most strenuous antipoverty efforts were expended during our greatest peacetime boom from 1965 to 1969. Nor was it an accident that public enthusiasm for the war on poverty waned as economic growth faded. Nor is it an accident that the current mean-spirited tone of public policy toward the poor followed years of anemic economic performance.

General grumpiness may be one contributing factor. But I think the main reason is that equality is a luxury good, one the nation buys when it prospers and gives up when belts must be tightened. Sluggish economic growth helped create the "me-first" society that tolerated and even applauded the reverse-Robin Hood income redistributions of the first Reagan term. America will patch the holes in its social safety net only when prosperity is restored. A more permissive monetary policy, less paralyzed by fears of inflation, is the surest route to faster growth. Creating more jobs should be our first priority. ∎

ALAN S. BLINDER IS THE GORDON S. RENTSCHLER MEMORIAL PROFESSOR OF ECONOMICS AT PRINCETON UNIVERSITY AND A VISITING FELLOW AT THE BROOKINGS INSTITUTION

DISPLACED WORKERS
Bearing the costs of a changing economy

During the last recession, the media focused its attention on the unemployed. The nightly news featured human interest segments portraying — but not analyzing — the plight of unemployed steelworkers and autoworkers. By 1984, however, GNP was growing rapidly and the unemployed had lost their media appeal.

What happened to the workers who lost their jobs in the dark days of the recession? A recently released study undertaken by the U.S. Department of Labor in January 1984 confirmed fears that the chances for re-employment among displaced workers were low.

According to the study, nearly 12 million workers aged 20 and over lost jobs because of plant closings or cutbacks between January 1979 and January 1984. The study focused on the 5.1 million workers in the group who had been employed at least three years in the jobs they lost. The study provides good evidence of the costs of structural change in an unregulated macroeconomy.

The following were some of its conclusions:

Displaced workers do not fit the white, male, blue-collar stereotype. Unemployment struck workers of both genders, of all racial and ethnic groups, and across all industries and occupations. Over one-third of displaced workers were women. Nearly half the workers surveyed had been employed in jobs outside the manufacturing, mining, or construction sectors. (However, these three sectors were disproportionately affected, since they account for nearly 30% of the workforce and 50% of the displaced workers.) One in seven displaced workers was a manager, executive, or professional. Five percent were the victims of government RIF's (reductions in force).

Their chances for reemployment were low. While displacement was distributed broadly across the labor force, reemployment was not. Of the 5.1 million workers defined as displaced between 1979 and 1983, only 3.1 million were reemployed by January 1984.

About 1.3 million were officially unemployed and seeking work, while the remaining 700,000 had left the labor force. (Many of those defined as "out of the labor force" were discouraged workers who might have continued to seek work if it were available.)

Age discrimination, racism, and sexism shaped the chances of reemployment in predictable ways. The younger the displaced workers, the greater their chances of finding new jobs. Nearly three-fourths of those between the ages of 20 and 24 found work by 1984, compared to two-fifths of those between 55 and 64. Sixty-three percent of whites found new jobs, compared to 42% of blacks and 52% of Latinos. And 64% of the displaced men found new jobs, compared to 53% of the women.

Workers who lost low- and semi-skilled jobs had the hardest time finding new work. The chances of reemployment were lowest for machine operators, laborers, clericals and service workers, roughly half of whom were

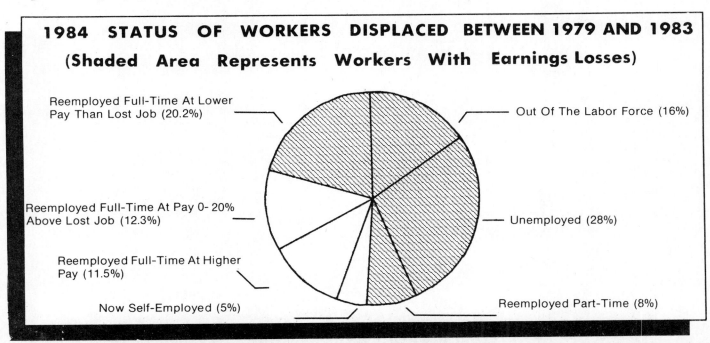

1984 STATUS OF WORKERS DISPLACED BETWEEN 1979 AND 1983
(Shaded Area Represents Workers With Earnings Losses)

- Reemployed Full-Time At Lower Pay Than Lost Job (20.2%)
- Reemployed Full-Time At Pay 0-20% Above Lost Job (12.3%)
- Reemployed Full-Time At Higher Pay (11.5%)
- Now Self-Employed (5%)
- Out Of The Labor Force (16%)
- Unemployed (28%)
- Reemployed Part-Time (8%)

Dollars & Sense, 38 Union Square, Room 14, Somerville, MA 02143.

reemployed by 1984. Not surprisingly, the outlook from the boardroom was better: three-fourths of displaced executives, managers, and administrators found new jobs.

The chances of finding a new job depended heavily on where you lived. Almost half of the displaced workers lived in the Snowbelt (the heavily industrialized states of the Midwest and Northeast). More than half of those surveyed in these areas had not returned to work by 1984.

Those who found new jobs often took cuts in pay or benefits. According to the survey at least half of the reemployed workers were earning less in their new jobs than in the jobs they had lost. Workers in ailing industries had the steepest decline in wages. For instance, among workers whose last job had been in manufacturing durable goods, median weekly earnings fell from $344 to $273. In addition, over a third of workers previously covered by health insurance had lost their coverage by 1984, often because their new jobs didn't offer health insurance.

Adding together workers whose earnings dropped and workers who hadn't gotten new jobs, over 70% of the workers displaced during the survey period were worse off in January 1984. The figure reveals that the devastation caused by the recession and by the structural changes taking place in the economy far overshadow the effects of the economic recovery.■

Source: *Monthly Labor Review*, June 1985

10

A Maddening Labor Mismatch

Despite lingering unemployment, the U.S. faces growing worker shortages

In the huge Hanover Room of downtown Atlanta's Hyatt Regency Hotel late last week, the air was filled with hubbub—and a sense of desperation. A total of 31 public and private corporations had set up interviewing tables to try to fill some 2,000 white-collar jobs, ranging from electrical engineer to word processor to bank teller, in the city's central business district. Some of the vacancies had gone unfilled for six months or more.

In Boston, the Burger King fast-food chain, which employs 160,000 people nationwide, took the unusual step of advertising jobs on MTV, the cable rock-music channel, to attract young prospective workers into its management program. In the throes of a rapid expansion, Burger King felt a strong need to try new avenues that might help ease its worker shortage.

In Chicago, Andy Frain Services, a supplier of ushers and ticket takers for concert halls and sports arenas like Comiskey Park, is faced with new recruiting headaches. Says Operations Director James Wronski: "The bonus of seeing a ball game or hearing a concert used to be enough to attract the workers we needed. We used to sign up half the kids we solicited for jobs. Now it's below 20%."

From shopping malls to corporate computer centers, from fast-food joints to high-tech industrial plants, a common plea is popping up all across the U.S.: HELP WANTED. APPLY WITHIN. Suddenly America is running up against serious labor shortages that are crimping many businesses and forcing corporate headhunters to work overtime. As a result, says Richard Kappus, an analyst at the New York State department of labor, companies are having to "do more, spend more and bend over backward to attract workers." The shortages are most severe in low-paying service jobs and in many positions that require technical skills. The maddening worker deficit has come about in part because of the low birthrate, or "baby bust," of the 1960s and early 1970s, which is causing fewer young Americans to enter the job market. That trend will continue over the next decade.

The labor shortages could worsen considerably this year as the U.S. economy starts to grow with renewed vigor. Government figures released last week showed that the gross national product expanded at a 3.2% annual rate in the first quarter of 1986, nearly five times as fast as in the last quarter of 1985. The sharp pickup in growth may prove to be quirky, but it got an additional boost late in the week when the Federal Reserve Board cut its discount rate, which is the interest charged on loans to member banks, from 7% to 6.5%, its lowest level in eight years.

But the economic statistics contain a striking anomaly. Even as business activity increases and worker shortages grow more troublesome, the number of Americans on the jobless rolls remains high by historical standards. The unemployment rate stands at 7.2%, which is less than the 9.7% registered in 1982 but still well above the 5.6% reached in 1979, near the peak of the last economic expansion.

For many worker-hungry employers, the jobless figures are a major mystery. "Who are these people who make up the unemployment statistics?" asks Thomas Anton, executive vice president of Troy, Mich.–based Kelly Services, the temporary office-help firm. "We're doing our best to find them because we can put them to work. Still, we don't get enough."

Part of the answer to Anton's complaint is that more than ever, the U.S. is suffering from a mismatch between the new jobs that are flooding the labor market and the people who are available to fill them. Many of those who are out of work are not in the right place with the right skills to take advantage of the increase in demand for workers.

One cause of the labor mismatch is a spiraling need for employees with new abilities, notably computer and word-processing skills. Kenneth Snyder, a vice president with the Louisville-based Humana hospital chain, faces a three-month delay in finding new computer programmers and systems analysts for the company, where the roster of such professionals has grown from fewer than 40 to about 150 over the past five years. Dewey Sadka, president of Temp Force, an Atlanta office-help firm, says that "word processing is a bottomless pit. I could place 100 people at IBM just like that as trainees."

In many areas the people who need jobs do not live where the openings are. Even as employers beg for workers in America's affluent suburbs, where the labor pool is shallow, unemployment rates among black youth in some inner cities run as high as 50%. Yet little or no mass transit is usually available to ferry the potential workers to the jobs.

Another fundamental force behind labor market mismatches is the shift in hiring demand from manufacturing to service industries. Of the 9.1 million U.S. jobs created in the past four years, 88% were in service categories such as clerical work, financial management and data processing. The Bureau of Labor Statistics projects that by 1995 service jobs in the U.S. will outnumber manufacturing positions by a ratio of 4.3 to 1 (the current ratio: 3.8 to 1). Many blue-collar workers and even some managers from the manufacturing sector appear to have difficulty in crossing over the line to fill new service jobs.

An even more profound cause of the labor drought arises from demographics (see chart). The baby bust shrinkage of the labor force is most marked among Americans 16 to 24 years old, many of whom are now entering the labor market for the first time. The Bureau of Labor Statistics projects that from 1984 to 1990, the number of workers in the 16-to-24 age bracket will decrease by 2.7 million, to 21.3 million; from 1990 to 1995, that group is expected to drop by an additional 1.1 million. Right now the thinning of the ranks of those workers is having its worst effect on low-wage, low-skill service industries, including fast-food and department-store sales. But eventually the impact of the labor shortfall is bound to spread. Warns Walter Cadette, a vice president and economist at Morgan Guaranty Trust: "McDonald's and Burger King's shortages today will be General Motors' and IBM's shortages tomorrow."

The dearth of many kinds of workers is putting upward pressure on salaries and making the $3.35-an-hour minimum wage all but obsolete in some areas. Says an Atlanta business development official: "I know places that pay bus boys $8 an

Average annual growth in the size of the civilian labor force

hour." Computer programmers who earned about $20,000 a year in 1980 now demand—and get—up to $38,000 annually in some cities, along with 12% to 15% annual raises. For low-level secretarial and data-processing jobs in the suburbs, wages can be 25% higher than elsewhere.

Unable to attract the youthful or specialized workers that they want, some employers are turning to senior citizens or the handicapped, among others. In Atlanta, one burger shop boasts an 80-year-old kitchen worker, while at a school for the deaf an information session on the jobs that deaf workers can effectively perform drew representatives from 20 local companies. Some firms are looking overseas for aid. Last October Grumman, the Long Island, N.Y., aerospace company, hired 28 engineers from Britain for six months to help design U.S. military aircraft. Says Miriam Reid, a Grumman spokeswoman: "We did it as a last resort. There's always been a short-

age of engineers, but it is becoming more acute."

Some employers are resorting to giveaways or other inducements to attract new workers. Like a pro baseball club, the Ann & Hope department store in Watertown, Mass., offers signing bonuses—as much as $300—to new employees. Veteran staffers who find new prospects for the payroll can also win up to $100. In Missouri's affluent St. Louis County, McDonald's recently offered free movie tickets to passersby in order to fill a hall with youngsters for a hiring spiel. In Dublin, Ohio, Denny Lynch, a vice president of Wendys International, says that the burger chain is looking into scholarships as a lure to start young people on an up-from-the-bottom career with the company.

Virtually all experts agree that more must be done to train and retrain potential employees. Many companies are instituting expensive in-house education programs to fill their more sophisticated openings. But some manpower specialists see a strong need to reinstate federal job-training funds that have been slashed by 58% during the Reagan Administration's tenure, to $3.3 billion annually. In some congressional circles there is tentative discussion about raising additional revenues to pay for the retraining of workers dislocated by foreign imports. But legislative action is not expected anytime soon.

Still other labor experts point to the doleful performance of the U.S. public education system as an area that badly needs shoring up. Says one job-placement executive in Atlanta: "There is a major gap between the business community and the schools. They need to produce a student who can get a first job." Money for improving education, however, is in short supply. As frustrations mount, the striking fact is that jobs in the U.S. are literally going to waste. —*By George Russell.* *Reported by Lee Griggs/Chicago and Frank S. Washington/Atlanta, with other bureaus*

11

Why America's Got So Many Jobs

By Peter F. Drucker

"Where have all the jobs gone?" has been the constant question in all industrial Western countries these past few years. But for the U.S., another question is at least as important—perhaps much more so—and yet it is never asked: Where have all the jobs come from? All developed industrial countries are losing jobs in the "smokestack" industries—even Japan. But only the U.S. economy is creating new jobs at a much faster rate than the smokestack industries are losing old ones, indeed at a rate that is almost unprecedented in our peacetime history.

Between 1965 and 1984, America's population aged 16 to 65 grew 38%, to 178 million people from 129 million. But jobs during that period increased 45%, to 103 million from 71 million. By this fall, they are likely to reach 105 million or 106 million, which would mean a rise of almost 50% since 1965. And more than half this growth occurred since the energy crisis in the fall of 1973—years of "oil shocks," of two recessions and of the near-collapse of the smokestack industries. Indeed the 1981-1982 recession, for all its trauma, barely slowed the rapid pace of new-job creation. At its bottom, in fall 1982, there still were 15 million more jobs than there had been in 1973, despite record unemployment.

In Japan, jobs these past 10 years have grown about 10%, only half the U.S. rate, to 56 million from 51 million. Western Europe has had job *shrinkage*. In Western Europe, there are now three million fewer jobs—after full allowance for cyclical unemployment—than there were in 1974.

High-Tech a Marginal Source

And the U.S. economy now has about 10 million more jobs than even optimists predicted 15 years ago. Such a careful and authoritative expert as Columbia University's Eli Ginzberg then thought that during the late 1970s and early 1980s the federal government would have to become the "employer of first resort" to provide jobs for the children of the "baby boom." But without any government help we have provided half as many again as needed to absorb the members of the baby boom. This was in order to accommodate what nobody foresaw 15 years ago—the rush of married women into jobs. Where have all these jobs come from?

They didn't come from the sectors that for almost 40 years through the 1960s provided virtually all the new jobs in the U.S. economy—government and big business. Government stopped expanding its employment in the early '70s and has barely maintained it since. Big business has been losing jobs since the early '70s. In the past five years alone, the Fortune 500—the country's biggest manufacturing companies—have permanently lost around three million jobs. Nearly all job creation has been in small and medium-sized businesses, and practically all of it in entrepreneurial and innovative businesses.

"Aha," everyone will say, "high-tech." But everyone will be wrong. High technology is tremendously important—as vision setter, pace setter, excitement maker, maker of the future. But as a maker of the present it is still almost marginal, accounting for no more than 10% of the jobs created in the past 10 years. And it is reasonably certain that its job-creation rate won't increase significantly until after 1990.

New-job creation mainly is in "low-tech" or "no-tech" businesses. One indication is Inc. magazine's annual list of the fastest-growing publicly owned businesses more than five years and less than 15 years old. Being confined to publicly owned companies, the list has a strong high-tech bias. Yet 80 of the 100 companies on the 1982 list were decidedly low-tech or no-tech—women's wear makers, restaurant chains and the like. And Inc.'s list of the 500 fastest-growing closely held companies is headed by a maker of exercise equipment for the home.

The most illuminating analysis, however, is a study of "mid-sized growth companies"—those with annual sales of $25 million to $1 billion a year—made by the consulting firm McKinsey & Co. A majority of these concerns aren't high-tech; a majority are manufacturers rather than services. These mid-sized growth companies grew three times as fast as the Fortune 250—the economy's big companies—in sales, profits and employment during 1975-1980. Even during the worst of the recent recession, when the Fortune 250 cut employment nearly 2% in one year, the mid-sized growth companies added one million jobs—or 1% of the country's employed labor force. And all that these companies have in common is that they are organized for systematic entrepreneurship and purposeful innovation.

For about 10 years now, the U.S. economy's dynamics have been shifting to entrepreneurial and innovative businesses—mostly low-tech or no-tech. In economics 10 years is a long time—long enough to talk of a "structural change." What explains this shift isn't clear yet. Surely there has been a sharp shift in values, attitudes and aspirations of a lot of educated young people—a shift totally different from the "Greening of America" we were promised 15 years ago, when the real change actually began. There are many people around now who are risk-takers and who want material success badly enough to impose on themselves the grueling discipline and endless hours of the entrepreneur.

But where does the money come from? A decade ago, we worried that there would be no capital available for new ventures—now it seems there is more venture capital than there are ventures. The biggest factor in the entrepreneurial explosion—and the one truly new technology—is probably a managerial breakthrough: the development since World War II of a body of organized knowledge of entrepreneurship and innovation.

Why is this new economy primarily an American phenomenon? While there are harbingers of a similar development in Ja-

Drucker on Management

The job-creation by entrepreneurial businesses in the U.S. bears a remarkable resemblance to the "atypical Kondratieff wave" of Germany and the U.S. after 1873.

pan, there are few signs of entrepreneurial dynamism in Western Europe.

The American development clearly disproves the most widely held and most serious explanation of the economic crisis of the past 10 years, and the most widely held and most serious prediction for the decades to come: the "no-growth" theory based on the "Kondratieff long wave" (named after the Russian Nikolai Kondratieff—born in 1892 and executed sometime in the 1930s on Stalin's orders because his economic model accurately predicted that collectivization would cut rather than multiply farm output).

According to the long-wave theory, developed economies enter a long period of inexorable stagnation every 50 years. The technologies that carried the growth in the earlier ascending stages of the "Kondratieff cycle" still seem to do very well during the last 20 years before the "Kondratieff bust." Indeed, they show record profits and can pay record wages; being "mature" they no longer need to invest heavily.

But what looks like blooming health is, in effect, wasting sickness; the "record profits" and "record wages" are already capital-liquidation. And then, when the tide turns with the Kondratieff bust, these mature industries all but collapse overnight. The new technologies are already around, but for another 20 years they can't generate enough jobs or absorb enough capital to fuel a new period of economic growth. For 20 years there is thus a "Kondratieff stagnation" and "no growth"; and there is nothing anybody—least of all government—can do about it but wait it out.

The smokestack industries in the U.S. and Western Europe do seem to conform to the Kondratieff cycle. In Japan, too, they seem to be headed the same way and to be only a few years behind. High-tech also conforms; it doesn't generate enough new jobs or absorb enough new capital yet to offset the shrinkage in the smokestack industries.

But the job-creation by entrepreneurial and innovative businesses in the U.S. simply isn't compatible with Kondratieff. Or, rather, it bears a remarkable resemblance to the "atypical Kondratieff wave" of Germany and the U.S. after 1873—25 years of great turbulence in these countries and of economic and social change, but also 25 years of rapid economic growth.

Ruling Out No-Growth Forecast

This atypical Kondratieff wave was discovered and described by Joseph Schumpeter (1883-1950) in his classic "Business Cycles" (1939). This book introduced Kondratieff to the West; but it also pointed out that the Kondratieff stagnation occurred only in England and France after 1873, the period on which Kondratieff based his "long wave." Germany and the U.S. also had a "crash." But recovery began almost at once, and five years later both countries were expanding rapidly and continued to do so up to World War I. And what made these two countries atypical and made them the growth economies of the late 19th century was their shift to an entrepreneurial economy.

There are massive threats in the world economy. There is the crisis of the Welfare State with its uncontrolled and seemingly uncontrollable government deficits and the resulting inflationary cancer. There is the crisis of the commodity producers everywhere, in the Third World as much as on the Iowa farm. Commodity prices for several years have been lower in relation to the prices of manufactured goods than at any time since the Great Depression—and in all economic history, there has never been a prolonged period of very low commodity prices that wasn't followed by depression in the industrial economy. And surely the shrinkage of jobs in the smokestack industries and their conversion to being capital-intensive rather than labor-intensive, that is to automation, will put severe strains—economic, social, political—on the system.

But at least for the U.S., the Kondratieff no-growth prediction is practically ruled out by what has already happened in the American economy and by the near-50% increase in jobs since the smokestack industries reached their "Kondratieff peak" 15 or 20 years ago.

———

Mr. Drucker is Clarke professor of social sciences at the Claremont Graduate School.

How Good Are The Price Indexes?

The use of inaccurate or incomplete information to estimate price indexes biases the measures from their true values and causes a variety of distortions in the economy and in the distribution of national income. Economists have identified several problems and issues in the construction and use of price indexes. Some issues are related to the calculation of real GNP estimates from current dollar estimates, while others relate to the use of price indexes to estimate changes in living costs.

One way that the methodology of constructing price indexes can affect the index value, and thus the estimated value of real GNP, is the use of prices listed in producers' price catalogs rather than prices actually paid by buyers. Tracking price changes from information on list prices can underestimate actual price declines in times of economic weakness if price discounting is prevalent. Similarly, tracking posted prices can underestimate inflation in boom periods if producers charge extra to allocate scarce supplies. The "transactions-list price" issue has been important historically in construction of the producer price indexes. It is of little importance with respect to the Consumer Price Index (CPI), however, because field workers traditionally have collected prices of consumer goods and services on an actual transactions basis.

The Bureau of Labor Statistics (BLS) has addressed this pricing weakness in its current comprehensive revision of the Producer Price Index (PPI) program. BLS is revising and improving the measurement of producer price changes to reflect adequately prices at which transactions actually occur. Currently, 191 out of the 493 mining and manufacturing four-digit industries in the Standard Industrial Classification (SIC), or almost 40 percent, are being calculated using procedures that adequately capture transactions prices. These 191 industries represent 57 percent of the value of all mining and manufacturing shipments. By 1986, all 493 mining and manufacturing industries will be calculated using the improved procedures. (Additional industries are brought into the system at six-month intervals.)

Other problems also bias the producer price indexes over the business cycle. These problems include adjustment for changes in the quality of products over time, reliability of reporter response, and other sampling and price measurement problems. Unfortunately, the net direction and magnitude of bias is unknown when all of these factors are taken into consideration.

The most widely used measure of inflation, and the one used for indexation purposes, is the CPI. Two frequently noted "shortcomings" of the CPI are the way it measures homeownership costs and its use of a fixed market basket. Critics of the CPI argue that these factors help explain why the CPI increased at a faster rate than some other indexes of inflation in the 1970s.

They also argue that the CPI overstated the rise in the cost of living in that period.

One reason the CPI may have overstated inflation is that, before last January, the official CPI treated the rise in the asset (investment) value of homeownership as an increase in the cost of living. In fact, a rise in housing values can represent an increase in wealth for homeowners who are not buying in the period of rising prices. This is because they could sell or refinance the housing asset or lessen other forms of saving to capture the capital gain associated with the housing price increases. The CPI also tends to be sensitive to mortgage interest rate changes and to attach too much importance to housing because mortgage costs are counted along with the purchase price.

The CPI is said to overstate cost of living increases because it tracks prices of a fixed market basket of goods and services despite changing consumption patterns. If consumption patterns change from the fixed, base-year market basket, then tracking the cost of buying the base-year basket will measure inaccurately the change in the cost of the more recently chosen market basket. Furthermore, if the prices of the original market basket increase faster than the actual goods chosen more recently, then the CPI will overestimate the increased cost of living.

Economists at the BLS are well aware of these "shortcomings." Starting with the January CPI for all urban consumers, BLS changed the way homeownership cost is officially measured. The new approach measures what a family would have to pay if it rented its home, filtering out the investment aspects of owning a home. Thus, wild swings in homeownership costs caused by volatile interest rates are eliminated. (In 1981, one-third of the rise in the CPI was caused by rapidly escalating mortgage interest rates.)

A major conceptual and measurement problem arises, however, in attempting to adjust for the changing market basket. Essentially there is no way of knowing whether a change in observed consumption patterns results in a higher or lower standard of living. A change can be caused either by varying prices or by a change in consumer preferences. For example, if the Smith family begins to skip its usual Sunday afternoon ride through the countryside because of rising gasoline prices, its standards of living is lower. If we want to use the CPI to index incomes to preserve living standards, the index should not count this market-basket change. If, however, the family foregoes the car ride so they can all go jogging together, then a measure used to index income should reflect this kind of market-basket change. This example illustrates that, in practice, there is no practical way to formulate the CPI so that it can be used exactly to index incomes to a particular living standard.

Reprinted from Federal Reserve Bank of Atlanta *Economic Review*, June, 1983.

An examination of employment and unemployment rates

The persistence of high rates of unemployment after more than two years of economic recovery has increased the controversy over what the best measure of labor market conditions is. The usefulness of the unemployment rate, the traditional measure, has been called into question; the employment ratio is the most frequently recommended alternative. Too frequently, the debate has implied that an absolute choice must be made between the two statistics. Such a view is mistaken, for no single measure can hope to provide a complete assessment of labor market conditions.

At the outset, it must be recognized that each measure suffers from some shortcomings. The unemployment rate has the most deficiencies, and because of them that rate has become an increasingly imperfect measure of labor market conditions. Analysts are therefore regarding the unemployment rate with increasing reservations, and some have suggested that the employment ratio be given more emphasis in the analysis of the labor market as it reflects demand pressures in the economy as a whole.

The two measures defined

The unemployment rate refers to the percentage of the civilian labor force that is seeking work but does not have a job.[1] This widely used statistic is not the only unemployment rate that the Bureau of Labor Statistics (BLS) regularly reports. A number of other unemployment rates, such as the percentage of household heads in the labor force who are unemployed, the percentage of teenagers in the labor force who are unemployed, and the percentage of the labor force out of work for fifteen weeks or longer are also available for evaluating labor market conditions. No matter whether the total or a segmental unemployment rate is ex-

amined, all these rates are intended to represent the proportion of labor force participants that offer labor for sale but are unable to find employment at the current level of wages. Thus, each measures the unutilized or excess supply of labor in the market at existing wages.

The employment ratio, in contrast, is defined as the proportion of the noninstitutionalized *population* in the working ages—16 years of age and older—that is employed, and it thus measures the extent of utilization of potential labor resources.[2] Employment ratios analogous to many of the published unemployment series may be constructed. These ratios measure the proportion of labor resources whose services have been purchased in the labor market.

A rate of unemployment supposedly indicates the extent of utilization of available rather than potential labor resources. The unemployment rate is also used to help assess the hardship experienced by workers who are willing to work and are available for work but are unable to find jobs. But whether the unemployment rate indicates hardship or need as precisely as one would like has come to be questioned. Its accuracy is impaired in several ways. The measured rate can be considered too low because it fails to include "discouraged workers", that is, the people who do not seek work if they do not believe they are likely to obtain jobs and thus leave the labor force temporarily or remain outside it. Similarly, the rate fails to include those who want to work full time but are forced to work part time because of economic conditions. In-

---

[1] The civilian labor force refers to all noninstitutionalized individuals 16 years of age and over who are employed or are without a job and seeking work.

[2] If the employment ratio were defined as the proportion of civilian labor force that is employed, it would simply be the mirror image of the unemployment rate. In that case, it could be obtained by subtracting the unemployment rate from 100. But then, any statistical or institutional factors that caused defects in the unemployment rate would cause the same defects in an employment ratio based on the civilian labor force. That is why the employment ratio uses the relevant population rather than the labor force in the denominator.

Reprinted from Federal Reserve Bank of New York *Quarterly Review*, Autumn, 1977.

Reprinted from Federal Reserve Bank of New York
Quarterly Review, Autumn, 1977.

stead, all part-time workers with jobs are treated as employed whether or not they would prefer full-time work.[3] The measured rate can be considered too high because of the expansion in the coverage of such programs as unemployment insurance as well as the rise in benefit levels. Applicants must remain in the labor force to receive these benefits even though they may not be seriously looking for jobs. Such behavior imparts an upward thrust to the unemployment rate. And the increases in these programs have also served to weaken the tie between the unemployment rate and "hardship".

Changing participation rates and their impact

The employment ratio avoids to a greater degree than the unemployment rate a statistical problem that is caused by changing labor force participation rates, *i.e.,* the proportion of the population 16 years of age and over who are at work or are looking for work. Changes in these participation rates have altered the composition of the labor force in recent years. The changes suggest that a basic structural alteration in the pattern of choice among work in the market, work at home, and the amount of leisure desired is under way, particularly in certain demographic groups. As a result of these changes, a larger proportion of the labor force now consists of women and teenagers. Indeed, the secular increase in labor force participation rates (see top panel, Chart 1) is attributable largely to this change in behavior by women and teenagers. And these groups in the labor force are among those that traditionally have experienced higher than average rates of unemployment. It is now recognized that for this reason alone a given rate of aggregate demand will be associated with a higher level of unemployment than in the past.[4]

Experience shows that rates of labor force participation respond to a host of influences. In the short term, the rate of business activity may have the most effect. On the one hand, the rate of participation in the labor force typically increases during upswings in economic activity because individuals perceive increased job opportunities. If, as sometimes happens, the growth of the labor force is faster than that of employment, the resultant increase in the unemployment rate should

not be construed as a sign of weakening economic conditions. On the other hand, if during an economic decline workers become discouraged and leave the labor force, the resulting tendency toward a lower unemployment rate should not be construed as a sign of improving economic conditions.

Changes in the long-term trend of labor force participation rates also affect the interpretation of the two measures. Should the rate of participation in the labor force and the age-sex composition of the population

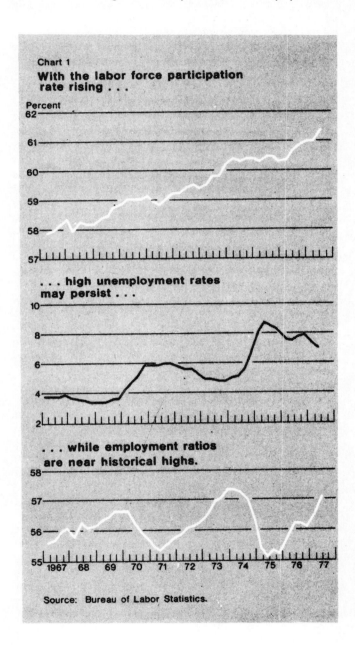

Chart 1
With the labor force participation rate rising . . .

. . . high unemployment rates may persist . . .

. . . while employment ratios are near historical highs.

Source: Bureau of Labor Statistics.

---

[3] It should be noted that this treatment of part-time workers impairs both the unemployment rate and the employment ratio, and also creates difficulties of interpretation with respect to both.

While it can be shown that an increasing proportion of the unemployment rate stems from the changing composition of the labor force, this by no means is the only or even the principal explanation for today's high unemployment rates. For further discussion of this point, see "The Changing Composition of the Labor Force" by Sharon P. Smith in this Bank's *Quarterly Review* (Winter 1976), pages 24-30.

remain constant for a considerable period, the unemployment rate and the employment ratio would suggest similar assessments of labor market conditions. However, if the labor force participation rate changes, the unemployment rate and the employment ratio can yield different assessments. Among all the possible scenarios, here are two. If the labor force participation rate is rising, then the employment ratio may suggest stable labor market conditions although the unemployment rate would be increasing. If the labor force participation rate is falling, the unemployment rate may suggest a strengthening of labor market conditions although the employment ratio would be declining. It thus seems clear that when changes in labor force participation rates occur, whether for cyclical or secular reasons, *both* the unemployment rate and employment ratio ought to be looked at to obtain more accurate appraisals of labor market conditions.

The relationships being discussed are highlighted in Chart 1, which shows quarterly data for the labor force participation rate, the civilian unemployment rate, and the employment ratio. During periods when labor force participation rates are more or less constant, as they were during most of 1970-72, a rise in the unemployment rate and a decline in the employment ratio suggest worsening labor market conditions. In fact, whenever these statistics move in opposite directions and participation rates are roughly the same, both statistics yield similar labor market appraisals. In recent years, however, it has been more typical for the labor force participation rate to rise—it went up strongly from 59.8 percent at the end of 1973 to 62.3 percent in September of this year. Consequently, the present employment ratio of 57.3 percent is associated with an unemployment rate of 6.9 percent; in 1973, the same employment ratio was accompanied by an unemployment rate of only 4.8 percent.

Characteristics of the two measures
The employment ratio is in general less subject to error than the unemployment rate. Because the impact of measurement error on the unemployment rate appears to be increasing, the unemployment rate is becoming the less reliable measure with which to assess labor market conditions.

Unemployment data are collected in a survey of households, and one individual usually responds for all members of the household. As a result, the recorded employment rate is affected by the accuracy of replies by the individuals who report on the labor force status of all members of the household. It has been observed that reports given by most households show higher unemployment when they have recently been added to the survey sample than in later interviews.

This is documented in a study by Robert E. Hall.[5]

Because of the difficulty of determining whether individuals actually are looking for and are available for work, a count of the employed is likely to be much more accurate than a count of the unemployed.[6] Moreover, because the employment figure is much larger than the unemployment figure, sampling errors that are to be expected in either statistic introduce a smaller possibility of error into the employment ratio than the unemployment rate. Seasonal fluctuations also are much smaller in employment than they are in unemployment.

In addition to these statistical problems, the unemployment rate is affected by institutional influences. Among the most publicized are those that occur as a consequence of unemployment compensation and of work registration requirements in certain welfare programs. To be eligible to receive benefits under the above programs, individuals are required to register as unemployed with the United States Employment Service or to register for manpower training.[7] These individuals are defined by the BLS to be unemployed, since registration with a public employment service is viewed as a means of actively seeking employment. However, these programs, like any income-maintenance plan, also create disincentives to seek employment in a more active fashion than by merely registering for employment to obtain benefits. As a result, it is likely that some recipients of benefits under these plans are voluntarily unemployed—that is, they basically choose not to work—and so would not be counted in a more precise measure of unemployment.

A number of analysts have attributed much of the present high rate of unemployment to Government benefits programs. Ehrenberg and Oaxaca, as well as Feldstein,[8] have suggested that a large portion of un-

[5] "Why is the Unemployment Rate So High at Full Employment?" *Brookings Papers on Economic Activity* (3, 1970), page 375.

[6] The BLS defines the employed as those who, during the survey week, worked either as paid employees or in their own profession or business, worked without pay for fifteen hours or more on a farm or a family-operated business, and those with jobs but not at work because of a labor-management dispute, illness, vacation, etc. The unemployed are defined as those who did not have a job during the survey week but were available for work and (according to the survey respondent) actively looked for a job at some time during the four-week period immediately prior to the survey.

[7] Some welfare recipients are exempt from these work registration requirements. These include certain categories such as the ill or incapacitated (with medical verification) and mothers or other members of the household charged with the care of children under age 18.

[8] See Ronald Ehrenberg and Ronald L. Oaxaca, "Do Benefits Cause Unemployed to Hold Out for Better Jobs?" and Martin Feldstein, "Unemployment Compensation: Its Effect on Unemployment", both in the *Monthly Labor Review* (March 1976).

employment is voluntary, because the high levels of unemployment compensation enable unemployed workers to engage in a longer period of search before taking another job or simply to enjoy leisure-time activities. Moreover, Feldstein believes that the present system of unemployment compensation costs some employers less in contributions to unemployment programs than the benefits that are paid to the employees they lay off. He concludes that this system thereby encourages employers to organize production so as to exaggerate seasonal and cyclical variations in unemployment and to create more temporary jobs than would otherwise exist.

Clarkson and Meiners maintain that the single most important factor contributing to the high level of unemployment is the change in certain welfare eligibility requirements.[9] They argue that the current overall unemployment rate has been inflated by as much as 2.1 percentage points because of the work registration eligibility requirements that were introduced in 1971 into the Aid to Families with Dependent Children (AFDC) program and into the food stamp program. In their view, these registrants represent a group of individuals who either are largely unemployable or have no need or desire to work but are counted as unemployed because they have to register to obtain benefits.

Clarkson and Meiners estimate a "corrected" unemployment rate by omitting from both the unemployment and the civilian labor force figures all those work registrants who have been required to register to be eligible for AFDC or food stamp benefits. This is undoubtedly an overadjustment since many welfare recipients actually do want a job. Indeed, nearly a fourth of all the AFDC recipients who register for work with the public employment service are exempt from registering. Moreover, a study of AFDC recipients indicates that nearly half of them have had recent labor market experience.[10] These facts cast doubt on the assumption that none of the welfare recipients are employable or seeking a job. In sum, while it appears that the work registration requirements of the welfare programs inflate the unemployment rate, the extent of overstatement is likely to be considerably less than the 2.1 percentage points suggested by Clarkson and Meiners.

An increasing awareness of the foregoing sorts of problems is reflected in the new unemployment insurance benefits bill signed into law on April 12, 1977.

[9] Kenneth W. Clarkson and Roger E. Meiners, "Government Statistics as a Guide to Economic Policy: Food Stamps and the Spurious Increase in the Unemployment Rates", *Policy Review* (Summer 1977).

[10] Robert George Williams, *Public Assistance and Work Effort* (Research Report Series No. 119, Industrial Relations Section, Princeton University, Princeton, N.J., 1975).

Under this legislation, individuals may be denied unemployment compensation if they do not actively seek work, do not apply for suitable work to which they are referred, or do not accept an offer of suitable work. Contrary to past practice, under the new law individuals may be required to accept positions that are significantly different in tasks and pay from their past jobs if the position is within the individual's "capabilities", if the individual is offered either the Federal minimum wage or more than the unemployment benefit, if the job does not entail unreasonable travel, and if it does not endanger the individual's "morals, health, or safety". It is too early to ascertain the extent to which the law may affect labor market statistics.

The need for further study
All in all, the unemployment rate tends to be inaccurate for both statistical and institutional—including legislative—reasons. In addition, the possible size of any error seems greater than for any associated with the employment ratio. In large part, this is because it is simply easier to identify clearly those who are working than to identify clearly those who want to work and are seeking work, since it is difficult to determine how many of the latter are in fact available for work. Further study of labor supply behavior under various income maintenance programs is necessary to formulate techniques that will eliminate from the unemployment numbers those who are really voluntarily unemployed.

Although at present the unemployment rate is a less accurate measurement than the employment ratio, this does not imply that the unemployment rate should be abandoned as a means of assessing labor market conditions. Instead, it calls for action to correct the shortcomings in all statistics relating to the labor market. For this reason, the Emergency Jobs Programs Extension Act of 1976 (Public Law 94-444) established a new National Commission on Employment and Unemployment Statistics. (The last major evaluation of employment and unemployment statistics was made fourteen years ago.) The new commission is charged with the responsibility of evaluating the present statistics as well as with making recommendations for their improvement.

In seeking the proper statistics to assess labor market conditions, the measure chosen should depend on the question being posed. For example, the Employment Act of 1946 calls for the Federal Government to take all feasible action to encourage the "conditions under which there will be afforded useful employment opportunities, including self-employment for those able, willing, and seeking to work, and to promote maximum employment, production, and purchasing power". To find out whether maximum—or full—

Chart 2

Relationship between the Consumer Price Index and the Employment Ratio

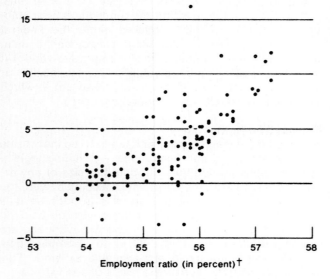

Percentage change in prices*

Employment ratio (in percent)†

*Change from previous quarter (at annual rate), 1948-77.

†By quarters, 1948-77.

Source: Computations based on data from the Bureau of Labor Statistics.

Chart 3

Relationship between the Consumer Price Index and the Unemployment Rate

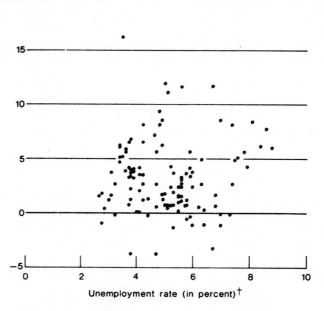

Percentage change in prices*

Unemployment rate (in percent)†

*Change from previous quarter (at annual rate), 1948-77.

†By quarters, 1948-77.

Source: Computations based on data from the Bureau of Labor Statistics.

employment has been achieved, the unemployment rate is conceptually the more appropriate measure, although its inaccuracies seriously compromise its relevance at the present time.

If, however, the primary interest is the relation between wage changes or inflation and the condition of the labor market, the employment ratio may be the better statistic to use because increasing inaccuracy of the unemployment rate has weakened the relationship between that statistic and excess demand. This has been pointed out by Geoffrey Moore[11] and is illustrated in Charts 2 and 3, which show a much stronger association between the percentage change in the consumer price index and the employment ratio than between the percentage change in the consumer price index

[11] "Employment, Unemployment, and the Inflation-Recession Dilemma", *AEI Studies on Contemporary Economic Problems* (1976).

and the unemployment rate. Of course, the observation of correlation between these statistical series does not prove the existence of any causal relationship between them.

If the unemployment rate included only the involuntarily unemployed, the rate could be interpreted as an indirect measure of the inflationary pressures resulting from excess demand. This, in fact, is the interpretation that underlies the Phillips curve relation. In that relation, wages are expected to rise when there is excess demand—which is taken to be indicated by a low unemployment rate—and the rate of wage increase is expected to be the faster the greater the excess demand. However, if the unemployment rate is increasingly affected by the inclusion of the voluntarily unemployed, this relationship becomes blurred and the employment ratio may provide a better indication of demand pressures.

Sharon P. Smith

Deficit Projections vs. Deficit Forecasts

The outlook for the federal government budget deficit over the remainder of the decade has received considerable attention in the press, in the most recent Presidential election campaign, and in discussions of appropriate economic policies. The data forming the basis for these discussions are usually deficit projections similar to those prepared each year by the Congressional Budget Office (CBO) and the Office of Management and Budget (OMB).

Both of these agencies are required, under the terms of the Congressional Budget Act of 1974, to construct medium-term projections of federal receipts, outlays and deficits. These projections are constructed for the limited purpose of providing a benchmark against which proposals for changes in federal outlays or taxes can be compared. The most recent projections of the federal deficit from these agencies are presented in Chart 1. It is evident from a quick glance that the two agencies project strikingly different paths for the deficit over the remainder of the decade.

Neither agency constructs these projections as forecasts of future federal budget deficits, although the estimates frequently are interpreted in that fashion. The purposes of this *Letter* are to explain the difference between a budget forecast and budget projections, and to indicate why it is inappropriate to use the latter as forecasts.

Budget forecasts

In many discussions of the medium-term (next 3 to 5 years) economic outlook or of proposed changes in fiscal policy, the economic forecast employed is based upon a forecast of federal receipts, outlays, or the budget deficit. For example, some analysts assert that interest rates on long-term securities are presently high because lenders are forecasting large federal government budget deficits through the remainder of the decade and thus anticipate that the government will have to finance them. These analysts predict that this large future borrowing by the government will drive up future short-term interest rates.

Such statements implicitly are based upon a forecast of future federal budget deficits, that is, the best guess about the size of the deficits that will actually occur at future dates given the information available at the time that the forecast is constructed. Alternatively stated, the forecast of future deficits is the forecaster's judgment about the most likely values for deficits at future dates.

A true forecast of government receipts, outlays, and the budget deficit cannot be constructed independently of a forecast of economic activity. The forecaster must make assumptions about the most likely future size of government programs, future tax rates, future monetary policy and all other factors that are believed to influence economic activity. Based upon these assumptions, budget deficits must be forecast *simultaneously* with future economic activity.

There are two reasons that economic activity and budget deficits must be forecast together. The first is that federal outlays and receipts, and hence the budget deficit, are affected by the state of the economy. If the economy slides into a recession, federal tax receipts decline even if tax rates stay the same since the tax base upon which those rates are assessed, such as adjusted gross income or corporate profits, declines. Similarly, in a recession, certain federal government outlays, e.g., unemployment insurance and social service payments, rise.

The impact of a recession on federal government receipts and outlays is to increase the size of the observed deficit even though no explicit policy actions have been taken by the Congress or the President. Conversely, if the economy expands rapidly, and the rate of inflation increases, federal receipts and outlays typically increase as the cost of items purchased by the government increases and as inflation increases the size, in dollars, of the base on which taxes are levied.

These induced effects of the economy on the budget tend to cushion the economy's decline when it is weak and restrain the economy when it is strong. Hence, the frequent reference to the "automatic stabilizer" aspect of fiscal policy.

The second reason forecasts of the economy and the budget cannot be done independently is simply

Reprinted from Federal Reserve Bank of San Francisco
Weekly Letter, July 5, 1985.

that the interaction between federal receipts and outlays and the economy is not a one-way street. Decisions by the Congress and the President to alter the amount of government purchases or the rate or base for various taxes affect the level of economic activity, at least in the short-run.

Budget forecasts vs. projections

The budget projections constructed by the CBO and the OMB are not forecasts as defined above. Instead of determining the future path of the economy and the future budget deficit simultaneously as required by a true forecast, these agencies *assume* a path of future economic activity and ask the question: what values will be realized for government outlays, receipts and the budget deficit if the assumed path of economic activity is to be realized and if government programs and tax rates are maintained at certain levels.

This technique does not guarantee consistency between the projections of economic activity and the assumed fiscal and/or monetary policy. In the words of the Congressional Budget Office: "These projections are not forecasts of the economy, based on assumptions about the maintenance of current policies. At times, the out-year projections have been viewed as goals while at other times they have incorporated average historical growth rates."

The contrast between the projection approach and a true forecast of future deficits can be seen in Chart 2 which gives the *economic assumptions* behind the CBO and OMB budget projections prepared last winter. Both agencies are required to make projections based on the same fiscal policy assumptions. CBO assumes an economic environment with less growth, more inflation, and higher market interest rates than the environment assumed by OMB. These differences in the assumptions about the path of the economy with the same policy settings are primarily responsible for the differences in the projections illustrated in Chart 1. In both cases, drastically different projections of future deficits could be produced by small alterations in the economic assumptions.

There is no basis for presuming that one set of assumptions represents a more likely path for economic activity than another. Indeed, the assumptions underlying both are suspect. The usual assumption is of relatively steady real growth over a five-year horizon. However, this horizon encompasses the average span of a typical peacetime business cycle in the U.S. In other words, a 5-year horizon often spans a period of considerable fluctuation in economic activity. Consequently, the underlying economic assumption of steady growth is often likely to be a poor forecast of the medium-term behavior of the economy. Because of such conditions, the budget projections are likely to be poor indicators of actual future budget deficits.

Current service concepts

Another reason that medium-term budget projections are apt not to represent future budget conditions is that they are typically constructed on a current services basis. Under the current services concept, future receipts and outlays are calculated under the unlikely assumption that the current laws and programs will remain unchanged.

Nondefense expenditures subject to the appropriations process are typically projected at their funding levels in the most recently completed fiscal year adjusted upward to keep pace with the projected rate of inflation. Defense expenditures have been treated differently at various times in the past within the current services budget concept. In the recent past, the CBO has prepared projections of defense expenditures based on the most recent Congressional Budget resolution. This builds substantial inflation-adjusted growth (5–6 percent per year) into the current projections of future defense spending, and, as a result, defense spending is projected to average in the range of 6.5 to 7.0 percent per year through 1990.

In contrast, OMB uses the Reagan administration's policy proposals for defense as the basis for its current services defense outlay projection. Under this definition, current services outlays for defense grow after adjustment for inflation as much as 10.6 percent in fiscal year 1986, but show inflation-adjusted growth declining to slightly over 5 percent per year in 1989 and 1990. These different treatments of defense spending result in a projection of $18 billion more in current services defense outlays by OMB in fiscal year 1990 than by CBO, even though the OMB projections assume lower future inflation rates than the CBO.

Conclusions
The medium-term budget projections prepared by the CBO and OMB are the results of a very precisely defined exercise. The rules of this exercise were constructed to provide a benchmark against which proposals for changes in outlays or taxes could be compared. These measures are not designed as, nor should they be interpreted as, forecasts of future federal outlays, receipts, or deficits.

Robert H. Rasche

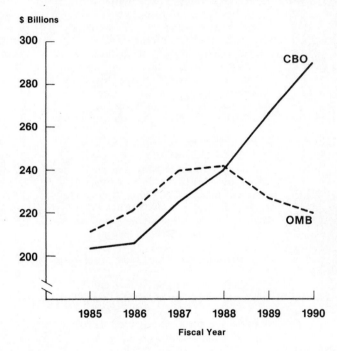

Chart 1
Current Services Deficit Projections

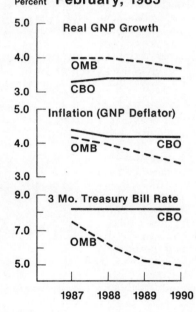

Chart 2
Economic Assumptions For Current Services Budget Projections
February, 1985

How You Can Track The U.S. Economy

Is the economy nearing the bottom of recession? Or will the upturn be delayed until early summer?

Economists and other professional forecasters follow dozens of indicators in search of the answers. But by keeping an eye on only a few key statistics compiled by government agencies, you can make your own educated guesses as to where the economy is heading.

To sort out the confusing array of figures that flow almost daily from Washington, here are some of the most important reports to watch—along with charts showing how the indicators have been acting recently, quarter by quarter. Note that all figures are seasonally adjusted except those for prices.

Gross national product— This is the broadest measure of the economy's performance. Issued every three months by the Commerce Department, it is the best estimate of the total dollar value of the nation's output of goods and services. Move-

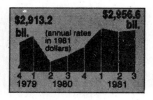

ments in many areas of the economy are closely related to changes in GNP, making it a good analytic tool. In particular, watch the annual rate of growth or decline in "real" or "constant" dollars. This eliminates the effects of inflation, so that the actual volume of production is measured. Remember, though, that frequent revisions of GNP figures sometimes change the picture of the economy.

Industrial production— Issued monthly by the Federal Reserve Board, this index shows changes in the physical output of America's factories, mines and electric and gas utilities. The index tends to move in the same direction as the economy,

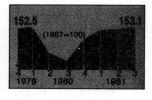

making it a good guide to business conditions between reports on GNP. Detailed breakdowns of the index give a reading on how individual industries are faring.

Leading indicators— This boils down to one number the movement of a dozen statistics that tend to predict—or "lead" —changes in the GNP. The monthly index issued by the Commerce Department includes such things as layoffs of

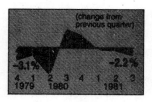

workers, new orders placed by manufacturers, changes in the money supply and the prices of raw materials. If the index moves in the same direction for several months, it's a fair sign that total output will move the same way in the near future.

Personal income— A monthly report from the Commerce Department, this shows the before-tax income received by people in the form of wages and salaries, interest and dividends, rents, and other payments such

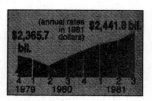

as Social Security, unemployment and pensions. As a measure of individuals' spending power, the report helps explain trends in consumer buying habits, a major part of total GNP. When personal income rises, it often means that people will increase their buying. But note a big loophole: Excluded are the billions of dollars that change hands in the so-called underground economy—cash transactions that are never reported to tax or other officials.

Retail sales— The Commerce Department's monthly estimate of total sales at the retail level includes everything from cars to a bag of groceries. Based on a sample of retail establishments, the figure gives a rough clue to consumer atti-

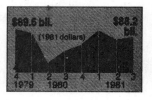

tudes. It can also indicate future conditions: A long slowdown in sales can lead to cuts in production.

Consumer prices— Issued monthly by the Labor Department, this index shows changes in prices for a fixed market basket of about 360 goods and services. The most widely publicized figure is for all urban consumers. A second, used in

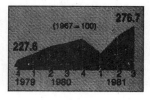

labor contracts and some government programs, covers urban wage earners and clerical workers. Both are watched as a measure of inflation, but many economists believe that flaws cause them to be wide of the mark.

Producer prices— This is a monthly indicator from the Labor Department showing price changes of goods at various stages of production, from crude materials such as raw cotton, to finished goods like clothing and furniture. An upward surge may

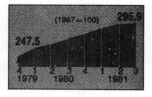

mean higher consumer prices later. The index, however, can miss discounts and may exaggerate rising price trends. Watch particularly changes in the prices of finished goods. These do not fluctuate as widely as crude materials and thus are a better measure of inflationary pressures.

Employment— The percentage of the work force that is involuntarily out of work is a broad indicator of economic health. But another monthly figure issued by the Labor Department—the number of payroll jobs—may be better for

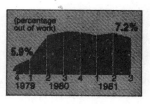

spotting changes in business. A decreasing number of jobs is a sign that firms are cutting production.

Housing starts— A pickup in the pace of housing starts usually follows an easing of credit conditions—the availability and cost of money—and is an indicator of improvement in economic health. This monthly report from the Commerce Depart-

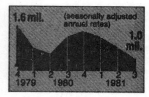

ment also includes the number of new building permits issued across the country, an even earlier indicator of the pace of future construction. □

Statements to Congress

Statement by Paul A. Volcker, Chairman, Board of Governors of the Federal Reserve System, before the Committee on Banking, Finance and Urban Affairs, U.S. House of Representatives, February 19, 1986.

I am pleased once again to appear before this committee to discuss the approach of Federal Reserve policy within the larger economic setting at home and abroad.

As you know, 1986 has begun with the economy continuing to move forward after more than three years of expansion. Today, more people are employed relative to the working age population than ever before recorded. Unemployment has continued to fall. Happily, the continuing expansion has so far been achieved while inflation has remained at the lowest rate in more than a decade.

Looking ahead, there are some highly encouraging signs as well. The larger employment increases in recent months are reflected in relatively confident attitudes by consumers. Manufacturing output as a whole, which had been sluggish during much of 1985, is again rising even though many areas continue to face strong competition from abroad. Lower interest rates and higher stock prices—buoyed, in part, by the action of the Congress in improving prospects for declining federal deficits in the years ahead—have made it less expensive to finance new business investment and housing. With few exceptions, excessive inventories, often in the past a harbinger of economic adjustments, appear absent.

While productivity growth has been rather disappointing, wage restraint in much of industry and lower commodity prices have kept costs under control. The sharp break in oil prices should be an important force cutting costs and prices in the period immediately ahead, in the process releasing real purchasing power to U.S. consumers. Moreover, changes in exchange rates and the welcome initiatives taken by the

Congress and the administration toward budgetary restraint offer the potential for dealing with two of the major, and interrelated, imbalances in the economy that I have spoken about with you so often—the enormous fiscal and trade deficits.

Altogether, the opportunity clearly remains for combining sustained expansion with greater price stability in the period ahead, building on the progress of the past three years. In my judgment, the present expansion—already longer than the postwar average for peacetime years—is not about to die from old age or sheer exhaustion. We do not have the pressures on capacity, the excess inventories, the accelerating costs and prices, or the rising interest rates that have typically presaged cyclical downturns in the past.

Yet, any claim that we live in an economy in which every prospect pleases would be idle pretense. There are evident points of economic pressure and financial strain, some of them aggravated by the sharp decline in oil prices. While the adverse trends are being changed, the deficits in our budget and trade accounts will take years to correct. And we have long since passed the time when we could, with any validity, insulate ourselves from the difficulties of neighbors and trading partners to which we are bound by strong ties of finance and trade.

Most of these threats, in magnitude and in combination, are unique, certainly in our postwar experience. They demand our full attention if we are to deal with them successfully.

Take, for instance, the trade problem. The dollar had risen to extraordinarily high levels by early 1985, with the effect of undercutting our trade position vis-à-vis major industrial competitors. At the same time, the relatively rapid growth in demand for goods and services in the United States, at a time of sluggish growth abroad, attracted a large volume of imports. The net result was to drive our trade deficit to a rate of close to $150 billion by the end of last year and to about $125 billion for the year as a whole.

Reprinted from the Federal Reserve *Bulletin*, April, 1986.

No doubt, given the extreme values the dollar had attained internationally in 1984 and early 1985, an adjustment in exchange rates has been a necessary part of achieving a better competitive equilibrium and of responding to destructive protectionist pressures. That fact was explicitly recognized in the meeting of the finance ministers and the central bankers of the five leading industrialized countries in September. By now, a substantial adjustment in exchange rates has been made, placing our producers in a stronger competitive position.

But we also know, from hard experience here and abroad, that changes in actual trade flows necessarily lag changes in exchange rates by a period extending into years, that currency adjustments can assume a momentum of their own, and that sharp depreciation in the external value of a currency carries pervasive inflationary threats.

No doubt, some depreciation in the dollar, after the rapid runup, could be absorbed without a sharp or immediate impact on domestic prices. But we cannot afford to be complacent. Inevitably, prospects for balance in our internal capital markets—and therefore prospects for interest rates—remain for the time being heavily dependent on the willingness of foreigners to place huge amounts of funds in dollars and on the incentives for Americans to employ their money at home. In essence, the financing of both our current account deficit and our internal capital needs—as long as the government deficit remains so high—is dependent on a historically high net capital inflow. Clearly, the *orderly* balancing of our demands for funds with supply in those circumstances requires continued confidence in our currency.

I recognize and appreciate the importance of the efforts that the Congress and the administration have made to place the budget deficit on a declining trend. I know that effort will continue to require the hardest kind of choices. But we can also see some of the potential benefits in improved market sentiment. The net result should be both to reduce risks of inflation and to make us less dependent on foreign financing in the years ahead.

At the same time, oil imports apart, improvement in our trade balance for the next year or longer is in large part dependent not on deprecia-

tion of our currency but on greater growth by our trading partners. More competitive pricing is of limited value when foreign markets are not growing strongly and when producers abroad do not themselves have expanding, profitable markets at home.

Prospects in that respect remain quite mixed. There have been signs of somewhat stronger growth in Germany and elsewhere in continental Europe. However, it remains questionable whether that growth will, in fact, be strong enough to reduce appreciably continued high levels of unemployment, now averaging more than 10 percent for the continent as a whole. In Japan, where unemployment is historically at much lower levels, growth by those same historical standards is sluggish, with the appreciation of the yen itself a restraining factor.

As appropriately emphasized at the September G-5 meeting, a better world equilibrium, including more rapid improvement in our trade balance, is clearly dependent on structural and other measures to deal with the sources of the imbalances. The Gramm–Rudman–Hollings legislation represents one important approach to that end. Stronger growth patterns in other leading countries are also directly relevant. The opportunities for policies to work toward that result this year appear to be greatly enhanced by the strongly beneficial effects of the declines in oil prices and the appreciation of currencies of other leading countries. Both developments reinforce the already strong prospects for price stability in those countries.

Should oil prices remain close to present levels, that development will also be a powerful force offsetting, and in the short run probably more than offsetting, the direct and indirect effects of the lower international value of the dollar on our overall price performance. At the same time, the effect is to release real purchasing power and cash flow to American consumers and oil-consuming businesses. The potential addition to real consumer income should work in the direction of offsetting the effects on purchasing power that some have foreseen in the full implementation of the deficit reduction program called for by the Gramm–Rudman–Hollings legislation over the course of this year.

With similarly beneficial effects for other consuming countries, that development is part of the basis for a sense of growing optimism about world economic prospects. But, of course, the effects are sharply adverse for energy producers, affecting important regions in the United States where energy production and exploration loom so large, and therefore prospects for investment as a whole. The added strains for certain already heavily indebted developing countries are even more acute. Moreover, the pervasive pressures on much of the agricultural sector in this country remain, although recent legislation by the Congress addressed—and should help stem—further deterioration.

These sectoral strains and imbalances point up the crucial importance of maintaining the essential safety and soundness of our financial system, and in particular our depository institutions. For a long time, that was something we in this country thought we could take for granted. And it was partly that feeling, combined with accelerating inflation and other factors, that contributed to much more aggressive lending behavior over the years—lending that has led to unanticipated problems in a period of disinflation and greater competitive pressures. Today, measures to protect the basic financial fabric necessarily assume a high priority, and that effort will require appropriate action by the Congress as well as by the regulatory authorities.

Finally, in surveying the economic setting for monetary policy, I must call your attention to the disappointing record with respect to productivity over recent years viewed generally, at least as recorded by the standard national statistics. Developments in that respect during 1985, when productivity for nonfarm businesses as a whole showed no growth, are hard to explain. In manufacturing, where recorded performance is substantially better than in other sectors, the slower productivity growth may be a reflection of the leveling of output. But other sectors were growing relatively fast, without reflection in productivity improvement.

Perhaps part of the seeming problem lies in the inherent difficulty in measuring the volume and quality of output in the dominant service sector of the economy. But the results do raise further questions about the growth potential of the economy as recorded by the GNP statistics—how fast can we expect the GNP to grow in a sustained way without excessive pressures on human or physical capacity. Over the past six months, for instance, the unemployment rate has dropped a full ½ percentage point—desirable in itself but accompanied by a recorded annual rate of output growth of only 2¾ percent.

In the end, it is largely productivity that governs prospects for growth in per capita income; together with growth in the number of workers, it sets a limit on our total economic growth. Fortunately, in developing monetary policies now, we do not need to reach precise judgments about our long-term growth potential; today, capacity utilization is still somewhat below, and unemployment somewhat above, average levels for periods of business prosperity. Recent productivity trends, nonetheless, do introduce an unwelcome cautionary note about the longer run.

MONETARY POLICY

Any description of the opportunities and risks in the current economic situation points up the fact that the formulation and implementation of monetary policy need to take account of a variety of sometimes conflicting objectives and criteria. In the current setting, other policy approaches—toward the budget, toward international finance, toward trade, and toward other areas—are obviously critical to the success of the common effort, just as the pervasive and indirect effects of monetary policy can bear upon the success of other policies beyond the strictly financial. Moreover, institutional and economic changes have strongly affected the behavior of certain policy guideposts—notably M1 and debt—relative to other economic magnitudes. Consequently, I do not believe that in current circumstances there is any escape from the need for a substantial element of judgment in the conduct of Federal Reserve policies.

That need was illustrated in 1985. Over the course of the year, monetary policy remained in a generally accommodative mode in the sense that pressures on bank reserve positions were both limited and little changed. The discount rate was reduced once in the spring, from 8 to 7½ percent, and most market interest rates declined 1 to 2 percentage points, generally reaching the lowest levels since mid-1979 or before.

As illustrated in charts 2 and 3, the broader

1. M1 target ranges and actual M1

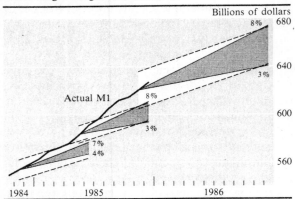

Monthly data.

monetary aggregates, M2 and M3, remained generally within the ranges targeted at the start of the year. At the same time, however, the narrowly defined measure of the "money supply," M1, grew persistently above the range set both at the start of the year and again after the range was reset in July. (See chart 1). That aggregate ended the year almost 12 percent above the year-earlier level, an historically high rate of growth.

In technical terms, that large "overshoot" was permitted in the light of a persistent and sizable decline in M1 "velocity"—that is, the relationship between M1 and the nominal GNP. That decline in velocity was apparent whether measured contemporaneously or with a one- or two-quarter lag between money and GNP. In other words, the exceptional growth in M1 seemed to be matched by an equally exceptional decline in velocity, suggesting that the high M1 growth in 1985 does not imply the same inflationary potential, at least for the near term, as in the past.

Less abstractly, the judgment of the Federal Open Market Committee as the year developed was that the rather strong restrictive action that would have been necessary to maintain M1 within its targeted range was not justified in the light of the different signals conveyed by the much more restrained growth in M2 and M3, the slower growth in overall economic activity, the margins of capacity that remained, and the continuing progress toward price stability. For much of the year, the dollar remained high, and that fact was another strong signal that monetary policy was not unduly liberal.

We were aware, of course, of some conflicting

evidence. During much of 1984 and 1985, domestic *demand*—the spending of consumers, businesses, and governments—continued to expand at a rate well beyond the rate of domestic *output*, measured by the GNP. In fact, the rate of demand increase, if maintained, would probably be beyond our long-term growth potential. In that sense we continued to live beyond our means, at the expense of a widening trade deficit.

Moreover, private as well as public debt continued to accumulate at a historically rapid rate, running above the "monitoring range" of 9 to 12 percent set out at the start of the year. The aggregate debt statistics, portrayed in relation to GNP in chart 4, exaggerate the problem to some degree. There has been massive issuance of tax-exempt securities in anticipation of tax law changes, for reinvestment in Treasury securities, in pending subsequent refundings, and for financing home purchases and industrial development. These activities lead to "double counting" in the aggregate statistics because both the new municipal debt and the debt acquired in employing the funds borrowed are included in the total. At the same time, substitution of debt for equity by businesses continued unabated, with about $100 billion of equity retired by a combination of stock repurchase programs, so-called leveraged buyouts, and as part of mergers and acquisitions.

The strongly rising stock market and lower interest rates had the effect of greatly increasing consumer wealth, measured by current market values, and lowering the cost of capital to business. Nonetheless, the trend of debt creation, with its implications of greater leveraging and

2. M2 target ranges and actual M2

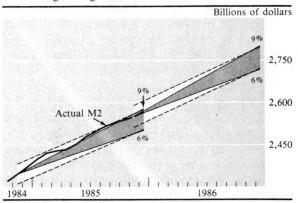

Monthly data.

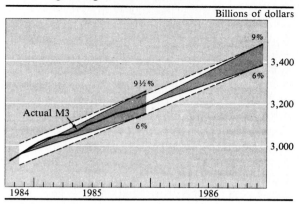

3. M3 target ranges and actual M3

Monthly data.

potential financial fragility, remains disquieting, particularly in an environment of progress toward greater price stability. Indeed, as I suggested earlier, there is already ample evidence in the financial area of the consequences for individual institutions of extended financial positions and unduly loose credit standards. The crises in the thrift industry in Maryland and Ohio, where federal insurance and supervision were absent, illustrated in an extreme form the consequences of essentially speculative lending and lax market practices.

A more pointed question for the deliberations of the FOMC has been the lasting significance of the sizable increase in M1. We are well aware, as I have often reported to this committee, of the long history and of the economic analysis that relate excessive money growth to inflation over time. The operational question remains as to what, in specific circumstances, is, in fact, excessive in the light of recent velocity behavior. That question is greatly complicated by the changed composition of M1, which now includes accounts that receive interest close to market levels and clearly have a large "savings" as well as a "transaction-oriented" component. The disinflationary process and the associated decline in market interest rates also have implications for the willingness to hold money.

Enough evidence has now accumulated since the peak inflation years to suggest the following two conclusions:

1. The long upward trend in velocity of 3 percent or so characteristic of most of the postwar period—when inflation and interest rates were generally trending upward—will probably not be typical of a world in which inflation and interest rates are trending downward and in which M1 has a growing savings component.

2. M1 may be more sensitive to short-term fluctuations in interest rates.

For 1985 specifically, our work strongly indicates that much of the unexpected decline in M1 velocity was a response to the sharp reduction in interest rates late in 1984, continuing at a lesser pace over much of last year. In a context of contained inflation, a generally strong dollar, and more muted economic growth, the decline in interest rates did not appear in itself to risk excessive economic stimulation, with renewed inflationary potential. Moreover, neither of the broader monetary aggregates, which remained within their target ranges, confirmed excessive monetary expansion.

Looking ahead to 1986, the FOMC decided to take account of the greater uncertainty associated with the relationship between M1 and economic activity and prices by adopting a relatively broad M1 target range of 3 to 8 percent. While wider, that range is centered on the same midpoint, 5½ percent, as the tentative 4 to 7 percent range that was set out last July. In fixing that range, the Committee anticipated that velocity would not drop at nearly the rate of 1985. Without some reversal of the sharp drop in velocity last year, growth toward the upper end of the range could well be appropriate. More broadly, the Committee agreed that changes in M1 would be evaluated in the light of the presence—or the absence—of confirming evidence of excessive

4. Ratio of domestic nonfinancial sector debt to GNP

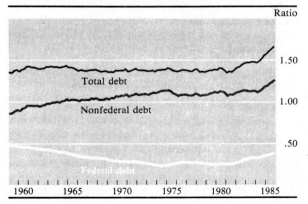

Monthly data.

growth in M2 and M3. For both those aggregates, the tentative growth ranges of 6 to 9 percent set in July were reaffirmed.

In establishing these target ranges, members of the Federal Reserve Board and the Reserve Bank Presidents anticipated that the economy would grow somewhat more rapidly than in 1985 and that the unemployment rate would continue to decline gradually. Views on the outlook for prices were rather mixed, with some anticipating measurable further progress toward stability, particularly in the light of the oil price decline, while others expected that the consequences of the lower exchange rate may, for a time, put stronger upward pressure on prices. While the "central tendency" of the projections for real growth is lower than that of the administration, so are most of the projections of prices by participants in the FOMC. The differences are not so large as to suggest, in themselves, inconsistency with the monetary growth targets; indeed, several Board Members and Presidents anticipated real growth in the area of 4 percent. I might also note that the somewhat lower unemployment rate generally anticipated by the Committee participants suggests more limited productivity growth than that implied by the administration projections.

Monetary policy is implemented day by day and week by week by determining the appropriate degree of pressure on bank reserve positions in the light of monetary growth, judged in the context of the flow of information about the economy, the outlook for prices, and domestic and international financial markets, including the value of the dollar in the foreign exchange markets. In the latter connection, circumstances now are, of course, very different from those during most of 1985. The potential inflationary implications of further depreciation of the dollar, while likely to be offset for some time by lower oil prices, need to be fully considered in the implementation of policy.

At present, with the various monetary aggregates at reasonable levels relative to their new target ranges, and taking account of the cross-currents in other factors bearing on policy implementation, there has been no occasion for significant change in the degree of pressure on bank reserve positions. As you know, both intermediate- and long-term interest rates have been declining to the lowest levels seen in years and the stock market has been ebullient. The justification, and the sustainability, of those developments lies in a combination of prospects for budgetary restraint, the favorable impact of lower oil prices, and improved inflationary expectations and performance. The challenge for monetary policy, insofar as it can contribute, is to help assure that those favorable prospects for maintaining progress toward stability can be a reality in the context of a growing economy. The implementation of policy will be conducted in the light of that objective.

RELATED APPROACHES

I referred earlier to the pressures in some areas of the credit markets growing in large part out of the backwash of overly aggressive lending policies in the earlier climate of accelerating inflation. Indeed, those concerns have been aggravated in more recent years by a continued highly aggressive approach by some institutions seeking high returns, with their own liabilities effectively underwritten by federal insurance. These problems, and appropriate responses to them, are too large a subject for me to deal with in the time available today; we have discussed them before on a number of occasions.

I do want to report, however, that the Federal Reserve has under way a number of initiatives to help deal with the problems more effectively. These initiatives include strengthening our force of examiners and supervisory personnel so that they are equipped to meet higher standards in the frequency and intensity of examination of member banks and holding companies. Certain regulatory steps have been undertaken as well. Specifically, we have issued for public comment a proposal for a framework of "adjusted capital–asset ratios" designed to supplement our present capital standards. The proposed standards are designed to take account of the different characteristics of bank assets and to incorporate allowance for off-balance-sheet risks that have been proliferating rapidly at major banks here and abroad in recent years. I know other regulatory agencies have comparable initiatives under way in the supervisory and regulatory area.

By its nature, this supervisory effort must be a continuing process, although it has particular relevance in this turbulent period.

Moreover, I can only emphasize to you again my longstanding concern that you act, and act soon, to modernize our basic laws governing the structure and nature of our depository system. After decades of little change in the legal structure, technological and market developments have together created a new competitive environment. That change, without a coherent legislative framework, has sown enormous confusion about the proper and legitimate role of banks, bank holding companies, thrift institutions, and their commercial and financial competitors. Regulatory decisions attempting to apply current laws, sometimes conflicting in themselves, are regularly challenged in the courts. The results are capricious as both regulatory bodies and the courts inevitably reach different conclusions in ambiguous circumstances.

The courts themselves in recent decisions have emphasized the need for fresh congressional guidance. I can only reiterate my own view that, without such a review, the banking and thrift industries are left adrift, driven to exploit perceived loopholes in present law, on the one hand, while, on the other hand, their basic and regulated business is undercut by commercial organizations and investment houses operating without the protections provided by the federal "safety net." The result is a clear threat not only to the coherence but also to the safety and soundness of the whole. Time is growing short.

From another perspective, the decline in oil prices has presented an enormous new challenge to a few countries that have been heavily dependent on oil resources for the development of their own economies. The problem is particularly acute with respect to Mexico, with which we have close trade and financial relationships, but it is certainly not limited to that country.

In the broadest terms, the initiatives outlined by Secretary Baker some months ago for managing a "second stage" of the international debt crisis provide a constructive and needed overall framework for dealing with problems. He emphasized the importance of achieving a solution in the context of overall financial and economic policies conducive to sustained growth. That solution, in turn, requires complementary actions by the borrowing countries, by creditors, and by multilateral development institutions alike.

In essence, the borrowing countries themselves—"Baker Plan" or not—appear to have the strongest kind of incentives to take those actions necessary to improve the efficiency and competitiveness of their own economies, including the development of their potentially vast non-oil resources. Those fundamental measures will be more effective, with faster results, to the degree those nations also have greater assurance of access to growing external markets for their products. Resistance to protectionism should, of course, be easier to achieve in a context of an expanding world economy, the prospects for which should be enhanced by the same decline in oil prices that makes the pressures more acute for oil-producing countries.

The restructuring process can be greatly assisted by cooperation with such institutions as the World Bank and the Inter-American Development Bank, which have funds available for substantially larger loan programs in support of fundamental economic adjustments, and with the International Monetary Fund. On that basis, I believe necessary margins of external private investment or loans can continue to be made available prudently to meet essential external needs. Indeed, without complementary policies by international institutions and creditors, the will to find constructive outward-looking solutions to the problems by the borrowers themselves will inevitably be undermined, and the adverse implications would extend far beyond the economic arena.

For some heavily indebted countries that either import a sizable portion of their energy requirements or are essentially neutral in that respect, recent developments should ease the task. But I do not in any way want to minimize the challenge for others—for Mexico, Ecuador, Nigeria, and Venezuela. What I do suggest is that the fundamental premises of the total effort by borrowers and creditors alike in managing the debt situation remain valid. I believe that, with will and wisdom, the basis remains for working through this inevitably difficult period in a way that ultimately will reinforce prospects for longer-term growth.

CONCLUSION

I conclude as I started.

With constructive policy responses, recent developments carry the potential for enhancing prospects here and elsewhere for a sustained period of growth in a context of price stability. Those are the common goals of the Congress, the administration, and the Federal Reserve.

But if those goals are to be actually achieved, we also must clearly recognize, and collectively deal effectively with, points of strain and danger, some of them stemming from the very successes of the past.

Economic history is replete with examples of countries that, in attempting to correct overvaluation of their currencies, failed to take advantage of their improved competitive positions. Too often, they lapsed into a debilitating and self-defeating cycle of external depreciation and internal inflation, at the expense of an eroding loss of confidence, higher interest rates, and impaired growth.

It would be foolish to presume that the United States is somehow immune from that threat—we had too much adverse experience in the 1970s to indulge in wishful thinking in that respect. Instead, in our monetary and fiscal policies, we need to be realistic about the danger and be fully sensitive to the need to maintain confidence in our currency.

Fortunately, the sharp decline in energy prices now under way should, for months ahead, help assure satisfactory price performance overall, making the job of maintaining progress toward stability much easier. But those lower prices are no unmitigated blessing. They create new uncertainties and stresses for some regions of the economy, for some financial sectors, and particularly for some important developing countries and trading partners. Those stresses need to be contained and dealt with in a constructive way, and we need to guard against conditions that might lead to a repetition of past energy shortages.

The sense of greater confidence about our fiscal prospects still needs to be converted into reality. Whatever the fortunes of the Gramm–Rudman–Hollings legislation in the courts or the merits of that particular approach toward the problem, the direction and broad spirit of the effort is essential if we are to correct deep-seated imbalances that, sooner or later, would only undercut our bright prospects.

The success of all our efforts is dependent in substantial part on complementary policies by other countries—their success in enhancing *their* growth and stability, in opening markets to others, and in helping to deal with points of strain in the international financial fabric.

Most other industrialized countries have, as a matter of priority, been deeply concerned with restoring price stability and reducing fiscal deficits. Remarkable strides have been made toward those goals. However, their growth, at least until now, has been heavily dependent upon rising trade and current account surpluses. Today, there appears to be a prime opportunity for encouraging "home grown" expansion, larger imports, and better international balance.

For the longer run, I welcome the call by the President to consider what steps might be desirable to achieve and maintain greater exchange rate stability internationally. No one should think that task is a simple one. It cannot in any way substitute for disciplined and complementary domestic policies among the leading nations. Indeed, meaningful progress would imply even greater demands on those policies and on international cooperation. But surely we have had enough experience, here and elsewhere, with the distorting effects of extreme exchange-rate volatility to make that effort to reexamine the international system worthwhile. In a fundamental sense, that is a corollary of the simple observable fact that the economic fortunes of all countries—including the United States—are inextricably interlocked.

We have come too far, and the stakes are too high, to fail to rise to the evident new challenges.

We have to recognize that depreciation of our currency does not in itself provide a fundamental solution, and is, in fact, a two-edged sword.

The budgetary effort must be sustained.

If we expect to benefit from the break in energy prices, we must collectively respond to the points of strain.

We need to be patient when patience is required. The trade and budgetary and financial problems will be with us for some time; at the same time, we need to be insistent in carrying through the measures to deal with them constructively.

In much of this, I recognize that the Federal Reserve and monetary policy have a vital part to play. Given the crosscurrents in the economy and sometimes conflicting signals among the guideposts to policy in today's setting, there will be a high premium on careful judgment. But through it all the basic objective does not change. We are convinced that sustained growth in the United States—and much more—is dependent upon maintaining progress toward price stability over time. And given our weight in the world, that same stability must be one of the foundation stones of a prosperous, integrated global economy. □

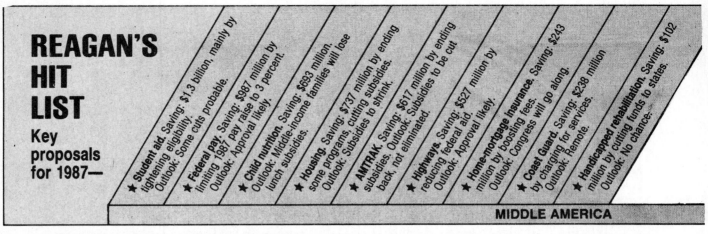

17

REAGAN'S HIT LIST
Key proposals for 1987—

★ Student aid. Saving: $1.3 billion, mainly by tightening eligibility. Outlook: Some cuts probable.	★ Federal pay. Saving: $987 million by limiting 1987 pay raise to 3 percent. Outlook: Approval likely.	★ Child nutrition. Saving: $683 million. Outlook: Middle-income families will lose lunch subsidies.	★ Housing. Saving: $737 million by ending some programs, cutting subsidies. Outlook: Subsidies to shrink.	★ AMTRAK. Saving: $617 million by ending subsidies. Outlook: Subsidies to be cut back, not eliminated.	★ Highways. Saving: $527 million by reducing federal aid. Outlook: Approval likely.	★ Home-mortgage insurance. Saving: $243 million by boosting fees. Outlook: Congress will go along.	★ Coast Guard. Saving: $238 million by charging for services. Outlook: Remote.	★ Handicapped rehabilitation. Saving: $102 million by cutting funds to states. Outlook: No chance.

MIDDLE AMERICA

WHERE BUDGET AX WILL FALL

■ The nearly $1 trillion budget Ronald Reagan presented to Congress in early February may be his toughest ever.

It certainly is the most stringent in terms of spending cuts. To comply with Congress's new budget-balancing law and get the deficit down to $143.6 billion for the 1987 fiscal year without raising taxes, the President wants to end or sharply reduce 40 programs—more than ever. In previous budgets, Reagan has proposed cutting more dollars, but never has his knife cut such a wide swath.

And the budget certainly will be one of the toughest to push through Congress. Even before receipt of the document, Republicans and Democrats alike had begun distancing themselves from it. Senator Slade Gorton (R-Wash.) accused the White House of trying "to cram cuts in vital and important services down the throats of the American people." Senator Bill Bradley (D-N.J.) said he doubted that "there are 25 votes in the Senate" for it.

Now a new obstacle of unknown dimension is compounding the difficulty. A U.S. District Court in Washington, D.C., ruled February 7 that a key part of the controversial Gramm-Rudman law that could force Congress to cut the deficit is unconstitutional. Though the court stayed the effect of its decision pending a Supreme Court review, probably by summer, the action created new confusion in the government and raised the specter of another year of budget gridlock.

Warned James Miller, the President's budget director: If the decision is upheld, "Congress might sit on its hands."

If the President's budget is

If the President has his way—and Gramm-Rudman survives—Americans in all walks of life will feel the pinch

enacted, it would hit almost every American, every section of the country and every sector of the economy. An analysis by *U.S. News & World Report* shows that the middle class, which by and large has avoided major pain in the past, would suffer this time. The poor, last clobbered in 1981-82, would take another hit. The elderly, though Social Security is left untouched, would get socked on medicare. Hard-pressed farmers would lose valuable credit subsidies, and big and small business would lose programs such as the Small Business Administration and direct loans from the Export-Import Bank, which they have fought to retain.

A few of Reagan's favorite programs not only escaped but won pledges of added support. Despite the record peacetime military buildup of the Reagan years, defense spending would get another boost. So would exploration of space and drug and law enforcement.

A smaller deficit is not the only item on the President's agenda this year. In his state-of-the-union address, Reagan proposed new domestic and international initiatives. He asked Health and Human Services Secretary Otis Bowen to come up with a plan to protect senior citizens from the high cost of treatment for catastrophic illness; Atty. Gen. Edwin Meese as head of the White House Domestic Policy Council to recommend reform of the welfare system, and Treasury Secretary James Baker to look into ways to moderate the volatility of international currency-exchange rates.

Though he has drawn a bead on domestic spending ever since taking office, the President was forced to prescribe his harshest medicine this year. The new Gramm-Rudman budget-balancing law mandates a $144 billion deficit for the 1987 fiscal year that begins next October 1 and a balanced budget by 1991. If the White House and Congress fail to agree on a budget, the law—if it stands—requires across-the-board budget cuts in October to drive the deficit down to the target. Half the cuts would come from the Pentagon and half from domestic spending. Social Security and programs for the poor would be exempt. Furthermore, the law stipulates that ultimately the comptroller general, who can be fired only by Congress, would decide whether and where to make the cuts. But the district court in Washington said that by granting this power to the comptroller general over the President, the law went too far, violating the constitutional separation of powers between Congress and the President.

To avoid the mandatory

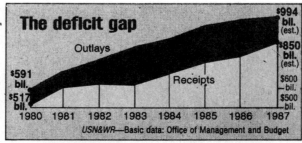

The deficit gap

Outlays

Receipts

$591 bil. $517 bil. — 1980 1981 1982 1983 1984 1985 1986 1987 — $994 bil. (est.) $850 bil. (est.) $600 bil. $500 bil.

USN&WR—Basic data: Office of Management and Budget

Yearly deficits are pushing the total federal debt from $935 billion at the start of Reagan's Presidency to a projected $2.3 trillion in 1987

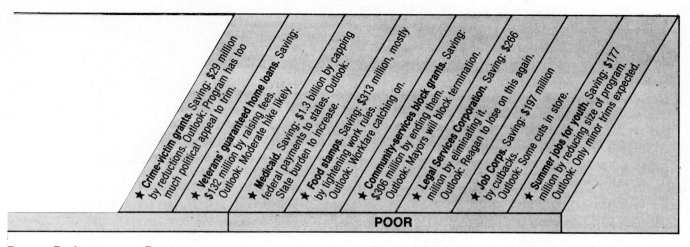

★ **Crime-victim grants.** Saving: $29 million by reductions. Outlook: Program has too much political appeal to trim.

Veterans' guaranteed home loans. Saving: $132 million by raising fees. Outlook: Moderate hike likely.

Medicaid. Saving: $1.3 billion by capping federal payments to states. Outlook: State burden to increase.

★ **Food stamps.** Saving: $313 million, mostly by lightening work rules. Outlook: Workfare catching on.

Community-services block grants. Saving: $306 million by ending them. Outlook: Mayors will block termination.

★ **Legal Services Corporation.** Saving: $266 million by eliminating it. Outlook: Reagan to lose on this again.

Job Corps. Saving: $197 million by cutbacks. Outlook: Some cuts in store.

★ **Summer jobs for youth.** Saving: $177 million by reducing size of program. Outlook: Only minor trims expected.

POOR

Gramm-Rudman cuts, Reagan proposed holding spending to $994 billion and collecting $850.4 billion in receipts. That will take some doing. His toughest task will be to get Congress to approve $22.8 billion of domestic-program cuts. Democrats, especially, will challenge Reagan's plan to save $10.7 billion by lopping non-needy beneficiaries from the rolls of social-service programs and imposing administrative reforms. Reagan wants to save an additional $2.3 billion by ending a slew of federal-aid and regulatory programs. Among them: The Economic Development Administration, the Interstate Commerce Commission, the Appalachian Regional Commission, Amtrak subsidies and urban-development grants.

It will be especially tough for Reagan to win backing for his proposal to raise $6.8 billion in extra revenue by selling some federal assets. In his budget, he hung a "for sale" sign on a variety of what he described as "commercial type" government operations that compete with services provided by the private sector. The President wants to sell five agencies that market federal electric power at subsidized rates in the Pacific Northwest, the Southwest, the Southeast and Alaska. Also on the sales counter are the Navy's oil reserves, a portfolio of government loans and surplus federal property. The Federal Housing Administration, which insures home mortgages, may be put up for sale in the future.

Reagan could have greater—though spotty—success with his plan to pick up $2.5 billion by imposing higher or new charges on users of a variety of government services, such as national parks and forests, the Coast Guard and Customs Service, inland waterways and federal loan guarantees.

The President's newest effort to rein in domestic government spending faces tougher going than previous attempts because it comes on top of cuts achieved earlier and exempts Social Security. If enacted in toto, which is unlikely, the result would be not only to abolish whole categories of aid but also to make it harder for people to qualify for the assistance that is left and to make them pay more out-of-pocket costs. But if successful, the result would be dramatic—the sharpest dollar drop in the deficit in history, from $202.8 billion in 1986 to a $1.3 billion surplus in 1991.

Reagan's difficulty will be in persuading Congress to go along with even minor parts of the plan. Congress hasn't bought earlier Reagan proposals to privatize government activities. Most of Reagan's domestic-spending cuts also have been rejected by Congress in the past.

But this year could be different. Even if Gramm-Rudman does not survive, congressional leaders say its spirit will. "Gramm-Rudman still lives," no matter what happens in the courts, said Senate Majority Leader Bob Dole. "The federal deficit is going to be center stage this session of Congress." That could force the White House and Congress to agree on a "grand compromise" on the budget in the months ahead. Domestic-program cuts would be a part of any deal. In all likelihood, so would a tax increase.

Key Republicans, as well as Democrats, see higher taxes as the adhesive necessary to seal a deficit pact. "The solution will be a revenue component to glue it all together," says Senator Pete Domenici (R-N.M.), chairman of the Senate Budget Committee.

Momentum is building in both parties to hold tax reform hostage until a deficit accord is reached. Among the Republicans, Domenici and Dole are insisting that any new tax be used to reduce the deficit before tax reform is taken up.

Defense spending could be a major sticking point. The President asked Congress for what he called a "bare minimum" increase in defense funding of 3 percent after adjustment for inflation. But the request touched off a firestorm of protest. Key legislators claim the increase being sought really is 8 percent because it is based on funding levels before they were lowered by Gramm-Rudman this year. Representative Les Aspin (D-Wis.), chairman of the House Armed Services Committee, condemned the Reagan request as a "shill."

The President plans to go to the people to defend his military buildup. He will deliver a televised speech to the nation, probably on February 19, and journey the next day to the island of Grenada. The visit to the site of the 1983 invasion will be to meet with Caribbean leaders, but the President hopes it also will remind Americans of the need for military strength. Congress isn't likely to be impressed. It already has scaled back the Reagan buildup, and further cuts in his plans seem inevitable.

If the Gramm-Rudman vise is allowed to threaten deep cuts in his defense program, Reagan may be inclined to look more favorably on higher taxes as an alternative. He already has hinted that he may bend his 1984 "no tax hike" pledge as a last resort. He told reporters he would be "willing to look at" a new oil-import levy if that is needed to win enactment of a tax-reform plan to his liking. That was interpreted on Capitol Hill as a signal that Reagan also may be willing to negotiate, at the proper time, on taxes to clinch a deficit agreement.

Congress will be pressured by voters to make a deal. One third of the Senate and all of the House are up for re-election this year. Polls indicate that

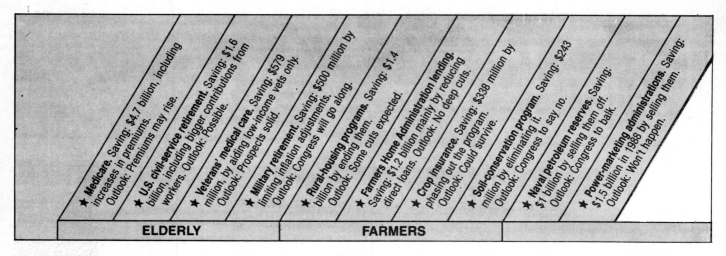

ELDERLY				FARMERS					
★ **Medicare.** Saving: $4.7 billion, including increases in premiums. Outlook: Premiums may rise.	★ **U.S. civil-service retirement.** Saving: $1.6 billion, including bigger contributions from workers. Outlook: Possible.	★ **Veterans' medical care.** Saving: $579 million, by aiding low-income vets only. Outlook: Prospects solid.	★ **Military retirement.** Saving: $500 million by limiting inflation adjustments. Outlook: Congress will go along.	★ **Rural-housing programs.** Saving: $1.4 billion by ending them. Outlook: Some cuts expected.	★ **Farmers Home Administration lending.** Saving: $1.2 billion mainly by reducing direct loans. Outlook: No deep cuts.	★ **Crop insurance.** Saving: $338 million by phasing out the program. Outlook: Could survive.	★ **Soil-conservation program.** Saving: $243 million by eliminating it. Outlook: Congress to say no.	★ **Naval petroleum reserves.** Saving: $1 billion by selling them off. Outlook: Congress to balk.	★ **Power-marketing administrations.** Saving: $1.5 billion in 1988 by selling them. Outlook: Won't happen.

voters rate the deficit as a top concern. Many lawmakers, therefore, won't want to tell constituents they failed to shrink the red ink.

The tricky political issue is which party gets the blame for raising taxes. "It will be a game of waiting for the other side to flinch," says Representative Leon Panetta (D-Calif.).

As the wheeling and dealing begins, here's how *USN&WR* assesses the impact of the President's budget on broad segments of the population and a look at what's likely to happen—

Middle Americans

Much more so than in the past, middle-income Americans will take a hefty hit if this budget takes hold. Reagan's main targets: Student and housing aid.

Some 600,000 college and graduate-school students stand to lose federal aid. Reforms would, among other things, tighten the definition of who is independent from his or her parents and cut off benefits to students who don't have a high-school diploma or the equivalent.

Many of the 4.3 million students receiving benefits would face much higher loan costs. Currently, the government pays the interest on guaranteed student loans (GSL) while the student is in school. A new rule would end this benefit, requiring the student to pay the interest when due. To cushion the blow, students would be given longer periods to repay their debts.

Middle and upper-income parents of about 10 million younger children would have to pay more for school meals as subsidies are eliminated.

The bad news for would-be homeowners is that an estimated 553,000 applicants for Federal Housing Administration home-mortgage insurance would have to pay more. Premiums would be raised to 5 percent from 3.8 percent, and the insurance would be limited to families with annual incomes of less than $40,000. The fee that ex-GI's pay for Veterans Administration home-mortgage guarantees would rise from 1 percent to 2 percent and higher later on.

Outlook: Many subsidies will be trimmed. User fees will be raised for mortgage insurance and housing loans. But neither the trims nor the fee increases will be as large as Reagan wants. In a large number of cases, political pressures will be so great that Congress won't be able to put together the majority needed to kill a program.

The elderly

Though Social Security benefits remain intact, senior citizens will find other benefits under fire. The 31 million elderly persons who depend on medicare would have to pay more for

What Reagan sought

The President's proposals and Congress's actions—

1981 **Reagan:** Seeks tighter rules for welfare and food stamps, limits on student loans, reduced school-lunch subsidies, large increase in defense spending, deep cut in personal and business taxes, end of main federal jobs program.

Congress: Gives the President almost all he asked for, including defense buildup and tax cut exceeding his request. Cuts new public housing deeper than Reagan sought, refuses to end some programs.

1982 **Reagan:** Proposes abolishing Departments of Energy and Education and slashing medicare, mass transit and other programs. Wants rent vouchers for the poor instead of new public housing, 13 percent boost after inflation in defense spending, user fees but no new taxes.

Congress: Accepts medicare cuts but rejects most other requests. Passes $98 billion tax bill that boosts certain levies and tightens tax code. Raises Pentagon budget by 7.6 percent while barring production of MX missiles and nerve gas. Raises gasoline tax 5 cents a gallon.

1983 **Reagan:** Seeks 10 percent defense boost, domestic-spending freeze and a standby tax if the deficit stays high. Also wants to cut welfare payments, child-support enforcement, vocational education. Would freeze payments to doctors under medicare, make the elderly pay

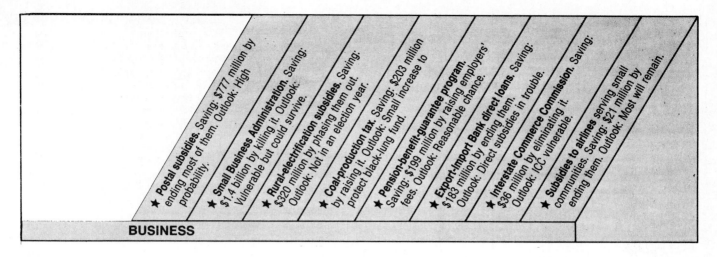

Postal subsidies. Saving: $777 million by ending most of them. Outlook: High probability.

★ **Small Business Administration.** Saving: $1.4 billion by killing it. Outlook: Vulnerable but could survive.

★ **Rural-electrification subsidies.** Saving: $320 million by phasing them out. Outlook: Not in an election year.

★ **Coal-production tax.** Saving: $203 million by raising it. Outlook: Small increase to protect black-lung fund.

★ **Pension-benefit-guarantee program.** Saving: $199 million by raising employers' fees. Outlook: Reasonable chance.

★ **Export-Import Bank direct loans.** Saving: $183 million by ending them. Outlook: Direct subsidies in trouble.

★ **Interstate Commerce Commission.** Saving: $36 million by eliminating it. Outlook: ICC vulnerable.

★ **Subsidies to airlines** serving small communities. Saving: $21 million by ending them. Outlook: Most will remain.

BUSINESS

health-care protection.

Monthly premiums for coverage of doctors' and medical bills would rise from the present $15.50 to $17.80 next year and higher later on. Patients would have to pay the first $100 of expenses, up from $75 now.

Many of the 19 million veterans who receive outpatient and hospital care at Veterans Administration facilities will lose out under a reform that restricts financial aid to lower-income families.

Military and civilian federal retirees would lose 1987 cost-of-living rises. Future hikes would be less than inflation.

Outlook: The elderly will have to pay higher premiums for medicare. VA health care will be limited to low-income veterans. Government retirees will lose cost-of-living pension increases for the year.

The poor

Low-income groups were hit hard when Reagan first came into office, but they have largely been spared recently. This time around, they aren't as lucky.

Employable welfare and food-stamp recipients would have to work to continue receiving assistance. Some 10.8 million people now collect welfare checks, and 19.5 million get food stamps. By putting the able-bodied to work, the President figures to save taxpayers $238 million in welfare and $313 million in food-stamp expenses.

Only the neediest 22,000 of the 40,500 youths now being trained by the Job Corps would stay in that program. Poor youngsters anticipating

federally subsidized summer jobs could find fewer available as the program is changed to give top priority to metropolitan areas with high youth unemployment. Low-income families would use vouchers to help pay for housing and special education in the marketplace. If Reagan has his way, both the Community Services block-grant program, which provides social services for the poor, and the Legal Services Corporation, which provides the poor with free legal aid, would go out of business.

Outlook: Congress is reluctant to take another whack at the poor. Requiring able-bodied welfare and food-stamp recipients to look for work

more for hospitalization but provide new catastrophic-illness insurance.
Congress: Approves major medicare revisions but not coverage against catastrophic illness. Rejects most other Reagan proposals. Gives Pentagon a 4 percent hike. Shelves standby tax.

1984 **Reagan:** Renews plea for rent vouchers, freeze on medicare payments to doctors, phase-out of mass-transit subsidies. Wants all able-bodied welfare recipients to work. Asks for power to veto items in spending bills. Seeks research on manned space station and acid rain and requests 13 percent spending increase for defense.
Congress: Agrees to medicare freeze, seed money for space-station and acid-rain research. Approves rent vouchers—along with some new public housing. Rejects $8 billion request for Central American aid. Gives Pentagon a 5 percent increase. Takes no action on line-item veto.

1985 **Reagan:** Wants simplified tax code with fewer loopholes and lower rates, curbs on student loans for middle class, reduced pay for federal workers, termination of Small Business Administration. Proposes to stop subsidies for Amtrak. Asks 5.9 percent increase for defense.
Congress: Rejects most Reagan proposals, although tax reform clears House and goes to Senate. Cuts Pentagon budget 6.2 percent after inflation. Approves aid to Nicaraguan rebels only for humanitarian needs. Passes Gramm-Rudman Act requiring yearly reductions in the deficit.

What Congress delivered

stands a good chance of acceptance.

Farmers

Farmers can't look for many breaks. The administration expects to hold price supports at the legal minimum, hoping that rising prices will boost rural incomes.

Other federal help would be trimmed back, with the elimination of conservation aid and crop-insurance subsidies. A housing-voucher system would be substituted for the present rural-housing program. Electric bills could rise as the Rural Electrification Administration, which subsidizes rates, is phased out. Farmers Home Administration credit would be cut sharply. A user fee would be charged on export loans.

Outlook: Rural-housing and crop-insurance programs will be sliced but not terminated. In the end, conservation aid may be funded near the 1986 level.

Business

If the President has his way, business-subsidy programs would be hit hard. But he has tried to kill some of them before and failed.

Once again, big business is being faced with the loss of direct export loans. The budget proposes to substitute an interest-rate subsidy for guaranteed loans.

Small businesses could not get subsidized direct loans, guarantees and disaster aid from the Small Business Administration, which would be abolished.

Businesses that now benefit from subsidized postal rates would pay higher mailing fees. A subsidy to airlines that serve small communities would end, too. Aid to business for energy research and development would be cut back.

A big cost for many firms would come from hiking fees they must pay to the government's Pension Benefit Guaranty Corporation to insure many retirement plans. Annual premiums would jump to $8.10 per worker from $2.60.

Outlook: Business may lose postal subsidies, export loans and the SBA. There also is a good chance that pension-insurance premiums will go up. But subsidies for local-service airlines, like many other programs that benefit business, probably will survive.

Defense and space

Reagan hasn't flinched in his zeal to build up the military. This year's budget seeks $311.6 billion in new spending authority. Defense Secretary Caspar Weinberger argued that the 8 percent jump is necessary to "regain some of the momentum that we lost," when the Pentagon got only $278.4 billion of the $313.7 billion it requested last year.

The biggest gainer would be the Strategic Defense Initiative, or Star Wars, which Weinberger calls "the President's highest priority." SDI is down for a 75 percent jump to $4.8 billion in 1987. When he first proposed SDI two years ago, Reagan hoped to spend $25 billion over five years, but Congress has given him only half his annual dollar requests.

Weinberger is reopening old battles over the MX and antisatellite (ASAT) missiles. Last summer, over his strenuous objections, Congress voted to cap the deployment of MX missiles at 50 and to end testing of ASAT. This year, Weinberger is asking for money to study ways to deploy another 50 MX missiles and for a big boost in ASAT funds.

The Pentagon's shopping list for hardware would allow the Army to buy 840 M1 tanks and 870 Bradley fighting vehicles, the infantry's controversial new troop carrier; the Navy to get four new attack submarines, one Trident-missile sub, two cruisers, three guided-missile destroyers, various other ships and 120 F/A-18 aircraft, and the Air Force to buy 48 F-15 fighter planes, 216 F-16 aircraft and 21 C-5 cargo planes.

In space, the President wants to keep funding for a manned space station to start operating in the mid-1990s.

Outlook: The President's defense request will be scaled back again. He may get more of what he wants for SDI than he has in the past, but both the MX and ASAT requests will be denied. The hardware list will be trimmed. The National Aeronautics and Space Administration probably will get money to build a new shuttle orbiter to replace Challenger, which exploded January 28.

The fate of each budgetary item and program will, if the past is any guide, only be finally determined by protracted negotiations between the White House and both houses of Congress, which will drag on for most of the year. But if Gramm-Rudman—or its spirit—survives, government spending as a percentage of gross national product is almost certain to decline, and the deficit should finally begin to move downward. Otherwise, it's likely to be business as usual—political gridlock and stubbornly high deficits. ■

by Monroe W. Karmin with Robert J. Morse of the Economic Unit and members of the magazine's Washington staff

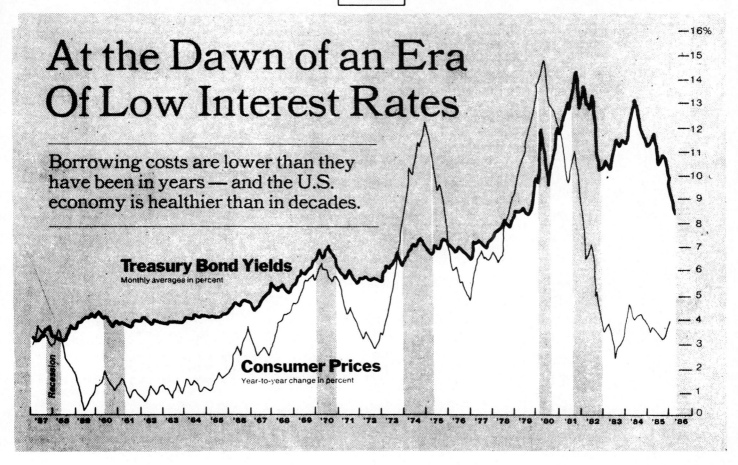

18

At the Dawn of an Era Of Low Interest Rates

Borrowing costs are lower than they have been in years — and the U.S. economy is healthier than in decades.

Treasury Bond Yields
Monthly averages in percent

Consumer Prices
Year-to-year change in percent

Recession

'57 '58 '59 '60 '61 '62 '63 '64 '65 '66 '67 '68 '69 '70 '71 '72 '73 '74 '75 '76 '77 '78 '79 '80 '81 '82 '83 '84 '85 '86

16% 15 14 13 12 11 10 9 8 7 6 5 4 3 2 1 0

By PETER T. KILBORN

WASHINGTON

A FEW years ago, with their children grown, Liz and Nelson Casmer bought a piece of land not far from their home in suburban Pittsburgh, planning to build a smaller house on it. But it was not until November, when interest rates made houses more affordable, that they found a buyer for the four-bedroom house they had owned for 22 years.

The Casmers then approached J. Roger Glunt, a Pittsburgh-area builder who specializes in single-family homes selling for $100,000 to $150,000 and whose business, he said, is now the best it has been in five years. Besides customers, he says he has banks pouring in the door. "They're flooding us with rate sheets saying, 'Hey! We've got money!'"

Next, the Casmers went to one of these lenders, Mellon Bank, which had knocked its rates for 15-year and 30-year conventional mortgages below 10 percent at the start of the year, sooner than most other lenders. "We are probably doing in the vicinity of $20 million a month in western Pennsylvania," said Gary Frauenhotz, executive vice president in charge of mortgage banking. "That compares with $3 million to $4 million a month a year ago." The bank granted the Casmers a 9½ percent, 30-year loan.

As Pittsburgh goes, so goes the nation.

• • •

Any economist, businessman or politician who just a few months ago predicted anything akin to the current combination of mortgage rates that dip into single digits, inflation of 3 to 4 percent and $15 oil could not have found a job even in that citadel of American optimism, the White House, or in the thousands of lesser institutions that trade on economists' foresight.

Yet the economy has delivered itself of just such a mix of extraordinary good news. And if the booming stock market is any indication, spirits across the land are soaring. Interest rates, dropping into territory not seen since the 1970's, have been the single most important set of numbers, buoying the mood and kicking off Wall Street's heady rise. And the good times — heralded by a new era of lower lending rates — seem here to stay awhile.

Some pessimists, of course, warn that it could all blow away in the summer breeze, with a dive of the dollar or a reversal of oil prices. Some also caution that if good times are coming, many narrower components of the economy — such as business investment or automobile sales — have yet to point that way.

But the fundamentals are overwhelmingly good. During the past year, interest rates have dropped 3 percentage points on average; many economists see them slipping still a bit more this year before they settle on a gentle low plateau for the balance of the 80's. Lending, more than any other force, makes the economy go 'round, and analysts now speak of an explosion of borrowing and spending to keep the economy growing for years.

None of the leading economic forecasters can see a recession for at least several years. Instead, they see growth of 3 percent annually, which is about what the economy requires to grow ad infinitum without giving rise to higher inflation. That means Ronald Reagan, with three straight years of economic growth under his belt, may now be presiding over the debut of the longest stretch of low-interest-rate prosperity since Eisenhower.

"All the ingredients that were so troublesome 5 and 10 years ago are falling into line," said Fabian Linden, consumer economist at the Conference Board in New York. "Lower interest rates mean there's money around to do all the things that money does. It buys factories. It buys houses. It buys cars. Lower interest rates mean we can use money more lavishly. Then we get oil. That's a tremendous serendipity. We appear to be moving into a new era of vigorous growth." Rarely, he said, has he seen such promise for prolonged growth — and lower interest rates are the key to his optimism.

"I can't foresee anything that would push us into a high-interest-rates, high-inflation kind of world." said Laurence H. Meyer, head of the St. Louis forecasting firm that bears his name. Compared to five and six years ago, said Peter L. Bernstein, of the consulting firm Peter L. Bernstein Inc., "interest-rate peaks are lower and the lows are lower: That is probably the way it's going to be." As a result, he said, "I think the world is going to have another boom. I don't know when it's going to come, but it's going to come big."

WITH a respectful eye on the rampaging stock and bond markets, considered by many to be the economy's best prognosticators, many economists are now beginning to invoke the aquatic metaphors of sea changes and tidal waves, creating images as strong as the Roaring Twenties, the Postwar Boom and the Soaring Sixties. The economy, they say, seems to have tamed the business cycle's 20-year pattern of pushing and pulling and settled onto a much more tranquil and healthy course.

The stock market certainly reflects the good times. Since the start of last year, the Dow has shattered one record after another, racing to almost 1,800 from what from what just a year ago seemed a not-so-bad 1,200. The message is clear: Investors figure that over the next two or three years, corporations will be harvesting profits, from big-spending, big-borrowing consumers, in magnitudes unknown since the last sustained booms of the 50's and the 60's.

What has happened is a massive change in the inextricable, often volatile, relationship of interest rates and inflation. The United States has completed four years of 4 percent annual inflation — one-third the rate that prices climbed in the 1979-1980 period. And over the past year or so, that sustained improvement has finally persuaded long-term lenders that they can begin to whittle down the inflation premium they build into the price they charge for money.

As a result, the homeowner's monthly payment on a 30-year, $100,000 mortgage has plunged to $840.87 at the 9½ percent level current in many parts of the country from $1,264.44 five years ago, when

the rate was 15 percent. That's about $5,000 extra a year to save and to spend, a boost to all beneficiaries of the homeowner's largesse — from furniture salesmen to travel agents.

And most other borrowers are reveling in the lower rates, from the corporations that borrow to expand their plants and work forces to the debtors of Latin America. The banks' prime lending rate, on which they base their loans, has dipped to 9 percent, less than half its 21½ percent peak in the winter of 1980 and 1981. Top-rated corporate bonds, over 15 percent at their highs in 1981 and 1982, were down to 10 percent at the end of last year and now are flirting with 8 percent. Automobile loans were 16 percent in 1981. Now they are a bit under 12 percent.

So-called "real" interest rates — the rate after deducting the inflation premium built in by lenders — have been cut in half in the last few years. So far, the only rates that have not budged much are those for personal loans, which seem mired in the high teens, and credit card balances, at nearly 19 percent. Bankers say that those loans cost them more to manage and that they are unsecured, by stocks, real estate or other property, so they are always high. But in time, they say, the tidal push of lower rates will force them down, too.

Over all, said David A. Wyss, economist at Data Resources Inc. in Lexington, Mass., each one percentage point decline in average interest rates adds one-third of a percentage point to the growth of the nation's economy in that year, provided it comes early on. Simply put, a three-point decline adds up to about $39 billion on last year's $4 trillion economy.

And the benefits of lower rates will be filtering through the economy for some time, analysts say. "The biggest impact is in the housing market," Mr. Wyss said, "and you should see a big surge there when the buying season gets going this spring. You should see more business investment, too, but that's a slower process because of the lead time in placing orders and changing attitudes. Then the dollar: Lower interest rates bring the dollar down, which chases imported goods out of the American market. Then you get exports up, but that doesn't happen in a hurry."

Businesses, he explained, went through wrenching adjustments to high rates and the high dollar. To bring costs in line with foreign competitors, many set up factories and supply lines abroad. It will take a while to convince them that the dollar and rates have settled down to stay, and then a while longer to get the domestic supply lines flowing again.

Behind the drop in rates, economists cite a confluence of forces pushing in the same encouraging direction for the first time in 20 years. Interest

rates, inflation, growth rates, and the exchange rates of currencies of major nations are in better balance than they have been in years.

They attribute the confluence mostly to two powerful sources. One is the apparent reversal in the course of the American budget deficits — the major culprit, many economists say, behind high American interest rates, the high dollar and major imbalances in the world economy.

Most politicians doubt that the deficits will fall to absolute zero five years from now as required by the Gramm-Rudman-Hollings balanced-budget law. But most of them, and the economists who sit in judgment, see the deficit falling from 5 percent of gross national product to well under 2 percent by 1990. Such a decline means that much less competition from the Government for credit and therefore, lower rates. Declining rates, moreover, help assuage the political pain of lowering the deficit.

Evidence of declining deficits feeds through the markets, causing lower rates, and lower rates reduce the Government's cost of borrowing to carry the deficits. The saving on Government interest payments means Congress will not have to cut popular Government programs as much as it would otherwise. Meanwhile, the Federal Reserve Board, which previously contributed to rate rises by tightening money-supply growth in order to slow inflation, has been cheered enough by lower inflation and progress on the deficit to relax its monetary policies.

The other major source of falling rates is the change in the international economic policies of the Reagan Administration, from a posture of indifference about how other nations manage their economies to a politically driven need to tell them what to do. It needs them to push their rates down along with American rates. Otherwise, the dollar would rise again, making imports rise , at the peril of American jobs. So far all major players in the exercise, from the Federal Reserve to the governments of Japan and West Germany, have been going along with the wishes of President Reagan and his principal agent of change, Treasury Secretary James A. Baker 3d.

The first big signal of the Administration's new policy was the five-nation statement in September that the dollar had climbed too high and that the group was prepared to drive it down. Then, a a week ago last Friday, the Federal Reserve , in concert with Japan and West Germany, cut the discount interest rate that it charges banks from 7½ percent to 7 percent — one-half its peak in 1981 and the lowest level since 1978.

Another signal could come during May's seven-nation summit conference in Tokyo. There, the Administration could disclose more of its thinking about setting up mechanisms to align economic policies, including the exchange rates of currencies.

"The cause of what we're seeing in interest rates is the change in our international economic policy," said Albert M. Wojnilower, chief economist of the First Boston Corporation, the investment banking firm. To try to halt the erosion of American jobs by a flood of imported goods, he said, "the United States is throwing its weight around."

There are some soft spots that worry economists. Consumer borrowers are not likely to be impressed by drops in rates that they do not pay. Banks still charge high rates on credit card balances and for personal loans, and many consumers are not reaping the off-setting benefits of falling mortgage rates.

Consumers relying on double-digit returns from money market deposit accounts and investments in corporate securities now receive half as much for their money as they did a few years ago. Those who have not switched into stocks have less to spend to keep the economy rolling.

Beyond that, the economy's midwinter burps have been many: the jump in the unemployment rate to 7.2 percent last month from 6.6 percent in January, last Friday's report of a sharp drop in the industrial production index for February, Detroit's somber disclosures that it has been producing too many cars, the lanquid state of retail sales, record levels of consumer and corporate debt, modest increases in capital spending, the report that the economy grew a mere 1.2 percent in the fourth quarter last year, evidence that the yawning American trade deficit continues to rise despite the decline of the dollar. Some economists point out that lower rates may reflect that persistent weakness in the economy.

Others, however, insist that weaknesses showing up in economic indicators this winter bode well for summer — and the summers beyond. Slow growth, by this reckoning, is safer than rapid expansion and will allow rates to tumble even further.

But some pessimism remains. "I think the conventional wisdom about everything getting better right now is full of baloney," said Sam Nakagama, a Wall Street economist and pamphleteer. "Oil producers' spending has to drop instantly," which is going to produce a severe deflationary shock," he said. "You've got a recession in the oil patch and in Mexico. You've got a farm recession." Lower rates and inflation eventually will mean a sounder economy, he said, "but we have to get there first."

Many businessmen, too, are not yet betting their resurgent profits on investments in factories and machinery to accommodate a prolonged new era of prosperity. The Dun & Bradstreet Corporation says manufacturers expect to raise capital spending this year only 5 percent, down drastically from 18 percent last year. And they are also unsure of what to expect of the battle between Congress and the White House over revising the tax system. Moreover, they say other forces in the economy have to settle themselves out, such as the still-rising tide of foreign competition and the course of the dollar.

AT General Motors, said David C. Monro, whose job at the company is to ponder the effects of economic trends on automobiles, "here's certainly been some intensive ruminating" because of sliding rates. He said he writes memos to senior management saying he still sees discouraging signs, although he expects the economy to do better, at least for the next year or two. But the big problem, he said, is that inflation is still a potential threat.

And some economists who have little argument with forecasts of a lively economy for a couple of years say the promise of a new era of prosperity stretching into the next decade is more murky. Mr. Wojnilower at First Boston says that the Administration's international economic policy, whatever it has done for current rates, could send inflation back up later.

The policy, he says, discourages price competition among countries in attempting to force the markets to level the exchange rates of currencies, and encourages countries to expand growth of their money supplies. Both factors, he said, pose the risk of higher inflation.

Like many analysts, he is most wary about the dollar. Despite all the efforts to control it, a binge of speculation could make the dollar sink, causing inflation. Or it could soar again, causing another rise of the trade deficit and the job losses the Government wants to avoid.

Barring these problems, economists say that a long-running engine of easy credit should accelerate evolutionary changes now at work in the nation. They see vastly more home building to meet the demands of the birth explosion of the late 1940's and 50's, more investment in factories and automation and more growth of service industries, which tend to offset the volatility of manufacturing.

From 1945 to 1960, Mr. Linden of the Conference Board says, 58 million babies were born, almost twice as many as during the preceding 15 years. "Those birth-boom kids, from now to the end of the century, are going to be, roughly, 35 to 50 years old," he said. "That's the most expansive phase of the life cycle. Income rises. Borrowing rises. Spending rises."

Home demand among the baby boomers is poised to explode, economists say, because they first started shopping for homes just as rates and real estate prices were soaring. Most economists predict that new home construction, which has been hovering around 1.7 million units annually, will rise to 2 million this year and remain there for at least several more.

David Reed, economist at the Hudson Institute in Indianapolis, said he doubts that the decline in interest rates alone will lead to the kind of extraordinary prosperity that followed World War II. But at the same time he expects better times than the nation witnessed during the high-rate, high-inflation immediate past.

"I think we are facing an extended period of moderate growth," he said. "In that sense, we are in a very different economy." ∎

THE BREATHING SPACE IN 'REAL' RATES

WASHINGTON

Many economists suspect that rates can still go down a bit more. They say the reason is based in part on the concept of the "real" interest rate, the one that remains after the expected toll of inflation has been removed from the "nominal" rate that people actually pay.

In the 1960's the real rate on the safest, long-term corporate bonds was 3 percent. Expected inflation added another 2 or 3 percentage points, so nominal rates on such bonds came to 5 to 6 percent.

Then, near the end of the 60's, real rates started climbing. Economists explain that rising deficits, the Federal Reserve's periodic tight-money policies and a strong economy then meant that money would become scarcer as Government competed with businesses and consumers for credit. Anticipating rising demand, lenders and investors raised the price they charge for money. At its peak in 1981, economists figure that the real rate on corporate bonds reached almost 7 percent.

During the same period, lenders became alarmed about double-digit inflation. Fearing it would persist for years, they demanded higher inflation premiums to put up their money long term. Nominal rates, as a result, rose mightily. In the bond market, top-rated companies often had to pay more than 15 percent to borrow from late 1980 until mid-1982. From then on, rates eased. Inflation has been no higher than 4 percent for four years, and Congress appears to have halted the rise in deficit spending, which means less competition for credit and lower real rates.

Laurence H. Meyer, head of Laurence H. Meyer & Associates in St. Louis, a forecasting firm, figures that on 9-percent corporate bonds today, the real rate is down to about 4 percent and the inflation premium is 5 percent.

A little more progress on inflation and the deficit could push all rates down a little more. Many economists predict a further drop of half a percentage point in rates this year. But anything more than that, next year and beyond, would require evidence of lower inflation than now and more cuts in the deficit.

But all that is possible, economists say. In the 1940's, leading corporations paid less than 3 percent to borrow. "In earlier times," said Geoffrey H. Moore, a business-cycle expert at Columbia University, "we would have thought today's rates and 4 percent inflation were high numbers."

The Fed Hasn't Changed Its Ways

By MILTON FRIEDMAN

There is an old story about a farmer who used his barn door for target shooting. A visitor was astounded to find that each of the numerous targets on the door had a bullet hole precisely in the center of the bull's-eye. He later discovered the secret of such remarkable accurancy. Unobserved, he saw the farmer first shoot at the door and then paint the target.

That is the precise counterpart of the way in which the Federal Reserve System hits its monetary bull's-eye. It simply repaints its target—a practice that a Wall Street Journal editorial writer recently applauded: "From all appearances arbitrary 'targets' will not interfere unduly with its vision, and at least that is something to be welcomed."

So what else is new? The Fed has not let "targets," arbitrary or not, interfere with its vision ever since it was first required—much against its will—to set them by a Joint Congressional Resolution passed in 1975. Its disregard of targets in favor of its typically myopic vision used to be labeled "fine tuning," and the Journal was among the Fed's severest critics when that fine tuning led to accelerating inflation and to erratic ups and downs in the economy and in interest rates.

The accelerating inflation was brought to an end in 1980, but the fine tuning has continued. Only the rhetoric has changed: from the October 1979 pledge of allegiance to controlling monetary aggregates, particulary M1; to the abandonment of M1 as a target in mid-1982; to the partial restoration of M1 in mid-1983; to its full acceptance in 1984 when M1 for a change hit its initial target; to the repainting of the bull's-eye in mid-1985 that the Journal editor welcomed so warmly.

Behind the rhetorical camouflage, the Fed has simply continued its fine-tuning ways, relying on whatever rhetoric served to rationalize its current policy. Indeed, the growth of M1 was more volatile during the 1979-82 period when the Fed pledged allegiance to M1 control than in any earlier period of comparable length, and so were the growths of interest rates and the economy. That volatility, by increasing uncertainty and therefore the demand for liquidity, contributed to the rapid drop in inflation, though at the cost of an unnecessarily severe recession.

More recently, as the accompanying chart shows, the relation long stressed by monetarists between monetary growth and subsequent growth in nominal gross national product has continued to prevail; if anything, it has been closer in recent years than it was earlier. The relation is far from perfect on a quarter-to-quarter basis, yet whenever monetary growth has risen or declined substantially for several quarters, nominal and real GNP have almost invariably followed suit, generally one to three quarters later, though sometimes after an even longer interval. For example, it took five quarters before the substantial and sustained decline in monetary growth from the fourth quarter of 1982 to the fourth quarter of 1984 was followed as usual by a sustained decline in the growth of nominal GNP.

In line with this pattern, the substantial rise in monetary growth since the fourth quarter of 1984 will almost surely be followed by a substantial acceleration in the growth of nominal GNP, perhaps already in its early stages, perhaps not beginning until the third or fourth quarter. Whenever it does begin, it will be some months or even quarters before the Fed recognizes that such an acceleration is under way. It will then step on the monetary brake, setting the stage for a subsequent deceleration—and so on, ad nauseam.

Fluctuations in nominal and real GNP reflect many forces other than monetary growth. However, they have been much exacerbated by the Fed's propensity, in former Chairman William McChesney Martin's graphic phrase, "to lean against the wind" that is blowing today, even though there is a "long and variable lag," as I put it 26 years ago, between the Fed's action and its effect on the economy, so that the Fed is as often as not leaning with rather than against tomorrow's wind.

Steady monetary growth is not a panacea. It will not solve the problems raised by high government spending, deficits and taxes; or by excessive regulation, protectionist legislation, and all the other ills the republic is subject to. But steady monetary growth is an effective insurance policy that, if it had been adopted two decades ago, would have avoided both the accelerating inflationary roller coaster of the 1960s and 1970s and the bumpy disinflationary roller coaster of the 1980s. And there is ample evidence that this is not simply hindsight. And if it were adopted now, it would have equally salutary effects for the future.

Monetary targets that meant something would contribute to both monetary and economic stability. Monetary targets that are repainted whenever the Fed regards it as convenient to do so serve only to confuse the public and to conciliate shortsighted congressmen and Wall Street Journal commentators.

Mr. Friedman, a Nobel Prize-winning economist, is a senior research fellow at the Hoover Institution, Stanford University.

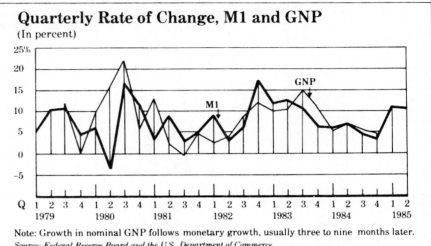

Quarterly Rate of Change, M1 and GNP
(In percent)

GNP

M1

Q 1 2 3 4 | 1 2 3 4 | 1 2 3 4 | 1 2 3 4 | 1 2 3 4 | 1 2 3 4 | 1 2
1979 — 1980 — 1981 — 1982 — 1983 — 1984 — 1985

Note: Growth in nominal GNP follows monetary growth, usually three to nine months later.
Source: Federal Reserve Board and the U.S. Department of Commerce

Rules plus Discretion in Monetary Policy— An Appraisal of Our Experience since October 1979

O ne of the oldest arguments in economic theory is whether monetary policy should be guided by rules or discretion. My object in this paper is to assess what we have learned about this subject since the famous Federal Open Market Committee (FOMC) meeting of October 1979. This is purely a personal assessment, not a Federal Reserve position.

Rules for monetary policy seem to have an intuitive appeal to many people. To some they seem to offer easy answers to complex problems. To others the rules offer a discipline which they think we would not impose upon ourselves.

All rules for monetary policy, whether they be based on the growth of money, the exchange rate, the price of gold or a basket of commodities, must rest on one of two assumptions. One assumption is that the behavior of the object to be controlled is predictably related to the nominal GNP. The only alternative assumption is that monetary policy should be directed solely toward controlling inflation and that the central bank should have no responsibility or concern for the level of employment or output.

I will argue that the events of recent years demonstrate that neither of these assumptions is viable. At the same time, our experience with monetary targeting, for all of its problems, has brought two substantial advantages to the conduct of monetary policy. First, monetary targeting automatically forces the FOMC to consider the longer-run consequences of actions taken to meet short-run objectives. This is an important discipline for the Committee. It reduces the risk of excessive reactions to temporary shortfalls in employment and output. Changes in the guidelines, while they may have to be made from time to time, require an overt decision by the FOMC and cannot be viewed as a casual matter. Second, monetary targeting has made it easier for the Federal Reserve to communicate its policies to the public and the Congress. It automatically injects into the dialogue with the Congress the long-run consequences

Frank E. Morris

President, Federal Reserve Bank of Boston. Remarks presented to The Money Marketeers, New York, New York, September 11, 1985.

Reprinted from Federal Reserve Bank of Boston
New England Economic Review, September/October, 1985.

of alternative policies in a way that no purely discretionary regime could do. These are advantages not to be discarded.

I conclude, therefore, that monetary policy should be one of rules, tempered by discretion. This is not a neat solution but the world is, unfortunately, too complex for neat solutions.

The Problems with Pure Rules Regimes

No one, to my knowledge, has demonstrated predictable relationships between the exchange rate, the price of gold, or the price of a basket of commodities and the nominal GNP. Thus any advocate of a pure rules regime in targeting these variables must necessarily assume that the central bank will concern

---

Policymakers should beware of any policy whose success requires a rapid change in the long-term expectations of the buyers of stocks and bonds.

---

itself solely with the inflation rate, regardless of the short-term impact on employment or output. The revealed unpredictability of the relationship of the monetary aggregates to the nominal GNP is leading some monetarist economists to the same position.[1]

This transition should not be difficult. Implicit in monetarist theory has always been the proposition that the public should accept any short-run consequences of a monetary rule, secure in the knowledge that in the long run, monetary growth rates are neutral with respect to employment and output. However, the monetarist long run is certain to be too long to be relevant for public policy unless some other policy instrument could assure a reasonably acceptable level of employment and output in the shorter run.

The supply-side-monetarist policy mix of 1981 was to have accomplished this. While a policy of gradually reducing monetary growth was to deal with inflation, the tax reduction program was to generate rapid and sustained economic growth. Most economists had difficulty in seeing how a monetary policy tight enough to bring down the inflation rate substantially could coexist with rapid economic growth. The reconciling element was to have been a massive

change in inflationary expectations, which would produce declining interest rates despite rapid economic growth.

In the event, we learned that long-term expectations do not change rapidly. It took a number of years of high inflation rates before the bond investor demanded an adequate inflation premium. It will take a number of years of low inflation rates for that premium to be eliminated.

Looking back to 1951 with our inflationary mindset, it seems amazing that the Federal Reserve could still be pegging government bonds at 2½ percent despite six years of rather strong economic growth following World War II. It was possible only because the long-term expectations of 1951 were still dominated by the experience of the 1930s. Policymakers should beware of any policy whose success requires a rapid change in the long-term expectations of the buyers of stocks and bonds.

The most critical recent demonstration of the need for discretion in monetary policy occurred in the summer of 1982. In the first half of 1982, M1 grew at a 7 percent rate, substantially above our policy range of 2.5 to 5.5 percent. During the same period, the nominal GNP grew at an annual rate of only 2.2 percent and real GNP declined at a rate of 2.8 percent.

Both Federal Reserve and private forecasters were predicting an upturn in the third quarter. The strong M1 growth in the first half was felt to presage such an upturn. As we moved into the third quarter, however, it became apparent that the widely forecast upturn was not occurring. The economy was still contracting. The FOMC responded by setting aside the M1 target, permitting interest rates to decline despite the M1 overshoot.

Sufficient time has passed to assess the wisdom of this judgment. Suspending the rule did not lead to excessive real growth or to a reacceleration of inflation.

Milton Friedman has argued that monetary policy should ideally be conducted by a few clerks at the New York Fed who should be instructed to provide a constant and low rate of growth of the money supply. He argues that Federal Reserve officials reject this advice only because it would eliminate their power. One can only speculate what would have happened if Milton's clerks were running monetary policy in the last half of 1982. The rate of inflation would probably be even lower than it is today, but the costs in terms of employment and output would have been prohibitive. Furthermore, the impact of a rigid monetary rule on an already shaky financial structure, both domestic and international, might have been catastrophic. It was a classic case of the occasional need for rules to be tempered by discretion.

In the last half of 1982, monetary policy was the only instrument that could have been applied quickly and powerfully in response to the unexpected weakness of the economy in the third quarter. In 1985, with fiscal policy almost completely immobilized, it is even more unrealistic to contemplate focusing monetary policy solely on inflation control.

What To Target?

Three years ago, I published an article in which I argued that we could no longer measure the money supply in the United States; that is, we could no longer distinguish balances held for transactions purposes from other balances. I argued that we could not assume that the historical relationship of M1 and M2 to the nominal GNP would prevail in the future.[2]

The reasons were simple. In the case of M1, we could not assume that interest-bearing "money" would behave in the same way as the old non-interest-bearing money. In the case of M2, we could not assume that deposits bearing market-determined rates would behave in the same way as deposits bearing regulated rates. To the extent that bankers kept the rates on money market deposit accounts reasonably in line with market rates, we should expect M2 to be much less interest-elastic than in the past.

In the place of M1 and M2, I argued that we should target on those aggregates that were sufficiently broad so as not to be impacted by financial innovation—specifically, total liquid assets and total, nonfinancial debt (hereafter, debt).

With the passage of three years, it is clear that financial innovation has, indeed, changed the behavior of M1 and M2, but factors other than financial innovation have also been at work which have affected the behavior of all the financial aggregates.

Goodhart's Law worked with amazing swiftness with respect to debt. No sooner had the FOMC adopted a monitoring range for debt than it became apparent that the very stable relationship which Benjamin Friedman of Harvard had found between debt and the nominal GNP over a number of decades had gone off the track. We can explain a large part of it. In recent years, the debt aggregate has been inflated by massive substitutions of debt for equity, in buy-out situations and in the actions of corporations to protect themselves against buy-outs. It has also been inflated

by advance refunding issues of state and local governments. These debt issues do not generate economic activity. However, even after making a rough adjustment for these factors, it appears that more debt is now required to generate a dollar of nominal GNP than was required in the 1970s.

In addition to financial innovation, M1 behavior has been impacted by large changes in interest rates which have dramatically changed the opportunity costs of holding M1-type assets. The introduction of the Super NOW account, which can pay a market rate, was expected to have reduced the interest-elasticity of M1. In fact, because of the way these accounts have been priced, the introduction of the Super NOW has increased the interest-elasticity of M1.

Bankers have been quick to reduce the rate paid on Super NOWs when interest rates declined, but loath to raise the rate when market rates rose. In contrast, when pricing money market deposit accounts, bankers promptly adjusted MMDA rates in both directions. (See Charts 1 and 2.) As a result of this pric-

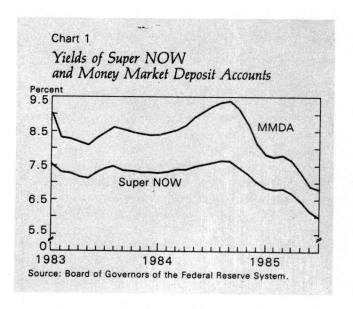

Chart 1

Yields of Super NOW and Money Market Deposit Accounts

Source: Board of Governors of the Federal Reserve System.

ing practice, the opportunity cost of holding Super NOWs can vary substantially. In early 1984 the opportunity cost of holding Super NOWs instead of money market mutual funds was about 1.5 percent and Super NOWs were growing at about a 30 percent rate. By the third quarter of 1984, the opportunity cost of holding Super NOWs had risen to 3 percent and the growth rate of Super NOWs fell below 10 percent.

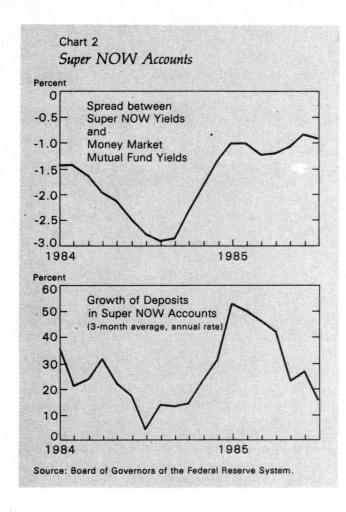

Chart 2
Super NOW Accounts

Percent

Spread between Super NOW Yields and Money Market Mutual Fund Yields

Growth of Deposits in Super NOW Accounts
(3-month average, annual rate)

Source: Board of Governors of the Federal Reserve System.

By early 1985, the opportunity cost had dropped to 1 percent and the growth rate surged to 40 percent. This interest sensitivity accounted for a significant part of the changes in M1 growth rates in 1984-85.

The M1/nominal GNP relationship has become even more unpredictable than I anticipated three years ago. In the autumn of 1983, prominent monetarist economists forecast that the economy would move into recession in the first half of 1984 and that the inflation rate would accelerate sharply in the second half.[3] The combination of two such seemingly contradictory events would have been most unusual in business cycle history. The forecasts were based on rules of thumb with respect to the lagged relationships of M1 growth, nominal GNP and the inflation rate, rules of thumb that had often been reliable in the past. In the annals of economic forecasting there can be few forecasts with such large misses. Instead of moving into recession, the first half of 1984 showed a real growth rate of 8.4 percent and, instead of a sharp

escalation in the inflation rate in the last half, the inflation rate actually declined. Forecasting the nominal GNP and the inflation rate on the basis of past M1 growth has become a chancy enterprise, indeed.

In three out of the past four years, the FOMC has either set aside the M1 target (1982) or rebased the target on the second quarter level (1983 and 1985). Only in 1984 did the original target set for M1 prove to be compatible with a reasonably acceptable outcome for the nominal GNP. This fact speaks volumes about the suitability of M1 as a target for monetary policy.

We have been pointing to financial innovation and large interest rate changes as the source of aberrant behavior by the aggregates. The information presented in the table and Chart 3 suggests a third factor. Shown on the table and chart are the cumulative deviation of velocity from the 1970-80 trend for M1, M2, M3, total liquid assets (L) and debt (D).[4] Although the amplitudes of the deviations differ widely, all of the aggregates showed larger than expected velocity gains in 1981 and much larger than expected velocity

Recent Behavior of Velocities: Deviation from 1970–1980 Trends

Percent

	M1	M2	M3	L	D
1981:I	1.9	6.3	5.0	3.7	2.1
1981:II	0.3	5.1	4.8	2.9	1.3
1981:III	1.7	6.0	4.2	3.2	2.1
1981:IV	0.2	4.1	2.1	1.0	0.6
1982:I	−3.9	1.6	−0.2	−1.5	−1.6
1982:II	−3.4	1.0	−1.1	−2.6	−2.3
1982:III	−5.1	−0.8	−2.8	−4.4	−3.8
1982:IV	−9.1	−2.3	−3.9	−5.5	−5.2
1983:I	−10.7	−5.4	−4.3	−6.0	−5.4
1983:II	−11.7	−5.1	−3.4	−5.4	−4.9
1983:III	−12.7	−4.7	−3.0	−5.5	−5.2
1983:IV	−12.6	−4.3	−2.7	−5.1	−5.3
1984:I	−11.5	−2.7	−1.3	−4.3	−5.0
1984:II	−11.5	−1.9	−1.1	−4.6	−5.5
1984:III	−12.2	−2.3	−1.9	−6.1	−7.2
1985:IV	−12.1	−2.9	−2.7	−6.5	−8.7
1985:I	−14.3	−4.6	−3.8	−7.5	−10.6
1985:II	−16.5	−4.8	−3.7	−7.5	−12.1
Mean Absolute Error 1970:I–1980:IV	1.0	2.2	2.2	1.6	0.7

Chart 3

Velocity of Financial Aggregates
Deviations from 1970-80 Trends

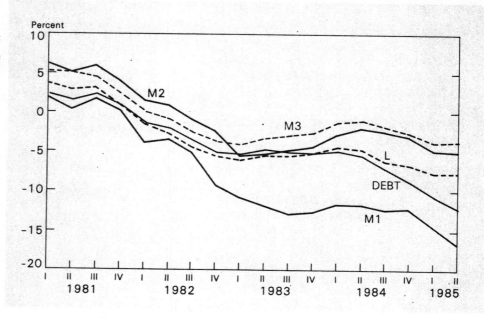

Source: See table.

declines in 1982-85.

This suggests a third factor at work which has affected all of the aggregates in different degree but in a similar fashion. Perhaps the third factor is the sharp decline in the rate of inflation, which since 1981 has led people to be willing to hold more financial assets relative to real assets and relative to income.[5]

If we are to target financial aggregates, which should we use? My answer is that the only ones we should use are those with a long track record and those whose character has not changed in recent years. This leaves out M1 and M2, since they are new aggregates, even though they bear old designations. The behavior of M3 since 1980 has been fairly good, but it has to be a very suspect aggregate in an era when the regulatory authorities are pressing banks and thrifts to improve their capital ratios. It is quite possible, in fact, that the fairly decent behavior of M3 has been a consequence of banks moving substantial assets off their books to improve their capital ratios. M3 may also not mean what it used to mean.

What about my two candidates of three years ago? I will confess that when I recommended total nonfinancial debt as a target three years ago, it never occurred to me that American corporations would be issuing vast quantities of debt for the sole purpose of retiring equity. I will not comment on the sanity of this in an already over-leveraged economy, but it is clear that if we are to utilize a debt target, we will have to differentiate debt that will generate economic activity from debt that will not.

This leaves me with total liquid assets. It seems to me that if we can no longer measure transaction balances, the next logical step would be to concentrate on controlling liquidity. I can emphasize how very personal a view this is by telling you that I doubt I could get two votes for this proposition on the FOMC, even if one of the votes were mine.

How has total liquid assets performed as a target during the last four years? Better than the rest. It had a disastrous year in 1982, when its velocity was 6.5 percent below trend. But 1982 was a disastrous year for all of the financial aggregates, with deviations from trend velocity ranging from -5.8 percent for debt to -9.3 percent for M1. In the other three years, the velocity for total liquid assets fell 0.7 percent faster than its trend, with the largest deviation being -1.4 percent in 1984.[6]

Since 1981 we have seen an increased willingness to hold liquid assets relative to income. This has impacted all of the aggregates. When the adjustment to a lower inflation rate has been completed, there is every reason to believe that the relationship of total liquid assets to the nominal GNP will be similar to that of earlier years. This, however, is not the case with the new interest-bearing M1. There is no basis for thinking that its future velocity will be similar to that of the old non-interest-bearing M1. We will need at least another decade of data before we can be confident in forecasting the velocity of the new M1.

To Sum Up

Asked the question "What have we learned since October 1979?" I would list the following:

1. A targeting procedure for monetary policy has great disciplining values which we should not discard.
2. There is no variable that the Federal Reserve can target which has a highly predictable relationship to the nominal GNP.
3. It is not feasible for monetary policy to focus solely on the price level, since there is no other policy tool available with which to deal with an unexpected weakness in the economy—à la 1982—or unexpected strength.

4. If one accepts the first three propositions, then it follows that the optimum monetary policy regime is one of rules tempered by discretion.
5. I would choose a total liquid assets rule for two reasons: (1) unlike all of the other aggregates its meaning has not been changed by the events of the past 10 years; and (2) if we can no longer measure transaction balances, controlling liquidity is the next best choice.

[1] See Milton Friedman's latest views in *Challenge*, July/August 1985.

[2] Frank E. Morris, "Do the Monetary Aggregates Have a Future as Targets of Federal Reserve Policy?" Federal Reserve Bank of Boston, *New England Economic Review* (March/April 1982). See also Frank E. Morris, "Monetarism without Money," Federal Reserve Bank of Boston, *New England Economic Review* (March/April 1983).

[3] See Edward Mervosh, *Business Week*, December 12, 1983, "Milton Friedman's Recession Forecast Sparks a Controversy:"

Milton Friedman, the Nobel laureate economist, is playing Scrooge this holiday season. While most economists and Administration officials are enjoying the steady diet of cheerful economic news coming from Washington, Friedman, the guiding light of monetarism, is gloomily predicting that the Federal Reserve is setting the U.S. up for a return to stagflation next year, possibly as early as the first half.

Friedman's scenario is based on straightforward monetarist analysis: By letting the money supply grow too fast from mid-1982 to mid-1983, the Fed has insured a sharp reacceleration of inflation at least by the second half of 1984. Beginning this summer, the Fed reined in the growth of the money supply, and Friedman argues that if the money growth continues its limp performance for another couple of months, the economy will be heading into a sharp slowdown or even a recession early next year. 'If money growth continues at its present rate for another two months, we are almost sure to have a recession in the first half of 1984,' he predicts.

Friedman holds out little hope that money growth will accelerate soon enough to head off the impending disaster.

See also: Walter Guzzardi, *Fortune*, March 19, 1984, "The Dire Warnings of Milton Friedman:"

Still, when Friedman takes his eye off the [tennis] ball to regard the economy, he is depressed. He forecasts a slow current quarter, with real growth of the gross national product running at an annual rate of only 1%; he also sees a strong possibility that by the end of this year inflation could reach an annual rate of 9%.

[4] I am indebted to my colleague, Richard W. Kopcke, for this analysis.

[5] This was suggested to me by Donald L. Kohn of the staff of the Federal Reserve Board of Governors among others.

[6] The velocity deviations from trend are measured fourth quarter to fourth quarter.

A Layman's Guide to the Keynesian-Monetarist Dispute

Peter D. McClelland

How curious it is that as the United States economy continues to recover from the worst recession since World War II, a Nobel laureate in economics favors the abandonment of countercyclical policy by the central bank,[1] while a Federal Reserve official argues that countercyclical policy has performed reasonably well in the recent past.[2] And why should the economics profession be so sharply divided on the merits of a tax-based incomes policy or the merits of wage and price controls?[3]

The answer must surely lie in sharply differing views about the causal processes of our economy. Regrettably, the key areas of disagreement are almost impossible to detect in either the popular literature or the textbooks written by these men and women. The following brief survey attempts to remedy this defect.

The best place to begin is where Milton Friedman and other monetarists usually begin: with the quantity equation of exchange, or

$$MV \equiv PQ ,$$

where M is the quantity of money in a society, V is its velocity of circulation (or the average number of times money changes hands in a year), Q is the quantity of real goods and services created and sold during that year,[4] and P is the average price of those goods. Every transaction in the marketplace is a two-way swap: the seller turns over goods or services valued at a price, and the buyer surrenders cash equal to that price. It must therefore *always* be true that the total value of cash turned over by buyers equals the value of goods and services received. That value, in turn, is nothing more than the sum of each commodity multiplied by its market price. This is why between the symbols MV and PQ one finds not an equals sign, but an equals sign plus a third line to indicate an identity. The relationship $MV \equiv PQ$ always holds.

A word of explanation concerning velocity. Economics has a long-standing tradition of illustrating complex mechanisms with oversimplified examples. Following in those footsteps, let us consider a medieval community in which the total sales in the village during a single year are as follows:

        4,000 pairs of shoes at $10 per pair = $40,000
        60,000 bushels of wheat at $1 per bushel = $60,000.

The value of PQ is thus $100,000, or ($10 × 4,000) + ($1 × 60,000). Suppose that the total money supply in this community consists of 20,000 one-dollar bills. This is then the value of M. The implied velocity [5] is

$$V = \frac{PQ}{M} = \frac{\$100,000}{\$20,000} = 5 .$$

Notice that V is calculated as a residual. We do not observe it directly in our medieval community (or anywhere else) but infer it from other data. If total transactions were $100,000 and the money supply was only 20,000 one-dollar bills, then on the average each dollar bill *must* have changed hands five times in the course of a year. All perfectly straightforward, one might think. Except that it is not. Lurking in this simple mathematics is a complicated problem that will become more apparent later on.

With the above equation in hand we can easily summarize the basic tenet of the monetarists. They make two assertions and one obvious inference. The assertions are (1) that V is "stable," and (2) that Q is not affected—or not affected very much—by M. (In more technical language this second point might be rephrased to read that Q is determined exogenously.) If these two assertions are granted, one can hardly deny what monetarists continually assert: that the main determinant of changes in the price level are previous changes in the stock of money. In

the equation $MV = PQ$, if V is stable and Q is unaffected by M, then P will tend to vary with M. Our problem is therefore to understand what is meant by the two assertions noted. If we can also understand why Keynesians challenge those assertions, we shall be well on our way to understanding the Keynesian-monetarist dispute.

What is meant by the statement "Velocity is stable"? This variable could change for several reasons. The most obvious relate to improvements in the financial institutions of a community. The development of the telegraph, clearinghouses, or commercial banks can accelerate the rate at which the stock of money changes hands. Monetarists readily concede this point—they could hardly deny it—but emphasize that the evolution of financial institutions takes time. No *sudden and large* change in velocity should result from this development if the institutions themselves do not change suddenly.

The main threat to the monetarists' position lies elsewhere. Consider again the example of the medieval village. Suppose that half of those 20,000 dollar bills were actually hidden away in mattresses as a means of storing wealth. In that case, while total velocity was 5, the actual velocity of active money (i.e., the money that is not in mattresses but out in the marketplace) would be ($100,000 ÷ $10,000), or 10. No problems arise for monetarists as long as roughly half of the money supply is held idle in mattresses. But suppose for some reason that 40 percent of this idle money, or $4,000, suddenly becomes active *and* takes on the velocity of other active dollars. Then 14,000 dollar bills would change hands on the average of 10 times a year and the value of PQ would rise to ($14,000 × 10) or $140,000. *Total* velocity (that is, the V in $MV = PQ$), as noted previously, is calculated as a residual. Since the total money supply (M) is unchanged but the value of PQ has risen from $100,000 to $140,000, total velocity now becomes

$$V = \frac{PQ}{M} = \frac{\$140,000}{\$20,000} = 7$$

How is this possible? In simplified terms, one can think of any community as having two "piles" of money, one idle and the other active. If some of the heretofore idle dollars are moved over into the active pile, then the supply of dollars bidding for goods and services increases, and the value of goods and services sold must also increase. In our example we achieved the seemingly odd result of an increase in total velocity (from 5 to 7) *not* because of an increase in the rate at which active dollar bills changed hands (that remained constant at 10), but rather because the proportion of the total money supply in active circulation increased [6] from 50 percent ($10,000 ÷ $20,000) to 70 percent ($14,000 ÷ $20,000).

The monetarists now have a problem. If large quantities of dollar bills jump back and forth between active and inactive piles, then clearly velocity will not be "stable." (In our example, when $4,000 moved over, V rose from 5 to 7.) Similarly, if the money supply were doubled *and* all of that extra money were added to the inactive pile, then prices would not tend to increase as the monetarists claim they should. The solution, as one might expect, is to argue that this does not happen. Monetarists usually make this point by claiming that the proportion of cash balances that people desire to hold is very stable.[7] This guarantees that the kind of jumping back and forth illustrated in the above example will not take place. It also means that when the money supply is dramatically increased, almost none of that new money will be held idle. If it is not held idle, it must be spent; if it is spent, it must increase the value of PQ; and if Q is relatively unaffected by changes in M, then the main impact must be to increase P. By this one assertion, then, the monetarists retrieve their central notion that changes in prices are largely determined by changes in the money supply.

Since the Keynesians challenge this conclusion, they must disagree with some of the premises in the above argument. One of the main premises in dispute is that the amount of money people want to hold idle cannot change significantly in the short run. Recall the speculative motive and the liquidity preference schedule of standard Keynesian analysis. The basic idea is that if the interest rate rises, the demand for idle cash by speculators will fall; if the interest rate falls, the demand for idle cash will rise.[8] In terms of the example used previously, this is equivalent to asserting that the movement of dollar bills between the two piles of active and inactive money is very sensitive—or at least quite sensitive—to changes in the rate of interest.

We have now clarified at least one major point of disagreement concerning how the economy actually works. The monetarists claim that the desire to hold idle cash is insensitive to interest rate changes (and to other factors as well); the Keynesians claim that the desire to hold idle cash is quite sensitive to interest rate changes. Notice two features. First, at the core of the debate is a question of fact concerning the responsiveness of certain decision makers: When interest rates fall, will the demand for idle cash balances increase by a lot or by a little? Second, when economists write about this dispute, the language chosen will usually include the phrase "the stability of velocity." What is seldom realized when the point is phrased this way is that the substantive issue is whether or not, over a short time period, large quantities of cash are moved between active and inactive balances in response to such changing economic variables as the rate of interest.

The second major puzzle is this: what is meant by the assertion that in the equation $MV = PQ$, Q is independent (or largely independent) of M; or to put the point in different words, that Q is determined exogenously? According to the monetarists, total real output (Q) in the long run is primarily determined by available technology and the supply of factors of production (usually lumped by economists into the four categories of land, labor, capital, and enterprise). Of negligible influence, they argue, is the supply of money. It follows that a large increase in the money supply—if it cannot affect Q, and if V is "stable"—must bring in its wake severe inflation.[9]

The Keynesians believe otherwise. The originator of this school of thought was puzzled by the existence of large-scale and sustained unemployment. Keynes knew only too well that according to classical price theory, if the supply of workers exceeds demand, then the price of workers—the wage rate—should fall until all those who want jobs at the prevailing wage rate can get them. Exit unemployment, one would think, except that it refused to exit in the 1930s. The most obvious answer to this puzzle became a central assumption of all Keynesian models. If wages are inflexible on the down side—if such economic forces as labor contracts and large unions prevent wages from being reduced—then whenever the demand for workers falls, the main effect will be rising unemployment rather than falling wages. How obvious the point appears in retrospect! In terms of elementary supply-and-demand analysis, if the demand curve falls and the adjustment cannot occur on the price (or wage) axis, then it must occur on the quantity (or employment) axis. The solution for unemployment is therefore to stimulate demand. An expansionary monetary policy can accomplish this through the conventional Keynesian mechanisms: an increase in the money supply should lower the interest rate; this lower interest rate should stimulate investment; the increased investment (through the multiplier) will stimulate income and consumption; and thus demand will be increased and unemployment reduced.

The monetarists refuse to accept the above as an adequate description of how our economy actually works. Leave the unemployment alone, they argue, and natural market forces will remove it.[10] If the demand for automobiles falls and workers are laid off in Detroit, the situation will be rectified by the forces of supply and demand. Some unemployed workers will find alternative jobs. Automobile producers will tend to cut prices or develop alternative devices to stimulate demand. If this unemployment is instead fought by an expansion of the money supply, the only result will be more inflation. Recall the point emphasized

earlier: that newly created dollars, according to the monetarists, are like hot potatoes—no one is willing to hold them very long. If they are not held, they must be spent. An expansionary monetary policy is therefore viewed as setting in motion successive rounds of spending and respending that are sure to drive prices up even if, in the process, the demand for cars is stimulated and unemployment in Detroit falls. Finally, that reduction in unemployment would have occurred *sooner or later* through the forces of supply and demand. To put it harshly, the monetarists might say, why bother to feed the horses in order to feed the sparrows when the sparrows will be fed anyway?

The key phrase is "sooner or later." The Keynesian rebuttal is that existing market forces will remove unemployment, at best, very slowly. Equally important, they assert that the main impact of spending and respending dollars should be the bidding for resources that are currently idle rather than for those that are already employed. This in turn implies that the principal impact of injecting new dollars into the spending stream should be a reduction in unemployment rather than a bidding up of the price level.

We have now arrived at the second main bone of contention between these two competing schools. Once again the central issue is a question of fact: How rapidly do labor markets adjust when unemployment occurs? The monetarists reply, "Very rapidly"; the Keynesians, "Very slowly." Here too the language usually used by economists tends to obscure the substantive point. Few would guess that the question "In the equation $MV = PQ$, is Q determined exogenously?" boils down to a dispute over speeds of adjustment in labor markets.

In review, and on close inspection, the main points of disagreement are remarkably uncomplicated. When extra money is created, the monetarists argue that almost all of it is sure to be spent. The Keynesians claim that it is far from clear how much will be spent and how much will be held idle. During a recession, whenever new money is created—and however much of it is spent and respent—the Keynesians believe, the main impact will be the bidding for otherwise idle resources. The monetarists believe that the main impact will be the bidding up of prices.[11] If these are the arguments, why can they not be resolved? The answer is what one might expect: because we lack the tools to prove conclusively which view more accurately portrays how our economy actually works.

If we cannot resolve the debate, we can at least understand two further implications of these conflicting positions. The first concerns the question of whether or not inflation and unemployment are inversely related. When one goes down must the other necessarily go up? The monetarists answer no. Since they argue that changes in the money supply mainly affect prices and not output, it follows that efforts to control inflation by controlling the money supply should not affect total output or, by implication, total employment. The Keynesians believe otherwise. Why they believe that stable prices and full employment are conflicting goals is not always clear. Some concede that when aggregate demand is stimulated, at least some of the spending and respending will bid for employed resources rather than unemployed resources, thereby creating upward pressure on prices. Others suggest that (1) prices are determined partly by wage costs and (2) wage demands tend to be more moderate in periods of high unemployment.

The second implication of the above arguments concerns the effectiveness of fiscal policy as a countercyclical tool. The Keynesian position is so familiar as hardly to bear repeating. If unemployment is caused by inflexible wages and falling demand, the solution is to increase demand. This the federal government can accomplish either by spending more itself or by cutting taxes, thereby giving the public more to spend. In either case the resulting government deficit will have a multiplied effect upon consumption (and possibly a stimulating effect upon investment), causing demand to increase and unemployment to fall.

The monetarists' position is more subtle. They begin by noting that any increase in deficit spending must be financed.[12] That is, before the government can spend more dollars it must first acquire those dollars from somewhere. If it acquires them by expanding the money supply—if the dollars to be spent are newly created dollars—then the anticipated impact will be that outlined above: rising prices and little change in total output and employment. If instead the government finances its deficit by borrowing dollars from the public, the anticipated effects are that (1) increased borrowing will drive up interest rates, (2) the rise in interest rates (perhaps reinforced by rising prices) will cause a cutback in consumption and investment, and (3) this cutback in spending by the private sector *will exactly match* the increase in spending by the government. Fiscal policy therefore has no effect upon the size of the pie, only upon its division between the public and private sectors. But suppose that deficit is financed instead by the printing of new money, as noted above. The same answer applies, argue the monetarists. Total output will remain virtually unchanged but prices will rise as the government uses newly created dollars to bid away goods and services from the private sector. The resulting inflation will be a disguised form of taxation. The public must surrender part of the pie to the government, not because income taxes or sales taxes have increased, but because higher prices force them to relinquish part of the share they heretofore had.

The reader by now should be able to anticipate the Keynesian counterattack. In a world of inflexible wages and economic recession, they argue, the size of the pie can be expanded by an expansion of demand. If government deficits are financed by borrowing procedures that raise interest rates, there is no reason why the resulting cutback in public demand should *exactly* equal the increase in government spending. More to the point, in a recession the appropriate monetary policy is to expand the money supply and *lower* interest rates. But why, one might ask, do Keynesians expect that the spending and responding generated by an expansionary monetary and fiscal policy will have its main impact upon unemployment rather than upon prices? And why do monetarists expect exactly the opposite? The answer is no more complicated than referring to a point made previously. *The substantive issue mainly concerns the speed of adjustment in labor markets.* The Keynesians believe that without government stimulation of demand, unemployment can remain a serious problem for a long time; with that stimulation, it can be alleviated. The monetarists take the opposite view. Disequilibriums in product and factor markets, they argue, should be treated in the same manner as the sheep of Little Bo Peep: leave them alone. The implicit belief is that, if left alone, imbalances will correct themselves; if meddled with, they may become worse.

Notes

1. See the article in this section by Milton Friedman entitled "The Fed Hasn't Changed Its Ways."

2. Also in this section see the article by Frank E. Morris, President of the Federal Reserve Bank of Boston, entitled "Rules plus Discretion in Monetary Policy—An Appraisal of Our Experience Since October, 1979."

3. See, for example, the articles in Section IX on a tax-based incomes policy.

4. The following analysis focuses exclusively on income velocity and ignores transactions velocity.

5. This assumes that all transactions involve an exchange of dollars and rules out the possibility of bartering with goods only.

6. Expressed in mathematical form, total velocity is the weighted average

$$V = \frac{MA(VA) + MI(VI)}{MA + MI},$$

where MA is active money, VA is the velocity of active money, MI is inactive money, and VI is the velocity of inactive money. Note that $MA + MI = M$ and $VI = 0$.

7. More correctly, what is assumed to be stable is the demand for real cash balances, or nominal cash balances adjusted for changes in the price level.

8. To review the behavioral premise, Keynesians assume that when interest rates are low (i.e., bond prices are high) many speculators will expect bond prices to fall and will therefore delay buying bonds, holding cash in the interim.

9. The key word here is "large." In the equation $MV = PQ$, if Q—or Gross National Product—increases gradually over time and P is to remain relatively stable, then the money supply should also increase at *roughly* the same rate as Q ("roughly" because gradual changes may also occur in V). This is why monetarists argue for a gradual expansion in M, rather than for a rigidly fixed money supply.

10. "Normal" unemployment, according to the monetarists, is determined by such factors as the interchangeability of job skills, the cost of labor market information, and the extent to which laws and organizations (such as unions) impede the free functioning of the labor market.

11. Notice the implied contrasting expectations concerning interest rate trends. If prices rise, interest rates should also rise to allow for expected inflation in the future. (A lender who normally receives 6 percent and now expects 10 percent annual inflation will demand 16 percent to compensate for being repaid in depreciated dollars.) Thus, if the main impact of an expansionary policy is on prices, interest rates will tend to go up as prices rise. If the main effect is lowered unemployed, then this kind of upward pressure on future interest rates should not occur, or at least not occur in any severe form.

12. Subsequent discussion focuses only upon deficits arising from increased spending. The arguments apply with equal force if that deficit is created by tax cuts.

WHAT'S PUTTING A STAKE IN THE HEART OF MONETARISM

BY ROBERT KUTTNER

The theory is a shambles: Money-supply growth, for example, has consistently outstripped goals without triggering inflation. And monetarism's main value to the Fed seems to be as a scapegoat

It is high time to give monetarism the decent burial it so richly deserves.

Monetarism, you will recall, held that inflation is always and everywhere a monetary phenomenon and that growth in the money stock closely parallels growth in real gross national product. Wise central bankers, says monetarist logic, will hold the economy on a stable course by targeting a steady, non-inflationary growth of the money supply rather than targeting interest rates.

Monetarism, please note, is partly descriptive, partly prescriptive, and deeply political. Traditional conservatives are obsessed with the money supply because monetarism logically points to laissez-faire as the best economic strategy. If money supply is really all that matters, then attempts by governments to engage in Keynesian macroeconomic manipulation, let alone forms of (gasp!) economic planning, can only make things worse. The optimal economic strategy, therefore, is to pick a money-growth target (Milton Friedman recommends 3%), stick with it, and leave the rest of the economy to the private sector.

SMOKESCREEN. Recent events have made a shambles of both theory and prescription. Not only has monetary growth sharply exceeded targets without triggering inflation, but the monetary aggregates seem to have taken on a life of their own. Moreover, although the Federal Reserve Board publicly embraced monetarism in 1979, the Fed gave up on its targets in 1982. Although the Fed nominally returned to a policy of setting monetary targets in 1983, it has missed them more often than not.

Further, the Fed doesn't seem to care very much whether it hits the targets. Most of the major Fed officials and Fed watchers now admit that the 1979-82 exercise in monetary targeting was less a devout conversion to monetarism than a useful smokescreen for the political pain of stringent disinflation. When Congress and the White House screamed that tight money and high real interest rates were strangling the economy, the Fed could shrug: "Don't blame us. We're just targeting the money supply."

When the dirty work was done, and disinflation threatened to turn into full-blown depression in 1982, Fed Chairman Paul A. Volcker could ditch formal monetarism and let the economy breathe. Despite dire warnings about the deficit, the Fed has continued to run a fairly loose monetary policy, mainly because it correctly perceives an absence of inflationary pressures on the economy. Friedman, using monetarist assumptions, predicted a recession in early 1984 followed by renewed inflation. Neither happened.

Why does the money supply wobble up and down independently of GNP growth and the rate of inflation? Richard W. Kopcke, senior monetary economist of the Federal Reserve Bank of Boston, provides the most convincing answer I have heard yet. Kopcke observes that if monetarism was ever a reasonable proposition, it has been undermined by financial deregulation, which has obliterated the distinction between the measured supply of "money" and long-term "investments." He notes that bankers offer depositors different yields on different accounts according to the bankers' expectations of where interest rates are headed. If they think money is getting tighter, they set attractive rates on long-term certificates of deposit in order to lock in depositors' money. If they think rates are dropping, they offer slightly better relative yields on super-NOW and money market accounts.

DELICIOUS IRONY. For monetarists and central bankers, the trouble is that money market and NOW accounts are part of M1 and M2—the ostensible money supply—and CDs are not. Kopcke, writing in the *New England Economic Review*, argues persuasively that a good part of the recent "inexplicable" swings in the money supply were reflections of changes in bankers' business strategies.

For example, from March to August, 1984, money in large time deposits grew at an annual rate of 23%. This occurred because bankers had deliberately widened the spread between CDs and money market accounts. M1 and M2, relative to GNP, declined accordingly. More recently, the apparent excessive growth of the measured money stock may reflect the fact that many depositors, waiting for predicted higher rates, are staying liquid by keeping more of their assets in demand deposits (which are counted in M1) rather than in CDs.

In short, the money supply is not a stable commodity that central bankers can target precisely. Instead, it substantially reflects the investment strategies of financial institutions and their customers. Monetary policy now exists in a Lewis Carroll world where the croquet mallets have become flamingos.

No wonder the money stock fails to conform to GNP growth. The most delicious irony of all is that this "rational expectations" reading of money supply leads to a Keynesian policy recommendation: If the apparent money supply in part reflects what people expect, the Fed is better advised to target GNP growth and to use interest rates as its instrument. Volcker, in effect, is doing just that. But he is too polite to abandon the monetarist pretense entirely. He may need it again to camouflage the next dose of disinflation. ∎

ROBERT KUTTNER IS ECONOMICS CORRESPONDENT FOR *THE NEW REPUBLIC* AND THE AUTHOR OF *THE ECONOMIC ILLUSION*

Comeback for Keynes?

*With monetarism now on the ropes, a new breed
of influential academics is again making a case for
government intervention in the economy.*

by Marc Levinson

No one has had a tougher decade than John Maynard Keynes. The renowned British economist, whose arguments for an activist government have been central to American politics since the New Deal, has been in disfavor. Academics who assert that the system works best without government intervention have dominated economics since the early 1970s. But now, economists have begun to pick apart the free-market theories and demonstrate that, in many cases, a dose of government involvement is just what the economy needs. Keynes is coming back.

This new economic research, in fields as varied as labor economics and trade theory, is not yet a unified body of thought. Rather, the new Keynesians are united only in opposition to the free-market economists who assert that, left to themselves, markets will allocate resources efficiently.

Economic research may be arcane, but abstract models demonstrating the irrelevance of government economic policy made Ronald Reagan's arguments for shrinking the size of government intellectually respectable. Similarly, theoretical research linking government intervention with superior economic performance could have a significant impact on future political thought—and, ultimately, the policies of the federal government. Advocates of government industrial policy, whose views have hitherto lacked intellectual standing, may find a whole new body of theory to buttress their case. Now, more than a decade after the free-market school became dominant, Robert Solow, who has preached Keynesian principles at the Massachusetts Institute of Technology since the 1950s, declares: "Within the last year or so, the pendulum in economics has begun to swing in the other direction."

The key to classical free-market economics is price flexibility. In an economy with perfect competition, the free-market advocates contend, wages and prices rise and fall freely. Unemployment, therefore, is seen as a temporary situation. Surplus labor should cause wages to fall until employers hire everyone who wants a job. The economy would thus automatically correct itself.

In the Keynesian world, however, markets are not always perfectly competitive. Wages and prices are "sticky," so the economy is not always self-correcting. Unemployment can persist indefinitely, and the economy will not operate at maximum efficiency. These economic imperfections give government a role: By stimulating or retarding investment, it can help achieve full employment and higher levels of output.

Although Keynes is popularly associated in the United States with deficit spending, his work in fact offers sophisticated reasoning for manipulating the money supply and using fiscal measures such as government spending and taxes to regulate the economy's output. These theories offered solutions to the problems of the Great Depression of the 1930s, and proceeded to dominate American economic policy for nearly four decades. As late as 1971, when President Richard Nixon proclaimed that "now I am a Keynesian," there was a broad consensus that the government should act to steady the course of the economy. But hardly had Nixon spoken when that consensus was dealt a serious blow. As the inflation rate climbed, unemployment rose as well—in direct contradiction to what Keynes, who died in 1946, had foreseen.

At the same time, a new generation of free-market economists began punching gaping holes in Keynesian theory. Their guru was Milton Friedman, then at the University of Chicago, who had long argued that the only proper government policy was to set a stable rate of money supply growth and leave the economy alone.

As monetarism came into its own, a younger group of free-market economists, led by Robert Lucas of the University of Chicago and Thomas Sargent of the University of Minnesota, propounded the idea that government intervention is useless, because it is nullified by the actions of individuals anticipating it. The "rational expectations" of people acting to maximize their economic welfare counteracts the government's intended results. Explains Lucas: "The proposition is not that economic policies do not matter. The question is whether the government can use monetary and fiscal policy to achieve higher levels of employment. The answer turns out to be no."

The Lucas and Sargent theories strongly guided conservative political thought in the 1970s. In 1981, monetarists assumed key policymaking roles in the Reagan Administration, and their voices were influential in urging that the government not use fiscal or monetary policy to fight unemployment. Slow but steady money supply growth would cure inflation, while increasing unemployment only temporarily, these economists argued; unemployment would drop as soon as the public became convinced the Federal Reserve was serious about stopping inflation. Instead of stimulating the economy, the government was advised to reduce regulations that hindered the workings of the free market and kept wages and prices from adjusting to the new low inflation environment.

But just as the stagflation of the 1970s dealt a blow to Keynesians, the events of the 1980s have been hard for monetarists to explain. Inflation has fallen only at the cost of persistent high unemployment, and even the impressive growth rates of 1983 and 1984 did not provide jobs for all those who wanted them. And despite monetarist warnings, double-digit money supply growth in 1985 did not send prices spiraling.

As a result of the monetarist failure, calls for government measures to spur economic growth are increasing. While deregulation to improve market efficiency in individual industries remains popular, economic theorists have been building the case that *laissez-faire* is not the best policy for the economy as a whole.

Asserts Harvard University economist Benjamin M. Friedman: "The events of the 80s have been devastating to the Lucas-style view. There's a new interventionist mood. The place you can chart that is in the research people are doing. The smart young guys are no longer trying to write dissertations saying government policies can have no effect. They're looking for explanations why, despite rational expectations, government policies can have an effect."

These new lines of research boast an analytical rigor that the Keynesianism of the 1950s and 1960s largely lacked. They feature impeccable mathematical models matching the sophistication and complexity of the monetarists' work, but their results are very different. Explains Columbia University economist Andrew Weiss: "What we're really doing is providing a theoretical underpinning for the assumptions of Keynesian economics."

The rational-expectations theorists generally started with assumptions of perfect competition, flexible prices, and efficient markets. By using a different set of assumptions, the new Keynesians have stood rational expectations on its head. For example, Princeton University economist Joseph Stiglitz has shown that if there is a rational expectation of additional unemployment tomorrow, companies will act so as to cause unemployment today, as well, by reducing planned investment. In such a case, the economy will move away from, not towards, full employment.

The causes of unemployment are the focus of much of the new work, since Keynes viewed persistent joblessness as the major ill that govern-

"IF A FIRM PAYS ONLY THE lowest wage at which it can obtain workers, workers have little fear of getting fired for nonperformance because they will always be able to find another job at that wage."

ment intervention in the economy could cure. Robert Lucas and his followers argue that long-term unemployment is voluntary, and that wages will fall until everyone who wants to work has a job. Earlier Keynesian theorists were unable to offer convincing explanations why this logic is wrong. But now, several such theories are under study. Suggests economist George Akerlof, of the University of California at Berkeley: "It may be that employers, for various reasons, find it profitable to pay wages above what is necessary to get their labor. That would give a reason for involuntary unemployment."

Three major arguments have emerged to show why, even in a perfectly competitive economy, wages might not fall to a level at which all job-seekers could find work. One model, advanced by Stiglitz and his Princeton University colleague Carl Shapiro, looks upon unemployment as a device to discipline workers. If a firm pays only the lowest wage at which it can obtain workers, workers have no fear of getting fired for nonperformance, because they will always be able to find another job at that wage. Paying higher wages means some workers will remain unemployed, but it also means that those who are hired are less likely to shirk on the job. If all employers act in their own self-interest and pay wages above the minimum, unemployment will be a permanent feature of the economy.

Weiss and Stiglitz argue that employers' lack of perfect information about workers' performance may cause companies to pay high wages. If employers reduce wages, the best workers will quit first, leaving an increasingly inefficient workforce. Another argument emphasizes the cost of turnover: because hiring and training workers is expensive, employers have reason to pay more than the lowest wage to keep the workers they have. In either case, private market incentives lead to wages that are too high to eliminate unemployment. "In these models, the market equilibrium is inefficient, so there's a role for government intervention," Andrew Weiss explains.

Trade policy is another area in which some theorists now postulate a role for government intervention. With perfect competition, economists have long known, free trade leads to the greatest possible economic welfare for the world. But researchers such as MIT's Paul Krugman contend that perfect competition is a rarity, so they have been using models that assume a particular good is produced by an oligopoly. In that case, a country may be better off if it restricts imports and promotes exports. Similarly, if a head start on technology is required to make a firm internationally competitive in the future, it may be wise for the government to protect that firm against foreign competition.

A fundamental tenet of Milton Friedman and his followers has long been that stock, bond and currency markets, left to themselves, will allocate resources most efficiently for the economy as a whole. The abandonment of fixed foreign exchange rates in 1971 and the subsequent move to floating rates reflected this free-market belief.

But the alleged efficiency of financial markets has come under sharp attack. Yale University economist Robert Shiller, for example, has shown that the allocation of capital by the stock and bond markets is not necessarily optimal for the economy. Several economists have developed scenarios in which market forces drive lenders and investors to make decisions that, while profitable for themselves, are not best for the economy as a whole. The volatile foreign-exchange rates of the last five years are a prime example of markets that work well for individual investors, but seem to produce results chaotic for the economy.

To explain such events as the strong dollar, some economists are shunning pure economics in favor of psychology. Keynes himself suggested that much market behavior is due to mass psy-chology rather than to underlying economic factors, and such economists as Shiller and Krugman share that view. This is heresy to classical economists, who believe that each individual operating in his own self-interest is the only force driving economic behavior. Researchers such as N. Gregory Mankiw, a 27-year-old Harvard professor, have gone so far as to argue that individuals may not always act to maximize their own welfare—an assertion that challenges the very theory behind rational expectations. For example, workers may choose to work less and enjoy more leisure as their wages go up, even if the wage increases are below the rate of inflation. The University of California's George Akerlof and Janet Yellin have shown that if individuals fall only slightly short of maximizing their own welfare, the economy as a whole can be thrown way out of kilter.

Finding justifications for government action is one thing; offering specific prescriptions is another. The younger economists whose research points up the benefits of a larger government role in the economy are well aware of the policy failures of the past, and understand that government intervention is easier in theory than in the real world. Among trade theorists, notes Paul Krugman, "There's a general sense of, 'Let's not apply this stuff too soon.' We all know something about the history of trade policy and what governments are likely to do in practice." Adds Yale's Shiller, "Even though markets are not efficient, it's not clear how the government can make them more efficient."

> "**If a head start on technology will be needed to make a firm competitive in the future, it may be wise for the government to act to protect that firm against foreign competition now.**"

Higher government spending is no longer seen as a cure for unemployment. "Supply-side" issues such as investment and capital formation play a far larger part in current Keynesian thinking than they did in the Johnson and Nixon years, when consumption was seen as more important. Says Massachusetts Institute of Technology economist Olivier Blanchard: "Keynesians were always ideological liberals at heart, and they believed the lower unemployment, the better. We don't believe that any more."

Many of the new interventionists are suspicious of fiscal policy, not for theoretical reasons, but on practical grounds. "Fiscal policy has been shown to be a very unwieldy instrument. There are so many actors involved, to think of it as an instrument that can be used to stabilize the economy is implausible," contends Stanford University economist John B. Taylor. Although most of Taylor's colleagues are unwilling to rule out fiscal policy so absolutely, they overwhelmingly reject the view of the 1960s, that taxation and spending can even out the economy's minor fluctuations. Says John Williamson, senior fellow of the Institute for International Economics in Washington, "The government should try some tuning, but it's excessive optimism to think that it can fine tune."

Monetary policy, once viewed as a secondary tool, has found its way to the center of Keynesian thought. In fact, a surprising number of the new Keynesians support rules to govern money creation. Unlike Milton Friedman, however, they would key money growth directly to inflation and unemployment, and would allow the Federal Reserve flexibility in making adjustments.

These new trends in economic research have yet to make themselves felt in political thinking, but their impact is only a matter of time. One area where they are likely to make a difference is in the debate over whether the federal government should have an "industrial policy" to favor the growth of certain industries.

Advocated by such economists as MIT's Lester Thurow and Harvard's Robert Reich, industrial policy has been attacked by those who ask why government can do better than the free market in directing the nation's economic future. Recent work by economists Jeremy I. Bulow of the University of Chicago and Lawrence H. Summers of Harvard provides one theoretical answer. They postulate an economy in which there are two types of jobs—"primary" jobs that pay more so workers won't shirk, and "secondary" jobs that pay less because employers can easily monitor worker performance. Everyone would prefer a primary job, but there are not enough high-paying jobs to go around.

In this model, the whole economy is better off if the government subsidizes creation of "primary" sector jobs and restricts imports of goods produced by the "primary" sector. Contends Lawrence Summers: "This suggests there is a coherent case on theoretical grounds that we should protect high-

> *"**T**O EXPLAIN SUCH EVENTS as the strong dollar, some economists are shunning pure economics in favor of psychology."*

wage industries." But, he warns, "That doesn't mean a political process which started out to do this would be successful in having subsidies based on considerations of efficiency rather than on political considerations. In some sense, this opens Pandora's box."

The new Keynesian economics is still in its infancy. But as it develops, it may begin to provide the intellectual base liberal politicians have lacked for two decades. "We still haven't decided what theories we like and what theories we don't," admits N. Gregory Mankiw. "That's the next step, before we go to Washington and tell people what to do." ∎

IS A TAX HIKE COMING?

IT SEEMS INEVITABLE. THE ONLY QUESTIONS NOW ARE WHAT KIND AND WHEN

It's high noon at Revenue Gulch, and Ronald Reagan is standing tall against taxes. "Over my dead body," he says. "My veto pen is ready."

Despite the tough talk, a major tax increase is on the way. Reagan may be sincerely opposed to higher taxes, but the arithmetic of the Gramm-Rudman Act is inexorable: The bill that the President embraced so enthusiastically is creating irresistible pressure for increased taxes. The only questions now are when, what kind, and how much.

Until Gramm-Rudman came along, Reagan probably could have blocked any tax increase. But the new law's rigid deficit-reduction targets have weakened his hand. Under current policies, the deficit for the fiscal year that begins next Oct. 1 will be at least $200 billion and perhaps as much as $220 billion. Gramm-Rudman requires that it be cut to $144 billion. Spending reductions of that magnitude, politicians of both parties agree, can't be made without savaging essential government services and gutting the Administration's defense buildup—political dynamite in an election year. There is a chance that the Supreme Court could invalidate the automatic features of the law. Even so, the deficit and the reduction targets will remain.

"Gramm-Rudman sounds great until you get down to the actual numbers," says Senator Bill Bradley (D-N.J.). "When Congress sees how many national parks will have to be closed and how much the cost of public transportation will increase, everyone will be considering tax increases."

The new tax debate has unsettling implications for Corporate America. Business is already worried by a House-passed tax-reform plan that raises corporate taxes by $140 billion over five years. Now the great revenue hunt of 1986 adds another level of uncertainty, vastly complicating business plans for future investment.

Reagan's crusade to lower tax rates makes increasing the income tax unthinkable. And because his tax-reform program eliminates a large number of

> 'A tax increase would . . . set back the economy and could even trigger a slump,' Reagan insists. But Gramm-Rudman's arithmetic is inexorable

deductions in order to offset a reduction in tax rates, there's little chance to raise significant amounts of money in the future through closing loopholes. What's left? Increasingly, tax experts are zeroing in on consumption taxes. Among the major options being discussed:

□ **A value-added tax.** Some prominent Republicans, including Senators William V. Roth Jr. (Del.) and John C. Danforth (Mo.), propose that the U.S. adopt a variation of a European-style VAT (page 52). Such a tax would amount to a sales tax but would be imposed at each stage of production. A VAT's main advantages are relative simplicity, uniform impact on all sectors of the economy, and the ability to raise enormous amounts of money. For example, a 7% levy could raise more than $90 billion a year. A major drawback to a VAT is its inflationary wallop, since it raises prices at each level. What's more, the idea faces stiff political opposition. Liberals protest that the burden will fall most heavily on lower-income taxpayers. Conservatives fear that a VAT could become a money machine that would fund a further expansion of government. And states, which depend heavily on retail sales taxes, are leery of the federal government intruding into their domain.

□ **Energy taxes.** With oil prices falling, energy taxes look increasingly attractive. An oil-import fee of $5 or more a bbl. would raise money and provide a prop to the sagging domestic oil industry. But politicians representing the Northeast would fight it. Instead, they favor a hefty increase in the federal gasoline tax. The biggest money-raiser would be a comprehensive oil tax combining an excise on all crude oil, imported or domestic, with an increased duty on imports of petroleum products. There are two problems with the energy tax schemes: They are subject to vicious regional political conflicts, and the amount of money they can pull in is limited—no more than $30 billion a year at a rate of $5 per bbl.

□ **Excise taxes.** The Treasury could raise cash without introducing a new tax by

Senators Roth, Packwood, Bradley: The Finance Committee will study a 'business transfer tax'—a VAT that could raise $90 billion a year

increasing existing federal excise taxes on alcoholic beverages, tobacco products, long-distance telephone calls, and airline tickets. But this kind of tinkering is unlikely to raise much more than $10 billion a year.

Before any of these schemes can become law, their backers must find a way to sell Reagan on any kind of tax hike—no small task. As a devotee of supply-side economics, the President believes that the preferred way to eliminate the deficit is by slashing nondefense spending and spurring the economy through further cuts in marginal tax rates. Supply siders insist that higher taxes would slow growth so much that revenues would actually decline. "A tax increase," asserts Reagan, "would . . . set back the economy and could even trigger a slump."

Reagan's antipathy to higher taxes may not be nearly as rigid as it appears. Twice during his Presidency, in 1982 and again in 1984, he railed against proposed tax increases only to endorse them in the end. Sources close to the White House believe that Reagan is taking a hard line now to wring maximum spending concessions from Congress but will ultimately be forced to bend. "It's the 'last resort' philosophy," notes GOP political strategist Lee Atwater. "Everyone knows that at some point there's going to be a tax increase." Adds former Office of Management & Budget official Lawrence A. Kudlow: "We'll have to go to revenue enhancement this year. The Gipper is simply going into his low crouch to protect himself."

Despite all of the Rambo-esque threats issuing from the Oval Office, many politicians are already giving serious thought to the shape of an eventual tax increase. And it's no accident that all the ideas currently under consideration are taxes on consumption. For years economists have complained that the U.S. tax system is biased against savings, and they remain concerned about a continuing decline in the personal savings rate, which dipped to 3.7% in the third quarter of 1985, the lowest since 1973. Money saved rather than spent would not be subject to the consumption tax. This increased incentive for savings could expand the pool of capital available for investment.

FIRST CHOICE. Many economists would like to scrap the income tax entirely and replace it with a consumption tax. But the current debate focuses entirely on new taxes as additions to the existing system, with or without tax reform. In terms of its economic elegance—as opposed to its political feasibility—a VAT ought to be the first choice.

In theory, a VAT is one of the simplest taxes imaginable. At each stage of production, a manufacturer or provider of services totals its gross receipts, subtracts the value of goods and services purchased (other than the labor of its employees), and applies a tax rate to the difference—the "value added" (chart, page 50). The tax would be imposed on imports and would be rebated on all exports. The system is easy to administer and difficult to evade because the invoices generated in the normal course of business contain all the information the Internal Revenue Service needs to calculate the tax due. In fact, the Treasury Dept., as part of a study of VAT, has drawn up a business tax return that is just 16 lines long.

A pure VAT—one in which all goods and services are subject to the same rate—also has the advantage of being economically neutral. No one sector of the economy is favored over any other. "It's a fairer kind of tax than anything else I can think of," says Harry Topliss

WHO WOULD BEAR THE BRUNT OF ADDITIONAL TAXES

BROAD-BASED OIL EXCISE TAX	Energy-intensive industries, including chemicals, electric utilities, heavy manufacturing, transportation
OIL IMPORT FEE	Energy consumers heavily dependent on imported oil, including chemical processors and utilities in the Northeastern states
RETAIL GASOLINE TAX	Transportation, travel, and tourism industries; highway and mall retailing, domestic auto makers
HIGHER EXCISE TAXES	Alcoholic beverages, tobacco products, long-distance telephone services
VALUED-ADDED TAX	All industries, except food, drug, and housing, which may gain exemption. Exporting industries—aircraft, computers, motion pictures, services—whose VAT payments are refundable to foreign customers

DATA: BW

Jr., treasurer of Scientific-Atlanta Inc.

Fairness is in the eye of the beholder. An all-encompassing flat-rate tax would be very regressive. According to Lawrence Chimerine, chairman of Chase Econometrics, "it would have more impact on lower-income groups and bigger families because they spend a bigger portion of their incomes." Organized labor, meanwhile, sees the VAT as one more distressing step away from the principle of progressivity. "We are not receptive to any variation on the VAT," says AFL-CIO President Lane Kirkland.

VAT boosters have ready answers. "You can make a VAT as progressive as you want by specifying exemptions or differential rates," says economist Alan Greenspan. "If you put a high enough rate on luxury goods, you can turn it into a progressive tax."

Some of the regressivity problems could be ironed out by making food and pharmaceuticals exempt from the tax. In addition, the European system of charging higher rates on some goods could be adopted in the U.S. A second way to make a VAT more equitable is by changing the income tax to reduce rates on middle-income taxpayers. Families at the low end of the income-tax scale would simply be dropped from the system. And the poor, who pay no income taxes now, would receive a cash payment to replace the VAT tax bite.

The VAT's inflationary potential is harder to deal with. At a minimum, the imposition of the tax will cause a one-time jump in the price level. The long-term impact is more problematic. It depends on how monetary policy responds to the new tax. If the Federal Reserve lets the money supply grow in an effort to keep the tax from slowing the economy as it sucks up consumer buying power, the initial price shock could become a spiral as workers try to get wage increases to cover the higher prices. On the other hand, the harder the Fed tries to fight the inflationary impact, the greater the risk of a recession.

Nariman Behravesh, chief economist for Wharton Econometrics, estimates that a 5% VAT would cause a 4%-to-5% "one-year pop" in the inflation rate while knocking two points off the growth rate. George F. Break, a University of California economist, disagrees: "With a skillful combination of fiscal and monetary policy, we would see no effect on output." Despite the VAT's inflationary potential, some business economists believe it's worth the risk. Says John M. Albertine, president of the American Business Conference: "If it were used to reduce the deficit and restore some of the capital incentives being taken away in tax reform, on balance the effects could be pro-growth."

STATES' NIGHTMARE. VAT advocates believe that the current economic environment is ripe for introduction of the tax. Says Donald T. Beldock, chairman of New York's Basix Corp.: "In a period of relative price stability . . . the risks of across-the-board price increases are less than at any time in recent memory." But other executives fear that in an era of disinflation and cutthroat competition, they—not their customers—would end up paying most of the tax.

VAT's similarity to a sales tax makes it a potential nightmare for the nation's governors. Concerned that the federal government could cut into states' favorite revenue source, many state and local officials strenuously object. "Stay out of those taxes that state and local governments depend upon," Kansas Governor John W. Carlin warns Washington. "A national sales tax or VAT would severely handicap the states at a time when we are being called on to do more."

Faced with the fact that a VAT is highly controversial, backers are trying to package the tax in a less threatening way. Enter the business transfer tax, or BTT. In the Senate, Delaware Republican Roth has introduced legislation that would impose a VAT-like tax on all stages of production and distribution. The big difference from a full VAT is that a BTT would not tax retail markups.

The BTT idea has attracted considerable interest from GOP moderates on the Senate Finance Committee. Chairman Bob Packwood (R-Ore.) remains interested in the concept but is preoccupied with trying to craft a "revenue-neutral" tax-reform bill. Although a majority of the committee clearly favors a tax increase, Packwood says, "I'm not moving anywhere without the President's lead."

Roth does not want to raise revenues. He would use the estimated $90 billion or more a year that a 7% BTT would bring in to pay for a big cut in income taxes, while retaining most credits and deductions, including the investment-tax credit and generous depreciation allowances. "I want to use the revenues from BTT to make American business competitive," he says. Some of Roth's colleagues, however, feel the exercise is pointless unless it reduces the deficit. Finance Committee members Danforth and John Heinz (R-Pa.) may introduce a version of BTT that will dedicate part of the tax take to deficit reduction.

OLD FAITHFUL. Business lobbyists were attracted to BTT because they felt it could fend off the corporate tax increases contained in the House tax-reform bill and because Roth's original bill allowed a credit against BTT for Social Security payroll taxes paid. But with BTT increasingly being viewed as an addition to, rather than a substitute for, existing taxes, interest has waned. "It's not getting good marks in the business community right now," concedes BTT-backer Charls E. Walker, a top lobbyist.

Some tax experts are leery as well. "BTT seems to be designed to look as if it raises revenue from the corporate sector, but it's really a hidden tax on consumers," asserts Michael Graetz of Yale law school. Although BTT has drawn interest from a scattering of Democrats on both House and Senate tax-writing committees, most reflexively attack the notion on "fairness" grounds. Democratic tax-reformer Bradley dismisses such a scheme as "nothing more than a tax on the middle class to pay for continuing tax breaks for business."

As an alternative to some form of a VAT, many lawmakers have fallen back on an old idea: energy taxes. Oil-state legislators, led by Senators Lloyd Bentsen (D-Tex.) and David L. Boren (D-Okla.), have introduced a bill imposing an import fee of $5 per bbl. on crude oil and $10 per bbl. on refined products. They claim this would bring in $15 billion a year. Struggling domestic producers, who would be sheltered from imports by such a tax, like the idea because it would allow them to raise prices above the world price. Many politicians find it attractive because, with oil prices soft, its inflationary impact would be minimal and it would discourage dependence on imported oil. Senator Malcolm Wallop (R-Wyo.) is pushing a measure that amounts to a price-support scheme for domestic producers. Under this plan, a floor of $22 per bbl. would be placed under the world price of oil, and a fee would be slapped on imports to bring them up to that price.

Easterners, who burn a lot of imported heating oil but who drive relatively few miles, would rather see higher taxes on gasoline. New Jersey's Bradley proposes tripling the current gasoline tax, to 27¢ per gal. That would also raise about $15 billion. Unlike the current federal gas tax, the new levy would go into general revenues. Felix G. Rohatyn, a partner in the investment banking firm of Lazard Frères & Co., thinks the gas tax could be boosted to as much as 50¢ per gal. and coupled with an import fee. "You could phase it in over two years," he says. "That would be perfectly bearable in terms of economic impact, and you'd get back to energy conservation."

Backers of higher gasoline taxes reckon that the idea might at least get a hearing at the White House because gasoline prices are falling and Reagan endorsed an increase of 5¢ per gal. in 1982. Former Council of Economic Advisers Chairman Martin S. Feldstein notes that a 15¢ increase would still leave the inflation-adjusted price of gasoline below its 1974 level.

Yet another approach is an excise tax on oil and natural gas, both domestic and imported. This plan could raise more revenue than competing energy-tax schemes and has the advantage of taxing all uses of petroleum equally. "With the price of oil falling, this seems the logical way to go," says Representative Richard A. Gephardt (D-Mo.). Another booster is Senate Majority Leader Bob Dole (R-Kan.). Thus far, though, neither the comprehensive oil tax nor an even broader excise tax on all energy use has caught on in Congress.

All of these revenue-raising plans will simmer on the congressional back burner for the next few months as the President keeps the political focus on spending cuts. But the tax schemes will come roaring back in the spring, when Gramm-Rudman requires Congress to vote on spending and revenue goals for fiscal 1987.

'SLAUGHTERED.' White House Chief of Staff Donald T. Regan is convinced that the budget-reduction targets, combined with the President's hard line on taxes, will force legislators to accept the painful domestic cuts that they have rejected in the past. And with this year's spending authority for the Defense Dept. already below the level of 1985, many politicians feel there is little room left for large cuts in the military budget. Says a Regan aide: "Is the platform for the next election going to be higher taxes and lower defense? We don't think so."

The President's aides are supremely confident that the tax-hike sentiment on Capitol Hill will not coalesce into action as long as Reagan remains adamant. Members of Congress, says one senior aide, "realize that if the President isn't with them on taxes, they're going to get slaughtered."

But the consensus view in Washington is that White House officials are deluding themselves. They may be able to stonewall for a couple of months, but tax-hike pressures will intensify as Gramm-Rudman's day of reckoning nears. If Congress and the Administration have not agreed to massive reductions in the deficit by Aug. 20, a process will begin that would lead to automatic budget cuts of $50 billion to $70 billion by Oct. 15.

The potential impact of those cuts, which the law applies indiscriminately to virtually all budget items, would be staggering. Massive layoffs would be required, not only in the federal bureaucracy but in the Coast Guard, the Federal Bureau of Investigation, and the air traffic control system. Defense budget authority would have to be slashed by $60 billion to $100 billion, forcing cancellation of weapons systems and cutting back on existing military forces.

Reagan intimates maintain that the President won't permit a defense cut of this magnitude for fear that it might send the wrong signal to Soviet leader Mikhail S. Gorbachev. In the scenario given the most currency in Washington, the President will yield to tax increases when faced with the reality that the only alternative is a defense cut on a scale that would make Jimmy Carter look like a gung-ho militarist. "In the end," says a senior Administration official, "a tax increase will be sold to Reagan as a way to save defense."

FLOGGING CONGRESS. Although Reagan enjoys nothing quite as much as flogging Congress, it will be hard for him to ignore a bipartisan "grand compromise" engineered by congressional leaders. Reagan's resistance to significant tax increases probably rules out something as sweeping as a VAT this year. More likely is acceptance of some kind of energy tax, which would permit the President to claim he kept his promise to oppose a general tax increase. "From the President's point of view, an oil-import fee is the least objectionable," says an Administration aide.

But the notion of a VAT will not fade away. Even if Congress and the Administration negotiate their way to meeting the 1987 Gramm-Rudman target, the law mandates four more years of deep deficit cuts. Ultimately, the revenue needs will exceed what any conceivable energy levy could generate. Some Republican strategists speculate that if a VAT could be used both to reduce the deficit and to pay for further steep cuts in income tax rates, even Reagan might be persuaded to take another look.

By Lee Walczak, Stephen H. Wildstrom, Richard Fly, and Ronald Grover in Washington; Joan Berger, Norman Jonas, and Elizabeth Ehrlich in New York; and bureau reports

TIME TO INCREASE TAXES?

Interview with Walter Heller, former chairman, President's Council of Economic Advisers **PRO**

CON Interview with Arthur Laffer, consultant, economist, Pepperdine University, Calif.

Q Professor Heller, why do you favor a tax increase?

Because it's the only responsible way of tackling the deficit. The plain fact is that this country is spending more than can be financed out of existing tax revenue. Even with spending cuts, the gap can't be closed sensibly without a tax increase.

Q Wouldn't a tax increase threaten the economy's health?

If the economy showed signs of going into a tailspin, which I do not foresee, you could put a tax increase on the books but postpone its effective date, as President Reagan proposed in 1983. A tax increase, moreover, would be less repressive to the economy than an expenditure cut. If you cut expenditures, you hit the economy dollar for dollar. Part of a tax increase comes out of savings and thus doesn't dampen the economy as much.

Q Could better enforcement of the law help collect more tax?

Yes. Many billions that should be collected are not. It's false economy for the White House to suggest cutting the Internal Revenue Service budget. But tight enforcement would be only a small contribution to solving the deficit.

Q Will higher taxes take the heat off Congress to cut spending?

Studies show that whether taxes are raised or lowered isn't the main determinant of how much Congress spends. As huge deficits show, spending hasn't been overly inhibited by the 1981 tax cuts—the main source of the deficit.

The cuts also didn't bear out the silly claim that a tax cut would pay for itself.

Q How big a hike in taxes would you like to see?

I would try to get 50 or 60 billion dollars more a year. That could come from energy taxes like an oil-import fee or gasoline taxes and from higher liquor and tobacco taxes. I would limit cost-of-living adjustments for middle-class benefit programs, including Social Security, as well as the indexing of tax rates to inflation.

Q What about a direct increase in income-tax rates?

I don't rule that out, but other sources would probably yield enough revenue and involve less controversy. You could also use the added revenue generated by a tougher minimum tax and loophole plugging to shrink the deficit.

Q Are you saying we should reverse the round of tax cuts for business and individuals that started in 1981?

That was the biggest tax cut in history and was coupled with the biggest peacetime defense buildup in history. And it gave us the biggest deficits in history. While I myself advocated a tax cut then as healthy, we went too far. We went head over heels and have suffered for it ever since.

> YES — "It's the only responsible way of tackling the deficit"

> NO — "We can get more revenue by increasing jobs and economic output"

Q Professor Laffer, why do you oppose a tax increase?

Because it will remove the pressure on Congress to cut spending. The real question is not whether we pay for government expenditures by raising taxes or increasing borrowing. The problem is to curtail the amount of money the government takes from the economy, the money it's taking in one form or another from all of us.

Q Isn't more revenue needed to contain the budget deficit?

We can get more revenue by increasing jobs and economic output. Taking people off welfare and putting them on the tax rolls as they go to work means more revenue. You don't encourage growth by raising taxes. President Reagan's 1981 tax cut led to a huge recovery. So far it has cost revenue, but that's because a tax cut takes time to pay for itself.

Q Americans seem to want most federal services. Shouldn't they be prepared to pay the taxes to support those services?

If, in the long run, tax receipts don't match spending for services people want, then people should be prepared to pay more. But even if you assume people don't want more spending cuts, which I don't believe, we should stress tax reform that lowers rates and also broadens the base on which tax is levied by ending many deductions and exclusions.

Q Is it possible to make spending cuts deep enough to balance the budget?

Spending cuts are important, but there's no way you can balance the budget without fast economic growth. Every 1 percent drop in the unemployment rate cuts the deficit by about 40 billion dollars a year. Monetary policies that lower interest rates and curb inflation also have a huge impact because interest payments on the debt go down. About half our deficit problem, in fact, relates to questions of the pace of growth and the level of interest rates.

Q Where, though, can spending reductions be made?

There's a panorama of ways to cut spending, none of which puts old people in the snow. A few examples: General revenue sharing of federal taxes with state and local governments makes no sense. The subsidy for synthetic-fuels development isn't needed. Pentagon procurement is out of whack. We could cut Small Business Administration loans and charge more for Rural Electrification Administration loans.

Q Isn't a tax increase inevitable in light of the recently enacted law that mandates annual reductions in the deficit?

I don't think so. This law will force a reduction in spending and a serious look at the programs we do and don't want. A tax increase, in any broad sense, is a dead issue.

The Fiscal Picture Improves, but . . .

By PAUL W. MCCRACKEN

"If this deficit is not brought under control, we risk losing all we've achieved—and more." This is not a comment from a critic of the president's fiscal strategy. It is the way the president himself described the situation in his February budget message. And he is right. While the overall economic performance has been good, these deficits have caused high interest rates, imposing severe distortions on some parts of the economy.

Improbable as it would have seemed only a year ago, the budget season's array of documents and projections has been producing some under-recognized good news. This may seem like a peculiar way to describe things to members of Congress whom the public seems to be telling to balance the budget, but in ways that involve no shrinkage in programs or increases in taxes. Yet, in fact, the fiscal outlook has improved almost unbelievably during the past year. It could be described as a 180-degree fiscal turnaround. And we are now within sight of a responsible budget once again.

Out of Control

This is dramatically evident if we look at projections of the deficit being made a year ago and those released this year. In each case these are on a so-called current services basis, which means simply that they reflect a "pricing out" of tax and spending programs currently on the books. The grim thing about the projected deficits a year ago was not only that they were too large but that given the tax and spending programs then on the books (and reasonable estimates about the course of the economy), the deficits were projected to be growing ever larger. We seemed then to be on a track leading us to $300 billion deficits by the early 1990s. In the quite literal sense the budget was out of control, and there was growing skepticism about whether the political will existed to get the fiscal operations of government back on a leash.

In his budget message a year ago, the president was only slightly less pessimistic than the Congressional Budget Office about the trend of deficits. He also was projecting rising deficits through fiscal 1988, with a deficit well above $200 billion by 1990—if the tax system and expenditure programs were unchanged. In retrospect it is small wonder that about the time the budget message appeared early in 1985 the dollar began to weaken in foreign-exchange markets.

The good news in these documents this year does not come from reaching further for improbably optimistic assumptions about the level of economic activity in order to project more revenue. These as-

sumptions have changed little, and both the administration and the Congressional Budget Office are actually assuming slightly lower revenues for, say, 1990 than they did a year ago.

The principal difference the year has made is that expenditure programs now on the books (current services) price out to almost $200 billion less spending by 1990 than was true a year ago. Despite the wails of anguish, whose decibel rating would suggest that the civilian budget is being eviscerated, outlays other than for interest and national defense are now projected for 1990 to be less than 4% below the projection for 1990 made a year ago. They are, in fact, still projected to rise more from 1985 to 1990 than the rate of inflation. A further increase in real terms is thus projected from 1985 to 1990.

The major changes that have occurred during the past year in the outlook for 1990's federal spending are to be found in outlays for national security and interest on the debt. Projected interest payments on the national debt are $71 billion lower, and outlays for national defense have been lowered by almost $100 billion.

The result is that programs now on the books point to a declining trend, to the $100 billion zone by the turn of the decade, rather than a rising trend to the $300 billion level, which is where the trend a year ago seemed to be taking us. This is a fiscal turnaround as significant and dramatic as it has been unheralded. Congress seldom gets many plaudits for effective labors, but it and the president have wrought a dramatic fiscal turnaround in one year—a near miracle.

In part this is a major dividend from dealing decisively with the high and rising rate of inflation inherited from the 1970s. Only a year ago the Congressional Budget Office, in its projections of interest costs, was assuming a rate of about 10% for 10-year Treasury securities in 1990. Interest-rate levels only a year ago indicated that this was a realistic and prudent assumption. Tardily, as usually has happened, market rates since have been adjusting to the markedly lower rates of inflation, and now the Congressional Budget Office is using a 7% figure for 1990. A difference of three percentage points on a national debt that, even with the improved fiscal out-

look, will exceed $2 trillion is consequential. This is the dividend from having resolutely pursued, earlier in this decade, policies to counter inflation—just as the stratospheric interest rates of the early 1980s were the inevitable result of a national policy of accepting rising rates of inflation in the 1970s. People then finally decided inflation was a reality, and interest rates adjusted upward. Finally, in 1985-1986, people have decided a better price-level performance is a reality, and interest rates have adjusted downward. The result of these lower rates and smaller deficits is a large saving of interest costs in the budget.

The budget problem is not, of course, finally solved. For one thing, there is a real question whether current programs make adequate provisions for national security as we head into the closing years of this century. We face an uncertain world in which an expansionist imperial power, whatever its rhetoric, is aggressively enlarging its empire by military and other means. It is a beguiling thought, skillfully nurtured by the U.S.S.R., that it could be reassured and pacified by our unilaterally disarming, but there is no credible evidence to support such a hope.

By the early 1990s current budget projections suggest that outlays for national security will be only about 6% of U.S. gross national product. In the 1950s after the conclusion of the Korean War the figure was almost 10%, and in the 1960s before Vietnam it was about 8%. The 2½% annual gain in productivity from 1955 to 1965 suggests that the economy readily carried this load and performed well. In any case the nation cannot afford not to spend whatever is required for its external security.

This year's projection of declining budget deficits is on the basis of current services—taking into account only programs now on the books. If between now and 1991 Congress sweetened some current programs and added some new ones, and it would be a considerable departure from history if this did not occur, such further actions net would increase the projected deficits beyond the current estimates. Moreover, while the projected deficit of $120 billion for 1990, made this year, is a dramatic improvement over the $296 billion estimated only a year ago, the goal for 1990 set by the Balanced Budget and

Projected Outlays, Fiscal Year 1990

(Current services basis; dollar amounts in billions)

| ITEM | ESTIMATES AS OF: | | PERCENT CHANGE |
	FEB. 1985	FEB. 1986	
National defense	$ 424	$ 327	-23%
Net interest	230	159	-31
Other	730	702	- 4
TOTAL	$1384	$1188	-14%

Source: CBO reviews of the Economic and Budget Outlook, February 1985 and February 1986

Reprinted with permission of Paul W. McCracken, Edmund Ezra Day Distinguished University Professor of Business Administration, the University of Michigan.

Emergency Deficit Control Act of 1985 (Gramm-Rudman-Hollings) is a deficit of $36 billion, and zero for 1991.

The budget job, therefore, is not yet finished. And here the impasse emerges. The remaining gap could be closed by further cuts in so-called civilian spending (outlays other than for national defense and interest on the debt). The fact that they are now projected in real terms to be larger in fiscal 1990 than in fiscal 1985 suggests that there is still some room here (particularly in light of growing evidence that some of these programs are counterproductive in their results). Yet it is difficult to see Congress approving further cuts large enough to do the job on the spending side.

That leads to tax increases. There are possibilities. Gasoline taxes in real terms are lower than before the oil crisis erupted, and far below those of most other countries. Individual income tax receipts are equal to only just over 10% of personal income, not a massive pre-emption (and certainly not a rationale for shifting taxes further against capital formation). Yet the president is probably right. Trying to close the budget gap with more taxes would relieve pressures for spending restraint. The result of tax increases could well be simply moving taxes and spending to a higher level, leaving us still with an unresolved budget deficit.

Line-Item Veto

There is a way out. The political arena is an arena of compromise—with all parties having to settle for some things they do not want to get some things they do want. The 1986 compromise fiscal package should contain two sets of things. Congress should support actions to reimpose the fiscal disciplines, discarded a half-century ago, by giving the president line-item veto authority, and by approving a constitutional amendment requiring a balanced budget. The president should then as a part of the package agree to additional revenue. The best evidence that this would be a good package is that both ends of Pennsylvania Avenue would get some of what they want, and would have to swallow some things they did not want.

To give teeth to the new process, a further provision might be added. For 12 months following any year that the budget is in the red, no salaries could be paid to members of Congress, the president, or members of his cabinet.

———————

Mr. McCracken, a member of the Journal's Board of Contributors, is Edmund Ezra Day distinguished university professor of business administration, the University of Michigan, and chairman of the Council of Academic Advisers, American Institute for Public Policy Research.

27

DEFICIT DEJA VU
Spending too much, or taxing too little?

Three months ago, the Gramm-Rudman deficit reduction bill was passed by both houses of Congress. This month, the bill takes effect as $11.7 billion is slashed from the 1986 federal budget. Beginning October 1, $60 billion or more will have to be trimmed from the 1987 budget in order to meet the Congressionally mandated deficit reduction targets. The domestic programs slated to fall under the Gramm-Rudman axe may lose up to 20% of their funding next year.

The enactment of Gramm-Rudman constitutes a significant step toward the time-honored (not to say hackneyed) conservative goal of balancing the federal budget. It also represents the culmination of a drastic — and dangerous — departure from the strategies conservatives have traditionally pursued.

Prior to 1980, conservatives generally argued that the federal government would have to cut spending before it could cut taxes. They used the possibility of future tax cuts as a bribe to persuade Congress to reduce domestic outlays. Everyone's tax burden could be lightened, they insisted, if only "wasteful" government expenditures like Social Security, education, and welfare could be eliminated.

Reagan has stood this conservative approach on its head. By cutting taxes and increasing military spending, the Reagan administration has spawned an atmosphere of crisis surrounding the deficit, which it has used to bludgeon Congress into cutting spending on other domestic programs. The attack on these programs is making it more and more difficult for the government to sustain its traditional functions.

ATTACKING THE STATE

According to conservatives, the free market operates best with little intervention from the state — whether in the form of taxes, regulation, or government spending. Yet state intervention is necessary in order to moderate and compensate for many of the inherent irrationalities of capitalism.

Through progressive tax policies and welfare programs, the government can redistribute income downward, reducing political tensions. It can use fiscal policy to offset cyclical downturns and prevent severe recessions. Thus the state plays a critical role in mediating — if not resolving — conflicts engendered within the system.

In addition, there are certain things the private market cannot or will not do which are necessary for a viable economy. The government must perform the tasks of developing infrastructure for transportation and communication, protecting the environment, educating the workforce, and so on.

The current deficit is primarily a result of Reagan's tax policies, and only secondarily the product of excessive government spending. The 23% income tax cut that he initiated in 1981 has cost the government roughly $100 billion a year in lost revenue, while military spending has increased by $30 billion a year over the same period.

Yet Reagan has chosen to define the deficit as a domestic spending crisis, rather than as a problem of lost taxes. In his view, the government's role in the economy must be pared down to a level which can be supported at the current level of revenue.

Unwilling to take the political risks of raising taxes or reducing military spending, liberals leapt onto the Gramm-Rudman bandwagon last fall. By accepting a measure that elevates the reduction of the deficit to the level of top national priority, they have allowed conservatives to set the agenda for the role of government in the economy.

ENTER GRAMM-RUDMAN

The initial version of Gramm-Rudman — the Balanced Budget and Emergency Deficit Control Act of 1985 — was introduced in the Senate as an amendment to a bill to raise the federal debt ceiling from $1.8 trillion to $2 trillion. Senate Republicans wanted to find a way to divert public attention from the fact that the huge national debt is largely the result of Reagan's own policies. Reagan's budget deficits have averaged $175 billion per year, reaching a record high of $220 billion in 1985. (The largest pre-Reagan deficit was $68 billion in 1980.)

The Republicans put their heads

The attack on domestic spending is making it more and more difficult for government to sustain its traditional functions.

Dollars & Sense, 38 Union Square, Room 14, Somerville, MA 02143.

89

together and came up with what sponsor Warren Rudman (R.-NH) blithely called "a bad idea whose time has come." The proposed amendment specified maximum budget deficits for each fiscal year between 1987 and 1991. Each year, $36 billion was to be chopped off the deficit, causing it to fall from $144 billion in 1987 to zero in 1991. For political reasons, social security was exempted from any automatic spending reductions, but with this exception the President was to be given broad discretion as to where to make the cuts. Conveniently, the Senate proposal delayed the enactment of spending cuts until after the November 1986 elections.

Once approved by the Senate, the amendment moved to the Democrat-controlled House. The Democrats made a number of positive alterations, but the overall thrust stayed the same. Aid to Families with Dependent Children (AFDC), Supplemental Security Income (SSI), Medicaid, child nutrition, and food stamps joined Social Security in being exempted from automatic spending cuts. Furthermore, half of the cuts were required to come from the Defense Department.

In addition, presidential discretion as to where to make the cuts was reduced. The final version stated that if Congress and the President failed to reach an agreement on some combination of these measures to meet the deficit target, automatic cuts in domestic and military spending would go into effect. Finally, the Democrats also insisted that the $11.7 billion in deficit reductions be made by March 1986, and that the 1987 cuts be voted in as of October 1.

Just how large are the deficit reductions required by Gramm-Rudman? Even under the best of circumstances, the amount will be substantial. The Congressional Budget Office has made two sets of projections to help estimate the amount of money that will have to be cut from the federal budget in order to meet the Gramm Rudman targets based on current spending and taxing policies (see table).

The "steady growth" projections assume a constant 3.5% rate of GNP growth through 1991. This is tantamount to assuming that the current recovery will last about twice as long as the average U.S. postwar expansion. If we accept the steady-growth hypothesis, in 1989 the government will have to spend $60 billion less than it did this year. The more plausible low growth estimates assume that there will be a mild recession starting in mid-1986 and ending in late 1987. Under the low-growth scenario, the deficit will have to be cut by $184 billion.

BUSINESS CYCLE BLUES

While the bill mandates shrinking the size of government, it also makes it nearly impossible for the government to spur economic growth. Furthermore, by eliminating fiscal policy as a tool for moderating the effect of recessions, Gramm-Rudman will surely hamstring the government's ability to provide an "automatic stabilizer" for the economy.

Normally, when unemployment rises, government spending on unemployment insurance and related programs goes up. Tax collections fall, since income has fallen. Generally, for every 1% increase in unemployment, the federal deficit jumps by roughly $40 billion. But by providing income to the unemployed, government spending props up demand—which in turn fuels a recovery. As workers are rehired, government expenditures drop and tax revenue rises until the deficit is reduced.

Under Gramm-Rudman, a downturn would still lead to an increase in the deficit for that year. To meet the deficit target for the following year, that year's deficit cut would have to be still larger. So, just as a recession begins, the government would have to lower its spending and/or increase taxes. Either action would reduce consumer income and lead to lower consumer spending—further deepening the recession.

While recessions have the valuable function of lowering labor costs and disciplining the labor force, even the most ardent capitalist does not look forward to a severe and prolonged depression. Consequently, Gramm-Rudman comes equipped with a "recession escape clause." If the Department of Commerce produces statistics indicating that economic growth in the two most recently reported quarters has been less than one percent, the majority leaders of both Houses must introduce resolutions that suspend the deficit ceilings for two fiscal years. But unless the resolutions are approved by majorities in both the House and the Senate, the deficit ceilings would remain in effect.

Anticipating recessions poses even greater problems. The bill requires Congress to consider the repeal of the deficit ceilings if either the Congressional Budget Office or the Office of Management and the Budget predicts a recession in the coming year. Unfortunately, the government has managed to consistently avoid predicting the onset of *any* recession in the past ten years. Hence, it seems likely that the government will wind up pursuing contractionary fiscal policies for the next five years, regardless of the state of the economy.

UNDERMINING TAX POLICY

The crisis mentality over the federal deficit has also increased the pressure to raise taxes. Members of both political parties now publicly argue that the passage of Gramm-Rudman has made tax hikes inevitable. But Reagan continues to insist that raising taxes is "not an option." Instead, he has seized

T*he current deficit is primarily a result of Reagan's tax policies, and only secondarily the product of excessive government spending.*

the opportunity to push for tax reform — consolidating tax brackets, closing loopholes, and eliminating some deductions. This move will do nothing to increase the amount of revenue raised through taxes. But what it will accomplish is the elimination of tax policy as a tool for adjusting the distribution of income.

Lower taxes and a simplified tax system could limit the role of local as well as federal government. In recent months, Reagan has pushed for eliminating the federal income-tax deduction for state and local tax payments. This would force high-tax states like New York and Massachusetts to cut back on their spending.

If public pressure to raise taxes does prevail, Reagan is most likely to accede to the taxes which are least progressive, such as the value-added tax or oil import fees. A White House official described the latter as popular with Reagan because "it's a tax that's not a tax." These are taxes on consumption, rather than income, and since poor people spend a larger proportion of their incomes on consumption, they are disproportionately affected.

Thus the two traditional functions of the tax system — to redistribute income and to provide revenue for the legitimate functions of government — are being undermined. Even the attempt to raise revenue through other means is aimed at reducing the role of the government in the economy. For example, the Reagan administration is plugging the sale of government assets as a way to raise federal revenue. Reagan is hoping to sell off the Bonneville Power Administration, and may also call for the sale of part of the government's $245 billion loan portfolio to private investors.

Such sales would do nothing to change the government's long-term revenue situation. Nor would the sale of government loans really reduce net federal borrowing from the private sector. The total amount of private capital tied up in projects determined by the goverment would stay the same. On the other hand, they would bring the Reagan administration closer to its goal of abolishing government operations that compete, however indirectly, with private profit-making.

HIDDEN AGENDA

Deficits have been with us more or less steadily since the 1920s. If the deficit were really the problem, raising taxes would be a reasonable solution. But Reagan is pushing a not-so-hidden agenda. He has vowed to meet the 1991 Gramm-Rudman deficit target while allowing the Pentagon to indulge in 3% real spending growth. And it looks like he'll have his way, since no one is likely to pose an effective challenge to the Reagan agenda: even when Congress had a chance to vote a 5% cut in the military last October, it refused to do so.

The Reagan budget proposal for 1987 targets some two dozen domestic programs. The Legal Services Corporation, Urban Development Action Grants, the Small Business Administration, and mass transit subsidies will all be subject to cuts. The Department of Transportation expects to lose $400 million that might have gone to building and repairing bridges and highways. The Education Department has announced that it may have to cut off aid to 68,000 middle-income students.

No matter what capitalists say, government is not a disposable item. Eliminating the public sector will have the eventual result of exposing the inadequacies of the capitalist economy and exacerbating the conflicts generated in the system. Nonetheless, working people have a long and difficult struggle ahead to win back the social and economic gains rolled back by Reagan.■

Definitions of Some Financial Aggregates

Item	M1	M2	M3	L
Currency in circulation	X	X	X	X
Travelers' checks of nonbank issuers	X	X	X	X
At commercial banks				
Demand deposits (except those due to domestic banks, U.S. Government, foreign banks, and official institutions)	X	X	X	X
NOW (negotiable order of withdrawal) accounts	X	X	X	X
ATS (automatic transfer service) accounts	X	X	X	X
At thrift institutions				
Demand deposits (at mutual savings banks)	X	X	X	X
NOW accounts	X	X	X	X
ATS accounts	X	X	X	X
Credit union share draft balances	X	X	X	X
At commercial banks				
Overnight RPs (repurchase agreements)		X	X	X
Small time deposits (less than $100,000)		X	X	X
Savings deposits		X	X	X
At thrift institutions				
Savings deposits (at mutual savings banks and savings and loan associations)		X	X	X
Small time deposits (less than $100,000)		X	X	X
Other				
Overnight Eurodollar deposits of nonbank U.S. residents at Caribbean branches of member banks		X	X	X
Money market mutual fund shares		X	X	X
At commercial banks				
Large time deposits ($100,000 or more), including large negotiable certificates of deposit			X	X
Term RPs			X	X
At thrift institutions				
Large time deposits ($100,000 or more)			X	X
Term RPs at savings and loan associations			X	X
Term Eurodollars held by nonbank U.S. residents at Caribbean branches of member banks				X
Bankers' acceptances				X
Commercial paper				X
U.S. Treasury bills and other liquid Treasury securities				X
U.S. savings bonds				X
Consolidation component[1]		X	X	X

Total credit = total credit-market debt owed by domestic nonfinancial sectors.

Monetary base = currency held outside the Treasury, Federal Reserve banks, and the vaults of depository institutions
+ reserve balances at Federal Reserve banks (current)
+ vault cash used to satisfy reserve requirements at all depository institutions (held two weeks earlier)
+ surplus vault cash at depository institutions.

1. Consolidation component: less cash items in the process of collection, interbank deposits, Federal Reserve float, and estimated proportion of demand deposits used by thrift institutions to service their transaction accounts.

Reprinted from Federal Reserve Bank of Dallas
Economic Review, January, 1985.

92

Financial Innovation and Monetary Policy

This article was adapted from a presentation made by Lyle E. Gramley, member, Board of Governors of the Federal Reserve System, at the XIX Meeting of Governors of Central Banks of the American Continent, Quito, Ecuador, March 22, 1982.

Innovation in financial markets has proceeded at an impressive pace for a quarter-century. Recently, the pace seems to be accelerating. While the implications of these developments for central banking are of most concern to the United States, they nevertheless are relevant for other countries as well. First, these innovations affect U.S. interest rates and credit conditions, which in turn have profound effects on financial markets around the world. Second, innovations beginning in one market are likely to spread eventually to others.

INNOVATIONS AND THEIR SOURCES

The key forces giving rise to financial innovation in the United States are found in the economic, interest rate, and regulatory environment of the past two decades. During most of the period since World War II, the U.S. economy has suffered from a rising rate of inflation. As borrowers and lenders came to expect inflation to continue, or even to accelerate, market interest rates moved progressively higher (chart 1).

Higher market rates of interest raised the penalty associated with holding deposits whose yields were limited by law or regulation. The yields that depository institutions could pay were limited by prohibitions or ceilings on the payment of explicit interest, and also by requirements to hold non-interest-bearing reserves, which reduce the rate of return on the investment of deposit proceeds. Moreover, the thrift institutions, which specialize in mortgage lending, were, and still are, severely limited in their capacity to pay prevailing market interest rates for deposits because they hold a substantial volume of longer-term assets acquired earlier, when inflation and interest rates were lower.

As the public has become increasingly sensitive to the earnings lost by holding non-interest-bearing or low-yielding deposits, they have become more adept at economizing on cash balances and more receptive to new kinds of financial investments. The increased financial sophistication of households and businesses, moreover, has been coupled with technological advances in computers and telecommunications that have reduced the cost of information and of transferring funds.

The innovational process stemming from these forces became evident during the 1950s. At that time, depository institutions did not actively seek deposits, but passively accepted the funds placed with them by the public. For individual institutions, deposit levels were determined exogenously, so that imbalances between deposit flows and net loan extensions were met by adjusting holdings of liquid assets, usually securities issued by the U.S. Treasury.

A heightened sensitivity to interest rate differentials developed during the course of the 1950s

1. Inflation and market interest rates

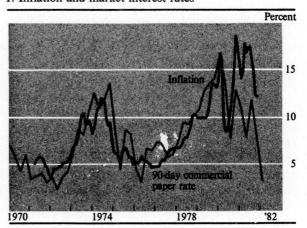

among larger business firms, and commercial banks found that they could no longer expect an automatic flow of business funds into non-interest-bearing checking accounts. Banks responded to their eroding liquidity position by issuing large-denomination negotiable certificates of deposit and making secondary markets for them. This was the first in a sequence of steps that ultimately led to dependence on liability management as the principal source of bank liquidity. The ability of banks to compete for these funds was at times hampered by deposit rate ceilings, but in the early 1970s the ceilings on large CDs were eliminated.

In the mid-1970s, banks began more aggressively to market instruments of very short maturity—such as repurchase agreements on securities and dollar-denominated deposits at their offshore branches. They also began to issue commercial paper through their parent holding companies. Rates paid on these instruments were not limited by regulation, nor was it necessary to hold reserves against them.

During the past decade, the financial sophistication of business firms has increased profoundly. Management of cash positions has assumed an important place in the duties of financial managers, along with their traditional role of ensuring the availability of capital for business enterprise. Considerable effort and investment have gone into the development of information systems, cash-forecasting methods, and techniques for transferring funds that enable firms to minimize their holdings of cash and, in the process, to maximize earnings on working capital.

Individuals as a group were slower than businesses to respond to the forces motivating changes in financial practices, in part because they lacked the necessary financial sophistication. In addition, the alternative financial investments available to individuals were, until recently, limited by minimum denominations on market instruments and the relatively high cost of securities transactions in small amounts. Since the mid-1970s, however, new institutions and instruments have emerged to compete for the savings of individuals. The most widely publicized of these are the money market mutual funds, which have grown explosively in the past several years (chart 2). These funds offer small savers the opportunity to invest indirectly in diversified

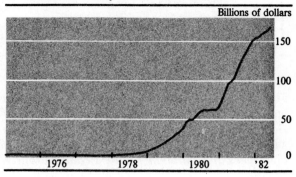

2. Growth of money market mutual funds

Billions of dollars

150
100
50
0

1976 1978 1980 '82

pools of large-denomination money market instruments such as commercial paper and negotiable CDs. Most of them permit the immediate withdrawal of funds by check or other convenient means. While money market funds are a repository for savings, they also can serve as transaction balances or as a very close substitute for them.

Other high-yielding investments have attracted considerable public interest as substitutes for money. A number of brokerage firms now offer "cash management" accounts, which combine the features of money market funds and margin accounts. Most of these allow for withdrawal of funds by check in any denomination, and also by debit card. The newest arrangements, "sweep accounts"—some of which are designed primarily for smaller businesses and others for individuals—permit funds to move automatically into or out of conventional transaction balances to investment accounts paying market rates of return.

The increased competition for savings of individuals has forced the financial regulatory authorities to accelerate the liberalization of ceiling rates on their small-denomination time deposits. Also, individuals may now hold checking accounts that bear interest (chart 3). The Monetary Control Act of 1980 authorized nationwide negotiable order of withdrawal accounts—checkable deposits earning 5¼ percent interest at commercial banks and at thrift institutions—beginning in 1981. These interest-bearing checking deposits now account for almost one-fifth of total transaction balances—that is, of the narrow measure of money, M1.

These innovations have particular relevance for monetary policy. First, transaction balances, as measured by M1, are growing much more

3. Growth of NOW accounts

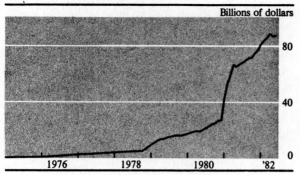

Billions of dollars

80

40

0

1976   1978   1980   '82

slowly than are other financial assets; the income velocity of M1 has approximately doubled in the past 20 years. Second, the differences between money and other financial assets have been narrowing. The new instruments have both transaction and investment characteristics. M1, the conventional measure of transaction balances, now includes interest-bearing checkable deposits that also have a significant savings component. At the same time, money market funds and cash management accounts, which are not included in M1, are also used partly for transaction purposes. Third, the distinctions among classes of financial institutions, and between financial and nonfinancial firms, have been blurred. To cite just one example, the retail firm of Sears Roebuck has become a financial conglomerate with a nationwide electronic funds transfer system, a savings and loan association subsidiary, a credit card company with more than 20 million customers, the capability to clear and settle third-party payments, a full-line insurance subsidiary, a nationwide network of more than 1,000 offices, and ready access to the commercial paper market. Sears has announced its intention to expand its provision of a wide variety of financial services to the public, including payments services.

The current process of financial innovation is far from complete. Technological advances have spurred changes in the structure of the financial services industry. Automated accounting systems, advanced telecommunications, computer-based cash management systems, and wire transfers of funds underpin some of the innovations already mentioned. Automation of data production and transmission will continue to shape the financial industry. We are, I believe, on the verge of a virtual revolution in electronic payment transfers, which will permit instantaneous flows of funds between financial instruments at very low cost.

IMPLICATIONS FOR MONETARY POLICY

Financial innovation in the United States has had important and far-reaching ramifications. It has raised questions about the appropriate definition of money, the precision of the Federal Reserve's control over the money stock, the meaning of changes in money balances, and the mechanism by which monetary policy affects economic activity. It has altered competitive relationships in the market for financial services. It has encouraged individuals and businesses to hold an increasing portion of their financial assets in forms not covered by federal deposit insurance, or at institutions not supervised or regulated by federal authorities. It has added to the risk exposure of many financial institutions. It has fostered the integration of financial markets, and in the process has altered the mechanism of credit allocation among sectors of the economy.

To deal comprehensively with even one of these issues is beyond the scope of a short paper. But I will try to suggest how financial innovation has affected the conduct of monetary policy in the United States.

The Definition of Money

The difficulties associated with defining money certainly are not new: the existence of money substitutes and "near monies" has always made it hard to decide which assets should be included in a particular measure of money. Traditionally, the issue has boiled down to drawing the line somewhere along a spectrum of assets ranked according to degrees of "moneyness," starting with balances serving as a generally accepted means of payment—having only a few investment characteristics—and moving successively to less liquid assets offering higher returns.

Innovation has made the dividing line between money and other financial assets conceptually more arbitrary. Assets with both payment and investment characteristics are more common;

moreover, the decline in the cost of shifting from one financial asset to another has widened the spectrum of assets held at any particular time to make payments.

From a purely theoretical standpoint, conceptual arbitrariness in the definition of money need not be a problem for monetary policy. After all, if a central bank can identify and control a monetary variable that is related in a reasonably stable way to economic activity and prices, it can accomplish its broad economic objectives even if the definition of that variable is arbitrary. If the definition of money appears arbitrary, however, it is more difficult for the central bank to maintain credibility with the public. Furthermore, when financial innovation proceeds rapidly, the appropriate concept of money on which to focus attention will almost certainly change, requiring periodic redefinitions of money that create still more credibility problems.

Controlling the Monetary Aggregates

Even more serious problems will arise if the process of innovation undermines the ability of the monetary authority to control money growth. Monetary policy in the United States is imple-

mented by setting targets for several monetary aggregates. The principal target has been the narrow money stock, M1, which comprises currency and checking deposits (chart 4). Studies at the Federal Reserve indicate that, despite its inadequacies, M1 is more closely related to economic activity and prices than are the more inclusive money aggregates.

Financial innovations have not, as yet, seriously compromised our ability to control M1. The Monetary Control Act of 1980 extended reserve requirements to all depository institutions, a step that helped to strengthen the link between reserves and M1.

We may, however, be on the threshold of serious problems of monetary control because of innovation. The proportion of money market funds used for transactions apparently is still quite small, but it may be growing rapidly. Moreover, the spread of sweep accounts may accelerate. Because these sweep arrangements transfer funds out of conventional transaction balances into investment accounts at the end of each business day, they effectively remove transaction balances from the reserve requirements of the Federal Reserve. To deal with this development, the Federal Reserve needs legislation authorizing it to impose reserve requirements on all

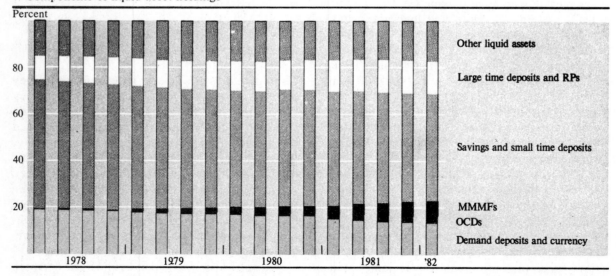

4. Components of liquid asset holdings

M1 is currency held by the public and demand deposits at commercial banks; other checkable deposits; and traveler's checks (included here with OCDs). M2 is M1 plus general-purpose money market mutual funds; savings and small time deposits; and overnight repurchase agreements and overnight Eurodollars (both included here with savings and small time deposits). M3 is M2 plus large time deposits; term RPs; and institution-only MMMFs (included here with large time deposits). L is M3 plus other liquid assets.

financial instruments that serve as the functional equivalent of transaction balances, regardless of the issuer.

A second kind of problem for monetary control arises if the money variable the central bank seeks to control, or at least a substantial part of it, pays a market-related rate of interest. For example, actions of the Federal Reserve to restrain the growth of bank reserves appear to have less immediate effect on M2 growth than they used to. The restraint on reserve growth increases market rates of interest, but rates on the nontransaction components of M2 rise as well. There is, consequently, little incentive to shift out of these elements of M2 into nonmonetary assets. Efforts to keep the growth of such a money variable within narrow limits could foster wider short-run fluctuations in interest rates. Eventually, of course, increases in interest rates may slow income growth and thereby moderate the demand for M2. In effect, such a process amounts to slowing the economy to slow money growth, a sequence the reverse of that contemplated in the use of a financial variable for monetary targeting.

Stability of Money Demand

In recent years, the principal problem that financial innovation has caused for monetary policy has not concerned the ability of the Federal Reserve to control the money stock. Rather, it has concerned the relationship among the money stock, economic activity, and interest rates.

Successful use of a monetary variable as an intermediate target of central bank policy requires relative stability in the relationship between money and economic activity. Before 1974, one could predict reasonably well the amount of M1 that the public would want to hold given the size of the economy and the level of interest rates. Since then, however, growth of M1 has been considerably slower, relative to the rise of nominal gross national product, than historical relationships suggested. More important, the period since 1974 has been characterized by greater short-run instability of money demand.

Estimates of shifts in the public's demand for money are imprecise, but studies by Federal Reserve Board staff suggest that they are too large to be ignored in the conduct of monetary policy. For example, over the four quarters of 1975, measured growth of M1 amounted to 5.1 percent. However, the demand for money—at given levels of nominal GNP and interest rates—may have declined about 3¾ percent during 1975. According to this estimate, *effective* money growth (the actual increase *plus* the downward shift in money demand) was nearly 9 percent over the four quarters. By contrast, the decline in money demand in 1977 is estimated to have added less than half a percentage point to effective money growth.

Shifts in money demand make it much more difficult to conduct monetary policy by setting targets for money growth. The Federal Reserve can, and does, try to estimate these shifts and take them into account in the formulation of monetary policy. But the estimates are necessarily imprecise, even for historical periods (chart 5). Worse still, at the time of change in growth of M1 deposits from a predetermined path an observer can never be sure whether it reflects a shift of money demand or the effects of change in economic activity on needs for transaction balances. The appropriate policy response is, of course, very different in the two circumstances.

Financial innovation has also affected the relationship between the more inclusive monetary aggregates and GNP. In past periods of rising market interest rates, growth of M2 (which includes savings and time deposits of individuals) tended to slow abruptly because funds were diverted from depository institutions to market securities. But the composition of M2 has

5. Error in money demand, based on FRB quarterly econometric model forecasts

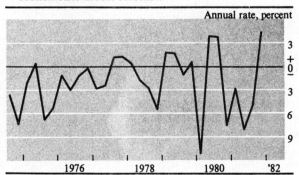

Annual rate, percent

6. Share of nontransaction M2 bearing market-related interest rates

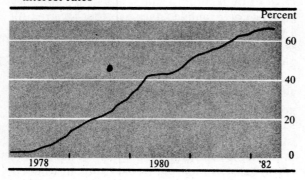

Percent

60

40

20

0

1978   1980   '82

changed materially since 1978; now, more than 60 percent of its nontransaction component consists of assets bearing market-related yields (chart 6). As noted above, such a composition affects the ability of the Federal Reserve to control the growth of M2 in the short run. Also, it tends to alter the relationship of M2 to GNP. Thus, even in the face of substantial variations in interest rates, the velocity of M2 has changed relatively little over each of the last three years, in contrast to the rather wide swings that used to occur.

The problems posed by the instability of money demand cannot be solved by making the monetary base the target. Such a step is unlikely to improve monetary policy. The monetary base is an arbitrary combination of the various components of the monetary aggregates. Its largest component is currency, whose magnitude has always been—and, I believe, always should be—determined by public demand. The remaining portion of the base, bank reserves, is basically a weighted sum of the reservable deposit components of the monetary aggregates, with the weights determined by reserve ratios. When the significance of movements in the aggregates is uncertain, so also is the significance of changes in the monetary base. Furthermore, there is little reason to think that stability in the growth of the monetary base will produce economic stability. Over the 1970s, yearly growth rates of the monetary base never deviated more than 1½ percentage points from their decade average. Nevertheless, the 1970s was a period of considerable economic instability.

Another suggestion is that we replace monetary aggregates by a broad credit aggregate as an intermediate target of monetary policy. This suggestion has some intellectual appeal. Some broad credit aggregates appear to be relatively closely and stably related to nominal GNP. Unfortunately, the suggestion seems impractical. The data on credit flows in the United States become available to the monetary authority with very long lags, and they are subject to large revisions. They could hardly serve, therefore, as a useful target for monetary policy.

Still another suggestion is that the Federal Reserve abandon its attempts to use quantitative targets as intermediate objectives of monetary policy, and instead seek directly to establish the level of real interest rates. From the standpoint of economic theory, this approach has some merit. From the standpoint of the practice of central banking, however, it has several deficiencies. First, the level of real interest rates is not directly observable; we observe only nominal interest rates and then infer what real interest rates might be by guessing the price expectations of borrowers. Second, it is extremely difficult to ascertain the real interest rates needed to produce the desired performance of the economy. The economic effects of a given level of real interest rates will change with the sectoral mix of GNP, tax rates, and the period over which monetary restraint is in effect. Third, and perhaps most important, public acceptance of monetary restraint is more readily achieved when the central bank focuses on reducing the growth of money and credit than when it sets interest rates openly and directly.

I believe, therefore, that the use of monetary aggregates as intermediate targets of monetary policy continues to be justified, despite the instability of money demand generated by financial innovation. Inevitably, however, the pursuit of monetary aggregate targets under present circumstances requires both judgment and flexibility. Short-run movements of the money stock have even less meaning as indicators of monetary policy than they once did. Moreover, monetary targets are best expressed in rather wide ranges; the Federal Reserve's present target ranges for money growth of 3 percentage points are certainly not too wide, given the kind of uncertainty that surrounds movements in the monetary aggregates. Also, we need to continue to use multiple targets, rather than to focus on any single measure of money. Indeed, greater weight may need to be given to the broader monetary aggregates in the future as a consequence of the relative instability of the demand for M1. Finally, we must stand ready to accept growth of money outside our target ranges—or to modify those ranges—when changes in the public's asset preferences warrant it.

Transmission of the Effects of Monetary Policy

The mechanism through which changes in monetary policy are transmitted to the nonfinancial sectors of the economy has also been influenced by innovation. Twenty-five years ago, monetary restraint worked partly through reductions in the availability of credit to potential borrowers. Financial markets at that time were less integrated, so that when inflows of deposits to depository institutions declined and liquid assets were drawn down, banks and thrift institutions were forced to reduce their lending to homebuyers, small businesses, and other borrowers who depended heavily upon them. The rationing process did not rely exclusively upon higher interest rates; on the contrary, nonprice rationing methods predominated in many sectors of the financial market. Usury laws and legislated ceiling rates on government-insured loans also acted to reduce the availability of mortgage credit and consumer installment lending. And statutory limits on the rates of interest that could be paid by states and municipalities blocked the flows of credit to those political subdivisions.

Innovations and regulatory changes have led to a gradual breakdown in the barriers to credit flows that existed in particular markets. As a result, monetary policy now transmits its effects to the economy largely through changes in real interest rates.

This shift in the channels of transmission of monetary policy has both positive and negative effects. It improves the efficiency with which money and capital markets allocate resources among competing uses. It also rewards savers more fully, thus encouraging saving for investment purposes.

But when monetary restraint does not result in curtailment of the availability of credit to potential borrowers, real interest rates may have to rise to much higher levels than they otherwise would to moderate aggregate demand. Such a development will be especially likely if monetary restraint is accompanied by an expansive fiscal policy. Moreover, the real interest rates confronted by different sectors of the economy are not the same, because expected price increases vary substantially from one sector to another. For example, wholesale prices of farm products generally are lower now than a year ago, in contrast to substantial increases in the wholesale prices of nonfarm products. The experience of sharply rising real interest rates, moreover, is one that farmers are unprepared to deal with. Before 1978, agricultural borrowers obtained funds principally from rural banks, whose lending rates were largely insulated from developments in the national money markets.

Higher interest rates in our money markets affect borrowers abroad as well as in our own country. The opening up of capital markets has increased international access to the U.S. financial system, and has made the effects of domestic monetary policy register more heavily and more rapidly abroad. The huge amount of dollar indebtedness of developing countries means that their debt service costs are powerfully affected by changes in U.S. interest rates. For the industrialized countries, the primary concern is that relative interest rates have a heavy impact on exchange rates in the short run. A sharp rise in U.S. interest rates, therefore, may confront them with the dilemma of accepting a depreciation of their currency relative to the dollar or taking steps to raise their own interest rates.

The Stability of the Financial System

Another way in which financial innovation may affect monetary policy is through its effects on the risks of enterprise. I would conjecture that innovation increases the risks of financial intermediation. Because it does so, it may limit the ability to use monetary policy aggressively to fight inflation.

In the United States, the risks of financial intermediation have increased for a number of reasons. First, some financial intermediaries, such as the thrift institutions, have been less able than others to adjust to rapid change. Second, fluctuating interest rates have tempted financial institutions with a high propensity to gamble to speculate in an effort to increase net interest margins. Moreover, it is difficult for supervisors and examiners to monitor and assess the interest-rate-risk exposure of a financial institution. Third, innovation has sharpened the competition among the suppliers of financial services, thus narrowing profit margins. Fourth, new forms of activity, such as foreign lending, have increased the chances for mistaken judgments. Fifth, and perhaps most important, reliance on liability management as a principal source of liquidity has increased the risk exposure of individual institutions. The problem of maintaining an·image of soundness has taken on critical importance, because sources of funding can evaporate at a mere hint of difficulty. Reliance on purchased funds has also intensified the interdependence among institutions. For example, if one institution appears to be in trouble, depositors may decide, out of an excess of caution, to remove funds from others.

The risks stemming from financial innovation have spread beyond financial institutions to the nonfinancial sectors of the economy. Interest rates in the U.S. economy have been more volatile in recent years—partly, in my judgment, because innovation has affected the way financial markets function. Interest rate movements have also become less predictable. As a consequence, banks and other lenders are seeking to avoid, or at least to minimize, interest rate risk—risk that they once accepted willingly. In the process, they have shifted the risks of fluctuating interest rates to other sectors, which may be less able to bear them. Futures markets for financial assets may help eventually to shift the burden of interest rate risk to those most willing and best able to bear it, but those markets are not as yet well developed.

Problems of this kind have not caused the Federal Reserve to deviate from a monetary policy designed to reduce inflation by gradually slowing the growth of money and credit. The process of financial innovation is not complete, however, and we cannot be sure of what the future will bring. At a minimum, concerns about the way innovation increases the fragility of the financial system will make it increasingly important to support policies of monetary restraint with aggressive use of fiscal policy to fight inflation. □

30

Examining the Recent Surge in M1

In recent months, many market analysts have questioned whether monetary policy is once again on an inflationary course. This concern has arisen in light of the recent rapid growth in the M1 monetary aggregate (currency plus all checkable deposits). Against a background of generally declining interest rates, M1 grew at an 11 percent annual rate from September 1984 to September 1985. This relatively high average rate of growth, however, masks two distinct episodes: M1 grew at a 7½ percent annual rate from September 1984 to April 1985, but then, in the five succeeding months ending in September, it grew at a substantially higher 16 percent annual rate. Naturally, this latter surge has attracted considerable attention, and led many observers to ask whether it is a sign of an overly expansionary monetary policy.

By some measures, it is not obvious that monetary policy has eased significantly since April. The Fed did reduce the discount rate by half a percentage point in May, but the resulting decline in the federal funds rate — which is often taken as an important indicator of the stance of monetary policy — by itself does not appear sufficient to explain the large increase in the M1 growth rate.

Several other explanations for the rapid growth in M1 have been offered. For example, some analysts have pointed to the recent problems at savings and loan associations and savings banks to argue that increased financial uncertainty has led to an increase in the public's holdings of liquid assets, such as demand deposits, that are part of M1. However, this and other explanations do not seem capable of accounting for all the growth in M1, especially from April onwards. In this *Letter*, we present evidence for a somewhat different explanation of the surge in M1.

We believe part of the explanation can be seen in the movements of the broader monetary aggregates. While M1 growth has picked up since April, the growth rate of M3 (which includes M1 plus MMDAs, money market funds, savings and time deposits, RPs and Eurodollar deposits) has actually slowed. In fact, the term components of M3, i.e.,

components that are not available on demand but that are investments that lock in funds for a fixed term to maturity — such as small and large CDs, term repurchase agreements (RPs), and term Eurodollar deposits — declined from May to August.

The behavior of these components resulted in part from sluggish growth in the demand for bank loans. In response, banks lowered the rates they offered on CDs and other term accounts. They changed the rates on Super NOWs and MMDAs much more slowly and kept the rates on NOW accounts at their regulatory maximum. The disparity in rate adjustments made it more attractive than before to hold funds in M1 and the nonterm component of M3 such as Super NOWs, NOWs, and MMDAs. The rapid growth in M1 relative to M3 thus appears to be a portfolio shift by the public out of term accounts into, among other things, M1 balances. This explanation of the recent rapid M1 growth implies that the surge does not indicate stimulative monetary policy. By the same token, if the portfolio shift should reverse itself in subsequent months, M1 growth could slow markedly (as it seems to have done through mid-October), but the slowdown would not indicate that monetary policy had turned restrictive.

The recent behavior of the monetary aggregates
While M1 growth accelerated after April, M3 growth actually slowed. M3 grew at a 9.4 percent rate from September 1984 to April 1985, but at only a 7.8 percent annual rate from May to August 1985. This deceleration was due mainly to the behavior of those components in M3 that are not in M1 or M2 (large CDs, term Eurodollars and term RPs). The level of these components was actually lower in August than in April, having *declined* at nearly a 3½ percent annual rate over the period.

The divergent growth patterns of the monetary aggregates are illustrated in Chart 1, which shows the monthly growth rates of M1 and those components of M3 that are not in M2 (M2 consists of M1 plus MMDAs, savings and small time deposits, non-institutional money market funds, and overnight

Reprinted from Federal Reserve Bank of San Francisco
Weekly Letter, November 15, 1985.

RPs and Eurodollars). Over the past year, the two growth rates have generally tended to move in opposite directions.

The major difference between the two aggregates shown in the chart is that the components of M3 minus M2 are generally term accounts, while none of the components of M1 has a term element. This suggests it may be useful to examine the components of M3 by splitting M3 into purely term and nonterm components. The term components of M3 consist of large and small time deposits, term RPs and term Eurodollars, while all other deposits are included in the nonterm component — this contains M1 (currency, demand deposits, other checkable deposits), savings accounts, MMDAs, etc. The dollar values of these two aggregates are shown in Chart 2. The divergence in their recent behavior is striking. The term component actually declined from June to August, while the nonterm component accelerated. In September, the term component picked up, but it is still below its June 1985 level.

An explanation for the portfolio shift

To understand the causes of this divergence in the components of M3, it is useful to begin by examining the banking sector. Chart 3 shows the rate of bank loan growth since September 1984. Notice that loan growth slowed in December 1984, fell sharply in January 1985, then picked up, but has been slowing again since May. This slowdown in loan growth is due to a reduction in loan *demand* rather than loan *supply*. The fall in the prime rate from 13 percent in August 1984 to 9½ percent in August 1985 supports this view. Bankers react to a slowdown in loan demand by reducing the rates they offer on their term deposits as their need for funds falls. Consequently, during the recent period of low loan demand, CD rates have declined relative to a very short-term rate such as the federal funds rate.

Chart 3 shows that the rate of growth of bank loans has changed in the same direction as the spread between CD and federal funds rates since December. In fact, from May through August, the 3-month CD rate was below the rate on federal funds suggesting that banks were not interested in tying up funds for a short term of around 3 months. This probably reflects expectations that loan demand will remain weak over the next few months.

The downward pressure on CD rates and rates on other term deposits has been reinforced by the reduction in the discount rate in May 1985. Rates on transaction balances — demand deposits, NOWs, and Super NOWs — have not fallen commensurately, so the rate reductions on term accounts lower the opportunity cost of holding highly liquid short-term assets such as M1.

The current rapid growth of M1 relative to M3 can be explained, then, as a portfolio shift by the public in response to the lower spread between the rates on term and nonterm accounts. In addition, the even faster growth in NOWs, Super-Nows, and MMDAs relative to demand deposits also seems to be a response to the fall in CD rates relative to rates on the interest-bearing components of M1 and M2.

Thus, the phenomenon of fast M1 growth from May to August reflected a shift out of term accounts. M3 was not greatly affected since the shift occurred within its components. Within M2, two opposing effects were at work: small time deposits declined because of the decline in rates, but MMDAs and savings accounts both grew extremely quickly. On balance, M2 grew much more slowly than M1. Of course, the effect of the portfolio shift toward nonterm accounts was most pronounced in M1 since that aggregate contains only nonterm deposits.

The near future and policy implications

In the near future, the shift out of term accounts is likely to slow and perhaps reverse for two reasons. First, if the economy picks up, the resulting increase in loan demand will lead to a rise in CD rates as banks scramble for additional funding. As the spread between the rates on term and nonterm accounts widens, funds should shift back into the former.

Second, if the economy does not pick up, we expect that banks will bring the yields on Super NOWs and MMDAs into line with other yields since they tend to adjust the rates on these accounts only with a lag of some months. This should lead to a slowdown in M1 growth relative to M2 and M3.

This reversal may have begun already. Chart 3 shows that the CD rate has risen relative to the funds rate, and Chart 2 shows that the term com-

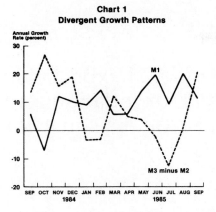

Chart 1
Divergent Growth Patterns

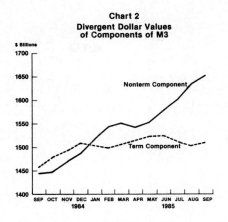

Chart 2
**Divergent Dollar Values
of Components of M3**

ponents of M3 have started to rise as the return on these accounts has become more attractive. Also, the rate of growth of nonterm accounts has fallen. Although developments in September do not provide conclusive evidence that the portfolio shift has reversed itself, they do seem to be consistent with the basic hypothesis of this *Letter*.

For policy purposes, it is important to realize that a large part of the recent surge in M1 represents purely a financial "disturbance" — in other words, a rearrangement of the public's portfolio that is not directly linked to spending, production, and employment outcomes in the economy.

Since such disturbances do not signal any change in real spending, the rapid M1 growth does not, by itself, indicate that monetary policy has become more expansionary. Nor does it indicate that monetary policy should be tightened to bring M1 into line with the Federal Reserve's target growth ranges. Conversely, a future reverse portfolio shift out of M1 that produces a large reduction in M1 growth would not signal a major contraction in monetary policy.

More generally, this analysis suggests one must be cautious in using M1 as a measure of the stance of monetary policy. Policy can only influence the funds rate directly, while the demand for M1 does not depend directly on the funds rate. The demand for M1 depends instead upon the difference between the return on M1 and the return on alternative assets, and these returns are likely to be generated by business conditions, loan demands, etc.

If, as this recent episode suggests, money holders are highly sensitive to small changes in the relative returns on different assets, substitution among the

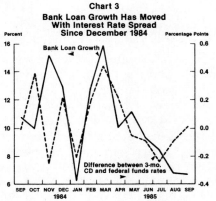

Chart 3
**Bank Loan Growth Has Moved
With Interest Rate Spread
Since December 1984**

different monetary aggregates is likely to be an important determinant of their relative growth rates, particularly over short periods. Therefore, for any level of very short-term interest rates, the quantity of M1 can vary significantly depending upon the state of the economy, expectations and other factors. Under these conditions, growth in M1 is not likely to provide a reliable signal of future spending plans.

Our analysis implies that while overall movements in interest rates continue to affect the demand for M1, movements in relative interest rates, such as have occurred recently, can lead to wide variation in the growth rate of M1 relative to the broader aggregates. During such periods, it may be difficult to interpret the meaning of any change in a particular monetary aggregate such as M1. However, as the general level of aggregate demand rises or falls, we would expect that all the monetary aggregates will tend to move together.

Bharat Trehan and Carl Walsh,
Economist and Senior Economist

31

Are the New Economic Models the Answer?

Economists are divided over the rational expectations challenge to mainstream solutions for inflation and unemployment. It is not just an academic squabble.

Martin Neil Baily

THE POLICY ADVICE offered over the years by most economists concerned with inflation and unemployment has been derived from a mainstream, or conventional, view of how the economy works. Recently, this mainstream view has been subject to a major challenge growing out of the work of Robert Lucas of Chicago, Thomas Sargent of Minnesota, and many of their colleagues and followers. The economics profession is now deeply divided and the debate between the two schools of thought has been vigorous and at times acrimonious.

A lot more than an academic squabble is at stake here. These are difficult and turbulent times for the economy of the United States and, indeed, for the whole world. Hyperinflations and massive unemployment both occurred prior to World War II, and to some degree were a cause of that war. If we are to recover from our current problems and avoid the disasters of the past, we will require wise economic counsel. And that can only be based on a sound understanding of the causes of economic fluctuations and inflation.

This article is occasioned by the recent publication of three volumes of collected papers that represent a coming of age of the new "rational expectations" or "equilibrium" model of the business cycle developed by Lucas and Sargent.* I will try to explain, first, the new ideas themselves; second, the criticisms of the mainstream approach by the new theorists; and, third, what I think is wrong with the new ideas. However, I do not intend to give a ringing endorsement of the old mainstream view. The last ten years have seen

* *Rational Expectations and Econometric Practice.* Robert E. Lucas, Jr., and Thomas J. Sargent, eds. University of Minnesota Press, Minneapolis, Minn., 1981. Vols I and II. *Studies in Business-Cycle Theory.* Robert E. Lucas, Jr., MIT Press, Cambridge, Mass., 1981.

steadily worsening combinations of inflation and unemployment. The time is right for new approaches. The intellectual ferment and the influx of new ideas from the rational expectations school have enriched our understanding, even though they have not convinced me there is a valid new framework for economic policymaking.

The new theory has three basic ingredients. The first is that prices and wages are determined competitively and adjust with complete flexibility to clear all markets; that is, supply always equals demand.

The second is that markets behave as if the persons trading in them use whatever information is available efficiently when they make the decisions that will determine their own income or profits in the future. This is what is meant by rational expectations. It implies that individuals and firms must have an intuitive understanding not only of how they are affected by economic events occurring in their own particular industry or market, but also of how general monetary and fiscal policy, and even worldwide economic events, will affect them.

The third ingredient is that observed cyclical fluctuations in the economy result from the short-run errors that individuals make. People do have limited information, since using today's information efficiently to forecast the future does not mean knowing what will actually happen.

With these three assumptions, it follows that in the absence of any major disturbance or shock the economy will operate efficiently—so that no one can be made better off without making someone else worse off.

At the level of the individual firm or worker, changes in the technology, movements in world trade, and even the weather may all create uncertainty and lead to layoffs and unemployment. Output and employment fluctuations may be quite large for particular firms or industries. In the aggregate these fluctuations will tend to average out, so that total output and unemployment will remain fairly constant. The unemployment rate in equilibrium—called the "natural rate"—results from frictional and structural adjustments that occur in individual firms and markets.

The Causes of Fluctuations

Fluctuations in the aggregate demand for goods are taken to be the main cause of observed business cycles, where output and unemployment for the economy as a whole deviate from their equilibrium or natural levels. The rational expectations economists see erratic and unpredictable government policy as the principal cause of such demand fluctuations. In particular, changes in the quantity of money induce cyclical fluctuations in the economy.

When the Federal Reserve Board acts to reduce the supply of money, there is less money relative to the amount of goods being produced. Money is scarce, and so the terms upon which goods and money are exchanged alter—the price level declines. (In practice this may mean that the rate of inflation has declined, not the price level itself. But that is only a complication and does not change the basic story.) An individual firm finds that the price it can get for its own product has declined, but at first it does not realize that the general price level has declined.

That is an important distinction, for if everyone knew that all prices had fallen there should be no effect on output or employment. After an across-the-board change in all prices and wages, firms would still maximize their profits at the same level of production. But because each individual firm believes at first that its own price has fallen relative to other prices, it cuts back its output.

An increase in the money supply runs this process in reverse, as firms believe their relative prices have risen and increase their output.

(This approach contrasts with the mainstream model, where tight money has no direct effect on the price level, but instead raises interest rates. High interest rates depress demand, particularly for houses and automobiles, and output falls. The inflation rate then declines slowly. Loose money lowers interest rates and encourages spending.)

The power of policy changes to affect real output is limited, however, because people soon catch on to

Martin Neil Baily is a senior fellow in the Brookings Economic Studies program. An earlier version of this article appeared in *Science* magazine, May 21, 1982, Vol. 216, No. 4548, pp. 859–862. Copyright 1982 by the American Association of Science.

the fact that the price level has changed. They go back to producing at their normal levels. Moreover, rational expectations theorists stress that changes in the quantity of money should not be viewed as isolated events, but as actions growing out of a particular policy regime. Private individuals then come to learn the way in which policy is made, and it is only the unanticipated government policy changes that can cause output to vary or unemployment to deviate from its natural rate.

This means, in particular, that any systematic rule for adjusting policy in response to events will have no effect on output or unemployment, once the private sector has learned of it. Thus in this model systematic stabilization policy is quite powerless to stabilize. This "policy ineffectiveness" theorem startled the profession and has influenced current thinking in Washington.

As well as presenting their own ideas, rational expectations theorists have been forceful critics of the mainstream model. Lucas and Sargent have frankly acknowledged the flaws in the models and the rather mixed results of empirical tests of them. But they are wholehearted proponents of their approach, nonetheless, because they believe that any alternative to it is intellectually bankrupt.

Keynes assumed that money wages were fixed. This assumption was subsequently replaced in the mainstream macro models by the Phillips curve, an empirically based relation in which the rate of change of money wages responds to any excess or shortage of labor, but only slowly. When coupled with another empirically based relation that links prices to wages, this provided the basis for models of the economy in which output, unemployment, and inflation evolve over time and move only slowly toward full employment levels, or the economy may become unstable. These models then make a case for stabilizing policy measures.

Attacks on the Old Models

Rational expectations theorists have attacked these mainstream models as being without a basis in the theory of individual decision-making. They point out that predictions made from a Phillips curve estimated through the 1960s proved inaccurate in the 1970s. This is clear evidence that these estimates had not uncovered a long-run structural relation of the economy. Moreover, these critics note that there is a serious inconsistency between the assumption of sticky or slowly adjusting prices made by mainstream economists when they talk about policies toward individual industries.

The slow adjustment or stickiness of the rate of wage and price inflation that is a feature of the mainstream models implies that many things are bought and sold at prices that are not at their market-clearing levels. In particular, wages adjust slowly so that jobs are rationed during recessions. This means that the unemployed are considered to be idle involuntarily. They would like to work at prevailing wages but cannot find jobs. Rational expectations theorists argue against this view, saying that except in periods of wage and price controls any firm can choose to change the price it charges or the wage it pays. If the firm chooses not to change or if workers refuse to accept a cut in pay then, almost by definition, any excess unemployment or slack capacity must be voluntary. Robert Lucas states that cyclical unemployment is a form of leisure.

An important implication of the mainstream models is that policy faces a trade-off between inflation and unemployment. Stickiness of wages and prices means, in the policy context, that an entrenched inflation has considerable inertia and cutting the inflation rate involves a prolonged recession. The new school concedes that tight money in the past has caused recession, but this is because such policy changes have been unexpected. What is needed, they argue, is a fixed policy rule, possibly embodied in a constitutional amendment, that makes policy constant and predictable by forcing the Federal Reserve Board to expand the money supply at, say, 4 percent a year. This is fast enough to accommodate real output growth but not to allow inflation. A balanced-budget commitment would also be needed in order to back up the monetary rule. Such a change in the way policy is made could stop inflation without serious recession, they say.

It is clear that things have gone wrong in the 1970s and new ideas are needed. But I do think the new school has gone off on the wrong track. The first problem with the new business-cycle model is that it does not fit the facts at all well. The theory makes very tight and specific predictions about the relationships among economic variables, and even the empirical tests run by advocates of the theory have found these predictions rejected by the data.

The two biggest difficulties the theory has with the facts can be explained fairly simply. The first is called the persistence problem. A typical recession lasts a long time. Business was clearly depressed from 1958 to 1962 and from 1975 to 1977. From 1931 to 1941 there was excess unemployment. But the new theory of the cycle makes excess unemployment a result purely of unexpected events. This should mean that unemployment fluctuates at random around its natural rate or equilibrium point. Instead, high unemployment in one year tends to be followed by high unemployment in the next year.

There are various attempts to deal with the persistence problem facing the new theory, but these strike me as unconvincing. The most plausible on theoretical grounds is to postulate that firms cannot adjust their output or employment without cost. Low output and employment levels this year follow low levels last year because the transition back to normal levels is costly. In practical terms, this is less convincing. There are adjustment costs, to be sure, but they are small. Employment and output in a typical firm or industry rise and fall very substantially from month to month in normal times, so why can they not be increased from year to year during a recovery?

More fundamentally, though, assuming that adjusting output and employment is costly gets you out of the frying pan and into the fire. The second major difficulty of the new theory comes about because it postulates that people's choices about how much to work or to produce are based only on wages or prices that are determined competitively in the marketplace. Their choices are never constrained by a shortage of jobs or customers.

However, the typical cycle is characterized by large changes in output and employment but by only small changes in wages and prices. In many industries the cyclical movement of prices is very hard to detect at all. This means that supply responses or elasticities must be very large indeed—big quantity changes result from small price changes. Yet from observing people or firms when prices or wages have changed for reasons unrelated to the business cycle, we do not find such large responses. Adding adjustment costs makes this problem even worse, because it says that the change in output or employment from a given price or wage change will be even smaller.

A third problem with the new theory is a conceptual one that was raised by Arthur Okun. He pointed out that the new models emphasize the rationality of behavior *despite which* there is a business cycle. The cycle occurs because of errors of expectation, but there is almost no analysis of the source of these errors or how they are eliminated. Okun thought the theory should explain in detail what people know, when they know it, and how they find it out.

Dealing With the Criticisms

Finally I turn to the new theorists' criticisms of the mainstream model. I agree with some of them. It is correct to say that the Phillips curve specification of the determinants of wage and price inflation collapsed in the 1970s and proved an unreliable guide to policy. The idea that the private economy alters its own behavior depending upon the way in which monetary and fiscal policy are made is an important one that had been largely ignored. It suggests that a resolute anti-inflation policy might work with less unemployment cost than is suggested by the past experience with haphazard anti-inflation policy.

The critics are also correct in asserting that simply assuming price or wage stickiness is not enough; one must understand why.

But to say that wage and price stickiness is not well understood does not mean that such behavior does not exist. The relentless upward movement of money wages during the mid-1970s in the face of a deep recession demonstrates the lack of wage responsiveness to excess unemployment and job rationing. The collapse of the simple Phillips curve model of wage and price behavior convinced Lucas and Sargent that a model based on perfect markets was appropriate. It convinced others to ask how the OPEC oil cartel, the worldwide shift in food prices, the slowdown in productivity growth, and the decline in the dollar have affected inflation. Lucas and Sargent ignore all these major events, claiming that excessive monetary expansion by an out-of-control Federal Reserve Board is the only cause of inflation.

On the theoretical side, there has also been some progress in understanding why wages and some prices fail to respond to short-run market imbalances. Farm prices do rise or fall depending upon supply and demand. But wages respond more to increases in the cost of living than to surpluses or shortages of labor. Recent approaches to understanding this pattern have stressed the differences between the markets for farm products and for labor. Most jobs last several years and employers treat their employees according to rules of fairness, responding perhaps to long-run changes in the economic climate but not to short-run conditions. The way to lessen the inconsistency in the mainstream view may be to improve the analysis of individual decision-making.

It is claimed that the assumptions about the formation of expectations that are made in the mainstream macro models are arbitrary and should be replaced with the assumption of rational expectations. This is tricky. How much rationality is appropriate in economic models? The proponents of rational expectations claim that their approach is merely an extension into the case of uncertainty of the usual assumption that people act in their own interest, but that is not true. They assume that people have an intuitive grasp of the way the whole economy works. They look at and use information on economy-wide variables such as the money supply and the deficit and they know how changes in these variables affect their own decisions.

In an economy subject to shocks and disturbances the price level would have to change substantially for full employment to be maintained. But the private sector supposedly knows in each period the best estimate of the price level that would ensure full employment and then sets individual price decisions relative to this as a benchmark. It is hard to believe that most product or labor markets are this efficient. There just is not any evidence to support the strong rational expectations assumption. There is an old-fashioned idea that when business and consumers fear or expect a recession they cut back their spending and actually induce the recession they fear. This is a hard idea to model formally, but it may be correct anyway. Volatile expectations can be a cause of instability.

Lessons of the Seventies

The "policy ineffectiveness" theorem of the rational expectations models was startling and challenging. But it is no stronger than the assumptions made. In an economy where the market always yields the best available outcome, it is not surprising that stabilization policy can do no good, and will generally do harm. The theorem simply says that the market is so clever it can actually offset the harm done by at least the predictable part of stabilization policy. But no one advocates stabilization policy on the grounds that it can be "effectively" harmful. The idea is to offset instability in the private sector. Even with the troubled 1970s, it is still true that our economy is much, much more stable than it was before World War II. Stabilization policy can probably take credit for much of this.

The lesson of the 1970s is that we do not have an adequate theory of inflation nor do we have policies, or at least acceptable policies, to combine stable output growth with price stability. That is a major inadequacy, and it means there is plenty of room to change or extend the mainstream model, but it does not imply abandoning the successful part of that model. Using monetary and fiscal policy to keep the economy on an even keel is profoundly conservative politically, contrary to the usual impression. It allows the free enterprise system to work well. Ⓑ

The deficit mess: How it developed, what might be done

WHAT REAGAN PREDICTED AND WHAT HAPPENED

When he campaigned for President in 1980, Ronald Reagan promised to achieve a balanced budget by the end of his first term. By 1982, however, his Office of Management and Budget conceded that large deficits would continue into the latter part of the decade. Most of the yearly shortfalls, in fact, have turned out to be more than twice as big as those first projected by the White House's budget planners.

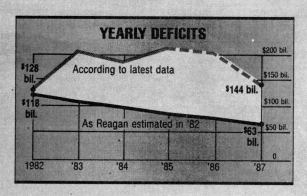

YEARLY DEFICITS

$128 bil.
$118 bil.
According to latest data
$200 bil.
$150 bil.
$144 bil.
$100 bil.
As Reagan estimated in '82
$63 bil.
$50 bil.
0
1982 '83 '84 '85 '86 '87

WHAT WENT WRONG

Even though budget cuts hit most domestic programs, federal spending as a share of the gross national product increased during Reagan's Presidency to the highest levels since World War II. Behind the surge: A sustained military buildup, a lack of controls over automatic boosts for Social Security and other entitlement programs and rising charges for interest on the debt.

According to Reagan's "supply side" plan, an improving economy would generate enough new revenue to offset losses caused by his 1981 tax cuts. Instead, the economy slumped into the worst recession since the Depression of the 1930s. The subsequent recovery has not been fast enough or strong enough to produce the tax dollars to meet the President's budget forecasts. Result: The federal debt has risen as much under Reagan as it did in all the other Presidencies combined.

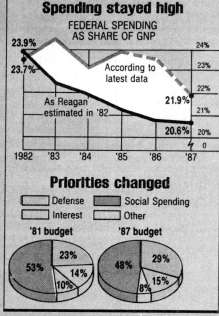

Spending stayed high

FEDERAL SPENDING AS SHARE OF GNP

23.9%
23.7%
According to latest data
24%
23%
As Reagan estimated in '82
21.9%
22%
21%
20.6%
20%
0
1982 '83 '84 '85 '86 '87

Priorities changed

Defense — Social Spending
Interest — Other

'81 budget
53% 23% 14% 10%

'87 budget
48% 29% 8% 15%

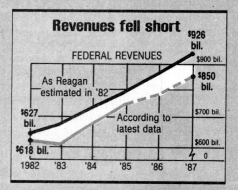

Revenues fell short

FEDERAL REVENUES

$926 bil.
$900 bil.
As Reagan estimated in '82
$850 bil.
$627 bil.
$800 bil.
According to latest data
$700 bil.
$618 bil.
$600 bil.
0
1982 '83 '84 '85 '86 '87

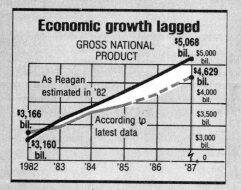

Economic growth lagged

GROSS NATIONAL PRODUCT

$5,068 bil. $5,000 bil.
$4,629 bil.
As Reagan estimated in '82
$4,000 bil.
$3,166 bil.
According to latest data
$3,500 bil.
$3,160 bil.
$3,000 bil.
0
1982 '83 '84 '85 '86 '87

THE BATTLE AHEAD: WHERE CUTS MAY COME

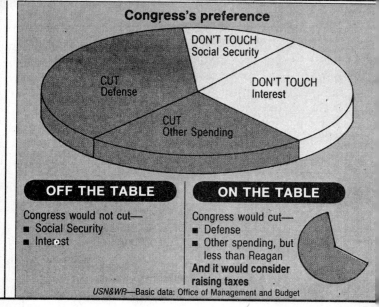

Reagan's budget

DON'T TOUCH Social Security
INCREASE Defense
DON'T TOUCH Interest
CUT Other Spending

OFF THE TABLE

President would increase—
■ Defense spending by 6.2%
President would not cut—
■ Social Security
■ Interest
Nor would he raise taxes

ON THE TABLE

President would cut—
■ Other spending by 6.4%

Congress's preference

DON'T TOUCH Social Security
CUT Defense
DON'T TOUCH Interest
CUT Other Spending

OFF THE TABLE

Congress would not cut—
■ Social Security
■ Interest

ON THE TABLE

Congress would cut—
■ Defense
■ Other spending, but less than Reagan
And it would consider raising taxes

USN&WR—Basic data: Office of Management and Budget

Federal Deficits 1986-1991

Deficit Projections and Targets

	Projections (billions of dollars)[a]					
	FY1986	FY1987	FY1988	FY1989	FY1990	FY1991
OMB current services						
February 1986	206	182	150	139	126	104
August 1985	243	253	256	244	238	n.a.
Change	-37	-71	-106	-105	-112	n.a.
CBO baseline						
February 1986	208	181	165	144	120	104
August 1985	212	229	243	264	285	n.a.
Change	-4	-52	-78	-120	-165	n.a.
Gramm-Rudman target[b]	172	144	108	72	36	0
Changes needed to achieve deficit target[c]						
OMB	-34	-38	-42	-67	-90	-104
CBO	-36	-37	-57	-72	-84	-104

Sources of Change in CBO Baseline Deficit

	Projections (billions of dollars)				
	FY1986	FY1987	FY1988	FY1989	FY1990
August 1985 baseline deficit	212.3	229.0	243.2	263.9	284.6
Change due to:					
(1) FY1986 appropriations	-10.5	-27.5	-42.2	-56.8	-71.0
(2) FY1986 sequestration	-11.4	-16.3	-18.1	-19.1	-20.3
(3) Net interest	+0.3	-7.3	-16.3	-30.9	-51.0
(4) Defense spending	0	-3.2	-9.5	-18.0	-28.1
(5) Other factors	+17.7	+6.6	+7.8	+4.7	+6.0
February 1986 baseline deficit	208.3	181.3	164.9	143.6	120.1

a. Figures are rounded to nearest billion.
b. Targets as specified in the Balanced Budget and Emergency Deficit Control Act of 1985.
c. Changes from February 1986 deficit projections.
NOTE: n.a. means not available.
SOURCES: Congressional Budget Office (CBO); and the Office of Management and Budget.

In August 1985, both the CBO and the OMB projected deficits of $200 to $300 billion annually in the absence of tax or spending policy changes. Yet, projections released by the OMB and the CBO in February suggest a different deficit path. Both the OMB and CBO projections show the deficit declining from over $200 billion in FY1986 to just over $100 billion in FY1991.

At least three developments since August have altered the deficit outlook. They are (1) partial implementation of the FY1986 budget resolution, (2) the passage of the Gramm-Rudman balanced-budget act and the sequestration of funds appropriated for FY1986, and (3) a brighter net interest payment outlook brought on, in part, by the interest-rate declines since last summer. The current policy defense concept has changed as well, although the CBO and the OMB view current defense policy differently. Last August, both the CBO and the OMB assumed 5% growth in real defense spending authority as representative of current policy, consistent with the FY 1985 budget resolution. In the February 1986 projections, the CBO assumed 0% real growth in defense authority, in view of Gramm-Rudman and consistent with its treatment of discretionary nondefense spending. The OMB assumed defense authority growth in line with the FY1986 budget resolution. Despite the improved outlook for deficits, projected deficits remain well above the annual targets outlined in Gramm-Rudman. Substantial deficit reduction, therefore, still requires policy actions.

Reprinted from Federal Reserve Bank of Cleveland *Economic Trends,* March, 1986.

Cyclically Adjusted Deficits

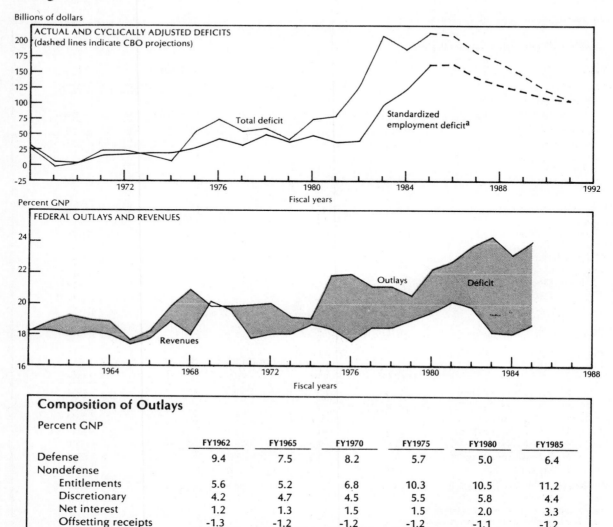

Billions of dollars

ACTUAL AND CYCLICALLY ADJUSTED DEFICITS
(dashed lines indicate CBO projections)

Total deficit

Standardized
employment deficit[a]

Fiscal years

Percent GNP

FEDERAL OUTLAYS AND REVENUES

Outlays

Deficit

Revenues

Fiscal years

Composition of Outlays

Percent GNP

	FY1962	FY1965	FY1970	FY1975	FY1980	FY1985
Defense	9.4	7.5	8.2	5.7	5.0	6.4
Nondefense						
Entitlements	5.6	5.2	6.8	10.3	10.5	11.2
Discretionary	4.2	4.7	4.5	5.5	5.8	4.4
Net interest	1.2	1.3	1.5	1.5	2.0	3.3
Offsetting receipts	-1.3	-1.2	-1.2	-1.2	-1.1	-1.2
Total outlays	19.2	17.6	19.8	21.8	22.2	24.0

a. Based on a 6% unemployment rate. These estimates are expressed on a unified budget basis, by fiscal year. They were provided by the CBO, based on NIPA estimates.
SOURCES: Congressional Budget office (CBO); and U.S. Department of Commerce, Bureau of Economic Analysis.

Federal budget deficits may be separated into two components for fiscal policy analysis—a structural component, which is attributed to tax and spending policies, and a cyclical component, which is attributed to changes in economic activity. A common measure, the standardized employment deficit, shows that structural deficits increased substantially in the 1980s and constitute the bulk of actual deficits. While CBO baseline projections show both total and structural deficits declining between FY1986 and FY1991, structural deficits are projected to fall by a smaller amount and account for nearly all of the projected deficit in FY1991.

The sources of structural deficits are debatable, but an historical view is illuminating. Throughout the 1960s and in the early 1970s, revenues tended to grow in line with outlays. Since the mid-1970s, outlays have grown more rapidly. As a percent of GNP, outlays currently are about 4 to 5 percentage points higher than during the 1960s and early 1970s, while revenues are at their historical levels, resulting in a large deficit. The composition of outlays, moreover, has changed since the mid-1960s. Currently, entitlements and net interest payments on the national debt are much larger as a percent of GNP than during the 1960s. Defense spending as a percent of GNP is below that of the 1960s, but has grown noticeably in the past five years.

Unless policy changes are made, CBO estimates suggest that the business cycle will not eliminate the deficit, and structural deficits will persist.

110

Deficit-Reduction Options

Alternative Deficits
in billions of dollars

	FY1986	FY1987	FY1988	FY1989	FY1990	FY1991
CBO baseline projections	$208	$181	$165	$144	$120	$104
Gramm-Rudman targets	172	144	108	72	36	0
Administration proposal						
OMB projections	203	144	94	68	36	-1
CBO projections	205	160	132	91	67	40

FY1987 Budget Alternatives
in billions of dollars

	Defense outlays	Nondefense outlays	Total outlays	Revenues	Deficit
CBO baseline	$284	$741	$1,025	$844	$181
Administration proposal (OMB)	282	712	994	850	144
Administration proposal (CBO)	298	713	1,010	850	160
Gramm-Rudman (CBO)	266	723	988	844	144

FY1987 Budget Alternatives
percent change from FY1986 levels

	Defense outlays	Nondefense outlays	Total outlays	Revenues
CBO baseline	5.2%	3.5%	4.0%	8.5%
Administration proposal (OMB)	6.0	-0.3	1.4	9.4
Administration proposal (CBO)	10.0	-0.1	2.6	9.1
Gramm-Rudman (CBO)	-1.9	0.9	0.3	8.5

SOURCES: Congressional Budget Office (CBO); and Office of Management and Budget (OMB).

The Gramm-Rudman Balanced Budget Act mandates deficit-reduction between FY1986 and FY1991, but does not specify how those deficits are to be reduced. Gramm-Rudman merely charges Congress and the President with arriving at a budget that meets the annual deficit targets. If Congress and the President fail to meet the targets, Gramm-Rudman (assuming its constitutionality) provides a means: automatic spending cuts divided evenly between the defense and nondefense portions of the budget.

The administration presented a budget last month that, according to the OMB, satisfies the Gramm-Rudman deficit target of $144 billion for FY1987. The proposal calls for continued growth in real defense authority, reductions in the nondefense portion of the budget, and no additional taxes. For FY 1987, OMB estimates a 6% increase in nominal defense outlays and a marginal decline in nondefense spending. CBO reestimates of the budget proposal indicate a larger (10%) increase in defense outlays, which, in turn, raises total outlays and the projected deficit.

The administration's budget represents a starting point from which Congress and the President can work as they attempt to forge a budget to meet the FY1987 target. The Gramm-Rudman procedure represents an alternative. This alternative implies a nominal decline in defense outlays and a small increase in nondefense spending.

A MESSAGE FOR REAGAN

Why the Deficit Must Be Slashed

By FRANCO MODIGLIANI

IT IS by now a familiar refrain that we need to cut the Federal budget deficit drastically. But the familiarity of the plea should not be allowed to diminish its force. It is long past time for President Reagan to lead the country in a rally against deficits.

While one can disagree with some of its policies, the Administration deserves credit for the steadfastness and courage with which inflation was fought and defeated, the pragmatic reliance on Keynesian fiscal and monetary policies in getting us out of that slump and back on a steady course and, last but not least, the courageous stand against the protectionist wave. It would be tragic if these accomplishments were forgotten and the President were to go down in history as a great spendthrift who sank the world in a sea of red ink.

The American people have traditionally supported sound fiscal policies and abhorred Government deficits. Thus, it is a great puzzle why they seem to have shed their concern at the very time when it would be most justified. For, in reaching levels unprecedented in peacetime, the deficit has become a serious threat to the well-being of younger and future generations of Americans as well as to other countries, both the developed ones and those struggling to develop.

My research of 35 years on individual and national savings supports the popular view: Deficit financing is very much like "enjoying it now and paying it later," by passing the bill to future generations in the form of higher taxes to cover interest and principal.

Moreover, total wealth held by the private sector (which includes capital, land and the national debt) is largely independent of the public deficit. Therefore, the deficit does in fact "crowd out" private production investments. More Government debt means less plant, equipment and housing, thereby reducing the future standard of life. It also turns out that the resulting future loss can be approximated by the taxes needed to service the public debt — interest and principal.

But many are unaware that, in addition to this gradually cumulating effect, the deficit has devastating immediate consequences.

Because of the unprecedentedly high level of interest rates (relative to the rate of inflation) reflecting the shrinkage of resources available for private investment, it has become nearly impossible for young people to acquire a home.

Because we live in an open economy with substantial freedom of capital movements, our high interest rates relative to the rest of the world enable us, in part, to make up for the reduced availability of domestic saving by borrowing abroad. But this reliance on foreign capital in no way reduces the burden on future generations. Though the stock of domestic capital and output may be less seriously impaired, part of that capital and part of the income therefrom will be claimed by foreigners.

But, in addition to this long-run burden, the huge inflow of capital is a major contemporaneous source of distress, because the import of capital and the trade deficit are two sides of the same coin — capital is imported through an excess of imports over exports. The endeavor of foreign investors to buy dollars to invest here leads to an appreciation of the dollar, making it harder and harder for American goods and services to compete, both at home and abroad.

The resulting trade deficit, now something like $130 billion a year, is playing havoc with large sectors of the economy, producing plant closings, mass displacement of jobs, widespread farm foreclosures, regional banking problems and emigration of industrial activity.

The deep malaise accompanying the trade deficit is in turn responsible for tremendous pressures for protectionist legislation. Resisting such pressure, as the President is valiantly doing, will be hard as long as our deficit is so large — but giving in would be tragic. As we learn from history, protectionist measures are sure to lead to retaliation, reversing the American-led trend toward a more open world economy that has contributed so much to the unprecedented growth of material well-being in the postwar period. In addition, protectionism might prove ineffective — leading to higher interest rates and a higher dollar. The answer to our loss of competitiveness is not protectionism but to cut the deficit deeply and quickly.

THE fourth deleterious effect of the deficit concerns the solvency and the very political and social viability of the debtor countries. These countries have no doubt over-borrowed and not spent productively all the proceeds of their borrowing. But the problem is immensely complicated by a circumstance for which they cannot be blamed. The interest rate at which they borrowed, which was low or even negative, has been raised to unprecedented levels by our budget deficit.

The economies of many of the debtor countries are cracking under the strain of servicing their debt, and growth has been replaced by contraction with the threat of social upheavals. In addition, we remain under the risk of some form of default which, in turn, could spark a domestic bank panic and the need for a huge injection of public monies.

The deficit and accompanying high interest rates also contribute to the current stagnation throughout the industrial countries, and in particular among the members of the European Common Market. In a world of considerable capital mobility, our high interest rates force these countries into a matching, relatively high, interest rate posture to avoid further devaluation of their currency, imported inflation and further deficit in the United States trade balance.

But a policy of high interest rates discourages investment and hence reduces aggregate demand and employment — unless offset by a large deficit American-style — a step that these countries are reluctant to take.

Unemployment in the Common Market averages around 11 percent — which corresponds to something like 13 to 14 percent in this country. No wonder these countries have been desperately pleading for an immedi-

ate slash of the deficit to reduce American and world interest rates, especially if accompanied, as it should be, by an easier monetary policy here as well as in Europe. In addition, as we tighten our fiscal policy, several of the Common Market members, particularly Germany and Britain, should loosen theirs.

Congress has, so far, failed to respond to the need for an immediate, deep cut in the deficit. The so-called Gramm-Rudman-Hollings amendment, which would bring the Federal budget into balance after five years, offers little hope. It merely instructs *future* Congresses to do the job that this one lacks the courage to face.

One must hope, therefore, that the President will take the lead in a crusade to cut the deficit deeply — perhaps by $100 billion — in this fiscal year. But if this initiative is to be effective, those involved in the process must renounce all the taboos as to what can and cannot be touched. This calls, first of all, for the President to recognize that cutting the deficit ranks higher than holding the line on taxes. And let's remember that we cannot really avoid raising taxes. If we refuse to pay them now, they will be paid by our children. ∎

Declining Deficits: A Little-Told Story

By Paul Craig Roberts

When David A. Stockman departed Washington, budget gloom and doom might well have packed up and left with him. The infamous "$200 billion deficits as far as the eye can see" were dead on Mr. Stockman's departure. Today both the Office of Management and Budget and the Congressional Budget Office forecast a 50% decline in the deficit by 1991 when it is projected to be about $100 billion, or 1.7% of gross national product. This deficit forecast is on a "current services" basis, which means that it is not dependent on any policy changes such as a tax increase or implementation of the Gramm-Rudman balanced-budget law.

Moreover, the substantially improved deficit outlook is not a result of more optimistic economic forecasts. The new budget contains no change in the real-GNP and unemployment-rate assumptions. Inflation and interest-rate assumptions are marked down a few tenths of one percentage point, and probably do not fully reflect the substantial drop in interest rates in recent months.

This is good news. It means that Gramm-Rudman will be easier to implement than anyone thought, and it means the deficit is on a declining path even if Gramm-Rudman comes a cropper.

Except for the Washington Times, the media have been slow to discover this enormous sea change in the deficit outlook. Even after the release of the budget, we continue to hear about "enormous federal deficits." Still the villain: "substantial increases for defense."

Clearly, what's being kept alive is the preferred story of conflict and failure featuring President Reagan and Congress locked in a senseless game of chicken over the budget while the country is destroyed by the deficit. This is as erroneous as the image of Mr. Reagan proposing ever higher defense spending while slashing social services to the bone.

Let's begin with the deficit forecast. OMB's figures were officially released on Wednesday, but the numbers were leaked at least a week in advance—to the studied indifference of much of the Washington press corps. CBO's deficit projections are not due for official release until later this month, but they have been available since the first week of February. (The Journal noted both the CBO and OMB estimates in a news story a week ago.) Usually the media can't wait to cite the numbers. In case you haven't seen them, the table below shows the deficit projections if existing government programs were maintained. One year ago OMB was forecasting a 1987 budget deficit of $246 billion and a 1990 deficit of $224 billion.

In addition to the official attitudinal change, three factors account for the marked shift in the deficit outlook from the budget of a year ago: Interest rates fell below projections, thus reducing debt service; the effect of the $11.6 billion taken out of the 1986 budget under Gramm-Rudman will be cumulative because it creates a smaller base for future spending; defense spending over the 1986-89 period was reduced $188 billion.

You had better let that last number soak in, because the media are reporting that Mr. Reagan's 1987 budget contains a 40% increase in defense spending over the next five years. What is not reported is that the base from which defense spending

Current Services Deficit
(in billions)

	1986	1987	1988	1989	1990	1991
OMB	206	182	150	139	126	104
CBO	209	178	164	146	123	107

grows has been slashed compared with last year's budget. To understand, think of it this way: Your boss tells you he is giving you a 40% raise but first is cutting your base pay. Last year's budget showed defense spending of $286 billion in 1986 and $392 billion in 1989. This year's budget shows defense spending of $266 billion in 1986 and $322 billion in 1989.

Hefty cuts in the defense base have been occurring for the past several years—a phenomenon that does not characterize other budget categories that are often described as being cut to the bone. The following comparison of defense spending in Mr. Reagan's 1985 budget with his 1987 budget shows a spending cut of $278.6 billion over the 1986-89 period (a similar reduction has occurred in budget authority). This has gone unreported. Instead, the media focus on the increase over the multiyear period from the new base.

Defense Outlays
(in billions)

	1986	1987	1988	1989
FY'85 budget	310.6	348.6	379.7	409.1
FY'87 budget	265.8	282.2	299.1	322.3
Difference	-44.8	-66.4	-80.6	-86.8

As the tables that follow show, the spending bases of other budget categories have moved up since the 1985 budget. Consider agriculture. The 1985 budget showed absolute cuts in agricultural spending over the 1985-87 period, producing heavy criticism of Mr. Reagan for his heartless treatment of the farmers compared with his bloated defense budgets. But no cut in farm spending occurred. Instead, agricultural spending about doubled—a fact that goes undetected in the 1987 budget that also projects a decline in farm support and

is taken as a continuing sign of Mr. Reagan's heartlessness.

Agricultural Outlays
(in billions)

	1985	1986	1987
FY '85 budget	14.3	12.0	11.9
FY '87 budget	25.6	25.8	19.5

Income Security Outlays
(in billions)

	1985	1986	1987
FY '85 budget	114.4	117.9	122.0
FY '87 budget	128.2	118.1	118.4

The greater the budget is overspent in any year, the higher the spending base is raised—thus making future restraint seem more severe. For example, the 1985 budget projected increases in spending on "income security" (mainly unemployment compensation, food stamps, housing assistance, disability and federal retirement). However, in 1985 the income-security budget was overspent, thus hiking the base and causing the 1987 budget to project absolute declines in spending on income security.

In other categories including Community and Regional Development, Education, Training, Employment and Social Services, and even General Government, the 1987 budget shows higher spending over the 1985-87 period than the 1985 budget envisioned.

Despite the facts, the picture has emerged that every year Mr. Reagan asks for more for defense than the previous year and less for everything else. The key to understanding the behavior of spending is to compare the spending projections in one year's budget with those in the previous year's budget. If the base is falling from one budget to the next, you will know that spending is being cut regardless of projections of increases. On the other hand, if the base is rising, you will know spending is growing despite projections of decreases.

As a result of the unexpected collapse in the inflation rate during 1980-82, the budgets of Mr. Reagan's first term contained unintended real spending increases. Correcting for this overspending has proved to be a difficult task, though we are now on the verge of accomplishing it. If monetary policy can avoid inflicting another recession in the 1980s and the media can resist the temptation to provoke a budget conflict, we will regain control over the federal budget, and our deficit problems will be behind us.

Mr. Roberts, a former assistant treasury secretary, is Simon professor of political economy at Georgetown's Center for Strategic and International Studies.

Last Defense Against Special Interests

By PHIL GRAMM

THE Balanced Budget and Emergency Deficit Control Act of 1985 — commonly referred to as the Gramm-Rudman-Hollings amendment — is a simple, straightforward plan to eliminate the Federal deficit over five years by forcing Congress and the President to do the job we were elected to do.

In a milestone vote of 75 to 24, the Senate concluded — after two weeks of debate — that this proposal is the best hope we have to reform an unworkable budget process and to assure that we, as a nation, stop mortgaging the future of our children. The amendment is now before a House-Senate conference committee.

If enacted, the measure would amend the budget process to create a cap on the Federal deficit, beginning at $180 billion in the fiscal year 1986 and moving downward in five equal steps to zero in the fiscal year 1991.

In each year, the President would be required to submit budgets with deficits no higher than the cap. Further, Congress would be barred from considering budgets with deficits that would exceed the cap.

The "teeth" in the bill come in the form of an across-the-board cut in Federal spending that would be imposed automatically if elected officials proved incapable of making the tough decisions necessary to reduce the deficit to the target levels.

This is, unquestionably, a tough cure, but for a truly awful disease. Consider the alternative.

The annual net payment of interest on the Federal debt now takes $140 billion from the total Federal budget. The deficit not only has gone unchecked, but actually has been encouraged by weak or crafty politicians and an array of greedy special interests who prefer to spend now and leave the bills for our children to pay.

The alternative to solving the problem, and soon, is clear. It means a

Phil Gramm is Republican Senator of Texas.

lower standard of living for our children and grandchildren; a surge in unemployment and astronomical interest rates; and, ultimately, high taxes and a repeal of the program that has stopped inflation and put eight million people to work.

The amendment has provoked howls of disapproval from only one segment of our society: Those who fear they are on the verge of losing their right to skim the Treasury. Political careers have been built on the idea that officials can, quite literally, buy votes with the taxpayers' dollars, and many who fight the amendment are fighting for their political lives.

And fight they should, because they are in danger. Either through the admittedly difficult process of enforced decision-making by the Congress and the President, or through the eminently fair procedure of across-the-board reductions, the special interests will lose their right to share the fruits of someone else's labor.

They say the amendment is a sure sign that the Reagan economic program has failed; that national defense and social programs would either suffer too much or not enough; that it would give too much power to the President, and that it is cleverly timed to clamp down only after the 1986 elections.

Take these allegations one at a time.

The Reagan economic program has created eight million new jobs, lowered taxes, crushed inflation, saved Social Security and put the United States on the path to a permanent economic recovery. That hardly smacks of failure. It has not fulfilled the promised balanced budget, but the Gramm-Rudman-Hollings amendment completes that promise.

IS IT fair? Extraordinarily so. If Congress were to prove unable to draw clear priorities for reducing the deficit, no individual program would bear the brunt of the reduction. Because its share of legally binding contracts is somewhat lower than

those of other departments, the Defense Department is slightly more vulnerable to reductions. (Is it not interesting — and disingenuous — how some critics who have built careers trying to strip national defense bare are suddenly bleating over national security?) Finally, Social Security is moved off-budget and treated as a free-standing, self-supporting trust fund, as it was intended to be.

Does it make the President more powerful? The trigger for across-the-board reductions is vested in economic forecasting conducted separately by the Congressional Budget Office and the Office of Management and Budget. A President's only function, indeed his only legal recourse, is to administer the statute in exactly the same manner that he administers a budget approved by the Congress.

In truth, both Congress and the President lose power under our bill — the power to bill future generations for indecision.

Have we somehow snookered political opponents by delaying the impact of the reductions — if any are made — until after the 1986 elections? Exactly the opposite is true. The process would begin operating the day the bill was approved, and would force the President to veto more bills in a few days than he has in the past five years to avoid an across-the-board cut.

If approved this year, the amendment would force the President to submit the toughest budget of his Presidency on Jan. 15, with a deficit no greater than $144 billion, which is $40 billion to $50 billion below the true deficit level that exists today. By May 15, Congress would have to adopt its toughest budget in history. Finally, unless we all did our jobs, we in Congress would be facing an across-the-board cut on Oct. 1, 1986, a month before Election Day.

Incumbents seeking re-election in 1986 would then have the final, crucial month of the campaign to explain their actions directly to the voters as they march to the polls. ■

Gramm-Rudmanizing the Economy

F. Thomas Juster
Director, Institute for Social Research
and Professor of Economics
The University of Michigan

Introduction

The economic policy legislation recently passed by the Congress and signed by the president, known as Gramm-Rudman-Hollings or more popularly Gramm-Rudman, is in principle one of the most far-reaching pieces of economic policy legislation ever enacted. It is also one of the most controversial, and has been roundly condemned by most economic policy-makers with academic credentials. It also appears to be widely regarded as bad legislation even by many of those who voted for it, who are essentially saying that while it is a bad piece of legislation it's better than the alternatives.

How Does Gramm-Rudman Work?

To understand the objections of many policy-makers to a piece of legislation like Gramm-Rudman, all one has to do is look at the process that the legislation calls for, and at the possible outcomes. Basically, the act says that federal government deficits must be reduced from their present level (estimated as roughly $190-$200 billion when the legislation was enacted) to zero over a five-year period. Thus deficits must be reduced by $36 billion annually over the next five years, going from $180 this fiscal year to $144 to $108 . . . . (During the first year to which Gramm-Rudman applies, FY 86, there is some slippage in that numerical calculation, but the general principle is as stated).

How is this to be accomplished? The first step, covering only part of the current fiscal year, has just been announced and involves cutting some $11.7 billion. It is being widely reported in the press as involving little hardship — just a few inconveniences here and there. But next year's problem will be different — and predictably much larger.

For future years, the president as usual will propose a budget to the Congress in late winter. The Congressional budget committees will then undertake the usual assessment of the president's budget proposal, modifying it to suit the preferences of the House and the Senate. At some point a conference committee will emerge with a budget that is agreeable to both House and Senate, and the president can either sign that budget or not. If the president signs a Congressionally-agreed budget, that document goes to the implementors of Gramm-Rudman to insure that it meets the law's requirements. If the deficit contained in the agreed budget does so, in the judgment of the implementors — the administration's Office of Management and Budget (OMB) and the Congress's Congressional Budget Office (CBO), as overseen by the General Accounting Office (GAO) — then it is enacted into law.

But if the deficit, as estimated by the tripartite Board of Overseers, is too large for Gramm-Rudman's requirements, then there is a complicated set of rules for deciding which expenditures are to be cut, and by how much. The rules exclude significant elements of the budget from being cut by way of Gramm-Rudman — Social Security, many other entitlement programs, some military programs — but everything else is more or less fair game. What the Board of Overseers does is simply to calculate how much must be cut to meet the Gramm-Rudman requirements, exclude the parts of the budget that are safeguarded from cutting, and then proceed to administer a "sequester" rule — if $15 billion must be cut and the eligible budget items total $450 billion, 3 percent must be cut from each of several thousand account numbers that govern federal government expenditures.

What happens if the president and the Congress cannot agree on a budget — that is, if either the two houses of Congress cannot agree on a conference committee budget that both houses will pass, or if the president will not sign a conference committee budget and the House and the Senate cannot override the president's veto? In that case the House and the Senate will presumably pass some kind of continuing resolution, which will authorize expenditures at their current levels or with some adjustment to current levels. That budget will then be Gramm-Rudmanized — the tripartite commission of OMB, CBO, and GAO will assess the deficit that is implied by the continuing resolution, exclude the parts of the budget that cannot be Gramm-Rudmanized, and do their thing on the parts that can.

How does the tripartite Board of Overseers work? The OMB obviously represents the president and the administration's position, the CBO represents the Congress's position, and the GAO is the referee. OMB and CBO each have to produce an estimate of what the deficit will be, given a set of laws that govern expenditures (either entitlements that can be drawn on by the entitlees, or discretionary outlays that are included in the current law), plus an estimate of tax revenue based on some set of assumptions about how the economy will perform during the next fiscal year. Estimates of both expenditures and revenue are to some extent judgments rather than facts — some people who are entitled to program support don't claim it, and tax revenues are clearly a function of a variety of economic activity variables. Thus the CBO and OMB estimates of the budget might well disagree. In that event, it is up to GAO to decide what shall be the operational deficit number before expenditures get Gramm-Rudmanized. The presumption is that GAO will split the difference between OMB and CBO estimates, although they don't have to.

What happens if the assumptions underlying either expenditure or revenue estimates are not realized during the fiscal year, as is almost bound to be true generally and looks to be likely during the current fiscal year? In that case, any shortfall in the Gramm-Rudman targets that occurs because expenditures or revenues or both are different from the GAO estimate will simply be added to (or subtracted from) the next year's target. That is, if expenditures are $10 billion more than expected and revenues are $10 billion less than expected, and thus the deficit is $20 billion higher than permitted by Gramm-Rudman, the next year's deficit reduction target will have to be $56 billion rather than $36 billion. And vice versa if the expenditure and revenue numbers are reversed—it will only have to be $16 billion lower. In the current situation, the estimated FY 86 deficit numbers have been growing steadily, and the $11.7 billion in cuts just announced will almost certainly not reach the Gramm-Rudman targets at the end of this fiscal year. Hence, next year's decline in deficit will have to be larger than $36 billion—possibly quite a lot larger.

Are there any safety valves in Gramm-Rudman? Yes there are—two. If the economy is determined to be in recession during the prospective fiscal year (or is forecasted to be in recession), then Gramm-Rudman is off. Of course, the $36 billion of deficit reduction that was forestalled because the economy was, or was forecast to be, in recession will have to be added to the following year's Gramm-Rudman target, which will then become a $72 billion reduction in deficit. Second, Gramm-Rudman is off if there is a war. As one senator is reported to have remarked in committee, "Is it OK if we declare war generally, or do we have to declare war on somebody?" It is unclear whether the spirit of Gramm-Rudman would be violated if the U.S. and, say, Iceland produced a mutual assistance pact which enabled either to declare war on the other without prior notice and without malice!

Does Gramm-Rudman put political pressure on either the president or the Congress to compromise their budget differences, or to dig in their heels? It's hard to tell. The president, who favors growth in military outlays and is adamantly opposed to a tax increase, may either have to acquiesce in a tax increase or face the likelihood that his defense budget will be Gramm-Rudmanized. The Congress, who would prefer to maintain social programs and other discretionary outlays at what they see as tolerable levels and are obviously reluctant to take the lead in suggesting a tax increase, may have to either face up to a tax increase or see the possibility that many of the social programs deemed most important will be Gramm-Rudmanized. Thus the president and the Congress have some incentive to agree on mutually acceptable levels of defense and non-defense outlays, since otherwise both get Gramm-Rudmanized and in roughly equal proportions. But, of course, if they could agree on some mutually acceptable compromise, there wouldn't have been any Gramm-Rudman bill in the first place. Or if they could agree that tax increases had to be part of any deficit reduction package, there also wouldn't have been any need for Gramm-Rudman.

Can Gramm-Rudman produce a recession all by itself? Technically, the answer is no. What happens is that OMB and CBO produce a deficit forecast based on the assumption that either expenditures or taxes or both will be adjusted to fit the stipulations of Gramm-Rudman. Hence if the economy were relatively weak before the application of Gramm-Rudman, reducing fiscal stimulus either by cutting expenditures or raising taxes or both might well produce a forecast of recession. But that forecast, if it was agreed to by the GAO arbiter, would eliminate the requirement for Gramm-Rudman in that particular year.

But that relatively benign scenario may not be a good description of what actually happens. Suppose GAO assesses the growth rate of the economy as 2.0 percent, given the cuts stipulated by Gramm-Rudman, and the cuts are made. The first quarter data come in and the growth rate is −0.2 percent. That's not a recession, although it's not very good. The next quarter comes in and the growth rate is −1.2 percent—but the previous quarter is revised from −0.2 percent to +0.1 percent. Is that a recession? Not by the "two consecutive quarters of negative growth" rule. The third quarter arrives at −2.0 percent. We are now clearly in recession, unemployment would have been rising for the past 5 or 6 months, and the year is three-fourths complete. The Gramm-Rudman cuts can be stopped, but the damage has long since been done and will predictably continue for awhile.

Forecasts that are contingent on specified cuts in spending or increases in taxes or both depend on how one assesses the combined effect of reduced fiscal stimulus and the presumably easier monetary policy that would accompany it. After all, lower deficits have some automatic offset, given the same monetary policy stance, in the form of less borrowing and therefore lower interest rates. And of course a smaller deficit is likely to have some impact on the trade balance, the value of the dollar, etc., leading to further complications in producing a reliable Gramm-Rudman forecast. But forecasts are always uncertain, and it is important to keep in mind that any forestalling of Gramm-Rudman in 198x just makes the problem twice as large in 198x + 1!

The Impact of Gramm-Rudman

What's basically wrong with Gramm-Rudman? The difficulty is that it signals a breakdown of the economic policy formulation process, transfers important decisions about national priorities to a computer (represented by the GAO's determination of the percentage cutback to be applied to each of the eligible expenditure categories), creates adverse incentives for the managers of public programs, and effectively assumes that there is no important impact of fiscal policy on macroeconomic activity.

Breakdown of the Policy Process. Budget decisions in any democratic society are political decisions, and are reflective of national priorities. Prior to Gramm-Rudman, the administration and the Congress had to find a way to reconcile their different perceptions of priorities, or to live with the political consequences if they could not come to agreement. Under Gramm-Rudman, political posturing is rewarded and responsible compromise is (probably) penalized.

Decision Making by Computer. Under normal circumstances, there is a slow but perceptible response of policy-makers to changing circumstances that dictate changes in emphasis of different types of public programs—defense vs. social programs, research and development vs. current services, health vs. education and training, jails vs. highways, etc. If the differences in priorities that have plagued the past several years of budget discussions cannot be reconciled, everything gets cut proportionately by way of the sequesters applied to eligible programs—fat along with muscle, wasteful programs along with efficient programs, etc. This process is not a tribute to rational decision-making.

Management Incentives. Under normal circumstances, public as well as private managers provide policy-makers with assessments of what can be accomplished with various levels of budgetary support. It is predictable that managers who can accomplish more with the same resources than those who are less effective will be greeted with enthusiasm by agency heads for their efforts at achieving economies—but such managers will then find their programs Gramm-Rudmanized to exactly the same degree as the inefficient. Once that happens, everybody has incentives to pad their budget requests and to exaggerate the dire consequences of not meeting their requests.

Fiscal Policy Impact. Gramm-Rudman effectively specifies that the fiscal tightening implied by gradual reduction in the size of the deficit is entirely independent of the level of aggregate economic activity, excepting the loophole provision that Gramm-Rudman is inoperative when a recession is in process or is forecast. Thus it calls for the same reduction in fiscal stimulus whether the economy is in a growth recession, with real growth rates in the 2 percent zone, or whether the economy is booming, with real growth rates in the 5 percent zone. Of course the aggregate economic impact of the Gramm-Rudman cuts can be offset, at least in principle, by other macro-economic policies: hence it is hard to forecast exactly how much impact on real growth rate would actually be felt by comparing the Gramm-Rudman budget process with the results of some other budget process.

An Overall Assessment

Given that there is so little genuine enthusiam for Gramm-Rudman, certainly among academic economists and even among many of its supporters, how did it become current policy? The answer seems clear enough: Gramm-Rudman has been agreed to by a majority of the Congress and approved by the administration because, unappetizing as it may be, it is judged better than the budget process that it replaces or supplements.

Why did the budget process break down? Political partisans would provide different responses. The Democrats would presumably say that Gramm-Rudman is the simple consequence of an ideologically rigid president refusing to recognize that the original vision of supply-side economics is a demonstrable failure. After all, they would say, the president promised that he could rebuild defense, maintain Social Security, cut taxes, and balance the budget. His critics pointed out (including the current vice-president, who coined the term "Voodoo Economics") that it couldn't be done except with mirrors. On the evidence, the critics were right.

On the other side, administration partisans would argue that the real problem is that Congressional Democrats refuse to recognize that non-defense programs are not worth what they cost in terms of social gain versus social cost, that there is enough waste and profligacy in these areas to balance the budget if only the Democrats would cooperate, and that the deficit problem facing the society results from a stubborn Congressional refusal to go along with the president's program.

Be that as it may, there seems to be overwhelming consensus that whatever the causes of the present roughly $200-billion-per-year deficit, they are having consequences for the future of the American economy and society that simply cannot be tolerated, and some way must be found to get the deficit under control. Since the normal process of political bargaining isn't working, some other process must be put in place that forces the outcome, even if it involves significant costs in terms of adverse side effects.

So far as this writer is concerned, the real culprit which has undermined the normal budgetary process, and which is therefore responsible for Gramm-Rudman, is the ideological position taken by the administration on taxes. Given the arithmetic of the total budget, there is simply no way that the deficit can be eliminated without a tax increase of significant proportions, or what is the equivalent, closing a significant number of tax loopholes.

A few relevant facts about federal government expenditures and receipts shows why virtually all serious budget analysts, of whatever political persuasion, have concluded that the deficit problem cannot be solved without a tax increase of some kind. Over the last three years, since mid-1982:

- Federal Government expenditures have grown by $238 billion, receipts by roughly $150 billion, and the deficit by about $88 billion—to its present level of $201 billion.

- Almost 80 percent of the spending increase—over $180 billion of the $238 billion—has come from three categories that the administration has declared off limits to budget cuts—roughly $80 billion in defense, $60 billion in Social Security, and almost $45 billion in interest on the (rapidly growing) national debt.

- All other expenditures of the federal government, leaving out defense, Social Security, and interest on the debt, come to $338 billion at present, have been roughly constant in real terms since mid-1982, and are mainly transfer payments to states and local governments and reimbursements under medicare and medicaid—items that have been strongly defended against further cuts by the Democratic House.

- The major discretionary item in the federal budget that has not either been declared off-limits by the administration or is not an entitlement program is nondefense purchases of goods and services—expenditures for items like highways, the criminal justice system, farm price supports, research and development, student loans, housing programs, airports and air traffic control systems, the Congress, the White House, etc.—and amounts to a little over $80 billion in total at present.

The numbers thus say that *either* we cut one of the off-limits programs, cut sharply into entitlements like medicare and medicaid, or face the simple fact that $200 billion in budget cuts cannot be obtained from $80 billion of discretionary outlays.

And finally, there is simply no credible evidence that we can "grow ourselves out of the deficit," as the supply-siders originally argued and as some continue to believe. Supply-side tax cuts did not increase tax revenues—they reduced them, and substantially.

If all that's true, tax increases must be brought into the picture, or else some other current untouchable—defense, Social Security, poverty entitlements—has to be reconsidered. But the politics of the 1984 election make tax increases an unpalatable budget choice, both for the president and the Congress. The president has made taxes his "make my day" issue—while the Congressional Democrats are not going to be found out in front on a tax increase given the political pummeling they received on that issue in the 1984 election. Perhaps Gramm-Rudman will force the tax issue, since it is likely to be a socially less damaging alternative than many of the others that will have to be faced by the budget protagonists this year and next.

January 1986

GRAMM-RUDMAN'S WEAK HAND LEAVES REAGAN HOLDING ACES

After a federal court ruled that the automatic budget-cutting provision of the Gramm-Rudman-Hollings balanced-budget law was unconstitutional, it was widely assumed in Washington that Congress could return to budget-writing—or wrangling—as usual. But as the lawmakers are quickly learning, the decision of a special three-judge panel did them little good. By leaving the deficit targets intact while sweeping away the hands-off enforcement mechanism, the court decision shifts budgetary power to the White House. The result could be a stalemate stretching to the eve of this fall's elections, and in the end the deficit for fiscal 1987 is likely to exceed the Gramm-Rudman target of $144 billion.

The Feb. 7 decision turned on a narrow point—but one with sweeping implications for the federal government. Gramm-Rudman, the judges wrote, violates the separation-of-powers doctrine by giving executive duties to the Comptroller General, whom the President appoints but only Congress can remove. That, the court said, makes the Comptroller a legislative official. Similar reasoning could invalidate a number of independent agencies, such as the Securities & Exchange Commission and the Federal Reserve Board, whose members can be removed by the President only for malfeasance, not because of policy disputes. Attorney General Edwin Meese III has hinted that he might attack the constitutionality of such agencies on these grounds.

SIGH OF RELIEF. But for now the Administration is focusing on budget concerns, and its first reaction to the ruling was an almost audible sigh of relief. President Reagan gets deficit targets without the threat of automatic cuts, one-half of which would have come from defense. He wants to keep pressure on Congress to write a budget that meets the 1987 deficit target without raising taxes or further scaling back his defense buildup. With the Supreme Court expected to uphold the lower court's decision, Congress is faced with cutting the budget the hard way—by passing legislation the President must sign.

That hurts Congress in two ways. First, automatic, across-the-board cuts buffered members from personal blame for unpopular reductions in domestic programs. Second, the elimination of automatic cuts removes a much-needed spur to get the Administration to the bargaining table early over defense spending and tax increases. "We are now in a stronger position to push for spending reduction as opposed to tax increases," says top White House strate-

> An election-year Congress is faced with making budget cuts the hard way

gist W. Dennis Thomas. At a Feb. 11 news conference, the President declared that any tax increase passed by Congress would be "vetoed on arrival."

The court ruling leaves Congress with a number of options, none of them very attractive. It could fix the constitutional flaw by making the Comptroller General removable only through the difficult process of impeachment. But that would defeat the purpose of giving a legislative-branch officer control of Gramm-Rudman's automatic cuts.

Congress could also press for an early budget summit with the President to fashion a "grand compromise." But with the threat of automatic cuts removed, the President can simply ignore such congressional pleadings. The most likely scenario is postponement of the inevitable. Says Senator Charles E. Grassley (R-Iowa): "I think Congress is incapable of really biting the bullet until the last minute, and then only under tremendous outside pressure." Adds a senior White House official: "I don't see what motivates Congress to be responsible now."

DAY OF RECKONING. The legislators, who have just 25 working days left before the Apr. 15 deadline for a preliminary fiscal 1987 budget resolution, will produce a document purporting to meet the $144 billion deficit goal. As it has for years, Congress' budget will include some savings on paper that will never become reality. Because House Speaker Tip O'Neill (D-Mass.) has said the President must make the first move on new taxes, the resolution won't call for any.

But this year, in contrast to previous years, a day of reckoning comes on Aug. 15, when the Congressional Budget Office and the Office of Management & Budget must project a fiscal 1987 deficit. These estimates will cut through the White House's and Congress' fudge factors and say that both sides have missed the target. Already the CBO says the President's 1987 budget underestimates defense outlays by some $15 billion. Under Gramm-Rudman's backup procedure, the projections will move swiftly to a joint House-Senate budget panel, which has just five days to send a resolution to the floor that really meets the $144 billion deficit mark.

With the election just around the corner, most House Democrats and many senators will be agitating for a modest tax increase so they don't anger voters by cutting services. Those up for reelection also don't want to disillusion constituents who won't understand why Congress can't meet its self-imposed deficit target. The President will have to choose between giving in to the wishes of Republican Party leaders and sticking to his guns, with control over the Senate possibly hanging in the balance.

Even if the Supreme Court upholds the Feb. 7 ruling, the deficit targets will remain, and politicians will feel compelled to meet them. "There may be a different hangman," says co-author Senator Phil Gramm (R-Tex.). "But it's the same noose." With opponents of spending cuts, tax increases, and big deficits all rounding up lynching parties, the election-year Congress has its hands full.

By Paula Dwyer and Richard Fly in Washington

The Tax Reform Controversy:
A Guide for the Perplexed

*Brian R. Horrigan**

INTRODUCTION

Widespread dissatisfaction with the personal income tax has produced an assortment of tax reform proposals from several quarters, including Congress, the Treasury, and some tax experts. All of these proposals would simplify the tax code by removing various deductions, exemptions, and exclusions, and would flatten the income tax brackets—that is, reduce the gap between the highest and lowest tax bracket. Some even go so far as to advocate one tax rate for all income above a personal exemption—a flat-tax system. The aim of all these proposals is to make the economy more efficient than it is under the present graduated tax bracket structure while producing the same amount of tax revenue. In broad strokes, the argument is that the existence of any tax brackets discourages work and saving by generating inefficiencies. And graduated tax brackets create disproportionately larger inefficiencies in the high brackets. By lowering the high end, while adjusting the rest of the tax system so as to keep tax revenues constant, people will be induced to work and save more, thereby generating more output. This expansion will broaden the tax base so that most of the tax brackets can be lowered, while still producing the same amount of revenue for government. Important efficiency gains can be had by simplifying the tax code, because elimination of deductions, credits, and exclusions also broadens the tax base, making possible lower tax brackets.

But the passage from proposal to law is proving to be a very rocky one, because these reforms also involve potentially major changes in the distribution of income. Many doubt that the trade-offs between the efficiency gains and the income distribution changes are worth making. After all, flattening the tax brackets means not just lowering the high end, but it may involve also raising the low end. And income distribution issues also touch those who have structured their investments according to the tax incentives in place now, such as mortgage interest deductions and the investment tax credit.

The central question, of course, is how much is to be gained and how much lost from enacting such reforms. As yet economists don't have a comprehensive answer to this question. At this stage there is only fragmentary evidence on the effects of simpler, flatter taxes. Nonetheless, economists have identified key elements of the economic consequences of tax reform, and this has helped focus the ongoing debate.

INCOME TAX RATES AND INEFFICIENCIES[1]

Not only are death and taxes inevitable—economic inefficiencies produced by income taxes are also inevitable. Economic inefficiencies arise because taxes drive a "wedge" between the wages and interest businesses pay and the wages and interest people receive. An example of this wedge is the difference between workers' gross salary (the worker's value to the firm), and workers' take-home pay (the worker's value of his own labor). These differences may result in an inefficient allocation of labor and capital, which would depress national income. And the higher the tax bracket, the larger the inefficiencies.

The tax reform proposals seek to reduce the overall inefficiencies by lowering and flattening the tax brackets to various degrees. But exactly how do these inefficiencies arise, and how can lowering and flattening the tax schedule help increase national income? Answers to these questions can be inferred, in part, by observing how people's work and saving behavior responds to changes in wages and interest rates, since changes in income tax rates change after-tax wages and interest receipts.

Labor Supply. People value both income and leisure, and they are willing to trade off the income they receive from additional work for

*Brian Horrigan is a Senior Economist in the Research Department at the Federal Reserve Bank of Philadelphia.

[1]For a discussion of these and other issues on the inefficiencies of taxation, see Ira P. Kaminow, "The Merits of Efficient Taxation" in this *Business Review* (November/December, 1981) pp. 15-22.

Reprinted from Federal Reserve Bank of Philadelphia
Business Review, May/June, 1985.

121

less leisure if wages are high enough. For example, suppose a firm offers a worker the opportunity to work 10 hours a week (a second job) at $10.00 per hour. From the firm's point of view, this worker will add at least $100.00 worth of value to its output per week. But suppose also that the worker is in the 40 percent tax bracket; from his point of view, he has to decide whether to give up 10 hours of his leisure activities each week for compensation of $60.00.[2] Income taxes drive a $40.00 wedge between what the firm sees as the value of 10 hours of work and what the worker sees as the value of 10 hours of leisure. A worker who would prefer to work 10 more hours for $100.00 may well be unwilling to work for $60.00, and as a result, he may refuse the extra work. The inefficiency arises because both the worker and the firm would have been better off if the tax brackets were lower—or zero—because the worker would have accepted the job. Since the existence of tax brackets affects all workers' decisions in similar ways, the inefficiencies tax brackets create may add up to substantial amounts, and they may make for considerably lower national income.[3]

Many people, of course, do not have much flexibility in deciding how many hours to work at a particular job. But there are instances where people can decide to work more or less time. For example, people can retire early, or make arrangements to work past a mandatory retirement age; people can work overtime, or work at second jobs ("moonlighting"); and self-employed people, like farmers or physicians, can decide to increase (or decrease) their workloads. Probably the most common example of choice about work is in the context of the family. In this case, it is not simply an individual's flexibility that allows for a labor supply response, but instead it is the household's flexibility. To a large extent, households have been characterized as having one member provide the primary source of income, traditionally the husband. Whether the other member of such a household joins the labor force (traditionally the wife, or the so-called secondary worker) depends on weighing the advantages of supplementing the primary income against the advantages of engaging in activities outside the labor force (such as child-rearing). And a major factor in that decision is the after-tax wage rate the secondary worker receives.

According to economic theory an increase in after-tax wages can influence people's decisions about how much to work in two conflicting ways. If a worker's tax rate goes down, he is likely to be inclined to work more hours, since for each extra hour worked he gets more after-tax pay. This is known as the substitution effect, because the higher a worker's hourly after-tax pay, the more income he would lose by not working, so he substitutes work for leisure. But if the worker's tax rate goes down he also may decide that, since he could get the same amount of pay for less work, he could cut back his working hours somewhat, and still get more income as well as enjoy more leisure. This reaction to a change in after-tax pay is known as the income effect.

In trying to predict the labor response to lowering tax rates, then, theory suggests that the substitution effect and the income effect work in opposite directions. But lowering tax brackets while keeping government revenues the same means that the income effect will not come into play for the typical worker in each income group. The average worker in each income group still gets the same take-home pay for the same number of hours worked because there is no change in the total taxes paid by such a worker. Lowering the tax brackets will affect only the decision about additional hours—lower taxes on additional hours makes working more and having less leisure more appealing for many workers.

In principle, then, lowering the tax brackets will increase hours worked—that is, it will increase the labor supply and, hence, national income. But how large could this increase be? Economists have tried to estimate the magnitude of the substitution effect. The estimates change as more data and better estimation techniques become available, but these estimates are far from perfect. For example, economists usually estimate responses to changes in wage rates separately for married men and married women—rather than for primary workers and secondary workers—because the available data are collected for married men and women. Also, economists cannot yet estimate the responsiveness of individuals like the self-employed and other special groups, because the data necessary

---

[2]Tax brackets here refer to the marginal tax rates people pay—that is, the rate on an additional dollar of income.

[3]Economists call society's loss of welfare from such inefficient resource allocation "deadweight losses." Since it is not possible to measure welfare losses directly, economists confine themselves to measuring losses in national income that arise from these inefficiencies. But there is no one-to-one correspondence between these inefficiencies and the level of national income. It is possible, under certain circumstances, to have an *increase* in welfare and a *reduction* in output. An example of what may seem perverse behavior is the case where higher wages induce workers to work less and enjoy more leisure. Though workers would be better off, output would fall.

to do so are not available. A number of different labor supply studies find that while the substitution effect is not very large for married men, it is substantially larger for married women.[4] Such studies imply that the magnitude of the substitution effect can be large. Thus, lowering the tax brackets can increase significantly labor supply and hence national income.

Saving. Another potential source of inefficiency of high tax brackets is their effect on saving and capital accumulation. People save for a variety of reasons—such as planning a nest-egg for retirement or for a bequest, accumulating enough funds for a large purchase, or setting aside something for the proverbial "rainy day." Since the quantity of saving determines, to a large extent, how much the national stock of productive capital can grow, inefficiencies that reduce saving will reduce domestic wealth, and they are likely to reduce capital formation and the level of output in the future.

Lowering the tax brackets increases the future after-tax return from savings. As with labor supply, an increase in the return on savings has conflicting effects on saving behavior. A rise in the after-tax return to saving—that is, the return to assets people buy with their savings—makes saving more lucrative because the future purchasing power of saving is higher. Therefore, people will reduce their spending, and they will save more—once again, the substitution effect. But the income effect also plays a role in saving decisions, and it works opposite to the substitution effect. The higher return on already accumulated savings means that people can consume more in their retirement years with the same saving strategy. Or else they can save less from now on, consume more until retirement and still attain their original desired consumption during retirement. But there is still a third influence on the saving decision—the wealth effect. The wealth effect exists because income tax reform in combination with a given tax scheme for corporate income will change the prices of assets, such as housing and corporate stock shares. If asset prices rise, then people will be wealthier, and they will want to consume more of their income—and save less; but if asset prices fall, then people will be poorer and they will want to consume less—and save more.

Economists generally have found the overall responsiveness of saving to its return to be small. But such estimates cannot be used with much confidence because the response of saving depends on the specifics of a given tax reform proposal.[5]

Less inefficiency, and with it more output, is the gain from lowering the tax brackets. But it may not be possible to lower all the tax brackets and still generate the same amount of tax revenue. In such a case, efficiency gains may be had by flattening the tax schedule—lowering the high end and increasing the low end—because inefficiencies at the high end are larger than those at the low end.[6] At the same time, widening the tax base by simplifying the tax code will increase efficiency gains by making it possible to lower all the tax brackets while collecting the same amount of tax revenues. So, substantial changes in the tax code inevitably will result in some people gaining and some people losing—the income distribution will change. Therefore, there is a trade-off between efficiency gains and changes in income distribution.

A decision to flatten the tax schedule and to simplify the tax code clearly will be influenced by how much is to be gained from doing so, that is, the size of inefficiencies of the current tax system. One way to get an idea of the importance of these inefficiencies is to estimate how much national income is lowered by the current tax system relative to a benchmark tax system.

HOW INEFFICIENT IS THE CURRENT TAX SYSTEM?

It is difficult to estimate by how much national income would increase if the tax schedule is flattened and the code is simplified. Because of the complexity of the issues and the limits of available data and of current economic method-

---

[4]See Jerry Hausman, "Income and Payroll Tax and Labor Supply," in Lawrence Meyer, ed., *The Supply-Side Effects of Economic Policy* (Federal Reserve Bank of St. Louis, May, 1981), pp. 173-202. Hausman analyzes 1975 data and finds that, if there had been no income tax at all, married men would have worked 8.2 percent more hours per year, and married women would have worked 18.2 percent more hours per year. A useful review of empirical labor supply studies can be found in Don Fullerton's article "On the Possibility of an Inverse Relationship Between Tax Rates and Government Revenues," *Journal of Public Economics*, Vol. 19, (1982), pp. 3-22.

[5]Summaries of the issue of how much savings react to changes in marginal tax rates can be found in: Robert DeFina, "The Link Between Savings and Interest Rates: A Key Element in the Tax Policy Debate," this *Business Review*, (November/December, 1984), pp. 15-21, and Lawrence Summers, "Tax Policy, the Rate of Return, and Savings," National Bureau of Economic Research Working Paper No. 995, (September 1982).

[6]This statement assumes that people's labor supply response to a change in wage rates is the same whether their wage rates (or tax brackets) are high or low.

ology, studies of the impact of the tax system have to make many assumptions and ignore a variety of important considerations. Despite these problems, advances have been made in the analysis of the consequences of tax reform, and further advances are certain to come. Two recent studies employ modern economic techniques to analyze closely some of the likely gains in national income by comparing the existing tax code to a flat-tax system, as a benchmark. Both studies estimate that a flat-tax system would lead to significant increases in national income. The estimates from these studies are not conclusive by any means, but they suggest that gains in national income could be large, and that flattening the tax schedule could yield important dividends.

The first study, by Hausman, estimates the effect of a flat-tax system, that is, a single tax rate for all taxable income on labor supply.[7] It ignores the effect of potential decreases in wages induced by increases in labor supply—so-called feedback effects—as well as changes in saving behavior. Examining combinations of single tax rates and personal exemptions that produce the same tax revenue, Hausman finds that both married men and women would increase their hours of work. For example, married men would increase their desired hours of work by 2 to 4 hours per week, depending on which combination of a single tax rate and personal exemption is analyzed. And married women would increase their hours worked by 4 to 8 hours per week. The combined increase in hours worked means that national income could have been 4 to 8 percent higher if the economy were operating under one of these schemes. This is between $150 to $300 billion, translated to 1984 income levels—a 4 to 8 percent rise in national income.[8] These income gains come both from the *flattening* of the tax brackets and from the *lowering* of the brackets made possible by the tax code simplification.

Auerbach, Kotlikoff, and Skinner (AKS) take a different approach to estimating the potential gains in national income from flattening the tax schedule.[9] They use an abstract but simplified economic model to simulate the effects of tax reform. These simulations do not rely on estimates from any one study, but instead they use "reasonable" values for the various income and substitution effects. Their study, unlike Hausman's, takes into account changes in wages due to feedback effects and changes in saving behavior. AKS find that converting from a set of tax brackets somewhat similar to those in the current income tax code (ranging from 23 to 43 percent) to a flat-tax system with no personal exemption produces an increase in national income of roughly 9 percent, which would have been about $340 billion if done in 1984. The hypothetical tax systems they analyze have no personal exemptions or tax deductions before or after flattening the tax brackets. Therefore, the improvement in efficiency they find is produced solely by flattening the tax brackets.

Estimating the Costs of Other Inefficiencies. There are some additional inefficiencies created by high marginal tax rates. One is that as marginal tax rates rise, so does the reward—and the temptation—to evade taxes. Though some tax evasion is due to unreported income from illegal activities, otherwise respectable people sometimes fail to report all or part of their income. The Internal Revenue Service estimates that if the tax law had been fully complied with in 1981, government would have collected about $95 billion more in tax receipts than it did—a 15 percent increase in revenue.[10] A reduction in the level of the tax brackets, among other things, would reduce the incentive to evade taxes, which would increase the tax base. Such an increase in the tax base would make it possible to have even lower marginal tax rates, increasing the potential gains in efficiency and in national income. A recent economic study finds that a 10 percentage point reduction in marginal tax rates could result in a 9 to 26 percent reduction in tax evasion, though other studies find more modest effects.[11]

[7]This study is reported in two articles by Hausman: "Labor Supply," in Henry J. Aaron and Joseph A. Pechman, eds., *How Taxes Affect Economic Behavior* (Washington, D.C.: The Brookings Institution, 1981), pp. 27-83; and "Income and Payroll Tax Policy and Labor Supply," in Lawrence Meyer, ed., *The Supply-Side Effects of Economic Policy* (May 1981), pp. 173-202.

[8]Hausman's work has been replicated with similar results for Swedish data by N. S. Blomquist in "The Effect of Income Taxation On the Labor Supply of Married Men in Sweden," *Journal of Public Economics,* 22 (November 1983), pp. 169-197. He concludes that "the progressive income tax [in Sweden, using 1973 tax data] decreases hours of work by 12 percent [relative to no taxes]. If a proportional tax was used to collect the same tax revenue, hours of work would decrease by only 6 percent [relative to no taxes]" (p. 190).

[9]A. J. Auerbach, L. J. Kotlikoff, and J. Skinner, "The Efficiency Gains From Dynamic Tax Reform," *International Economic Review* 24 (February 1983), pp. 81-100.

[10]These numbers are cited in Congressional Budget Office, *Revising the Tax Code,* 1983, p. 3, and "The Underground Economy's Hidden Force," *Business Week,* (April 5, 1982), pp. 64-70, and "Unearthing the Underground Economy," by K. Bacon. *Wall Street Journal,* (February 4, 1985).

[11]See Charles T. Clotfelter, "Tax Evasion and Tax Rates: An Analysis of Individual Returns," *Review of Economics and Statistics,* (August 1983) pp. 363-373.

Another source of inefficiency is the high costs of compliance and collection that stem from the complexity of the tax code. According to government surveys, in 1982 about 40 percent of all taxpayers paid for professional assistance in filling out their tax forms, and taxpayers collectively spent approximately 300 million hours filling out their tax forms. A recent economic study of the income tax compliance costs, by extrapolating from a sample of Minnesota taxpayers, estimates that in 1982 U.S. taxpayers bore between $17 and $27 billion in compliance costs—5 to 7 percent of the income tax revenue collected by the federal and state governments.[12] To that must be added the costs of operating the Internal Revenue Service and the court system that deals with the legal controversies created by the tax code. A wholesale simplification of the tax code would reduce these costs.

A variety of evidence suggests that there are solid income gains to be had from flattening the tax schedule and simplifying the tax code. And some analysts argue that a flat-tax system has some special advantages. But such major reforms of the tax system could result in important changes in the existing income distribution. What trade-offs might there be between efficiency gains in national income and changes in income distribution?

---

[12]Reported in *Revising the Tax Code*, pp. 2-3. Also see Joel Slemrod and Nikki Sorum, "The Compliance Cost of the U.S. Individual Income Tax System," *National Tax Journal* (December, 1984), pp. 461-474.

WHAT MIGHT TAX REFORM DO TO INCOME DISTRIBUTION?

If so many inefficiencies could be reduced or eliminated by a flatter, simpler tax system, why is there resistance to tax reform? For one thing, there is broad concern about whether such reforms would alter key aspects of income and wealth distribution. An important concern expressed by the public and legislators is whether flattening the tax schedule means abandoning progressivity.

There is a loosely defined public consensus that the tax system ought to be progressive, meaning that people with higher incomes pay a higher proportion of their income in taxes—*average* tax rates rise with income. One might think that the only way to have a progressive tax system is to have graduated tax brackets, that is, to have tax brackets rise with income, but this is not so. Even a flat-rate income tax would be progressive as long as a personal exemption is allowed.

For example, suppose the tax code allows an $8,000 exemption for each family and imposes a 20 percent tax rate on all income above the exemption. (Table 1 shows the average tax rate created by such a tax system for families with different income levels.) Even though every taxpayer is in the same tax bracket, the average tax rate rises with income. A flat-tax system can be progressive because a personal exemption that is the same for all families exempts a larger percentage of the income of lower-income families from taxation than the percentage of the income of higher-income families. Only if there

---

TABLE 1
A SIMPLE CASE OF PROGRESSIVITY WITH A FLAT TAX

Exemption: $8,000 per family
Tax rate on all incomes: 20%

Income	Taxable Income	Taxes	Average Tax Rate
$8,000 or less	$0	$0	0.0%
10,000	2,000	400	4.0
15,000	7,000	1,400	9.3
20,000	12,000	2,400	12.0
30,000	22,000	4,400	14.7
50,000	42,000	8,400	16.8
100,000	92,000	18,400	18.4
1,000,000	992,000	198,400	19.8

NOTE: This example is strictly illustrative and does not represent a revenue-neutral tax reform proposal.

UNIQUE FEATURES OF FLAT TAXES

While some of the recent tax reform proposals advocate partial flattening of the tax brackets and partial simplification of the tax code, other proposals advocate going all the way to a completely flat, completely simplified tax system. Though such an extreme proposal may strike some as unprecedented, there are many flat-tax systems in operation here in the U.S. already: the states of Illinois, Indiana, Massachusetts, and Pennsylvania impose a flat tax on income, and the cities of Cleveland and Philadelphia impose a flat tax with no personal exemption on wage income.

Flat-tax schemes have a number of unique features that no tax system with graduated tax brackets can have. In particular flat-tax schemes eliminate the bias in the current tax system against taxpayers with fluctuating incomes, eliminate the incentive to manipulate income to take advantage of tax rate differences, and eliminate the pattern of taxes and subsidies that depends on martial status.

Income Variability. Under a graduated income tax system, a taxpayer with a variable income will end up paying more taxes than a taxpayer with a steady income, even if they both have the same *average* income over time and the same deductions. When the taxpayer with a variable income has a high income year, her taxes go up by more than they go down in a low income year because the higher income is taxed at a higher bracket than the low income. Although the current tax code deals with this effect by allowing those with fluctuating incomes to "income average," the method in the current tax code is only partially successful. (An income averaging method that did eliminate all the effects would involve very complex record-keeping and laborious computation.) As a result, there is some economic inefficiency in that people will leave or refuse to enter occupations that are characterized by fluctuating incomes. Under a flat-tax system, people with fluctuating incomes will not pay more taxes because their high income and their low income are taxed at the same tax rate, as long as income is higher than the allowed personal exemption.

Tax Rate Manipulation. Graduated income taxes create incentives to rearrange income so as to pay taxes in a lower tax bracket. For example, some taxpayers transfer income-producing assets to their children so that the income from those assets are taxed at their children's (lower) tax rate. And taxpayers earning relatively high incomes near retirement have an incentive to postpone realization of income until after retirement when almost certainly they will be in a lower tax bracket. Similarly, taxpayers have an incentive to avoid realizing capital gains until they are in a lower tax bracket so as to reduce their taxes. And there is an incentive to realize capital losses in order to shelter other income. Because the graduated tax brackets distort such decisions, they cause inefficiencies. A flat-tax system diminishes greatly the incentives to manipulate tax bracket differentials.

The Marriage Tax/Subsidy. Under the current tax system, a couple will generally find that their taxes rise or fall after they marry: a feature called "marital non-neutrality." This non-neutrality is created by graduated tax rates and the fact that married people and single people are not allowed to use the same tax schedule. The change in taxes that results from marriage depends on the balance of income between the spouses. If one spouse earns most of the family's income, the tax liability will fall after marriage, producing a "marriage subsidy;" but if two people with similar incomes marry, they would pay more taxes jointly than singly, a "marriage tax." Generally, the more nearly equal the incomes of the couple, the greater the marriage tax. The tax code was revised in 1981 to reduce the marriage tax, but the revision does not eliminate it.

There are only two ways to eliminate completely the marriage tax/subsidy. The first is to allow each person to file a separate tax return regardless of marital status. The shortcoming of doing so, however, is that households with the same joint income can pay very different tax bills, depending on the distribution of income between the spouses. The other solution is to have a flat-tax system. As long as both members of the couple have taxable income, their joint tax bill will not depend on marital status or the distribution of income between the two.

is no personal exemption will a flat-tax system not be progressive—in which case all families pay the same average tax rate.

Within limits, a flat-tax system can be made more progressive while yielding the same amount of revenue as the current tax system by increasing the personal exemption and the tax rate at the same time. As the personal exemption and the tax rate rise together, the system becomes more progressive both because more low-income families are removed from the tax rolls, and because higher-income people pay an increasingly higher average tax rate. But in order to keep revenues constant, making the system more progressive also requires a higher tax rate, which increases inefficiencies and reduces national income. Thus, there is a trade-off between progressivity and national income—more progressivity means lower national income.

Progressivity and efficiency also are affected by tax deductions, credits, and exclusions (DCEs), such as deductions for interest payments, child care expenses, state and local taxes, energy tax credits, and tax exempt retirement accounts. The more DCEs the tax code allows, the smaller is the tax base, and the higher the tax brackets must be to generate the same revenue. For instance, the IRS calculates that the personal income tax base in 1979 was only 44 percent of total personal income—52 percent excluding the personal exemption from total income. Reducing the DCEs improves efficiency and increases national income because it allows for the same tax revenues to be raised with lower tax brackets. At the same time, reducing DCEs tends to increase the progressivity of the tax system, for any tax schedule, since higher income people tend to use more DCEs than do lower income people.[13]

The two main tools of recent tax reform proposals—flattening tax brackets and reducing DCEs—work in the same direction on efficiency, but in opposite directions on progressivity. While flattening the tax schedule increases efficiency (and national income) and *reduces* progressivity, reducing the DCEs also increases efficiency but it *increases* progressivity.

Perhaps, then, it is possible to use these tools together to reap the efficiency gains without major changes in progressivity. Hausman's study contains an example of how this could be done (see Table 2). In his analysis of different feasible flat-tax systems that raise equal revenue, Hausman estimates how the average tax rate for different income classes would be affected by a flat-tax system with no DCEs other than a personal exemption. Hausman finds that, in 1975, a flat-tax system with a personal exemption for each family of $1,000 or more reduces the average tax rate of *all* income classes compared to the actual average tax rates. Moreover, with a family

---

[13]According to data from the *Statistics of Income-1982* (Washington, DC: GPO, 1984), those taxpayers whose adjusted gross income (AGI) is in the $5,000 to $15,000 range have itemized deductions which amount to 7 to 8 percent of AGI, on average. Those with AGI in the $20,000 to $30,000 range take about 13 to 15 percent of their AGI in itemized deductions. And those with AGI of $40,000 or more take about 20 to 22 percent of their AGI in itemized deductions.

TABLE 2
FOUR REVENUE-NEUTRAL FLAT-TAX STRUCTURES

Exemption Level Per Family	Flat-tax Rate	Average Tax Rate at These Income Levels			
		$4,000 (7,720)	$8,000 (15,440)	$16,000 (30,880)	$24,000 (46,320)
$0	14.6%	14.6%	14.6%	14.6%	14.6%
$1,000 (1,930)	15.4	11.6	13.5	14.4	14.8
$2,000 (3,860)	16.9	8.5	12.7	14.8	15.5
$4,000 (7,720)	20.7	0.0	10.4	15.5	17.2
1975 Tax Code	Graduated brackets (14% - 70%)	11.9	14.7	17.3	18.8

These data are computed by J. Hausman in "Income and Payroll Tax Policy and Labor Supply," in *The Supply-Side Effects of Economic Policy*, ed. by L. Meyer, Federal Reserve Bank of St. Louis, 1981. The calculations are based on the 1975 federal income tax system. The income levels and the exemptions are in 1975 dollars while the numbers in parentheses represent what the income levels and the exemptions would be in 1984 dollars. The first column shows the different exemptions Hausman uses in his analysis. The second column shows the tax rate needed to maintain the same tax revenue as the personal exemption rises. Naturally, a higher tax rate is required as the personal exemption increases. The next four columns show the average tax rate for taxpayers in the four income levels.

exemption of $2,000 a flat-tax system would have been *more progressive* at lower-income and middle-income levels than the 1975 income tax system. However, even though every income class receives a reduction in its average tax rate, higher-income families receive a larger reduction in their average tax rate than lower-income families. Hausman's estimates suggest that it may be possible to flatten the tax schedule and simplify the tax code at the same time, so that all income groups reap at least some of the benefits of the gains in efficiency, and progressivity is retained.

But progressivity is only one of the areas of concern. Even if every income class gets a reduction in its average tax rate, still there may be winners and losers within each income class. If all the DCEs are wiped out and tax rates are reduced, those who rely on DCEs more than average may end up with an increase in their average tax rate. Furthermore, since many DCEs were added to the tax code presumably to further certain social goals, the direct beneficiaries of those goals are likely to become financially worse off. And people who have organized their finances mindful of the DCEs—for example, by buying a house or making certain types of investments—are concerned that the elimination of DCEs will make them financially worse off. Three examples help illustrate some of these concerns about the effects of flattening tax brackets and simplifying the tax code.[14]

Homeowners. Many homeowners are concerned that if the deductions for interest payments and property taxes are eliminated, their tax bills will rise regardless of which income class they are in. But several other factors might offset the loss of the interest deduction. For example, all the tax reform proposals provide a larger personal exemption. Also, since homeowners tend to have higher than average incomes, they would pay a lower tax rate on their income. In addition, the tax reform may well reduce interest rates, thereby reducing the burden of mortgage payments on homeowners.[15] Such a reduction in interest rates at least partially would offset the loss due to the elimination of the interest deduction, though it is not clear by how much interest

rates might fall as a result of tax reform. Finally, homeowners are concerned that tax reform would lower the value of their homes. If the after-tax mortgage costs become substantially higher, house prices are likely to fall even if homeowners end up with at least as much after-tax income. But such a fall in house prices could be reversed as people demand more housing when the reductions in inefficiencies result in more income. Thus, no one is quite sure whether the benefits would outweigh the losses for homeowners.

Charitable Deductions. The government allows donations to nonprofit organizations engaged in charitable, educational, religious, or cultural activities to be deducted from taxable income. The rationale for allowing such deductions is to reduce the cost to the taxpayer of making such beneficial donations, and thereby to stimulate charitable donations. A number of economic studies have verified the stimulating effect of this deduction. Therefore, people who in one way or another benefit from the activities of these institutions are likely to become worse off if the deduction is eliminated, because this will have a depressing effect on charitable donations. However, the depressing effect of eliminating the deduction for donations will be offset to some extent by the rise in incomes following the adoption of a flat-tax system.

State and Local Taxes. Many of the proposals—including the Treasury proposal—plan to eliminate the federal deductibility of state and local taxes. Many state and local government officials have expressed grave concern and opposition to the elimination of this deduction. They are concerned that if state and local taxes are no longer deductible, these taxes will be more costly to the taxpayers. As a result, they fear that the taxpayers may demand state and local tax reductions, or even relocate to states or municipalities with lower tax rates.

The loss of the deduction of state and local taxes will hit the higher-income taxpayers in high-tax states like New York harder than it will hit the higher-income taxpayers in low-tax states like Mississippi. (Lower-income taxpayers usually do not itemize their deductions, so the

---

[14]See "Wealth Changes and the Flat Rate Tax," by Robert Tannenwald, *New England Economic Review,* (January/February, 1983), pp. 5-17, for a more detailed description of the redistributional issues involved and what might be done to mitigate them.

[15]Eliminating the personal interest deduction increases the after-tax cost of borrowing which decreases demand for

it. This decrease in demand in turn tends to lower interest rates. If lowering the tax brackets elicits more saving, the interest rate will fall some more. And corporate tax reform—such as eliminating the corporate interest deduction—could make interest rates fall by enough to offset the loss of the personal interest deduction for homeowners.

loss of this deduction would not affect them much.) The loss of the deduction to high-income taxpayers in the high-tax states would be at least partially offset by the lowering of the top tax brackets. This lowering of the top brackets would benefit high-tax states more since the citizens in high-tax states also tend to have higher than average incomes. To the extent that the offset is only partial, the tax burden on high-income families in high-tax states and cities will be higher following adoption of a flat-tax system. Furthermore, to the extent that the loss of deductibility leads to state and local tax revenue reductions, the services provided to residents may decline. People who use state and local government services more intensively would be affected adversely by such changes.

CONCLUSION

Tax reform proposals which advocate flattening the tax schedule and simplifying the tax code have become the center of controversy. The rationales for these proposals are that they increase labor supply (especially among higher-paid workers and secondary workers), encourage saving, reduce the incentive to escape taxes via tax evasion or tax avoidance, and reduce the cost of administering and complying with the tax code. Recent economic studies suggest that the efficiency gains could be significant.

Many are concerned that flattening the tax schedule and simplifying the tax code would injure the poor, abandon progressivity, and benefit only very high-income families. But converting to a flat-rate income tax need not entail abandoning progressivity, since, by varying the personal exemption, it is possible to make even a flat-tax system approximately as progressive as the current system. And some recent economic estimates indicate that if the tax code is simplified and if the personal exemption and the tax rate are chosen appropriately, not only will national income be larger, but the increase in national income will be distributed in a way that makes every income group better off.

Even if it is possible to make every income group better off, major changes in the tax system will create winners and losers within each income group, because people's financial well-being depends in varying degrees on their ability to use the deductions, credits and exclusions provided for in the current tax code. Homeowners are concerned that their after-tax housing costs may rise, and that housing prices may fall. Charitable institutions and their constituencies are concerned that there will be a major decline in charitable donations. And state and local governments worry that state and local taxes will become more expensive to their taxpayers, forcing major adjustments in their operations.

Though some of the impact of distributional effects of tax reform may be cushioned by the resulting overall gain in income, at this point no one knows precisely how the distribution of income and wealth will change. But that there is a trade-off is clear. The more the tax brackets are flattened and the more the tax code is simplified, the larger the gain in efficiency and in national income—but also the greater the chance that income and wealth distribution will change, and the greater the uncertainty about how they will change. This trade-off is at the heart of the controversy about any tax reform proposals.

CURRENT TAX PROPOSALS

There are a number of flat-tax proposals under active consideration: the Administration proposal; the FAST—"Fair and Simple Tax"—proposed by Congressman Jack Kemp and Senator Robert Kasten; the "Fair Tax" proposed by Congressman Richard Gephardt and Senator William Bradley; and Senator Dennis DeConcini's flat-tax proposal, which implements the proposal advanced by economist Robert Hall and Alvin Rabushka.[a] All four of these proposals raise the personal exemption, flatten and lower tax

	Tax Rates	Personal Exemptions:		Zero Bracket Amount:			Maximum Income for Family of 4 to Pay No Taxes
		Taxpayer and Spouse	Dependent	Single Persons	Heads of Households	Married Couples	
Current Tax Code	11-50%	$1,080[1]	$1,080	$2,480	$2,480	$3,670	$8,070
Administration	15, 25, 35%	2,000	2,000	2,900	3,600	4,000	12,000
Bradley-Gephardt	14, 26, 30%	1,600	1,000	3,000	3,000	6,000	11,200
Kemp-Kasten	24%[2]	2,000	2,000	2,600	2,700	3,300	14,125
DeConcini	19%	4,500	1,800	NONE			12,600

[1]These are the personal exemptions and standard deductions for 1986 under current law, as estimated by the Treasury Department.

[2]The Kemp-Kasten bill allows a deduction of 20 percent of wage income below the FICA ceiling ($41,700 in 1986), but adds in an extra 20 percent of income above the ceiling. Effectively, there are two marginal tax rates: 19 percent below $41,700 and 29 percent above it.

brackets, and simplify the tax code, but they differ in degree. All these proposals are designed to raise the same amount of revenue as does the current tax law under the assumption that economic behavior (for example, labor supply and savings) *will not change* in response to the tax reform. They all modify corporate taxation also, but that issue goes beyond the scope of the current article.

[a]Robert Hall and Alvin Rabushka, *The Flat Tax* (Stanford, CA: Hoover Institution Press, 1985).

Capital Gains Treatment	Major Deductions Kept	Major Deductions Eliminated	Indexation of Tax Brackets
60% exclusion from tax base; distinction made between short and long term gains; no indexation of basis, capital losses deductible up to $3,000 against ordinary income.			YES
50% exclusion; capital losses deductible up to $3,000; depreciable assets not eligible for the exclusion; no indexation prior to 1991.	Mortgage interest on primary residence plus other interest up to $5,000 over investment income, charitable contributions, IRAs, KEOGH accounts, medical expenses (over 5% of AGI), exemption of municipal bond interest, employee business expenses, casualty losses.	Income averaging, all state and local taxes, secondary-worker deduction, dividend exclusion	YES
Exclusion eliminated; capital gains treated as ordinary income; no indexation of basis; capital losses deductible up to $3,000 for a married couple.	Mortgage interest and personal interest up to the amount of passive investment income,[3] real-estate taxes, state and local income taxes, charitable contributions, IRAs, KEOGH accounts medical expenses (over 10% of AGI), mortgage interest exemption of municipal bond interest, employee business expenses.	Income averaging, non-mortgage interest over investment income, secondary-worker deduction, dividend exclusion.	NO
Investors may choose to: (1) treat capital gains as ordinary income with the basis indexed to the price level; or (2) exclude 40% of gains from taxation, with no indexation. subject to 6 month holding period; capital loss deductible up to $3,000 against ordinary income.	Real-estate taxes, charitable contributions, IRAs, KEOGH accounts, medical expenses (over 10% of AGI), mortgage and educational loan interest, employee business expenses.	Income averaging, all non-mortgage, non-educational interest, secondary-worker deduction, dividend exclusion, state and local income taxes.	YES
Capital gains, dividends, and interest not taxed at the personal level; all capital income is taxed at the business level.	NONE	ALL	YES

[3]The Bradley-Gephardt bill only allows deductions to be charged against the 14 percent rate, so the deductions are, in reality, tax credits equal to 14 percent of the amount of the deductions. Mortgage interest in excess of the amount of passive investment income is treated as a tax credit at the 14 percent rate, but all interest expenses are fully deductible against passive investment income.

Who Needs This Sort of Tax Reform Anyway?

President Reagan last week sent his budget to Congress for the fiscal year starting Oct. 1. The numbers indicated that things are still in pretty much of a mess. So what do you suppose some leading U.S. senators are doing this week? Arguing about how tò "reform" the tax law.

One ground rule of this reform game is that the resulting bill be "revenue-neutral," raising not a penny of additional revenue to shrink those big deficit numbers that came out last week. The legislators are supposed to somehow juggle existing revenue and spending around to produce a bill that will be both less complex and more equitable. Don't hold your breath.

The House of Representatives, of course, went through exactly the same ex-

Speaking of Business

by Lindley H. Clark Jr.

ercise last year. President Reagan didn't like the result very much, but he felt that he had to grit his teeth and urge House Republicans to vote for it. Without such a shove from the president the bill presumably would have gone down to defeat, and Congress might have decided simply to forget the whole silly exercise.

The main thing the president wanted was lower tax rates for individuals, beginning with a maximum rate of 35%, compared with the present 50%. Whether lower tax rates are more equitable or not, they surely do help to persuade the public that this is sound legislation.

The House didn't quite achieve Mr. Reagan's objective. The top rate under the House bill would be 38%, not 35%. But they got the maximum rate down to that level in pretty much the way that the administration's tax experts had proposed: by socking it to the corporations.

In 1981 the Reagan administration reasoned that cutting individual tax rates would encourage savings and investment. But the administration was broad-minded enough to figure that businessmen needed some incentive to pour more money into plants and equipment. Business got a variety of tax incentives to invest.

The incentives probably were a little overdone. They were passed in a year when the inflation rate was only beginning its fall from double-digit levels. Congress figured that some additional incentive was needed to offset the inflation. Actually the rate of price rise continued to diminish, so there may be some reason to take away part of the 1981 goodies.

In practice, Congress took almost all of

them away. One Washington specialist was asked how the administration and Congress decided to do this. "They knew what they wanted to do for individuals, and they knew what it would cost," he replied. "So they tagged the corporations with the cost."

In testimony before the Senate Finance Committee, Murray L. Weidenbaum, the first chairman of President Reagan's Council of Economic Advisers, summed up the House bill this way:

"It would make it more difficult for American firms to compete, even as international competition is growing more fierce. The numerous blows to savings, investment and research and development would slow down the modernization of American plants.

"Corporate taxes would be raised by about $140 billion over the next four years, further straining our ability to compete. Many of the companies hardest hit by imports—those in capital-intensive heavy industry—would have their tax burdens increased most substantially. This is an unusual switch from the old proposition that you don't kick a man when he's down.

"The proposed changes in bank taxation would come at a time when those institutions are wrestling with the difficult debt problems of the private sector. For example, deductions for bad-debt reserves are eliminated, except for relatively small banks. Finally, the claim of tax simplification violates any truth in labeling law."

The House measure actually adds complications to the tax law. Moreover, it would make so many changes in existing law that it would create a great deal of new business for tax lawyers and accountants, at least until the public got adjusted to the new rules of the game.

To be sure, Mr. Reagan has said that he would not sign a tax bill if the final product looked like the House version. So one of the certainties that the Senate must deal with is that its version must be different. It's likely to be different, all right, but the early sparring doesn't indicate that it's likely to be a lot better.

Very early the Senate Finance Committee got into the matter of deductions for state and local taxes on sales, personal property, income and real estate. The House had floundered around in that area for quite a while, too, and finally retained all the deductions.

One trouble is that those deductions cost a fair amount of revenue. That's one reason why the House couldn't get the top income tax rate any lower than 38%. Also, the deductions are defended by some states as though they were apple pie and

motherhood. Some high-income-tax states reason, possibly correctly, that they would lose some people and some businesses if their high income levies no longer could be deducted on federal returns.

Well, Sen. Bob Packwood, chairman of the Finance Committee, knows that politics is the art of compromise. He suggested that the Senate might end the deduction of sales and personal property taxes but keep the deduction for income and real estate taxes. At last report the suggested compromise hardly pleased anyone. Some senators were unkind enough to point out that Sen. Packwood's home state of Oregon has neither a sales nor a personal property tax, so the finance committee chairman really wouldn't be giving up anything.

Several senators were upset because the House bill would take away tax breaks for oil, timber and other natural resources. The whole exercise looks more like smoke-filled-room politics than high-minded reform.

Several senators, convinced that the budget deficits are much more important than this so-called reform, are actually proposing President Reagan's no-no, tax increases. A few of them think the president eventually will accept some increases to get what he wants otherwise, but no one can be sure.

There are, of course, lots of things wrong with the present tax law. Just when investment should be a high priority, the law encourages individuals to borrow and spend by allowing deduction of interest payments. Real estate taxes on first homes may be politically untouchable, but payments on second and third homes shouldn't be.

Real simplification and reduced rates could wipe out a lot of the special provisions for both individuals and businesses; many of these were put in to offset the high rates. Actually overhauling the tax law in an intelligent way would take time, perhaps a lot of time. Mr. Weidenbaum suggests that congressional and Treasury staffs begin a careful review of the tax law while Congress and the administration continue to struggle to get the budget deficits down. The benefits and costs of each provision, present or proposed, could be carefully weighed.

Tax reform is an important objective, but it won't sink the republic if we don't get it this year or even next. The kind of tax reform that the House passed last year, and that the Senate seems likely to pass this year, on the other hand, could do a great deal of damage.

Yes, Tax Reform, But Not Very Much

By WILLIAM NORDHAUS

TAX reform: The words conjure up the image of a modern-day Sisyphus, forever condemned to push weighty proposals up the hill, only to see hordes of well-heeled, oil company lobbyists hurl the nuggets back down to the Brookings Institution from which they were launched.

In defiance of the laws of political gravity, President Reagan put his shoulder to the task of tax reform. The purposes of the President's proposal were two: to introduce a system with as broad a tax base as possible; and to reduce as much as possible marginal tax rates.

After months of labor, the House Ways and Means Committee has completed its drafting. What is the outcome? Has tax reform been advanced by the Committee? Or has the Committee unwittingly given comfort to the tax deformers?

At the outset, note that the Committee proposal follows the grand design of the President's plan. Mr. Reagan's proposal greased the skids of reform by raising revenues from corporations (mainly by trimming investment incentives like the investment tax credit), and using these revenues to reduce personal taxes. The bill adopts this philosophy. In addition, the bill accepts many of the President's individual proposals, ranging from taxing unemployment compensation to curbing the shifting of income within families.

Where has the Committee left its mark? It has corralled support by retaining certain popular tax preferences (like deductibility of state and local taxes and of mortgage interest on second homes). Moreover, in a kick to the President's shins, the House Democrats raised the top tax rate from 35 percent to 38 percent.

But the House changes are only small wrinkles on a garment fashioned by the Administration. For better or for worse, most of the credit or blame for the House bill lies on the President's shoulders.

Will the bill enhance the efficient operation of the economy? Will it lead to more saving and swifter economic growth? How will tax reform affect the budget and trade deficits?

William Nordhaus, professor of economics at Yale University, struggled in vain for tax changes as a member of the President's Council of Economc Advisers during the Carter Administration.

Notwithstanding the public cries of alarum or hosanna, voices loudly amplified in the service of advocacy, the tax bill will have but a modest economic impact in coming years. Just as the 1981 supply-side tax cuts failed to lift personal saving, raise revenues or produce an outpouring of innovation—similarly, the 1985 reforms will add little to the tax code's simplicity or perceived fairness.

What will be the impact on the overall efficiency of resource use in our economy? The proposal takes significant steps toward efficiency, tending to equalize the treatment of lightly taxed and heavily taxed activities.

For example, under current law, the tax on investments in tractors is 8 percent, while the tax on investments in farm structures is 39 percent. This senseless discrepancy promotes wasteful investment patterns. The current bill would tend to align tax rates across such different investments.

In addition, the bill provides a modest reduction in the marginal tax rates faced by households, with the most sizable reduction occurring at high incomes.

Taken as a whole, these reforms will provide a small fillip to the nation's productivity. Studies indicate that the gains from such reforms are in the order of one-tenth of 1 percent of national output — worth harvesting, but unlikely to ignite an explosion of entrepreneurial activities.

The major drawback of the tax plan is its impact on saving and investment. By curbing investment incentives, raising corporate taxes and lowering personal taxes, the plan will tend to depress the already-dreary national savings rate.

How will this occur? First, according to Committee staff estimates, the bill raises corporation taxes, and lowers personal taxes, by $25.2 billion per year over the next five years (the figure for the President's proposal is $24.5 billion per year). This boost to disposable personal income will increase personal consumption outlays by a sizable fraction of the $25 billion — say $20 billion, for illustrative purposes.

AS LONG as the Federal Reserve in practice targets inflation and unemployment, this $20 billion increase in consumption will increase total spending and require the Fed to raise interest rates, thereby "crowding out" interest-sensitive spending on housing, business investment and consumer durables. High interest rates may in addition keep the dollar and the trade deficit higher longer than otherwise. On balance, the change will lower the national saving and investment rate by as much as one-half percentage point.

Clearly, a lower national savings rate is as welcome as a Thanksgiving ice storm. Yet the current tax bill will inexorably reinforce the long-term trend toward national profligacy.

The harm done to saving reminds us that the tax-reform effort ignores today's central concern — the Federal budget deficit. Is Washington simply rearranging deck chairs on the Titanic as the fiscal iceberg looms dead ahead? Or are these separate issues?

At first blush, the deficit might appear a severable issue. On further thought, perhaps not. If either the Gramm-Rudman budget-balancing bill or good sense prevail, the nation will inevitably need to raise taxes in coming years. Has the tax-reform bill depleted the easy sources of raising revenues? Will tax increases of future years simply undo today's progress toward a more efficient tax system? I think yes on both counts. Surely, orderly decision-making would include a modest tax increase along with the tax reform.

What is the net impact of the House bill? In adding up the pluses and minuses, I believe the improvements in the tax system outweigh the costs to saving and deficit reduction. But the Senate should attempt to correct the flaws in the House bill.

First, the Senate should resist the temptation to cut personal taxes further at the expense of corporations. Indeed, the increase in corporate taxes should be pared as much as possible to protect our dwindling savings rate.

Second, the Senate should attack important pro-consumption provisions — deductibility of interest, of entertainment and other phony business expenses, and of fringe benefits like health and life insurance. Moreover, the Senate should not fall prey to affected industries — oil, timber, banks—who cry "wolf" at every hint of equal tax treatment.

Finally, the Senate should tilt toward raising rather than reducing revenues; higher taxes today will reduce needed tax hikes tomorrow.

Jean Baptiste Colbert, the 17th Century French statesman, once remarked that raising taxes is like plucking a goose — you want the maximum number of feathers with the minimum amount of hiss. How remarkable it is that a tax bill with so many worthy provisions provokes so few hisses — and these mostly from the plump waddlers destined to lose their fair share of feathers. The President and Congress should ignore the hisses of the plump in designing a tax code for the entire flock. ■

Tax Reform: Harmful if Passed

By Martin Feldstein

As the Senate Finance Committee begins its deliberations on tax reform, one thing should be easy for the otherwise divided senators to agree on: The bill passed by the House is bad tax policy and deserves to be scrapped. Even with the changes that the president has requested, the House plan would take our tax laws in the wrong direction.

The House bill, in addition to all of the sweetheart special provisions that were added to woo individual congressmen and their key constituents, is bad tax policy for four fundamental reasons:

● It would hurt our nation's economic performance. The immediate effect of its sharp reduction in the incentive to invest would likely be to push the economy into recession. Over the longer term, the reduced level of investment in plant and equipment would slow the growth of real incomes and reduce the international competitiveness of U.S. industry.

● It is not tax reform. The original goal of a fundamental reform to broaden the personal tax base and reduce tax rates has been abandoned. All of the major tax-code provisions targeted by tax reformers for so long—the deduction for interest on home mortgages and consumer loans, the exclusion of employer-paid health insurance premiums and other fringe benefits, and the deduction of state and local tax payments—have now been judged to be either socially desirable or politically untouchable. What remains is not tax reform but a tax reshuffle that would raise corporate taxes by about 30% in the near term and more than 50% by the 1990s.

Two Sets of Returns

● It is not tax simplification. For most taxpayers, there would be no change in tax reporting requirements. But many upper-income taxpayers would have to prepare two sets of tax returns—one return for the regular income tax and another for the greatly expanded minimum tax.

● It is the wrong way to help low-income taxpayers. An across-the-board increase in the personal exemption is an extremely costly and inefficient way of reducing the tax burden on low-income families. The president's proposal would be even more costly than the House plan, raising the cost of the personal exemption by $48 billion a year by 1990.

It would be best if the Senate could drop the whole idea of major tax reform in 1986. The nation would be better served if Congress concentrated on deficit reduction and passed only a modest tax bill that tightened the minimum corporate tax and took poor working families off the tax rolls by an expanded earned-income credit.

But if a more grandiose tax bill is politically inevitable, the Senate should be guided by these four suggestions:

● Target the change in the personal exemption. Taking the poor off the tax rolls can be done at a small fraction of the $40 billion-plus annual cost of the administration's plan by targeting the increased exemption. Raising the personal exemption to $2,000 only for taxpayers in the new 15% bracket and to $1,200 in the 25% bracket would cut the revenue cost in half—saving more than $20 billion a year. The tax reduction could further be targeted more effectively to families by increasing the exemption only for dependent children.

● Preserve the deduction for state and local taxes. The most convincing argument for eliminating the deduction has been that doing so would raise more than $30 billion a year in additional federal revenue that could be used to reduce personal tax rates. Unfortunately, that tempting arithmetic is based on a false premise. If the current deduction were eliminated, state and local governments would be pressured by voters to rely more heavily on taxes and fees paid by businesses. The Treasury could lose more because of the resulting increase in deductions by businesses than it gains by eliminating the personal deduction.

Eliminating only the sales-tax deduction would also produce much less revenue than traditional calculations suggest and might also easily lose revenue. States and localities that now use sales taxes would be under substantial political pressure to shift to income taxes or property taxes that lo-

Board of Contributors

Those eager to raise taxes on corporations to finance a cut in personal taxes should know that the 1982 and 1984 tax bills rescinded almost all of the business tax cuts enacted in 1981.

cal residents could deduct from their federal income tax. Since a larger share of those taxes would be paid by individuals who itemize and who are in relatively high tax brackets, the Treasury might end up losing more revenue from these increased deductions than it gained from eliminating the deduction for sales taxes.

● Maintain the incentive to invest. The administration's proposal and, even more so, the bill passed by the House would substantially reduce the incentive to invest in productive plant and equipment. They would divert a larger share of our nation's scarce capital into shopping centers, office buildings, vacation homes and larger

houses for upper-income taxpayers. This reshuffle of investment incentives would hurt the economy in both the near term and the more distant future.

Direct experience and analytic studies indicate that the investment tax credit is a particularly powerful incentive. The ITC is also more cost-effective than other tax changes as a way of stimulating investment because it immediately reduces the out-of-pocket cost of investing in new equipment.

Eliminating the ITC and using the resulting revenue to cut the corporate tax rate or increase depreciation allowances would have the net effect of depressing investment.

However, if the ITC is to be eliminated, depreciation rules should be modified to maintain as much as possible of the current incentive to invest. The administration's proposal to index depreciation is relatively cost-effective and deserves to be enacted. But even with this indexing, the administration's proposed depreciation lives should be shortened in order to maintain current incentives.

Those who are eager to raise taxes on corporations to finance a cut in personal taxes should bear in mind that the combination of the 1982 and 1984 tax bills rescinded virtually all of the business tax cuts enacted in 1981, leaving projected 1988 corporate tax payments only $4 billion below what they would have been if there had been no tax legislation beween 1981 and 1985. By contrast, 1988 personal taxes will be lower by $191 billion. This record hardly justifies a major hike in corporate taxes to finance another cut in personal taxes.

● Raise revenue. Some new revenue will be needed to finance the desirable changes in the personal income tax: reducing the tax burden on low-income families and lowering the high marginal tax rates. Even more revenue will be needed to achieve the important budget goals of a $144 billion deficit in fiscal 1987 and lower deficits in future years. Although these deficit reductions cannot be responsibly achieved without substantial spending cuts as well, the public now recognizes by a 2-to-1 margin that taxes will also have to be raised if the deficit is to be brought down.

The decline of more than 20 cents a gallon in the price of crude oil provides the most logical candiate for a revenue increase. A 15-cent to 20-cent increase in the gasoline tax would raise $15 billion a year. Supplementing this with a modest $3-a-barrel tax on imported oil would yield at least an additional $5 billion while helping to offset the adverse effect that the combination of the oil-price drop and the hike in the gasoline tax would otherwise have on U.S. oil producers, oil-service firms, and banks with loans to these companies.

Value-Added Tax

Tax indexing should be changed to adjust tax brackets only for the excess of inflation over 3%. Shrinking the automatic future tax reductions in this way would not violate the president's opposition to a tax hike, but by 1991 it would save about $55 billion a year in revenue. A parallel 3% floor on the indexing of various benefit programs, including Social Security, could produce another $55 billion a year by 1991. Yet both taxpayers and benefit recipients would be protected completely against the adverse effects of inflation above 3%.

Although a value-added tax has much appeal, there are also many serious problems. Since the combination of an energy tax that recaptures only part of the recent decline in the price of oil and a modest 3% floor on future indexed tax reductions could together raise $75 billion a year by 1991 while targeting the increase in the personal exemption could yield an additional $25 billion, I believe it is premature to think about a value-added tax.

In short, if we must have a tax overhaul this year the Senate should reject both the House's anti-investment plans and the president's request to squander more than $40 billion a year on an indiscriminate doubling of the personal exemption. While a minimum tax on all corporations would increase both fairness and revenues, the tax incentive for investment in plant and equipment should be strengthened by improved and indexed depreciation rules. The tax burden on the poor should be eliminated by carefully targeted measures. Finally, the Senate should remember that the fundamental responsibility of the tax system is to raise enough money to pay the government's bills.

Mr. Feldstein, past chairman of the president's Council of Economic Advisers, is a professor of economics at Harvard.

43

Proposal for an Anti-Inflation Package

Sidney Weintraub

A spillover from Proposition 13 in California has been a revival of the old-time religion of slashing government expenditures and banishing inflation from the land. This is a monstrous delusion. Incomes policy will be imperative even under Spartan budgets.

Suppose we succumbed to the present fervor for curtailing government spending? With current pay trends, any prospective cutback would be dwarfed in a short time by the income bulge. Economy-wide, employee compensation is running about $1.3 trillion per annum. An 8 percent annual pay hike will add $100 billion. At 10 percent the figure is $130 billion. In five years the pay balloon will compound to $600-$800 billion—about half the current aggregate and well above projected federal outlays of $500 billion for fiscal 1979.

Support has materialized for a tax-based incomes policy (TIP), as originally proposed by Dr. Henry Wallich and myself, and for the variants of Drs. Okun and Seidman. Public awareness of the ideas has widened. In the United Kingdom a version of the concept is on the parliamentary docket for enactment.

On the premise that the "carrot" and the "stick" will both influence conduct, the following package reflects my own concept of the proper legislative design for TIP.

1. *Amend the Davis-Bacon Act*. According to law, prevailing wages must be paid on current government or government-assisted construction. The government is thus already operating an incomes policy. Labor and business now lobby for contracts which create jobs, and shortly thereafter there are strikes for higher pay, involving raids on the public purse. A new clause, however, can require that, over the life of the contract, average pay increases for all personnel are not to exceed 5 percent per annum.

A construction authorization incomes policy (CAIP), should help hold the line on construction excesses. Penalties can include disallowing overpayments on the corporate income tax form, and remanding sums equal to the excess above 5 percent to the government.

2. *Amend government procurement contracts*. CAIP can be applied to government procurement generally, especially to defense contracts, where pay increases are paid for by the public.

3. *Reduce personal income taxes*. Reduce the personal income tax by a credit of 2 percent on employee compensation, with a minimum tax reduction of $200 and a maximum of $300 on all incomes rising by 5 percent or less per annum. This borrows from the original Okun proposal. Largest percentage benefits would redound to wage earners' advantage and help induce wage restraint.

4. *The (modified) Wallich-Weintraub TIP*. All business firms employing 500 or more employees or having an annual wage and salary bill of five million or more, are subject to the following tax provisos:

a. For average employee wages that increase by not less than 3 percent nor more than 5 percent per annum, the firm's tax rate will be lowered by (at least) 2 percent below the standard corporate tax rate.

b. If the average annual pay increase exceeds 5 percent, the firm will be subject to progressive penalty tax rates.

Essentially, (b) is the original Wallich-Weintraub TIP. Proviso (a) is inserted (from Dr. Seidman) with the 3 percent floor intended to preclude greater rewards to firms that beat down pay levels; it dispels any possible allegation that TIP is a plan to "create slave labor." It should also encourage pay moderation to foster price stability. Restriction to large firms should render the proposal administratively feasible. Others may prefer to include only firms that are even larger in size.

5. *TIP-CAP: A productivity bonus*. Firms reporting average value-added per employee surpassing the economywide 2-3 percent trend of the past might be

granted a pay prerogative above the 5 percent norm. Calculations would have to be made for average product corrected for price level inflation (CAP, or Corrected Average Product). This would be a bit more complicated than TIP calculations, but would involve only simple subtractions (of cost of materials from sales receipts) and applying standard price level indexes as a deflator.

This would be a productivity bonus. Perhaps one-third of the superior productivity increase above 6 percent might be added to the 5 percent standard increase. Not all of the productivity gain should be commanded by employees, however, for the firms should be motivated to reduce prices.

6. *TIP supplements.* Various supplements can be attached to TIP-CAP to assure compliance. For example, certain firms might be in cash-flow financial straits if their 5 percent settlement offer were rejected by labor, resulting in a strike. Such firms might be cleared for a government-guaranteed loan to meet fixed charges. Clearly, loan availability would have to be monitored to prevent collusion.

Labor, in rejecting a settlement at 5 percent (or a trifle more) might be subject to penalties ranging from mild to stringent, depending on strike duration and the (vague) national interest. Labor specialists should promote this discussion.

7. *Amending the anti-trust laws.* To allay objections that prices are absolved from sanctions, the Federal Trade Commission (FTC) might be mandated to report quarterly on trends and profit margins, especially among the 2,000 largest firms, measured in terms of sales or employment.

Firms reporting extra productivity improvement should be expected to lower prices. Where there is evidence that they are not doing so, the FTC might be empowered to report and to seek remedial policies.

Profit margins have been declining. Until contrary evidence emerges, further action can be deferred.

8. *Government employees.* Average pay increases for federal employees would be limited to 5 percent per annum, with corrections every two or three years if the private sector trend exceeds this norm. State and local employees would be brought under the same 5 percent tent through the leverage of federal grants or other federal aid programs.

Conclusions

These appear to be the essential legislative provisos to accomplish a firmer match-up of money, wage and salary trends to the productivity norms. None of them does violence to the market economy; mostly, they invoke the tax laws and, confining them to the largest firms, they spell only minor complications. They are modest by way of intervention in the market system. If successful, they ought to capture the big prize of full employment without inflation. Over the past decade a workable policy of price level stabilization would have enhanced GNP by $50 to $150 billion per annum. Inflation drift will inflict equal or greater annual losses in the future.

Chancellor of the Exchequer Healey, in the United Kingdom, is reported to advocate a 5 percent ceiling on annual pay hikes. Sanctions involve denying government loans to firms that puncture the norm, and refraining from government purchases from violators.

The Healey program is a cousin of TIP, more attuned to the widespread nationalization of industry and capital market structure in the United Kingdom. The Healey program, if enacted, should practically subdue their rapid inflation. The recent 10 percent inflation rate under 10 percent pay hikes speaks volumes compared to the 25 percent rates under the 25 percent pay explosion of recent memory. England has learned some concrete incomes policy lessons from its hard knocks. We should not wait for catastrophic price bursts to complete our own education.

44

Can Tax-Based Incomes Policies Work?

As inflation has grown more and more serious, it has become fashionable to talk about a tax-based incomes policy (TIP) as a possible device to moderate it. I am very sympathetic to the idea of an incomes policy, but I find it difficult to see how TIP can be implemented. The following are the most difficult problems, as I view them. (The issues are thoroughly explored in *Curing Chronic Inflation*, Arthur M. Okun and George L. Perry, eds., Brookings Institution, 1978.)

Coverage. About 13 million firms filed federal tax returns in 1975, including 10.9 million sole proprietorships, 1.1 million partnerships, and 2.0 million corporations. In addition, there were 0.5 million returns of nonprofit organizations and over 78,000 governmental units. Most of the business firms have no employees, many report no net income, and only a relatively small number of large businesses keep personnel records. Yet, if a tax penalty (for firms that grant too high a wage increase) or a tax subsidy (for firms that hold wage increases down) is to be designed, the law must be explicit about how every one of these units is to be treated.

A penalty would be easier to administer than a subsidy, because it could be limited to large firms. But as I shall indicate below, I am not persuaded that it is feasible to measure average wage changes for all economic units in a manner that would be satisfactory for a tax-based wage penalty or subsidy.

As for the subsidy approach, I assume that we would not ask the average farmer, or the average corner drugstore owner, or most self-employed professionals who have a few employees, to report manhours on a tax return. Moreover, many firms with only a few employees might be denied a subsidy if they happened to shift to higher-paid workers. To avoid the problems that the small firms would have, the wage subsidy would probably be given to all employees in such establishments and to the owners as well. This is not fatal for the wage subsidy plan on administrative grounds, but it would mean that a substantial fraction, if not a majority, of all workers would get the subsidy whether they conformed with the wage guideline or not.

The economic unit. The unit for tax accounting purposes is a legal entity which, in our complex economy, often bears little relationship to the unit which enters into wage bargains with its employees. Large corporations generally file consolidated returns that include the operating results of many, but not necessarily all, of their subsidiaries. So far as wages are concerned, the branches or subsidiaries of a large firm in this country often bear no relationship to one another or to the parent firm. Accordingly, the rules would have to be flexible enough to permit the unit of calculation to be relevant to the wage-setting process. Under wage controls, the business firms themselves made this decision and I assume the control agency could modify the decision if it was deemed necessary. But for purposes of a wage subsidy or penalty, definite rules would have to be set out either in the legislation or in the regulations so that labor and management knew exactly what wage bargains they were dealing with. However, I am not aware of any usable guides to the writing of such rules.

It would be necessary to prescribe other rules to make inter-year wage comparisons for new firms, mergers, spinoffs, sales of facilities, changes in product mix, and other types of abnormal situations in which the wage data would not accurately reflect changes in average wages. This is what is referred to in tax language as "the excess profits tax problem": that is, the problem of estimating the tax base when it depends upon events and conditions in two or more adjacent years. The decisions made for the excess profits taxes in the United States were the subject of extensive and time-consuming litigation every time the tax was used, and no one on the government or the business side was ever satisfied. I can imagine a set of arbitrary rules that economists or tax administrators might agree to, but Congress would find it difficult to accept such rules. (One example: it has been suggested that, for new firms, a base year wage structure might be constructed from averages for other firms in the same industry. But the only data of this type that do exist are those of the Bureau of Labor Statistics and they could not possibly be applied to a particular firm.) In the end, the legislation would be complex and, like the excess profits tax, would impose unforeseen costs on business which would lead to further legislation and litigation to moderate those costs.

Timing of penalty or subsidy. From an administrative or compliance standpoint, it would be much easier to impose a penalty or provide a subsidy after the end of the accounting period. If the proposal is for a penalty based on profits, it should be possible to rely on the business firm to take the penalty into account in its wage decisions.

Just the opposite is true for a subsidy to workers accepting a wage increase below the guideline percentage. To appeal to workers to accept the constraint, the subsidy must be prospective and must be incorporated into the current tax withholding tables so that the workers will have immediate tangible evidence that their disposable income will not be impaired by the policy. (Two sets of withholding tables would be required, but this is only a minor complication compared to the others.)

The basic problem is that labor and management would find it extremely difficult to incorporate a prospective subsidy into their wage bargaining and, incidentally, to come to an agreement in a few weeks before the beginning of each year. Unless the bargaining unit were coterminous with the unit for determining the subsidy, no worker or group of workers would know whether the deal they made would actually trigger the subsidy until negotiations were completed with the other bargaining units in the same firm. Management would have the same problems: how could it be sure that the construction workers would accept a wage increase that, together with the agreement with coal miners, would trigger a subsidy to both groups?

I conclude that a retrospective penalty on profits based on wage changes is feasible. For prospective subsidies to workers, there are numerous pitfalls and I frankly do not see how they can be overcome to the satisfaction of labor and management.

Prices. The original tax-based incomes policies were to increase profits taxes of firms with excessive wage increases, so that prices were not involved at all. Others have suggested that, to be even-handed, it would be necessary to provide penalties against firms with above-average price increases. Unfortunately, any kind of tax penalty or subsidy that depends upon a change in average prices of particular firms is simply impractical. All the problems of constructing price indexes would emerge—treatment of new products, quality change, measurement of costs to be passed through, etc.—and there is really no solution to most of them. I leave it to the reader to judge whether a tax-based incomes policy can be applied to wages and not to prices.

Controls versus tax-based incomes policies. I believe it is not productive to argue whether tax-based incomes policies are another form of controls or not. The question is which approach is feasible, and what are their relative costs.

It is true that a tax-based incomes policy can be disregarded by any firm and its workers if they wish. But the rules and regulations must be written so that all economic units in the country understand them and make their decisions accordingly. Even if it is agreed that some of the rules must be arbitrary, I doubt that it will be possible to arrive at such arbitrary rules through the tax legislative process as we know it today.

Under controls, Congress avoids the hard decisions and lets the controlling agency make the arbitrary rules. One reason why controls seem to be more acceptable than tax penalties or subsidies is that relatively few firms are ever involved in disputes under controls, whereas a tax penalty or a subsidy would apply to all or a large number of firms and the perceived hardships and disputes would be numerous. Both devices lead to capricious results, but I am at a loss to understand why their proponents believe that tax-based incomes policies would be more acceptable to labor, management, the public, and Congress.

JOSEPH A. PECHMAN
Director of Economic Studies, The Brookings Institution. The views expressed are the author's and do not reflect those of the officers, trustees, and other staff members of The Brookings Institution.

45

A Tax-Based Incomes Policy (TIP):
What's It All About?

NANCY AMMON JIANAKOPLOS

SUBJECT corporations to higher corporate income tax rates if they give pay raises which are too large. This is the essence of a plan devised by Governor Henry C. Wallich of the Federal Reserve Board and Sidney Weintraub of the University of Pennsylvania.[1] Their proposal to use the tax system to curb inflation is called "TIP," an acronym for tax-based incomes policy. As inflation continues to plague the economy, many economists feel that the traditional tools of monetary and fiscal policy are inadequate to handle the situation and have recommended direct measures to stop wage and price increases.[2] The Wallich-Weintraub plan has received considerable attention as a policy measure which might be capable of dealing with the problem of inflation.[3]

Before adopting a program such as TIP, it is important to understand clearly how the proposal would operate and, more importantly, whether it would achieve the desired results. The first part of this article describes the functioning of TIP and the rationale for such a program as envisioned by Wallich and Weintraub. The rest of the article is devoted to an assessment of whether TIP would accomplish its stated objectives.

HOW WOULD TIP OPERATE?

According to the plan presented by Wallich and Weintraub, TIP would be centered on a single wage guidepost established by the Government.[4] The acceptable percentage wage increase could be set somewhere between the average increase in productivity throughout the economy (asserted to be around 3 percent) and some larger figure which incorporates all or part of the current rate of inflation. The ultimate aim of the guidepost is to bring wage increases in line with nationwide productivity increases.

The TIP guidepost is directed at wages only, although the tax is levied on corporate profits. The basic assumption behind TIP is that monetary and fiscal policies have been ineffective because they have not been able to prevent labor from obtaining wage increases in excess of productivity gains, even when there is significant unemployment in the economy. Furthermore, Wallich and Weintraub contend that empirical evidence supports the view that price in-

---

[1]Wallich and Weintraub first collaborated on this idea in Henry C. Wallich and Sidney Weintraub, "A Tax-Based Incomes Policy," *Journal of Economic Issues* (June 1971), pp. 1-19.

[2]See, for example, "Another Weapon Against Inflation: Tax Policy," *Business Week*, October 3, 1977, pp. 94-96; "Debate: How to Stop Inflation," *Fortune* (April 1977), pp. 116-20; Lindley H. Clark, Jr., "Uneasy Seers: More Analysts Predict New Inflation Spiral or Recession in 1978," *Wall Street Journal*, December 2, 1977.

[3]See, for example, U. S. Congress, Congressional Budget Office, *Recovery With Inflation*, July 1977, p. 40; U. S. Congress, Joint Economic Committee, *The 1977 Midyear Review of the Economy*, 95th Cong., 1st sess., September 26, 1977, p. 76; "Well-Cut Taxes Should Be Tailored," *New York Times*, December 21, 1977.

[4]Unless otherwise noted, all descriptions of TIP in this article are based on Wallich and Weintraub, "A Tax-Based Incomes Policy"; Henry C. Wallich, "Alternative Strategies for Price and Wage Controls," *Journal of Economic Issues* (December 1972), pp. 89-104; Henry C. Wallich, "A Plan for Dealing With Inflation in the U.S.," *Washington Post*, August 21, 1977; Sidney Weintraub, "An Incomes Policy to Stop Inflation," *Lloyds Bank Review* (January 1971), pp. 1-12; and Sidney Weintraub, "Incomes Policy: Completing the Stabilization Triangle," *Journal of Economic Issues* (December 1972), pp. 105-22.

Reprinted from Federal Reserve Bank of St. Louis *Review*, February, 1978.

creases have been a constant markup over unit wage increases. Therefore, if wage increases can be kept down, price increases will also be held down.

The corporate income tax system would be employed to enforce the TIP guidepost. Corporations which grant wage increases in excess of the guidepost would be subject to higher corporate income tax rates based on the amount that wage increases exceed the guidepost.

In order to understand how TIP would operate, consider the following example. Suppose the guidepost for wage increases is set at, say, 5 percent for a particular year. In the base year, Corporation A had a total wage bill of $100,000 and in the following year granted increases which brought its total wage bill to $108,000 — an 8 percent increase. Assuming no change in either the number or composition of the employees, this 8 percent increase is 3 percentage points above the guidepost. This excess would then be multiplied by a penalty number. If, for instance, the penalty was set at 2, the corporate tax rate of Corporation A would be increased by 6 percentage points (3 percentage point excess times penalty number of 2). Thus, instead of paying 48 percent of its profits in taxes, the existing corporate tax rate, Corporation A would have to pay 54 percent of its profits, as a penalty for acceding to "excessive" wage demands.

Wallich and Weintraub argue that because of competitive forces this additional tax could not be shifted forward to prices.[5] They, therefore, believe that such a tax penalty would cause corporations to deal more firmly with labor. In their view the penalty would ultimately restrain the rate of wage increases and, hence, reduce the rate of inflation.[6] Since wage increases would be curbed, corporations would not have higher costs to pass through in the form of price increases, thereby eliminating a major "cost-push" element of inflation. Furthermore, since the increases in incomes of workers would more closely approximate increases in productivity, there would be smaller increases in spending, reducing the "demand-pull" aspect of inflation.

Wallich and Weintraub acknowledge certain difficulties in computing the corporation's wage bill. One method which they believe would overcome many of these difficulties would be to construct an index of wages, rather than using the gross dollar figure. Using this method, wages, fringe benefits, and other related payments would be computed for each job classification and skill level and divided by the hours worked at each level. These wage figures would then be combined into an index weighted by the proportion of each of these classifications in the entire corporation. Changes in this index would then be compared to the guidepost in order to assess whether the corporation would be penalized.

Administrative problems are not neglected by Wallich and Weintraub. They recognize that the tax laws must be specific and "airtight" in order to avoid loopholes. However, it is argued that TIP would not involve establishing a new bureaucracy. Most of the data necessary to administer TIP are already collected for corporate income tax and employee payroll tax purposes.

One of the principal merits of TIP, in the view of Wallich and Weintraub, is that it would not interfere with the functioning of the market system. They argue that there would be no direct controls or distortions to the pricing mechanism. Firms would still be free to grant large wage demands, but would face the penalty of a higher corporate tax rate.

Rather than a short-term plan to curb inflation, TIP is envisioned to be a long-term means of reducing the rate of price increase. However, TIP is not intended to function by itself. Both Wallich and Weintraub see it as a supplement to "appropriate" monetary and fiscal policies. In addition, if labor contends that TIP would hold down wages while allowing profits to increase, Wallich proposes the implementation of an excess profits tax. This could be accomplished by increasing the basic corporate tax rate to keep the share of profits in national income constant.[7]

WOULD TIP WORK?

The TIP proposal has two principal objectives:

(1) to curb inflation, and

[5]See Richard A. Musgrave and Peggy B. Musgrave, *Public Finance In Theory and Practice* (New York: McGraw-Hill Book Company, 1973), Chapter 18, pp. 415-29, who contend that empirical evidence is inconclusive in determining whether the corporate income tax is shifted.

[6]Studies by Yehuda Kotowitz and Richard Portes, "The 'Tax on Wage Increases': A Theoretical Analysis," *Journal of Public Economics* (May 1974), pp. 113-32, and Peter Isard, "The Effectiveness of Using the Tax System to Curb Inflationary Collective Bargains: An Analysis of the Wallich-Weintraub Plan," *Journal of Political Economy* (May-June 1973), pp. 729-40, analyze the effect of TIP on an individual firm and conclude that theoretically TIP should lead to lower wage settlements for an individual firm.

[7]Other adjuncts proposed for TIP include a payroll tax credit designed to entice workers to accept lower wages. See Lawrence S. Seidman, "A Payroll Tax-Credit to Restrain Inflation," *National Tax Journal* (December 1976), pp. 398-412.

(2) to avoid interfering with the functioning of the market.

Given these aims of TIP, one can analyze whether TIP will, in fact, be able to accomplish its goals. Other issues raised by TIP, such as the costs of implementation and the ability of firms to avoid the tax penalty of TIP, will not be discussed here.[8]

Would TIP Curb Inflation?

TIP is based on the assumption that most of the inflation in the economy is of a "cost-push" nature. Inflation occurs, according to this framework, because labor is able to attain wage increases in excess of increases in productivity. Business is not capable of resisting, or finds it does not pay to resist, labor's demands. Faced with higher costs, businesses pass these costs through in the form of higher product prices. As prices rise, further wage increases are granted, forming the basis of a wage-price spiral. TIP is proposed as a measure which will intervene in this process and bring inflation to a halt.

As the Congressional Budget Office stated in a recent study, the assumption that inflation is the result of "cost-push" is "a conjectural notion at best."[9] A major challenge to the concept of "cost-push" rests on empirical evidence supporting an alternative theory of the cause of inflation. According to this other view, ongoing increases in the general price level (inflation) are primarily the result of excessive increases in the rate of monetary expansion.[10] Lags exist between the time when the money stock is increased and when prices rise. In this framework, the observed relationship between the rate of wage increase and the rate of price increase is explained as part of the adjustment process through which prices increase in response to increases in the money stock. This view does not deny the "cost-push" phenomenon,

but contends that it is consistent with the view that inflation is ultimately caused by money growth.[11]

When the stock of money is increased faster than the rate of increase in production, people find themselves with larger cash balances than they desire to hold. In order to bring their cash balances down to desired levels, they will spend the money, thereby bidding up prices on goods and services, and the general price level will rise. As long as the stock of money increases faster than the demand for money, inflation will persist, even if TIP manages to hold down wages temporarily.

Conversely, just as inflation is caused by excessive growth of the money stock, the only way to stop inflation is to reduce the growth of the money stock. As the rate of monetary expansion is reduced, people will have cash balances below their desired levels. They will reduce their rate of spending in order to build up these balances. As spending (demand) falls, the rate of inflation will decrease. Prices are "sticky," and just as it took several years to build up the current rate of inflation, it will take several years for inflation to wind down. One of the by-products of reducing inflation is a temporary idling of resources, since prices do not tend to be flexible in the short run. This is a cost of reducing inflation which must be borne, just as there are costs imposed on society as inflation mounts.

The idea that there are certain "key" wages in society, such as union wages, to which other wages and prices adjust, confuses the *motivation* for increasing the money stock with the *cause* of inflation.[12] If certain unions are able to attain large wage increases, even in the face of falling demand, the prices of the products produced by this labor will increase. As prices increase, less of this product will be demanded and the use of the resources (labor and capital) which produce this product will be decreased. Unemployment will rise as resources are freed to work in the production of other products whose prices are lower. The relative prices of products will change, but the average price level will be unchanged.

[8]For a discussion of implementation problems, see Gardner Ackley, "Okun's New Tax-Based Incomes-Policy Proposal," Survey Research Center, Institute for Social Research, The University of Michigan, *Economic Outlook USA* (Winter 1978), pp. 8-9. Although Ackley deals with the anti-inflation proposal put forward by Arthur Okun, he notes that the critique also applies to the Wallich-Weintraub proposal.

[9]Congressional Budget Office, "Recovery With Inflation," p. 41.

[10]Empirical support of this view for the period 1955 to 1971 is presented by Leonall C. Andersen and Denis S. Karnosky, "The Appropriate Time Frame for Controlling Monetary Aggregates: The St. Louis Evidence," *Controlling Monetary Aggregates II: The Implementation*, Federal Reserve Bank of Boston, Conference Series No. 9, September 1972, pp. 147-77. Additional evidence for the period 1971 to 1976 is found in Denis S. Karnosky, "The Link Between Money and Prices — 1971-76," this *Review* (June 1976), pp. 17-23.

[11]See Leonall C. Andersen and Denis S. Karnosky, "A Monetary Interpretation of Inflation" in Joel Popkin, ed., *Analysis of Inflation: 1965-1974*, Studies in Income and Wealth, Vol. 42, National Bureau of Economic Research, Inc. (Cambridge, Massachusetts: Ballinger Publishing Company, 1977), pp. 11-26.

[12]This argument draws on Armen A. Alchian and William R. Allen, *University Economics: Elements of Inquiry* (Belmont, California: Wadsworth Publishing Company, Inc., 1972), pp. 684-85.

However, if the Federal Reserve policymakers keep a close watch on these "key" industries and see an increase in idle resources (unemployment) in these industries, they may take actions to alleviate the unemployment by increasing the money stock. The increases in spending resulting from monetary expansion will bid up average prices and return relative prices to a position similar to that prior to the granting of the wage demands. It was as a consequence of the excessive wage demands that policy actions were *motivated,* but it was monetary expansion which *caused* the subsequent inflation.

Some proponents of TIP base their support on the belief that TIP will reduce *expectations* of inflation. Lower expectations of inflation in the future, according to this view, will lead to lower demands for wage increases and eventually lower prices. However, expectations of inflation do not cause inflation.[13] It is ongoing inflationary forces in the economy, excessive rates of monetary expansion, which lead to expectations of future inflation. Curbing inflationary expectations requires curbing the underlying forces which cause them.

Wallich and Weintraub agree that TIP is a supplement to, not a substitute for, "appropriate" monetary and fiscal policy. However, the character of their "appropriate" monetary policy is questionable. In the basic article which outlined TIP, Wallich and Weintraub stated, ". . . the proposal is conceived as a supplement to the familiar monetary-fiscal policies so that the economy might operate closer to full employment without the inflationary danger of excess demand and 'overheating.' "[14] Indeed, in a later article Weintraub is more specific: "Given a suitable incomes policy to align wages (and salaries) to productivity, monetary policy would be released to make its contribution to full employment. . . Full employment requires ample money supplies for its sustenance."[15] Thus, it appears that "appropriate" monetary policy, in the view of Wallich and Weintraub, is expansionary; however, a restrictive monetary policy is necessary to curb inflation.

This disparity in determining the appropriate character of monetary policy points out another problem with TIP. Given the lag time involved in the func-

tioning of monetary policy, it might appear in the short run that TIP is, at least temporarily, holding down prices. If, at the same time, the Federal Reserve increases the rate of monetary expansion, inflationary pressures will actually be augmented. An incomes policy, such as TIP, gives policymakers the illusion of taking corrective measures against inflation when, in fact, reducing the rate of monetary expansion is the only way to accomplish that goal. In summary, it appears that TIP would not be effective in reducing inflation and could make matters worse by fostering inappropriate monetary policy.

Would TIP Interfere With the Market?

Wallich and Weintraub argue that TIP would not interfere with market pricing because no ceilings are placed on any wages or prices. TIP operates through the tax system, yet it is based on a *single* guidepost for every firm and industry. They contend that a single guidepost is appropriate because in competition all comparable workers would earn the same wage. TIP, therefore, is only imposing what competition would achieve.

The problem with this argument is that it is only true if all industries are in equilibrium and remain there. In a growing, changing economy, equilibrium prices and wage rates are changing. Prices and wages are constantly moving toward new equilibria; hence, there is no reason to believe that each sector in the economy would be at equilibrium when TIP was imposed or would remain there afterward. In the U. S. economy, demands and tastes of consumers are constantly shifting and the technology and products offered by business are also changing. As a consequence, the equilibrium prices of some goods are rising (houses, for example) while others are falling (electronic calculators). In addition, some firms are growing, making large profits, and seeking additional labor, while others are declining, earning very little profit, and contracting their labor forces.

Imposing a single wage guidepost would distort the price system. It does not matter whether the guidepost is imposed through the tax system or by direct fines and penalties. Those firms which are growing or are adapting to changing consumer tastes have an incentive to hire scarce resources (capital and labor) away from other firms, but they would be penalized either through a lower rate of return, if they grant "excess" wage demands, or by a barrier to growth if they adhere to the guidepost. Consequently, in some instances labor would not be compensated in accord

[13] Weintraub supports this contention in Weintraub, "Incomes Policy: Completing the Stabilization Triangle," p. 116.

[14] Wallich and Weintraub, "A Tax-Based Incomes Policy," p. 1.

[15] Weintraub, "Incomes Policy: Completing the Stabilization Triangle," p. 110.

with the demand for its services. In other cases, firms would not be able to attract all the labor they desired. Relative prices would, therefore, be distorted by the establishment of a single guidepost for all firms and industries.

The TIP proposal would lead to a misallocation of resources. Prices, when allowed to operate freely, offer signals of where demand is increasing and where demand is falling. Resources move to those industries or firms where they will receive the highest compensation. The TIP proposal would obscure these price signals and, hence, resources would not move to where they would be used most efficiently. The economy would suffer since production would be lower than it would be otherwise.

The distortions in the economy caused by TIP could have a very long lasting effect. Capital (plant and equipment) is allocated by the market to those firms which have the highest rate of return. The TIP proposal would reduce the rates of return of those firms which are growing, and capital would not be adequately allocated to them. Capital generally tends to have a relatively long life. Once it is misallocated, as a result of TIP, it would not be easy to reallocate it to a more efficient use. Thus, TIP could have serious long-term consequences, as a result of the distortions it would cause in the price system.

CONCLUSION

TIP is an incomes policy designed to reduce inflation without interfering with the market system. The essence of the proposal is to subject corporations to higher corporate income tax rates if they granted pay increases in excess of a single Government-mandated guidepost.

TIP would not be successful in reducing the rate of inflation because it is based on the premise that inflation is largely a "cost-push" phenomenon — higher wages leading to higher prices, which lead to still higher wages. Inflation, however, is caused primarily by excessive growth of the money stock. The TIP proposal, therefore, deals only with the symptoms of inflation, rather than attacking inflation at its root.

TIP would distort the market pricing system because the imposition of a single wage guidepost would not allow relative prices to adjust fully to change. This would lead to inefficiencies and a lower level of production than would be otherwise attainable.

Inflation is a serious problem, and there are no magic solutions. There may be a temporary reduction in the apparent rate of inflation with TIP, but eventually leaks will develop in the system and prices will rise anyway. The only way to stop inflation is to reduce the rate of monetary expansion.

Union Settlements and Aggregate Wage Behavior in the 1980s

This article was prepared by Robert S. Gay of the Board's Division of Research and Statistics. Anne Peters and Maura Shaughnessy helped prepare the data.

Since 1979, at least 3 million union members in the United States, one out of every six, have accepted labor contracts that freeze or reduce wages and fringe benefits or alter work rules. Initially, such deviations from traditional union wage practices were confined to a few financially troubled firms. But as the economy went through back-to-back recessions during the early 1980s and unemployment climbed to postwar record levels, deviations from customary practices appeared with increasing frequency in union contracts and often were negotiated on an industry-wide basis. By 1982, wage freezes and pay cuts had become as commonplace as wage increases in major collective bargaining settlements. Moreover, despite the rebound in economic activity and in profits since late 1982, managements have continued to press for cost-reduction measures, and wage cuts and freezes remained prominent features of union negotiations in 1984.

These developments coincided with an unusually large reduction in aggregate wage inflation. As recently as mid-1981, the rate of wage increase averaged close to double digits, whereas just three years later, wage adjustments had dropped on balance to less than 4 percent—the smallest rate of increase since the mid-1960s. The change in the size of union settlements has been even more dramatic. Average wage adjustments exclusive of cost-of-living payments during the first year of new union contracts dropped from about 10 percent in 1981 to 2½ percent during 1983 and the first nine months of 1984 (chart 1).

In summarizing recent union wage developments, the discussion will focus on three issues. First, what were the nature and extent of nontra-

ditional bargaining and how much did it contribute to the unusually sharp reduction in wage inflation during the past several years? Similar contract modifications have occurred with some regularity in the past, but the recent episode clearly involved unprecedented numbers of workers and industries. Under some conservative assumptions, aggregate wage inflation would have been at least ½ percentage point higher in 1983 and 1984 in the absence of pay cuts and freezes. This estimate could be substantially larger if nontraditional bargaining had a major influence on other wage decisions. For the most part, however, the evidence suggests that spillovers outside of traditional channels have not been widespread. In industries that were less severely affected by the recession, both unionized and nonunionized, wage changes generally have shown fairly typical cyclical responses to rising unemployment and lower inflation.

Second, what factors contributed to the recent changes in union wage practices? Exceptionally large and prolonged declines in output and employment in many unionized industries often precipitated unscheduled reopenings of contracts and modifications to traditional wage formulas. That adversity was not solely cyclical. It stemmed also from longer-term influences, such

1. Union settlements and aggregate wage change

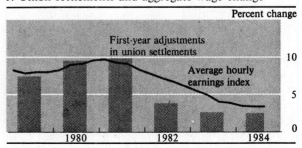

Hourly earnings index is the change from four quarters earlier; first-year adjustments are annual data, except 1984, which represents the first nine months.
SOURCE. Bureau of Labor Statistics.

Reprinted from the Federal Reserve *Bulletin*, December, 1984.

as the secular rise in the relative wage of union workers and intensified competition from domestic nonunion or foreign firms, and from the relaxation of barriers to entry under deregulation of the transportation and communications industries.

Third, what aspects of recent settlements may reflect permanent changes in union wage determination and what aspects may prove transitory? Unions have shown no tendency to abandon certain key features of traditional contracts—multiyear settlements and escalator clauses. However, many union workers appear to have scaled back their expectations for annual improvements in real wages and have shown a willingness to experiment with profit-sharing and various cooperative labor–management programs to enhance productivity. These innovations may endure if competitive pressures persist.

UNION WAGE PRACTICES AND DISINFLATION

By the 1970s, the basic institutional features of union wage determination were well established. Multiyear contracts had become the predominant format for labor negotiations, and formal cost-of-living adjustment (COLA) provisions had spread to cover a majority of union workers. Prospective wage settlements were fairly predictable as many large unions adhered to a policy of negotiating identical fixed increases in each contract year—often referred to as the annual improvement factor—plus COLAs. When annual improvement factors were established during the 1950s and 1960s, they were perceived as paralleling productivity trends, but by the 1970s they had become more a matter of custom than a projection of current or future productivity performance. To the extent that COLA formulas did not pass the full increase in prices through to wage increases, first-year wage increases in succeeding contracts were adjusted to make up the difference—a so-called catch-up adjustment. In contracts without escalator provisions, negotiators had to build into future adjustments their expectations for inflation over the course of the contract or include contingency clauses for reopening the agreement.

These wage-setting practices often were cited as a major factor underlying the persistence of wage inflation in the United States. In particular, three-year contracts with staggered expiration dates, often buttressed by escalator clauses, were viewed as building inertia into the wage-determination process, thereby limiting the response of inflation to aggregate demand policies designed to reduce it. Some observers extended the inertia argument beyond union agreements by noting contract-like regularities in nonunion wage practices.

One rationale for attributing a central role in the inflation adjustment process to overlapping, multiyear contracts rests on the presumed importance of wage comparisons. In this view, workers' notions of an equitable wage have a major influence on wage-setting practices. Such notions may be based on wages paid to other, similar workers or on expectations of real wage gains that have been ingrained by experience. Given workers' perceptions of equity, union leaders feel pressure to emulate other settlements or to retain traditional guaranteed wage increases in escalated contracts; otherwise, they risk a rejection of the contract by their memberships. Thus key contracts reached in a bargaining round often appeared to set the tone for subsequent settlements, especially in related industries, even if economic conditions had changed in the interim.

Factors other than wage comparisons also influence union settlements. Negotiators ultimately must take into account current and prospective macroeconomic conditions as well as longer-run trends in their own industries. Evidence from the postwar period up to the 1980s indicated an asymmetric sensitivity to macroeconomic conditions: union wages were highly responsive to inflation but relatively insensitive to slack demand.

A closer look at the traditional features of multiyear contracts discussed above reveals why union wages were not very responsive to cyclical fluctuations in demand. First-year negotiated wage changes under new settlements, which dictate only a portion of all union wage adjustments in any given year, are fairly sensitive to unemployment. But that cyclical responsiveness is overwhelmed by the rigidities introduced by fixed wage increases that were scheduled under contracts negotiated in previous years, when economic conditions may have been decidedly different. In contrast, COLA clauses generate far less wage inertia than deferred adjustments. Many COLA formulas call for frequent reviews, making union wages highly responsive to price changes. Thus to the extent that macroeconomic policies designed to curb inflation in fact do so, COLAs help to moderate wage adjustments with only a brief delay.

Important aspects of the cyclical response of union wages have changed in the 1980s. To illustrate the changes that have occurred, chart 2 displays data on the components of union wage changes—first-year adjustments, deferred adjustments, and COLAs. For most of the period since 1968, the data relate the traditional story told above. First-year adjustments under new settlements show the greatest cyclical variance, albeit with some delay, while the deferred component displays relatively little variance. The inertia generated by deferred increases under earlier settlements can be seen most vividly in the years when total effective wage change decelerated sharply, as it did in 1972 and 1982; in those years, deferred increases accounted for an unusually large proportion of the average change in union wages. The contribution of COLAs rose dramatically during the 1970s—from only 5 percent of wage changes received by union workers in the late 1960s to about one-third in 1977–78. Part of that secular trend was attributable to a higher average inflation rate during the 1970s; but, more important, COLA provisions were added to many contracts early in the decade so that the proportion of union workers covered by such provisions rose from about 25 percent to around 60 percent.

2. Effective union wage change and its components

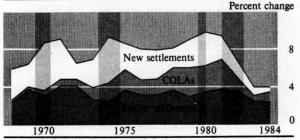

Percent change

New settlements

COLAs

8

4

0

1970   1975   1980   1984

Annual data; 1984 represents first nine months at annual rates. Shaded areas denote recessions.
SOURCE. Bureau of Labor Statistics.

EMERGENCE OF NONTRADITIONAL BARGAINING

The deceleration in union wage changes since 1980 has differed from past patterns in two key respects. First, the reduction in the size of first-year adjustments was exceptionally large after 1981, primarily because an unprecedented number of union workers accepted freezes on base wage rates or pay cuts. Second, the COLA component also declined sharply. Most of the reduction in COLAs can be traced to the general deceleration in price increases rather than to deferred or forgone payments under some union contracts.

Even though a contraction in activity in some unionized industries began as early as mid-1979, relatively few workers agreed to contract reopenings or deviations from traditional patterns until late 1981. According to data from the Bureau of Labor Statistics on major settlements that cover only bargaining units of 1,000 or more workers, about 35,000 workers took wage cuts or freezes in 1980. A separate tally from press reports and other published sources that was made by the Federal Reserve Board staff put the figure at 67,000 workers; this estimate includes salaried employees who agreed to terms similar to those granted by their union coworkers and other workers at nonunion firms. Often these early contract modifications took the form of a temporary deferral of scheduled wage adjustments or COLAs, and they generally were confined to financially troubled firms with recent records of poorer profitability than other companies in their industries. As the period of slack demand lengthened, however, wage cuts and freezes not only became pervasive but also were frequently negotiated on an industry-wide basis and extended over the life of multiyear contracts.

In 1981, roughly 190,000 union workers, or 8 percent of those reaching new settlements in the private sector, accepted first-year wage cuts or freezes, according to the data from the Bureau of Labor Statistics shown in table 1. By 1982, that figure had climbed to almost 1.5 million. The corresponding figures from the tally by the Federal Reserve Board staff were 365,000 workers in 1981 and 2.3 million workers in 1982. Many of the larger agreements broke with traditional wage-setting practices by eliminating guaranteed

147

1. Distribution of workers by first-year wage adjustment in major collective bargaining settlements, 1980–84
Percent except as noted

Wage adjustment	1980	1981	1982	1983	1984 (first nine months)
Decrease	0	5	2	15	6
No change	0	3	42	22	21
Increase					
0–4 percent	4	3	9	14	33
4–8 percent	25	9	23	39	37
8 percent and over	71	81	24	10	3
MEMO:					
Mean adjustment (percentage change)	9.5	9.8	3.8	2.6	2.5
Number of workers (thousands)	3,790	2,382	3,257	3,089	1,447

SOURCE. Bureau of Labor Statistics, *Current Wage Developments*, various issues.

annual increases over the life of the contracts. This new format became the standard for union workers in the automobile, trucking, and rubber industries in 1982, and was adopted in 1983 by the aluminum, metal container, shipbuilding, copper mining, and farm machinery industries. Significant deviations from the industry standard were negotiated at companies with particularly acute financial problems. All told, more than two-fifths of workers covered by large new settlements accepted first-year wage freezes in 1982, and in manufacturing the proportion was one-half.

In 1983, the distribution of first-year union settlements shifted even more dramatically toward wage cuts. Settlements in the steel, airline, and meatpacking industries called for initial wage reductions ranging from 10 to 20 percent. In addition, half of unionized construction workers signed new agreements calling for pay reductions or freezes. Altogether, about 1.1 million workers under large union contracts in the private sector accepted wage cuts or freezes in 1983. The tally by the Board staff found that at least 1.3 million employees were subject to new wage cuts or freezes in 1983. Modifications to past wage practices continued to be a prominent feature of union negotiations during the first nine months of 1984, despite the strong rebound in overall economic activity and profits over the preceding year. About one-fourth of the 1.5 million workers negotiating new contracts accepted initial wage cuts or freezes. In the construction industry, the average wage adjustment was about 1 percent, the lowest figure recorded for the industry since the Bureau of Labor Statistics began publishing these data in 1968.

Chart 3 puts the recent period in historical perspective. Although wage cuts were common during the Great Depression, the experience with distressed bargaining after World War II is more instructive because by that time modern institutions of collective bargaining were well established. Two other episodes of distressed bargaining occurred during the postwar era: one during the 1953–54 recession and another in the late 1950s and early 1960s. Both episodes were highlighted by the spread of wage cuts or freezes to a substantial portion of the unionized workforce in a few select industries. Usually, these industries were undergoing extensive structural change at the same time.

In the early 1950s, the textile industry faced considerable excess capacity, largely as a result of foreign competition, technological advances, and the introduction of synthetic fibers. To forestall plant closings, union workers accepted pay cuts. Despite these revisions to pay scales, industry employment continued to decline over the next two decades. During the late 1950s and early 1960s, the meatpacking industry also experienced structural upheaval. Nonunion firms

3. Union workers receiving no wage increase or a wage cut

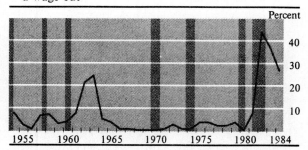

Annual data for collective bargaining agreements covering 1,000 or more workers; 1984 represents first nine months. Shaded areas denote recessions.
SOURCE. Bureau of Labor Statistics, *Current Wage Developments*, various issues.

paying wages below the union scale had entered the market by building highly efficient production facilities. Unionized companies, which had once dominated the market, generally failed to keep abreast of technological and marketing advances, and cost disadvantages threatened their long-term viability. Contracts eventually were reopened in 1962 and 1963, and pay and work rules were changed.

Wage cuts were rare outside the meatpacking industry in the early 1960s, but decisions not to increase negotiated rates for base wages were fairly common. Some observers viewed the prevalence of moderate settlements at that time as evidence of success of the wage–price guideposts program or attributed it to a tougher stance taken by management after a period when unions had extracted fairly generous wage increases. Concern arose among union workers about the impact of automation and the employment problems caused by closures of outmoded plants. Despite all the factors restraining wage adjustments, the extent of pay cuts and freezes in union settlements did not approach that recorded during the past three years.

Apart from a few instances, most situations of distressed bargaining during the postwar period

before 1982 were specific to individual firms or plants. Almost invariably, these situations involved financially weak firms, and managements were able to convince workers that changes in labor contracts were necessary to assure the firm's survival or to avoid plant closure. Cyclical layoffs even on a large scale generally did not provoke extensive modifications to traditional wage formulas. A prime example is the experience during the 1974–75 recession. Negotiations for most major multiyear settlements were completed before the severity of the recession was evident. Yet, although employment and output fell sharply in many industries, existing contracts were not reopened, as they have been recently. The reason for the sharp contrast between the experiences of 1974–75 and 1980–84 apparently was that in the earlier period, union workers did not perceive job losses to be permanent.

As discussed earlier, the COLA component of effective union wage changes also has declined precipitously since 1981 after a decade of increase. The observed contributions of COLAs to total effective union wage changes are the product of three factors: (1) the proportion of union workers covered by COLAs; (2) the recovery rate—the extent to which COLA formulas pass

2. Factors affecting COLA components of effective union wage changes, 1968–84

Percent, except as noted

Year	Portion of total due to COLAs (percentage points)	Proportion of union workers covered by COLAs	Recovery rate[1]	Price change[2]
1968	.3	23.6	34	4.7
1969	.3	25.0	26	6.1
1970	.6	25.9	67	5.5
1971	.7	27.8	92	3.4
1972	.7	40.6	59	3.4
1973	1.3	39.4	47	8.8
1974	1.9	39.2	48	12.2
1975	2.2	51.5	68	7.0
1976	1.6	59.4	73	4.8
1977	1.7	61.2	58	6.8
1978	2.4	60.4	55	9.0
1979	3.1	58.9	51	13.4
1980	2.8	58.1	58	12.5
1981	3.2	58.2	67	8.7
1982	1.4	56.7	70	3.9
1983	.6	57.6	53	3.3
1984: first nine months[3]	1.1	57.3	53	4.1

1. The data for 1968–80 are Federal Reserve Board staff estimates of the passthrough of price changes into wage adjustments under COLA clauses based on data on the average size of cost-of-living adjustments for workers who actually received payments during the calendar year as a percent of the December-to-December change in the consumer price for urban wage earners and clerical workers (CPI-W). After 1980, the data are estimates by the Bureau of Labor Statistics, which are based on the change in consumer prices over the actual period of the COLA review.

2. December-to-December change in the CPI-W.

3. Nine-month change at a compound annual rate.

SOURCES. COLA contribution and recovery rates after 1980 are from Current Wage Developments, various issues; COLA coverage is from Monthly Labor Review, vol. 107 (January 1984), p. 31, and previous January issues; price change data are from the Department of Labor.

the change in consumer prices through into wage increases; and (3) the rate of change in consumer prices. Historical data on these factors affecting the COLA contribution are presented in table 2. Note that the diminished role of COLAs in total union wage adjustments recently cannot be attributed to union workers giving up COLA provisions in their collective bargaining agreements. COLA coverage has remained fairly stable at just under 60 percent since 1976. Even in distressed situations, union workers showed little willingness to eliminate entirely contractual provisions indexing wages to movements in the general price level. The only major exceptions to this generalization have appeared in contracts negotiated for airline and food store workers, in which abandonment of escalator clauses has reduced COLA coverage from around 70 percent of the union workforce in these industries to less than 20 percent over the past four years.

Instead of abandoning COLA provisions altogether, some unions agreed to defer or forgo some payments (as in the auto and steel contracts), or to divert payments to help defray the rising costs of fringe benefits (as in the Master Freight Agreement), or to lengthen the period between reviews, which in effect reduces employers' total costs. In addition, some settlements, notably in the steel industry, set limitations on COLAs so that payments are based only on increases in consumer prices in excess of a threshold inflation rate. Most of the alterations to COLAs appear to be temporary and are often scheduled to terminate before the expiration of the contracts.

All of these modifications to COLA provisions should affect the recovery rate. Estimates of the recovery rate are shown in column 4 of table 2. In the early 1980s, COLA formulas on average compensated workers for roughly two-thirds of the rise in consumer prices. Modifications to COLA formulas lowered the recovery rate to around one-half in 1983. These data suggest that modifications to COLAs accounted for perhaps ½ percentage point, or one-fifth of the deceleration in the COLA component of total effective union wage changes. The remainder was attributable to the general slowdown in price increases.

IMPACT OF CONTRACT MODIFICATIONS ON AGGREGATE WAGE INFLATION

The unprecedented number of wage cuts and freezes after 1981 coincided with a halving of the

3. The deceleration of wages, 1979–84

Percentage change

Measure	1979	1980	1981	1982	1983	1984 (first nine months)
Employment cost index, wages and salaries[1]						
Private nonfarm	8.7	9.0	8.8	6.3	5.0	3.9
Union	9.0	10.9	9.6	6.5	4.6	3.3
Nonunion	8.5	8.0	8.5	6.1	5.2	4.2
Manufacturing	8.6	9.4	8.7	5.6	4.3	4.1
Union	9.4	11.0	8.9	5.8	3.6	3.9
Nonunion	7.9	7.9	8.3	5.6	4.7	4.3
Nonmanufacturing	8.8	8.8	9.0	6.5	5.5	3.9
Union	8.5	10.8	10.2	7.1	5.5	2.7
Nonunion	8.8	8.1	8.6	6.2	5.5	4.2
Hourly earnings index[2]						
Private nonfarm	8.0	9.6	8.3	6.1	3.9	3.1
Manufacturing	8.7	10.9	8.8	6.0	2.7	3.3
Construction	6.9	7.7	8.3	5.4	1.5	1.2
Transportation and public utilities	9.0	9.3	8.5	6.1	4.3	3.1
Trade	7.5	8.7	6.9	5.4	4.7	2.4
Services	7.6	9.3	9.1	7.0	4.9	4.1
Finance, insurance, and real estate	7.7	10.1	8.0	7.7	6.0	3.9
Major collective bargaining agreements[3]						
Total effective wage change, private sector	9.1	9.9	9.5	6.8	4.0	4.0
First-year adjustments under new settlements, private sector	7.4	9.5	9.8	3.8	2.6	2.5

1. December to December; data for 1984 are from December 1983 to September 1984 at a compound annual rate, not seasonally adjusted.

2. Fourth quarter to fourth quarter; data for 1984 are from 1983:4 to 1984:3 at a compound annual rate.

3. Wage adjustments put in place during the calendar year, except for 1984, which covers only the first nine months.

average rate of wage inflation from 9 percent in that year to around 4 percent recently (table 3). At least two aspects of this wage deceleration contrast with the experience in previous postwar downturns. First, union wage change actually began to decelerate long before there was any sign of a slowdown in nonunion wages. Second, wage inflation fell more rapidly in the union sector than elsewhere—from 11 percent in 1980 to about 3¼ percent thus far in 1984.

As indicated by the data from the employment cost index, the slowdown in union wage inflation began in 1981. Even so, wage adjustments for union workers on balance exceeded those received by nonunion workers, as they had throughout most of the past decade. By 1982, however, union wages on average were rising at about the same rate as nonunion wages. Much of this early deceleration probably was attributable to smaller COLAs in contracts with escalator clauses, as consumer price increases slowed from 12½ percent in 1980 to just 4 percent in 1982. Not until mid-1982 did a substantial number of union workers actually forgo scheduled wage adjustments or COLAs. As the cumulative total of workers negotiating wage cuts and freezes rose, the average change in union wages fell below that for nonunion workers and has remained below it over the first three quarters of 1984. During the past two years, changes in union wages have averaged about ½ to 1 percentage point less than those in nonunion wages.

The direct influence of distressed bargaining also can be seen in wage data by industry. Wage cuts and freezes were particularly prevalent in manufacturing, construction, and transportation; and these industries also showed the greatest deceleration in average wage changes, especially after 1981. According to the hourly earnings index, wage adjustments in manufacturing fell from 11 percent in 1980 to around 3 percent during the past two years. In construction, where wage cuts and freezes in union contracts were widespread in 1983 and 1984, wage changes have averaged only 1 percent lately, compared with about 8 percent in 1981. The direct influence of distressed bargaining is less noticeable in the aggregate wage index for transportation, communications, and public utilities—probably because wage settlements at public utilities were well above average in recent years while wage cuts

and freezes were confined largely to trucking firms and airlines.

Distressed bargaining also appeared to have some limited influence on other wage decisions. For example, many union contracts contained provisions requiring "equality of sacrifice" from nonunion counterparts at the same firm. Also, once wage cuts or freezes were negotiated in certain key contracts, other, similar settlements soon spread to industries in the same "sphere" of union wage setting, in a pattern that has been evident for many years. The automobile settlements set precedents for revised agreements in automotive parts, truck manufacturing, and farm and construction equipment; the master steel settlement influenced negotiations in nonferrous metals and metal containers; and intercity trucking settlements were imitated in local trucking agreements, by truckers at retail food stores, and at bus companies.

Even in these examples, it is difficult to distinguish whether the behavior followed a pattern set by one industry or was the independent responses of the individual industries to acute financial problems all of them faced. The contracts negotiated within traditional spheres of influence clearly were tailored to fit the economic conditions of each industry. The steel contracts, for example, cut pay substantially (although the reductions are to be restored over the contract term) and limited COLAs for two and a half years, whereas related settlements merely froze base wage rates. Settlements for truck and bus drivers also have varied widely according to market conditions and companies' fortunes. In short, even within traditional spheres of imitation, there has been considerably greater diversity of wage settlements than in the past.

Outside distressed industries, union settlements also moderated after 1981, but the deceleration appeared to be no greater than might be expected during a period when inflation dropped sharply and unemployment rose. For those workers who received wage increases, first-year adjustments under new settlements exclusive of COLAs dropped from 11 percent in 1981 to 4.2 percent in the first nine months of 1984. This slowdown can be explained largely by reduced inflationary pressures, which mitigated demands for catch-up increases and moderated expectations of future inflation. With consumer prices rising less than 4 percent annually during the past two and a half years, union workers who received wage increases enjoyed, on balance, fairly substantial gains in real wages. Indeed, the rise in real wages over the life of contracts expiring recently is a key factor in the virtual disappearance of initial wage increases in excess of 8 percent in 1984. Thus the unionized workforce divided into two camps during the early 1980s: in industries afflicted by sweeping changes in product market conditions, heightened competition spurred employers and unions to reduce labor costs; in industries facing less stringent product market pressures, negotiators stuck with traditional wage-setting practices.

Wage decisions in unrelated, nonunionized industries also did not appear to be influenced greatly by the extraordinary developments in the union sector. Nonunion wages rose less rapidly than union wages in 1980 and 1981, as was the case throughout most of the 1970s. If strong spillovers from union to nonunion wages existed, the persistent widening of union–nonunion wage differentials over more than a decade could not have occurred. After 1981, when pay cuts and freezes became widespread for union workers, increases in nonunion wages declined, but the reduction was far less than that for union workers. Apparently, nonunionized employers did not feel that product market conditions warranted drastic measures to cut costs; indeed, employment in many nonunionized industries in the service-producing sector continued to rise during the back-to-back recessions of the early 1980s.

A crude calculation may be made of the impact of distressed bargaining on aggregate wage inflation. Roughly 3 million union workers were directly covered by wage cuts or freezes. Spillovers to nonunion workers might double the number of workers affected to 6 million, or about 8 percent of private nonfarm payroll employment in 1983. A realistic assumption is that these workers received no increase in wages on balance. (Small wage adjustments generated by COLAs in many contracts that froze base wage rates probably were counterbalanced by steep wage cuts in some other contracts.) If, instead of having their wages frozen, these workers had received wage increases of 5¼ percent, commensurate with traditional formulas (a 3 percent annual improvement factor plus COLAs), the

average wage change for all workers reported in the employment cost index would have been 5½ percent rather than 5 percent in 1983. In other words, recent modifications to traditional wage formulas may have held down overall wage inflation since 1982 at least ½ percentage point per year. This estimate understates the impact on aggregate wage inflation because the definition of contract modifications used here is confined to freezes on base wage rates and pay cuts.

FACTORS INFLUENCING RECENT SETTLEMENTS

Developments leading up to the recent wave of wage cuts and freezes were complex in their origins and varied across industries, but many of these situations had common characteristics. Frequently, the affected industries were among those hardest hit, in terms of sales and profits, by the prolonged slump in economic activity. Yet the problems facing financially troubled firms were not solely cyclical in nature. At least three developments that evolved during the 1970s probably would have forced unions to modify their traditional wage formulas even in the absence of the back-to-back recessions during the early 1980s.

First, wage dispersion across industries widened dramatically over the past decade as average union wage increases consistently exceeded average nonunion wage increases. By the early 1980s, the union–nonunion wage differential had reached a historic high. Second, productivity trends deteriorated markedly across a wide range of industries, particularly after 1973. As a result, real wage increases for many union workers tended to outstrip productivity gains, exacerbating cost pressures on prices. Third, new competition emerged. For heavily unionized "smokestack" industries, the challenge came from foreign suppliers that made dramatic inroads into U.S. markets. In several highly unionized industries less subject to import competition, domestic nonunion firms paying lower wages captured an increasing share of the market. For the airline and trucking industries, the new competition has been the result of deregulation, which effectively removed barriers to entry into basically competitive markets. The twin recessions of the early

1980s and the strengthening value of the dollar relative to foreign currencies clearly added to these burgeoning market pressures on unions and hastened modifications to traditional wage practices.

Layoffs and Plant Closings

Almost invariably, unions have accepted major contract modifications only when bankruptcy, extensive plant closings, or massive layoffs were an immediate threat. Job losses were particularly widespread among union workers during the early 1980s. Table 4 shows cumulative declines in employment from peak levels (usually in 1979) to the recession lows for numerous heavily unionized industries in which wage cuts and freezes became widespread. In many cases, including automobiles and steel, more than one-third of the prerecession workforce was laid off. In the meatpacking, trucking, and airline indus-

4. Job losses in selected industries receiving wage concessions

Percent

Industry	Cumulative change in employment	
	Prerecession peak to recession trough[1]	Prerecession peak to July 1984
Copper ores..........	−50.4	−51.3
Construction..........	−29.8	−4.6
Metal cans............	−28.8	−27.1
Primary aluminum......	−37.7	−24.1
Fabricated structural metal.............	−29.5	−23.5
Farm machinery........	−48.4	−43.2
Construction machinery..	−59.6	−44.0
Metalworking machinery	−28.6	−19.0
Motor vehicles and equipment	−35.7	−17.4
Blast furnace and basic steel products	−43.7	−41.2
Meat packing plants	−17.2	−12.0
Tires and inner tubes	−27.9	−20.7
Trucking and trucking terminals	−17.3	−4.8
Air transportation	−5.4	4.7
Food stores............	...[2]	13.5
Ship and boatbuilding....	−20.7	−10.9
Total private nonfarm	−4.4	4.9

1. Peaks and troughs are specific to the individual industries. The absolute decline in employment totaled about 4 million in the industries listed; private nonfarm employment fell 1.9 million between February 1980 and December 1982.

2. There was no trough for this industry.

SOURCE. U.S. Department of Labor, *Supplement to Employment and Earnings* (July 1984), and recent monthly issues of *Employment and Earnings*.

tries, the overall declines in employment undoubtedly understate the adversity faced by union workers, because the number of nonunion jobs expanded or at least contracted less than the number of union jobs. By 1982, many union workers had been separated from their former jobs for nearly three years, and prospects for regaining them were highly unfavorable. Indeed, by mid-1984, after one and one-half years of economic recovery, employment in these industries generally was still well below prerecession levels.

A puzzling question is why crisis situations must develop before unions are willing to modify traditional wage practices. One possible explanation is that unions do not perceive the wage–employment tradeoff, especially in the short run. Under some circumstances, this lack of perception is understandable. If the short-run elasticity of demand for union labor is low, as some evidence suggests, employed workers must sacrifice a lot in wages to generate a small gain in employment for their unemployed counterparts. Elasticities of labor demand tend to be low when unions effectively control their jurisdictions and when the ratio of labor costs to total costs is low. For many of the industries in which wage formulas ultimately were altered, including steel, autos, meatpacking, and tires, the ratio of labor costs to total costs is one-third or less. A sizable wage cut, even if fully passed through into prices, would translate into only a moderate reduction in product prices, which in turn would stimulate output and employment only a little in the near term. Thus low short-run elasticities of labor demand may account in part for the reluctance of unions to accept cost-reduction measures until they saw clear signs of a long-term crisis.

Institutional considerations also can forestall or even preclude contract modifications during recessions. Workers often distrust their companies' claims of financial distress. Lacking membership support, union leaders are reluctant to recommend pay cuts that would alienate their members and threaten their leadership within the union. Moreover, revisions to customary wage formulas in even one firm often are viewed by union leaders as undermining union strength because they can subject the union to demands for equal treatment by other organized firms.

A key role in union decisionmaking is played by senior workers, who generally constitute a majority and whom seniority systems insulate to some extent from layoffs. Unless the job security of senior workers is threatened, a consensus in favor of contract reopenings and revised settlements is unlikely to emerge. The jobs of senior workers rarely were threatened during the postwar period before the 1980s, and the responsiveness of wages under multiyear contracts to cyclical changes in economic conditions was sharply limited. By contrast, crisis situations that threatened senior workers—imminent threats of bankruptcy or permanent plant closings—extended far beyond marginal firms during the early 1980s and afflicted a much greater number of industries.

Long-Run Influences

Although massive layoffs were the catalyst for recent changes in collective bargaining, a confluence of developments during the 1970s had added to market pressures on unions and probably would have forced modifications to traditional wage formulas in any event. These difficulties included high domestic labor costs, a narrowing or even the elimination of the U.S. productivity advantage, and the failure of some unionized industries to adapt quickly to changes in technology and in consumer preferences. As these problems evolved, numerous unionized industries became increasingly vulnerable to import and nonunion competition, which in turn eroded union bargaining power.

In key manufacturing industries, the new competition came from imports. During the 1970s, foreign suppliers made steady inroads into U.S. markets formerly dominated by domestic firms. For example, by 1982, foreign cars accounted for 28 percent of total U.S. auto sales, compared with only 9 percent in 1968. The import share for steel almost doubled over the same period to 22 percent (table 5). Likewise, imports of apparel, tires, leather goods, and machine tools rose sharply as a share of domestic sales. The sharp increase in the foreign exchange value of the dollar beginning in late 1980 put added pressure on domestic producers by reducing the relative price of imported goods. Since late 1982, the

5. Import penetration ratios

Percent

Industry	1968	1981
Food and kindred products	1.0	4.2
Tobacco manufacturers	.3	2.0
Textile mill products	5.2	5.9
Apparel and related products	4.2	13.7
Lumber and wood products, except furniture	8.3	8.7
Furniture and fixtures	1.6	4.8
Paper and allied products	5.8	6.4
Printing, publishing, and allied products	.6	1.0
Chemicals and allied products	2.3	4.4
Petroleum and coal products	3.9	6.8
Rubber and miscellaneous plastic products	3.0	7.7
Tires and inner tubes[2]	2.3	11.7
Leather and leather products	8.9	24.7
Stone, clay, and glass products	3.0	5.1
Primary metal products	8.8	14.5
Steel[3]	12.2	21.8
Fabricated metal products, except machinery and transportation equipment	1.7	3.9
Machinery, except electrical	4.0	3.9
Metalworking machinery[2]	4.8	16.3
Machine tools[2]	14.6	29.4
Electrical machinery, equipment, and supplies	4.0	8.0
Transportation equipment	5.7	14.8
Motor vehicles and parts[2]	5.7	21.7
Measuring, analyzing, and controlling instruments; photographic and optical goods; watches and clocks	4.9	11.3
Miscellaneous manufactured commodities	10.6	23.6
All manufacturing industries	**4.3**	**8.4**

1. Import penetration ratios are defined as imports divided by total industry shipments plus imports. Changes in industry classifications as of 1972 affected import penetration ratios in a few industries, notably petroleum; basic trends for most two-digit industries, however, are not distorted by comparing figures for 1968 and 1981.

2. Data are from the Census of Manufactures, 1967 and 1982.

3. Data are from the American Iron and Steel Institute, 1967 and 1982. Exports are netted out in this volume-based data.

SOURCE. Bureau of Labor Statistics, except as noted.

strong recovery of aggregate demand has bolstered sales of domestic producers but has not stemmed the tide of imports. Indeed, the U.S. merchandise trade deficit reached record levels during the first three quarters of 1984.

In a number of industries in which imports are not a factor, the emergence of nonunion competition eroded union bargaining power. Unionization in construction, meatpacking, and retail food stores shrunk during the 1970s, and the deterioration appeared to accelerate during the early 1980s. For the highly unionized airline and trucking industries, deregulation effectively removed barriers to entry into basically competitive markets, and new low-cost nonunion firms offering discount rates have thrived. Whatever its source, the heightened competition exacer-

6. Ratio of hourly earnings in selected industries to average for private nonfarm production workers

Industry	1969	1973	1977	1981	1983
Trucking[1] (Master Freight Agreement)	1.31	1.59	1.63	1.73	1.63
Autos[2]	1.39	1.45	1.57	1.70	1.67
Steel[3]	1.34	1.42	1.64	1.81	1.67
Rubber[4]	1.38	1.33	1.38	1.53	1.54

1. Straight-time hourly wage rates are specified in Master Freight Agreements.
2. SIC 3711, motor vehicles and car bodies.
3. SIC 3312, blast farmers and steel mills.
4. SIC 301, tires and inner tubes.
SOURCE. U.S. Department of Labor and Master Freight Agreements for various years.

7. Productivity growth in selected industries, selected periods

Average annual percentage change

Industry	Productivity growth[1]		
	Earlier period		1973–81
	Change	Years covered[2]	
Motor vehicles and equipment	3.7	1957–73	1.9
Steel	1.8	1947–73	.8
Tires and inner tubes	4.0	1947–73	2.9
Primary aluminum	4.4	1947–73	−.3
Farm and garden machinery	2.5	1958–73	.5
Intercity trucking	2.7	1954–73	.3
Air transportation	7.5	1947–73	2.6
Metal cans	2.3	1947–73	3.8
Copper mining, crude ore	3.7	1955–73	2.2
Retail food stores	2.8	1958–73	−.6
Construction machinery	2.1	1958–73	.1
Machine tools	1.5	1958–73	−.7
Meatpacking	3.2	1967–73	3.2
Fabricated structural metal	2.3	1958–73	−.4
Total private nonfarm	2.5	1947–73	.6

1. Output per employee hour.
2. The period covered was determined by the availability of data.
SOURCE. *Productivity Measures for Selected Industries, 1954–81*, Bureau of Labor Statistics Bulletin 2155 (December 1982).

bated the cyclical decline in union employment and undoubtedly was a major influence on workers' perceptions of their firm's long-term prospects. More important, greater competition in product markets made it more difficult for businesses to pass on higher costs into prices.

Underlying these fundamental changes in product markets were marked cost differences between union firms and their competitors. During the 1970s, wage increases varied considerably across industries, and the dispersion of wage rates widened dramatically after a decade of relative stability (chart 4). The causes of the increased dispersion in wages are open to debate, but it is clear that many of the union workers granting wage cuts or freezes in the early 1980s were among those who had received the largest wage increases during the 1970s. For

4. Dispersion of average hourly earnings across industries

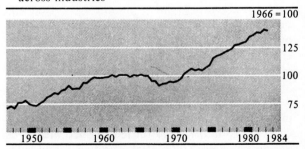

The summary statistic plotted is the coefficient of variation for average hourly earnings in 44 three-digit industries for which data are available since 1947; data are indexed to equal 100 in 1966. A similar widening in interindustry wage differentials during the 1970s was evident for a larger sample of 120 three-digit industries for which data are available since 1958. Weighting the earnings data by industry employment also did not change the basic pattern of dispersion.
SOURCE. U.S. Department of Labor.

example, union wage scales in autos, steel, rubber, and trucking—industries recently marked by wage cuts and freezes—climbed from a level 30 to 40 percent higher than the average wage for all private nonfarm production workers in the late 1960s to a level 50 to 80 percent higher in 1981 (table 6). In the meatpacking industry, older unionized plants paid substantially higher wages than the new nonunion plants with advanced technology, and large settlements in the construction industry during the early 1980s undoubtedly widened the wage gap between union and nonunion workers.

Many industries in which labor contracts were modified recently also experienced a slowdown in productivity growth after 1973 (table 7). One consequence of that slowdown was a compounding of cost disadvantages for unionized firms in these industries relative to foreign or domestic nonunion competitors. Before the 1970s, strong productivity gains appeared to warrant annual increases in real wages of 2 to 3 percent that were embedded in union wage formulas. For nearly a decade after 1973, however, few heavily unionized industries experienced productivity gains of that magnitude, yet traditional annual improvement factors remained largely intact. At the same

155

time, foreign producers, particularly in Japan, were able to raise productivity substantially, thereby narrowing or even eliminating the U.S. advantage in production efficiency.

LONG-RUN PROSPECTS FOR COLLECTIVE BARGAINING

Traditional union practices governing wage determination and other key outcomes of collective bargaining underwent sweeping changes during the early 1980s in response to heightened competition in many unionized markets. This response was the inevitable result of the significant widening of union–nonunion wage differentials or, in the case of import-sensitive industries, the worsening of labor cost disadvantages vis-à-vis foreign producers during the 1970s. Union wage-setting practices remained stable as long as trend productivity growth matched the annual improvement factor built into traditional wage formulas. But when productivity gains slowed, the use of mechanistic formulas resulted in settlements that were at odds with the market conditions facing individual firms or industries. After the longer-term consequences became evident in the form of declining market shares, affected unions began to modify traditional wage formulas and to experiment with alternate approaches to wage administration in an effort to lower costs. Which modifications in recently negotiated contracts are likely to be enduring features of union settlements during the remainder of the 1980s? What are the implications for union wage behavior?

If the only change in union wage determination were that workers did not recoup traditional wage adjustments that were forgone, then the moderation in wage inflation would be transitory. Wage *levels* would be indefinitely lower than they would have been without the recent wage cuts and freezes, but future wage *changes* would be indistinguishable from those in the past; that is, the past relationship between union wage behavior and its basic determinants—inflation and unemployment—would reemerge as modified contracts expire. There are some indications, however, that the structural upheaval in many unionized markets has redirected the attention of union workers to the long-run adverse

consequences that higher labor costs have for employment—a development that could presage longlasting changes in traditional union wage practices.

One fundamental change could be the scaling back of annual improvement factors. The absence of this factor from so many contracts during the past several years suggests that workers no longer automatically expect real wage improvements of 3 percent annually and will accept more modest goals in order to preserve jobs. Other joint efforts by labor and management to curb costs can be seen in recent contract provisions that diminish the economic impact of published wage scales. Such cost-saving provisions include two-tier wage systems under which new hires are paid less than incumbent employees for doing the same job, measures to hold down the rapid rise in benefit costs, and the elimination of costly work rules.

A survey by the Bureau of National Affairs found that nearly 6 percent of the 1,800 nonconstruction agreements reached between January and July 1984 specified some sort of dual pay plan. The potential savings from lower pay for new hires will vary depending on the size of the wage differential, on labor turnover rates, and on the extent to which new hires remain at the lower pay scales. Some observers of industrial relations fear that two-tier schemes could affect morale and productivity adversely if they create animosity between new hires and incumbents. Perhaps for that reason, many of these plans are temporary or graduated systems that allow new employees to progress to top-tier or regular wage scales over a specified period of time.

Negotiators also have sought to curtail the rapid rise in benefit costs, particularly the costs of medical plans. Union contract provisions covering medical plans often are specified in terms of benefit coverage rather than benefit costs. As medical costs rose, they were absorbed automatically by employers in addition to any negotiated improvements in benefit coverage. To curb rising costs, negotiators have turned to such measures as employee-paid deductibles and so-called cafeteria plans, under which employees are offered a choice of medical plans varying in cost and coverage while employers pay for a fixed dollar amount of their cost. These provisions are meant to encourage workers to avoid unnecessary medical expenditures and excessive insurance coverage. Improvements in benefits also have been scaled back or eliminated, and in some contracts a portion of COLAs has been diverted to help cover benefit costs.

A potentially more far-reaching change may be found in union agreements to lift work rules that have evolved over the past five decades. There is a growing consensus that many contractual rules governing the performance of work are no longer appropriate, particularly for industries faced with rapid technological change or increased competition.

Two major types of work-rule changes are being negotiated. One type leaves the existing organization of work intact but makes it more efficient. Examples include allowing management greater flexibility in scheduling work, relaxing the use of seniority in job assignments, and reducing the number of separate job classifications by combining duties and eliminating superfluous jobs. Generally, work-rule changes of this type give only a one-time boost to the level of productivity, unless they signal an ongoing effort to increase flexibility in the workplace. More fundamental changes involve revamping the organization of work entirely. An example is the introduction of team work, whereby workers learn all of the jobs in their work areas rather than perform narrow job functions, the usual practice. These developments may mark an emerging trend away from the traditionally adversarial atmosphere of U.S. labor–management relations toward a more cooperative framework with a long-term commitment to enhancing productivity.

Other innovations negotiated recently include profit-sharing arrangements and new job security provisions. Both of these innovations may be viewed as evidence of the new emphasis that unions are placing on preserving jobs. Because profits are heavily influenced by cyclical fluctuations in demand, profit-sharing plans tend to make labor compensation more sensitive to the ups and downs of the business cycle. Greater flexibility in compensation and prices could tend to smooth out cyclical fluctuations in sales, production, and employment. More stable employment in turn could reduce the costs of job security provisions such as lifetime employment guarantees or income maintenance plans for workers who are laid off because of plant closings. Over the longer term, preserving jobs will depend on remaining competitive; so managements often have offered new job security provisions in return for union commitments to negotiate improvements in productivity.

Whether profit-sharing plans will have a major influence on the cyclical behavior of union wages depends on (1) the proportion of the union workforce covered by profit sharing; (2) the size of bonuses as a share of total compensation; and (3) the extent to which bonuses replace other features of union settlements such as guaranteed wage increases and COLAs, which contributed to wage inertia in the past. Although the number of plans indexing compensation for union workers to company performance has increased sharply since 1980, overall coverage under these plans is still fairly low. Only about 10 percent of the workers in large bargaining units were covered by profit-sharing plans as of late 1983. Moreover, the size of bonuses under existing plans has yet to become a substantial proportion of total compensation. Thus, unless more unionized industries adopt profit-sharing plans and unions continue to accept bonuses in lieu of guaranteed wage increases, the impact of such plans on the cyclical behavior of aggregate union wages will be limited.

Although unions and management may continue to experiment with alternative forms of wage administration, there is no evidence of either a permanent move toward shorter contracts or a willingness to abandon COLA clauses. A recent survey found that management would strongly oppose any legal restrictions on the duration of collective bargaining agreements. The disadvantages of short-term contracts cited by management include an increase in the time and money spent on negotiations, an increase in the incidence of strikes, and adverse consequences on employee morale and productivity. Some of these objections may not be warranted, but it is clear that U.S. employers still feel that multiyear contracts are extremely important to maintaining stability in labor–management relations. At the same time, unions have been very reluctant to eliminate COLA provisions, even during a period of duress. Thus wage changes under multiyear agreements probably will remain highly sensitive to inflation.

5. Wage changes

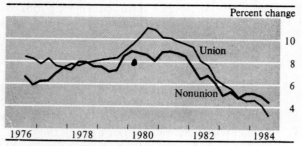

Percent change

Union

Nonunion

10
8
6
4

1976   1978   1980   1982   1984

Change from four quarters earlier.
SOURCE. Employment cost index, Bureau of Labor Statistics.

Nevertheless, the secular developments that led to the unprecedented wave of wage cuts and freezes recently may keep downward pressure on union wage changes. Apart from a few cases of steep wage cuts, recent modifications to traditional wage formulas have not yet substantially narrowed labor cost disadvantages. During the past two years, the rise in union wages on balance has averaged only ½ to 1 percentage point less than the rise in nonunion wages. That compares with a widening of the overall union–nonunion wage differential of perhaps 10 percentage points during the 1970s (chart 5). Given remaining cost disadvantages, the highly competitive conditions in many product markets are likely to persist. In unionized markets subject to foreign competition, domestic firms still have incentives to shift production abroad. In other unionized industries, recent inroads by nonunion firms have reduced the ability of unions to maintain wage premiums for their members. Barring any concerted actions to raise protectionist barriers or toward the reimposition of regulation, which merely would postpone market adjustments, these factors imply a sustained moderation in the rise of union labor costs in the years ahead and perhaps some reversal of the widening in union–nonunion wage differentials that took place during the 1970s. □

47

The "Share Economy": Can It Solve Our Economic Ills?

A new theory says inflation and unemployment both can be stabilized by "making workers' pay more flexible."

Interview With Martin Weitzman, Economist

A professor of economics at Massachusetts Institute of Technology since 1972, Martin Weitzman, 43, is the author of *The Share Economy* and has been a consultant to the World Bank and the International Monetary Fund.

Q. Professor Weitzman, your proposal for a "share economy" has been called the best economic idea since the theories of Keynes. Just what is a share economy?

A The idea is that instead of trying to deal with our major macroeconomic problems—unemployment and inflation—exclusively by sledgehammerlike manipulation of the money supply, tax rates, the size of the budget, etc., we should attack the problems at the source by making workers' pay more flexible.

Q. How would you do that?

A By keeping the predominant part of a worker's pay—the base wage—as it is today but having a substantial part of pay linked directly to profitability per employe. A worker's pay would be divided into two parts—one, a base wage; the other, a part that would depend upon the fortunes of the company.

Q. Which are you talking about—sharing profits or sharing revenues?

A Theoretically, it doesn't make much difference. Either provides incentives for the employer to want to expand production during good times and to want to resist layoffs during bad times.

Q. How would those incentives work?

A With the current wage system, the company wants to hire workers up to the point where what the worker is contributing is at least equal to the amount that the worker is being paid.

When you have something like profit sharing, it is like the pie of revenue is effectively being divided into two parts: One fixed fraction is going to labor; the other fixed fraction is retained by management for everything else—paying off capital, stockholders and the rest. Now, if a pie is being split in that way, it's in management's interest to make the pie as big as possible.

Under the wage system we now have, there's a definite limit on how many workers managers want to hire and how big they want the pie to be because as it gets bigger they have to pay more in fixed amounts to labor. When some fraction of the pie is being paid to labor—no matter how many workers there are—and managers retain the other fraction, they naturally want to make that pie as big as possible.

Q. What would happen under your system if the economy slid into a recession?

A Employment would remain at about full employment; there would be incentives to cut prices; there might be some buildup of inventories, or there might be some attempt to sell the output at lower prices. The crucial point is that the way an economy with widespread profit sharing would absorb recessionary shocks would be not to contract employment but to maintain employment at the full-employment level.

Q. How could you persuade companies not to fire workers if sales didn't demand them and to hire more during boom times?

A Well, sales are never such that they don't really need more workers on *some* terms—never, ever. Any airline company could aggressively expand if it could only lower its price to its customers. The automobile industry, which is pretty concentrated, is still very competitive; they'd love to be able to lower their prices and compete more aggressively with Japanese imports.

What prevents them from lowering their prices and increasing their volume is their high costs. If you could shift over some of that cost so that the worker is getting perhaps about the same amount but the base wage is lower and the difference is made up by profit shares, the company would be induced to expand volume and lower price.

Q. Then take-home pay would fall in a recession and rise when business picked up?

A There would be some movement in money pay for the average worker, which there isn't now under a fixed wage. But if this sort of thing could be widespread enough, 80, 85 percent of a worker's pay could be in the form of a base wage. Probably 15 to 20 percent in the form of profit sharing would be enough to perform this miracle of stabilizing employment. So we are not talking about huge changes in paychecks.

Q. How does the business cycle fit in?

A Today, wages are sticky. We've got a system where the average worker can be sure of the money pay that he is receiving as long as he has a job. That is all right in some ways, but it's very bad in some other ways. It's very bad because it throws the entire burden of adjustment in an economy on the employment side and on the price side. So we've stabilized the median worker's money income, but we've destabilized employment and we have destabilized the price level.

Actually, in terms of randomness, the average worker has more uncertainty under the present system. Look around at the uncertainty out there: Interest rates are highly variable; prices can jump around a great deal. Look what's happened to young people trying to buy a house: They're priced out of the market now. So in terms of purchasing power, in terms of real income, the present system introduces a great deal of variability.

I don't think that's the end of the world, but it's better to have less variability. What is a very serious detriment to the current system is unemployment because not only is that bad for the unemployed, not only does that have very harmful social effects, but it's also bad for the employed: They have to pay the burden. Each percentage point of unemployment contributes some 30 billion dollars to the budget deficit and loses 80 billion dollars of national income. Unemployment represents a loss—a real loss of production—and that's where the crime is.

Q. How much of unemployment today is related to economic fluctuations and how much to the advent of new technologies?

A The introduction of new technology is causing only a fraction of unemployment. Assume there is that kind of frictional unemployment; it's still something that could be avoided. In an ideally functioning economy with a tight labor market and a hungry demand for labor, those high-tech companies or whoever would be sending buses to the rust belt to pick jobless people up and bring them on board. That's the kind of situation I'd like to see, and that's what I think perhaps widespread introduction of profit sharing could bring about.

Q. How do you define full employment?

A If you had a high-enough fraction of profit sharing, we might be able to get down to 2 percent unemployment.

Q. What about workers in a declining industry? Aren't they still going to be fired?

A Any system that wants to grow has to have a mechanism for taking workers or resources out of a declining industry and transferring them to an advancing industry. That's what capitalism is all about. You can't fossilize workers or resources in any particular industry or sector. Now, the way that occurs under a set-wage capitalism is simple: The worker gets the boot. The way that happens under the share system is that the worker is never actually laid off. If there's a strong-enough profit-sharing component, the company doesn't find it in its self-interest at any given moment of time to lay the worker off.

Q It might go broke, though—

A No. Instead, they're going to resist pay increases. If managers can successfully resist the pay increases, they still will want to keep as many workers as they can at the existing base wages and profit shares. But the workers themselves are going to say: "Hey, what are we doing here? We're getting $2 an hour less than we could make somewhere else where the profit share is larger." When that differential becomes great enough, they move on.

And other companies under this kind of system are eager to soak up labor. The transference takes place under conditions of a tight labor market. There won't be the kind of interim unemployment or malaise that affects the community when its industry is going down.

Q Does that leave the low-efficiency workers on the payroll?

A It could. If one views managers or employers as so clever that they can see who are the hard-working workers and who are not—and pay them accordingly—then what's the difference? If a worker is working at two thirds the efficiency of another, he or she is only getting two thirds of the pay anyway. Under that circumstance, it doesn't make any difference, all in all, which one leaves. If managers can't tell what kind the worker is, then—yes—I suppose there might be some of that.

Q What would happen to unions?

A Unions will have less ability to set a fixed-total money wage. If this kind of sharing becomes more widespread—as it is in Japan—the unions' fate is tied a bit more to the fate of their company. Now, I think that's a good thing.

The traditional union concerns are still there—procedures about fair practice, about who is laid off, about due process and all that sort of thing. The negotiating about what is to be the base wage and what is to be the profit share and how is it to be defined—that's still there. I assume it's going to be tougher for a union to lock into a high level of base pay because the company is going

to be able to offset that demand to some degree with profit sharing.

Q Could and should your system be promoted through government actions?

A I would be in favor of having profit-sharing income by an average worker treated, up to some reasonable level, the same way as long-term capital gains. On the most basic level of common sense—and also with a lot of highfalutin mathematical economics—you can show that it would flex up workers' pay. It would make it so that there would be a big incentive for that automobile worker to let some part of the pay be dependent upon the performance of the company.

Q Would the idea work for small firms?

A I don't see why not. As a matter of fact, where it is working today, of course, is with really small businesses, with partnerships or with a single person. I mean lawyers, doctors in self-practice, farmers—they're on profit sharing; they share profits with themselves. A doctor or a lawyer doesn't put himself out of business when there's a recession; he makes out with a smaller income. □

48

SHOULD CONGRESS RAISE THE MINIMUM WAGE?

The Working Poor Deserve a Raise

**By SAR A. LEVITAN
and ISAAC SHAPIRO**

ECONOMISTS are predicting continued economic growth and prosperity for the foreseeable future, and that is good news. Unfortunately, the millions of Americans who work for the minimum wage are not sharing this prosperity. The real value of the minimum — which was designed to protect the working poor by placing a floor under their meager earnings — is now at its lowest level since 1955.

At $3.35 an hour, the minimum wage is still at the same level it was in January 1981. In that same time, the cost of living has risen by 26 percent, so that a full-time, year-round minimum wage worker currently earns income equivalent to only 76 percent of the poverty level for a family of three.

Nearly 8 million workers are paid at or below the minimum wage level (some employers simply ignore the law and pay sub-minimum wages, while some 10 million non-supervisory workers, primarily in retailing, service industries and agriculture, are not covered by the minimum wage). Almost half of minimum-wage workers are 25 years or older, and one of every four is a head of household.

Whether or not a minimum-wage worker is poor, and many are not, income from a higher minimum wage would provide much-needed assistance. And the higher wage would do the most good for the people who have suffered the greatest from the erosion of the minimum and who most deserve support — the working poor.

Throughout most of the 1960's and the 1970's, full-time, year-round work at the minimum wage provided enough income for a family of three to escape poverty. For this same family to escape poverty now, however, the minimum wage would have to rise to $4.38 an hour. In 1984, 2.1 million individuals worked full-time throughout the year but remained in poverty, including 1.2 million heads of households. Millions more live in these impoverished families.

Sar A. Levitan is director and Isaac Shapiro is research associate of the George Washington University Center for Social Policy Studies.

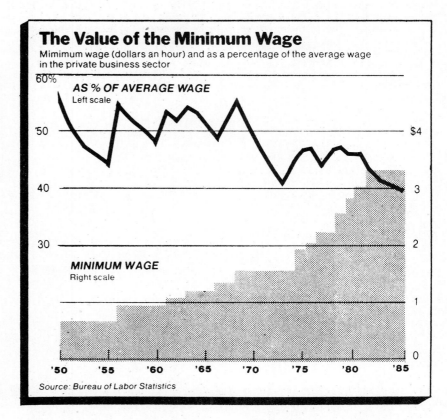

The Value of the Minimum Wage

Mimimum wage (dollars an hour) and as a percentage of the average wage in the private business sector

AS % OF AVERAGE WAGE
Left scale

MINIMUM WAGE
Right scale

'50   '55   '60   '65   '70   '75   '80   '85

Source: Bureau of Labor Statistics

An adequate minimum wage reinforces the work ethic. A worker earning a reasonable minimum not only gains economic independence but also moves his family above the poverty level. Greater work effort also boosts productivity and cuts the welfare rolls.

Opponents of the minimum wage argue that it reduces employment opportunities. President Carter's Minimum Wage Study Commission estimated that a 10 percent increase in the minimum wage would decrease teen-age employment by 1 percent. The employment loss for adults is less, because young workers tend to be laid off before older workers and because a smaller proportion of adults work at the minimum wage.

The minimum wage may indeed cause some job loss, but its positive income and work-incentive effects outweigh this loss. The current challenge is for Congress to establish a minimum wage that strikes the right balance between loss in employment and a rise in earnings. The minimum wage is now so low that we could raise the minimum substantially without significant job loss.

A rise in the minimum wage would not adversely affect the economy. It has little effect on inflation, because most workers earn substantially more than the minimum. The last time the wage was increased, in January 1981, some 5.5 million workers potentially benefited by $2.2 billion annually. This, however, was only two-tenths of 1 percent of total worker compensation in 1981.

Rather than proposing an increase

in the minimum wage, the Reagan Administration has advocated a sub-minimum wage for youths. Teen-age unemployment is disturbingly high, particularly among black teen-agers, but a sub-minimum wage for youths is not the right answer.

A youth sub-minimum would encourage employers to hire teen-agers instead of adults, and would lower the earnings of employable youths. Also, it would be of least help to the youngsters who need the most help — disadvantaged youths do not live in the areas where new jobs might be created. Moreover, many of these young people, lacking job skills, need training before employers will hire them.

Despite these arguments, the Administration continues to seek legislation that would establish a lower minimum wage for young people, thus detracting attention from the deterioration of the minimum wage. Labor unions have not pushed for raising the minimum wage because of their concern that the legislative package might include the sub-minimum wage for youths. To break this impasse, the minimum wage could be raised for adults but held, on a trial basis, at its existing level for youths.

THE purchasing power of the minimum wage should be raised by modest annual increments — say, 5 percent annually — until it is equivalent to its traditional level of half the average hourly earnings in private industry. In current dollars, the target level is $4.36 an hour. The minimum wage is now 38 percent of the average hourly wage, its lowest level by this measure since 1949.

In the absence of Congressional action, the minimum wage will continue to wither. The notion that state action will supplant Federal policy is false. Only three states have a minimum higher than the Federal standard.

Congress should raise the minimum wage to assist the working poor and other minimum-wage earners. This would be the surest way to increase their income without raising the Federal deficit. More working Americans would then share in the benefits of continued economic growth. ■

SHOULD CONGRESS RAISE THE MINIMUM WAGE?

An Increase Would Hurt Teen-Agers

By MARVIN H. KOSTERS

IS it time once again to raise the minimum wage? It has indeed fallen since it was last raised in 1981, after adjustment for inflation and relative to average wages. But we should look carefully at the consequences of raising the minimum.

The most obvious effect is that some workers would get higher wages. If this were the whole story, raising the minimum wage would be a very promising strategy and there would be no reason to settle for a small increase. Since this is only part of the story, it is essential to consider the other, less direct effects.

First, research on previous increases has established that the argument is no longer about *whether* but about *how much* a rise in the minimum wage reduces employment. Proponents of an increase argue that the job loss is small as a percent of those employed, and emphasize the gains in earnings and income for those remaining employed. How large the gains are compared with the losses is therefore a critical question.

Because a larger fraction of teen-age workers earn wages near minimum levels, research has focused on how teen-age workers have been affected. Much of this research shows fairly small effects on teen-age employment; an increase in the minimum of, say, 10 percent would result in 1 percent to 3 percent fewer teen-agers employed.

This might seem like a small price to pay. But those teen-agers losing jobs lose *all* of their earnings. Some who remain employed would benefit. But some teen-agers are not covered by the minimum wage and many already earn wages higher than the minimum. Others would have their hours cut back, so only a fraction would actually get 10 percent higher earnings. Thus, what initially might seem a small price to pay turns out to

Marvin Kosters is director of market and regulation studies at the American Enterprise Institute for Public Policy Research.

be a hard bargain. For every extra dollar earned by those who benefit, more than 50 cents is lost by those harmed. Moreover, those who lose are teen-agers whose earnings capability is already poorest.

But the story does not end here. When fewer jobs are available, teen-agers face difficulties in developing valuable work experience. In addition, minimum wages encourage employers to emphasize work that contributes to their revenues and to skimp on on-the-job training.

Comparisons of the earnings history of teen-age workers covered by the minimum wage and those who are not show noticeably smaller earnings gains for covered workers. In other words, as a result of less on-the-job training, the overall gains to teen-agers who do get jobs are much smaller than the higher pay they receive. A higher minimum wage means fewer jobs, and more of the jobs that remain are "dead end" jobs.

Curiously, the same people who would raise the minimum wage think nothing of subsidizing education and, at the post-secondary level, paying hefty tuition fees along with the "work" that schooling entails. Some young people, however, choose work instead of schooling. Why should those workers willing to "pay" — in the form of lower current earnings for jobs with more training content — be prevented by the minimum wage from making such arrangements?

The traditional justification for a legal minimum wage — to enable a worker to earn wages sufficient to support a family — is usually less applicable for teen-agers than for adults. For most families the major benefits of teen-agers' jobs are the work discipline acquired, the contribution to a developing sense of independence and, in many cases, diversion from antisocial activities. Two-thirds of those earning wages near or below the minimum are adults, however, so the effects on family living levels of higher minimum wages for adults deserve examination.

REGRETTABLY, data on how many poor families might benefit from a higher mini-

mum wage are scant. Estimates show that only about 6 percent of household heads work for wages at or below the minimum, and about 10 percent of households with poverty-level incomes may include a year-round full-time worker. While some of these families would benefit from a higher minimum wage, the cost to a poor family of a lost job would be extremely high.

Despite data limitations, certain generalizations are possible. First, the principal reasons for low incomes are not low wages but the absence of work for those who are employable and the absence of transfer payments for those who are not. Second, income from sources other than earnings, especially transfers, is so broadly distributed today that the link between earnings and levels of living has been greatly weakened. Most analysts agree that raising minimum wages is a remarkably ineffectual policy for reducing poverty or reducing income inequality.

Finally, it is useful to look beyond workers most directly affected by minimum wages and consider developments in the economy as a whole. The highly favorable growth in employment in recent years when the real minimum wage was declining did not come at the expense of average wage levels. Average real wage levels have increased by 2.1 percent since 1981, compared with a decline of 1.8 percent in the three years after 1973, when the real minimum wage increased by the same amount as it has recently declined.

Both the detailed examination of the effects of minimum wages on particular groups and general performance in the economy point to a simple conclusion: however well intentioned, boosting the minimum wage is not a policy that deserves support. ∎

The Economics and Politics of the Supply-Side View

F. Thomas Juster
Director, Institute for Social Research
Professor of Economics
The University of Michigan

Economic policy is, at least for the moment, set on a course which is distinctly different from the past. What are the prospects that the new policy will successfully produce the set of outcomes that its proponents hope to achieve—a reinvigorated economy with a smaller but more effective public sector; an incentive structure designed to produce more effort, saving, and investment; a business climate more conducive to innovation and productivity growth; and a sharply lower rate of inflation?

Seldom has an economic experiment been put in place with less conventional credentialing by professional economists. This is partly because supply-side policies represent a political statement at least as much as an economic perspective, partly because aspects of the supply-side view of economic life are not testable by assessing their consistency with the facts of economic life: supply-siders argue that many such facts are irrelevant because they come from a world where important expectational forces were substantially influenced by demand-side considerations.

What I judge to be the theoretical core of supply-side economics can be summed up in the following proposition:

1. Entitlement programs have eroded work incentives; cutting back on those programs will restore incentives and reduce the tax burden on the working and investing population.

2. The tax system is biased against effort, saving, and investment; reducing tax rates; especially marginal rates, will have a substantial effect on labor supply, saving, and investment.

3. Economic progress has been significantly impeded by an antibusiness climate of regulation designed to protect consumer and employee groups against various risks: many of these regulations not only require large and unproductive investments, but have adverse cost/benefit ratios in terms of protection offered versus the costs of obtaining it.

4. The stubbornness of inflation forces is largely due to the expectational climate built up by the demand-side oriented fiscal and monetary policies followed by past administrations: modifying the expectations of decision makers will thus permit a much more rapid reduction in inflation rates, at less social cost, than would be predicted from past history.

In addition to the economic content of supply-side ideas, there is a strong political content as well. Supply-siders and their political allies are apt to believe that government in general is too big and inevitably inefficient, that an impersonal monetary policy is the only effective way to control the macroeconomy, that free markets are the only way to allocate resources efficiently under any and all circumstances, and that politicians of any persuasion are not to be trusted to carry out promises. Many of those who

favor the current set of supply-side policies do not necessarily buy the economic underpinnings, or at least not all of them. Rather, they see supply-side theory and practice as a way to achieve other desirable objectives, and are willing to overlook its shaky intellectual foundations.

Whether or not supply-side policies will work depends ultimately on the adequacy of its economic underpinnings; from that perspective, the political content that is the basis for much of its support is largely irrelevant. Thus the basic question is: what can be said about the central analytical themes of supply-side economics?

Entitlements and Incentives

There is a good bit of evidence to support the general thrust of the supply-side argument—that entitlement programs have sapped work incentives. Most economists would probably agree with the view that extended unemployment compensation benefits reduce people's willingness to seek work or to accept work that is less well paid than their previous occupation, and that the welfare system with its extremely high implicit marginal tax rates has discouraged people from entering or staying in the labor force, etc.[1]

The argument here is not whether such programs tend to reduce work incentives—they almost certainly do. Rather, it is a question of magnitude—is the incentive reduction aspect of the programs a major defect or a minor blemish? Moreover, is the incentive reducing effect sufficiently important to outweigh the income distribution aspects of the program? On the latter issue, economic analysis will not do much good, and value judgments are at issue.

The proposition that reducing marginal tax rates will have a significant effect on labor supply and effort for the working population is much more dubious. Here, there is quite a lot of evidence and general agreement among economists: the effect of reduced marginal tax rates on effort is quite minor, and much of the evidence suggests that there will be no effect at all. In fact, one can make a case that reducing marginal tax rates will actually cause less work effort rather than more—people may choose to work as many hours as needed to maintain a satisfactory consumption level, and increasing their after-tax income will make it possible to realize the consumption goal with fewer hours.

---

[1] Incidentally, it is also true that some entitlement programs appear to have had major unintended effects on family structure—divorce, for example—which may be much more important than the labor supply effects.

Saving and Investment Incentives

It is true that the tax system is biased against saving and investment, relative to alternative tax systems that one could imagine. But that's a long way from saying that modification of the tax structure along the lines proposed by supply-siders will cause a great upswelling of saving and investment. There is a good bit of empirical evidence here, although much of it speaks only indirectly to the issue. On the whole, I would assess the potential impact of supply-side policies on saving decisions to be substantially weaker than the potential impact of such policies on investment decisions.[2].

On savings, there really is no persuasive evidence at all that personal or national saving rates would be impacted by modifications of the personal income tax structure, as argued by the supply-siders. Saving behavior is influenced by a lot of factors, and after-tax rates of return do not loom large among such influences as best we can tell from the empirical evidence. In fact, as is true for labor supply responses, it is at least as plausible that increasing the after-tax rate of return on saving will cause people to save less rather than save more, and for the same reason—if people have wealth targets, they can reach them more easily with a higher rate of return on saving than with a lower one, and may therefore be induced to save less.

For investment, expected rates of return are crucial. But one needs a good deal more than a favorable tax structure to produce a favorable investment climate—business firms do not add to capacity without a robust forecast of higher sales, regardless of the tax climate for business profits, and the capital deepening that might result from a more favorable after-tax rate of return is a subtle and long-term effect that might or might not be importantly influenced by the tax structure.

Regulatory Climate

What may be potentially the strongest weapon in the supply-side arsenal is the impact of a change in the regulatory climate on private investment and on incentives to take risks. The evidence for the negative impact of present and prospective regulation on risk taking and investment decisions is not so overwhelmingly strong that one can confidently conclude that a change in the climate will produce a major impact on investment. However, the argument seems entirely plausible on theoretical grounds and has some empirical support. Business decision makers do seem to perceive the regulatory climate as one with a great many land mines, and tiptoeing through those mine fields does not seem conducive to bold investment strategies of the sort that we probably need in order to

---

[2]See F. Thomas Juster, "Saving, Economic Growth, and Economic Policy," in the Summer 1981 issue of ECONOMIC OUTLOOK USA.

revitalize the economy. I would make the case by simply noting that bureaucracy generally stifles innovation, and whatever desirable social effects might be achieved by a vigorous regulatory climate, it is quite likely to create a distinct lack of enthusiasm for entrepreneurial adventure.

Inflation and Expectations

An important underpinning to the supply-side view of life is the role given to expectations in influencing a variety of decisions. Much of our recent economic history is consistent with the view that wringing inflation out of the U.S. economic system is likely to be a long and painful process, involving very substantial losses in real income and output for a very modest gain in lower inflation rates. Supply-siders argue that this history is largely irrelevant, since it results from a widely held expectation that economic policy will be used to prevent a serious or prolonged recession. And with an expectation that the government will bail the system out of any temporary weakness, no one has any incentive to modify behavior.

I am certainly not one to quarrel with the view that expectations have a lot to do with behavior. On the other hand, I would feel a lot more comfortable with the central focus given to expectational forces by the supply-siders if they showed any interest in actually studying expectations, or how expectations change in response to events, or what forces appear to influence expectations. But like most macroeconomists, supply-siders seem quite content to infer the force of expectations from observing consequences that could in theory be explained by expectational phenomena—a scientific procedure which has the great merit of avoiding conflicts between theory and data, but the great demerit of being untestable because it cannot discriminate among hypotheses.

Some of the expectational forces alleged to be important by supply-siders seem to me quite plausible, others much less so. For example, I think it is probably true that the stubbornness of inflationary forces in the U.S. economy is a consequence of the widespread expectation that policy will not tolerate extended periods of economic weakness. But it remains to be seen whether changing those expectations will have a major or only a minor impact on the cost of decelerating the inflation rate.

In other areas, the expectational views of supply-siders seem to me simply implausible. For example, it is alleged on theoretical grounds that the prospect of lower taxes on future income will shift labor supply from the present, when income is taxed at a relatively high rate, to the future, when income will be taxed at a lower rate. The notion that people will buy more present leisure because they expect tax rates to decline in the future is one that I find a little hard to relate to anything I think I know about behavior.

One should be careful not to single out supply-siders for criticism on this count. For example, most macroeconomists appear to believe that people make saving, labor supply, and retirement decisions on the basis of their expectations about social security entitlements in the distant future. Thus they calculate a variable called "social security wealth" and assume it represents a decision parameter in the household utility function. Perhaps so, but I doubt it. People do have expectations of retirement income, and there is likely to be some influence on what they do currently in terms of what they expect. But I doubt that the computed actuarial value of future pension rights, properly discounted to the present, is a very good representation of that expectational structure. One indication of this problem is that pension rights, and even more so changes in those rights, are pretty hard to calculate: for example, there is an enormous advantage to continuing work between the ages of 62 and 65, in terms of the value of future social security benefits, but that is not even realized by many of those who have written on social security problems, let alone by the potential recipient.

Summing up the pluses and the minuses, it turns out that what many see as the most important elements in supply-side economic policy—the impact of changes in tax rates on labor supply and the flow of saving—are the elements that are most in conflict with what we know about behavior, and the least likely to be effective. The other parts of the program—the effect on incentives of cutting entitlements, the effect on the expectations of price and wage setters of changing the government's role in setting limits to recession—seem more promising but represent views supported by evidence that is shaky at best and often either casual or impressionistic.

51

DID REAGAN'S 1981 TAX INCENTIVES WORK?

The Vaunted Investment 'Boom' Is a Bust

BENJAMIN M. FRIEDMAN

DESPITE the latest negative flutterings of scattered indicators, the idea has taken hold that America in the second half of the 1980's is on the move again economically. Prices are more nearly stable, incomes are up and unemployment is at least steady.

Surveys show that most people think there is more to the current wave of good economic news than a typical expansion of the business cycle. People expect this expansion to last and to bring a long-term renewal of gains in productivity and overall standards of living.

These high hopes for the economy's longer-run prospects hinge critically on the widespread belief that business capital spending — which is linked to productivity growth — is booming. But where, in fact, is this boom?

Indeed, business capital spending has recovered sharply from the depths it reached at the bottom of the recession in 1981 and 1982. Gross spending for new plant and equipment last year was $425 billion, up 20 percent from the $353 billion that business spent the year before. More important, net investment — investment spending beyond what was needed to replace old structures and equipment — rose even more dramatically, from $50 billion in 1983 to an estimated $107 billion in 1984. Surely America is in the midst of a well-publicized boom in capital spending, building today the foundation for tomorrow's rapid growth. Right?

Wrong. What is missing in this analysis is a sense of how high is up. The development that has attracted so much attention lately is the large increase in investment spending from the recession-depressed level of 1983.

The $50 billion that American business spent on net additions to its productive capacity in 1983 amounted to only 1.5 percent of that year's gross national product. That performance made 1983 the second-worst invest-

Benjamin M. Friedman is professor of economics at Harvard University.

U.S. Capital Spending

Net nonresidential fixed investment, in billions of dollars and as a percentage of gross national product

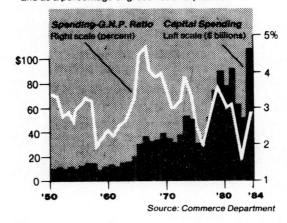

Source: Commerce Department

ment year in the nearly four decades since World War II. Only in 1975, after the sudden four-fold increase in oil prices had not only squeezed economic activity but also rendered obsolete many kinds of energy-intensive capital goods, was the nation's net investment rate that low.

The much heralded improvement of our investment rate, to an estimated 2.9 percent of gross national product last year, was welcome. But climbing off the basement floor is not the same as scaling new heights.

For example, the economy's average investment rate during the decade following the Korean War was only slightly lower — 2.4 percent of gross national product. The prevailing attitude then was different, however. Most people recognized that so little investment fell far short of what our major trading partners and competitors abroad were doing, and also fell short of what we needed to achieve our own aspirations for continuing economic growth.

By 1964, this widespread dissatisfaction led to public policy initiatives aimed at stimulating business capital spending. Prominent elements in that package included lower corporate tax rates, accelerated depreciation and an investment tax credit. In response, business invested more. The economy's net investment rate rose

to 2.8 percent in 1965 and 3.9 percent on average for the remainder of the 1960's — more than half-again as much as before.

HARD economic times in the 1970's eroded most of these gains, as the average net investment rate during the decade dipped to 2.7 percent. The real disaster was the recession of 1981 and 1982. The collapse of net investment from 3.1 percent of total output in 1981 to 2 percent in 1982 and finally only 1.5 percent in 1983, was part of the huge price the country paid to slow inflation.

Now, during the vigorous recovery from that recession, the net investment rate has leapt all the way up to 2.9 percent — only slightly better than the performance of the 1950's.

Building for a lasting renewal of American economic growth will require a much more substantial improvement in investment, one that goes well beyond the current, quite ordinary cyclical recovery. The promise held out by the Reagan Administration to justify the business tax cuts enacted four years ago was that they would produce just such an investment boom. Along the way, a continuing Federal budget deficit that swallows more than half the nation's private savings has gutted this promise. With no end to the deficit in sight, the prospects for our economy's achieving a genuine investment boom are hardly promising.

Individuals and businesses in the United States consistently save about 7 percent of the nation's gross national product, and the combined surpluses of state and local governments are currently adding another 1 percent. Hence, there is ample saving to finance both strong business investment and a healthy pace of homebuilding, without relying on inflows of capital from abroad. Instead, as a result of a Federal deficit now running more than $200 billion per year, or nearly 6 percent of G.N.P., both business investment and homebuilding are far from adequate despite record foreign capital inflows.

Current policy initiatives both help and hurt. The effort in Congress, now apparently stalled, to compromise on about $50 billion a year of spending cuts deserves support. But even if it is successful, it will still leave a Federal deficit equal to nearly 4 percent of G.N.P. At the same time, abolishing the investment tax credit, as the Reagan Administration has proposed as part of its tax reform package, will render investment in new equipment more expensive. Moreover, if tax reform turns into tax reduction, it could offset most or even all of the spending cuts.

Opening the way for a genuine investment boom will require a more significant slashing of the Federal deficit than what is now on the table. Carrying through on the proposed spending cuts, balancing this tighter fiscal stance with a less restrictive monetary policy and keeping the tax reform revenue-neutral are all essential parts of the strategy, but together they will not be enough. In the absence of spending cuts that go well beyond what the public seems to want, a significant increase in taxes that do not discourage investment will also be necessary. ■

52

Impervious Saving Behavior

One argument made a few years ago by proponents of large federal tax cuts was that the resulting massive federal deficits could automatically be financed by the private sector. In part, the argument relied on the hypothesis that the fall in tax rates would create an incentive for the private sector to increase its saving rate, and that the increase in private saving would finance the federal deficits and obviate any increase in market interest rates.

Such arguments no longer appear in the financial press because the reality is that we live in a country of deficient domestic saving. This deficiency is easily measured. It is simply the difference between gross *private domestic* investment and gross domestic saving in our national income accounts. Gross saving is the sum of gross private saving (personal and business) and the saving of the government sector.

In the second quarter of this year gross *private* saving totalled $663 billion. Added to the $54 billion surplus of state and local governments and the $167 federal deficit—the "dissaving" of the federal government, we find that the gross saving of the entire economy in the second quarter of 1984 amounted to $550 billion, at an annual rate. In contrast, gross private domestic investment totalled $626 billion. Domestic investment therefore exceeded domestic saving. The balance of about $76 billion was made up in essence by borrowing from abroad. Foreigners can be viewed as having provided about 12 percent of the funds needed to finance U.S. private investment in the second quarter, or as having financed about 45 percent of the federal deficit.

How the private sector sees the government
Before the proponents of large federal tax cuts made their claims about probable private sector responses to increased federal deficits and higher after-tax rates of return, they should have studied the post-war behavior of gross domestic private saving. Despite recent economic events such as changes in federal income tax rates and high real interest rates, the gross domestic private saving rate whether measured as a percent of GNP or of national income has remained relatively stable.

From 1975 to 1983, gross domestic private saving as a percent of gross national product varied between 16.5 percent and 18.2 percent. In the last three years, its rate has moved narrowly between 17.1 and 17.3 percent. The same stability does not describe the government saving rate. Since 1975, federal, state and local financial positions combined have yielded a government saving rate (as a percent of GNP) that has ranged from about zero in 1979 to negative 4 percent in 1983. Gross domestic private saving, has, then, seemed insensitive to the financial position of the government sector as well as to the extraordinarily high level of real interest rates in recent years. (See Chart 1.)

While the gross domestic private saving rate has been relatively stable, its two components— personal saving and business saving have not. As noted by Edward F. Denison three decades ago, personal saving and corporate saving often appear to move in opposite directions. In a sense, the personal sector appears to incorporate the saving behavior of the corporate sector in its own decisions to save and to consume. This is not unreasonable. Since the non-business (personal) sector "owns" the corporate sector, it considers corporate saving, composed of undistributed corporate profits and depreciation of corporate and noncorporate business, a close substitute for personal saving. This implies, as noted by Denison, that personal consumption expenditures are unaffected by corporate dividend behavior.

The offsetting saving behavior of the personal and corporate sectors leads to stability in the gross private domestic saving rate. The relationship is clearly observable in the two saving rates in just the last few years (Chart 2). Business saving as a percent of GNP grew from 12.6 to 13.7 percent between 1981 and 1983. Personal saving as a percent of GNP, on the other hand, fell from 4.6 to 3.6 percent from 1981 to 1983. The net effect was to produce gross private saving rates (as a percent of GNP) of 17.24, 17.07, and 17.30 percent in 1981, 1982 and 1983, respectively.

Domestic private saving has truly been impervious to the level of real interest rates in recent years and to the financial status of the federal government,

Reprinted from Federal Reserve Bank of San Francisco
Weekly Letter, September 28, 1984.

169

whose deficits have nearly tripled during the period from 1981 to 1983. While the personal sector seems to continue to incorporate the saving status of the business sector in its own saving decisions, it appears to have disregarded the financial status of the government sector.

Not internalizing government financial behavior
The debate over the effect of the federal government deficit on the real economy centers on the degree to which taxpayers recognize any current and future costs associated with paying for government expenditures with the sale of bonds rather than through immediate taxation. At the local community level, one might argue that taxpayers quickly recognize that bond issuance will involve a future financial burden to the local residents. These residents would alter their saving behavior in recognition of the future financing burden. In a sense, bond finance may be viewed as deferred taxation. A similar argument applied to federal deficits has gained popularity recently among some academic economists. However, it is difficult to observe any major change in private domestic saving behavior in response to the outbreak of large federal deficits.

The stability of the gross private saving rate in the face of federal budget deficits amounting to 5-6 percent of GNP, and expected to remain in the 3-4 percent range for the next several years, is inconsistent with recent arguments promoted by some academics that current federal deficits, entailing future principal and interest servicing costs, are equivalent to and interpreted by consumers as future taxes. Their argument presupposes that consumers realize that the only real "tax cut" is a government spending cut. Since they recognize this equivalence, according to the argument, they would not have interpreted recent personal income tax cuts as real tax cuts. Instead, they would have recognized the need to obtain additional interest-earning assets in order to pay for the future costs of servicing the increased federal deficit and saved *all* of the tax cut. The result should be a rise in the gross private saving rate. Chart 1 shows that in 1969 and 1975, for example, the gross private saving rate and the government saving rate moved in opposite directions, as suggested by the theory. Recent facts, however, do not support this argument. Between 1981 and 1983, the gross private saving rate averaged 17.20 percent compared with an average saving rate of 17.18 percent of GNP between 1975 and 1980. The tax cut and resulting

federal deficits do not appear to have disturbed the general stability of the gross private saving rate.

The saving gap
The apparent insensitivity of the gross private saving rate to changes in after-tax rates of return means that gross domestic saving likely will fall short of gross private domestic investment if the federal government goes substantially into deficit. The resulting shortfall may be called the "domestic saving gap." This gap totalled about $34 billion in 1983 and was closed by importing foreign capital, observable in our large and growing current account deficit.

The existence of both large federal deficits and large current account deficits has sometimes led to the claims that the former "causes" the latter. This is not necessarily true. The current account deficit could decline significantly, that is, the saving gap could close, even in the face of large federal deficits if domestic private investment would decline —the textbook case of "crowding out." Eliminating the domestic saving gap therefore requires either a fall in domestic investment or a reduction in the federal deficit.

But is the current saving gap necessarily pernicious, something to be avoided? Not necessarily. What we observe in the United States is that capital investment is more cyclical and more interest-sensitive than private saving. Hence, the saving gap is altered by cyclical swings in investment. For example, between 1978 and 1982, the ratio of gross private domestic investment to GNP fell from almost 18 percent to 13.5 percent, while the gross private saving rate was 17.3 and 17.1 percent.

The cyclical recovery beginning in late 1982 coupled with the reduction in after-tax interest costs of business capital investment and the resulting pick-up in investment led to the emergence of a saving gap and the need for the U.S. to import capital to finance what has turned out to be almost a capital investment boom in 1984. The saving gap currently reflects the very strong cyclical growth in business capital investment as well as the deficit status of the federal government. But unlike earlier recoveries, the saving gap is not expected to decline because the government saving rate is not expected to become less negative as it did between 1975 and 1979.

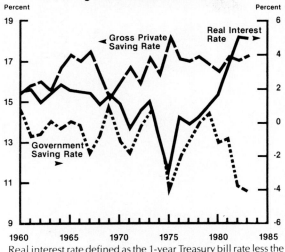

Chart 1
Saving and Real Interest Rates

Real interest rate defined as the 1-year Treasury bill rate less the annual rate of change in the GNP price deflator.

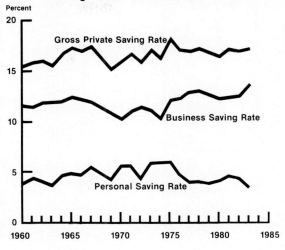

Chart 2
Saving Rates as a Percent of GNP

In part, the present situation is not unlike what occurred after the Civil War, when rapid U.S. economic growth and a declining price level led to massive importation of foreign capital. From 1861 to 1899, the United States was more often than not a financial capital importer. Only in nine years during this period did the United States experience a capital outflow. And not until the end of the 19th century did the United States turn from importing to exporting financial capital. This comparison of saving behavior in the 19th century with that in 1984 is meant simply to emphasize the fact that rapid economic growth and low inflation is often accompanied by capital importation, particularly if rates of return on real and financial investments are higher than they are abroad, which now appears to be the case.

The stability of the gross domestic private saving rate in the United States means that a significant pick-up in capital investment would lead to a cyclical shortfall of private domestic saving available to finance private investment. The private saving gap can be filled either by saving in the government sectors or by importing of foreign capital. In the long-run, it makes a considerable difference how the private saving gap is closed. Interest payments on the federal debt to foreign bond holders represent a real future tax burden to U.S. citizens. One could argue that the heavy importation of foreign capital is financing current government consumption and not private invest-

ment and hence the deficit represents the mortgaging of future income to pay for this excess consumption.

Tax policy implications

Changes in neither the personal income tax structure nor real after-tax interest rates have affected the U.S. gross domestic private saving rate. As a result, a large and possibly structural, that is, non-cyclical, domestic saving gap has emerged, resulting in U.S. dependence on foreign capital to finance both capital formation and the deficit of the federal government.

Should aggregate tax policy be changed to reduce the saving gap? This is obviously a sensitive and politically charged question, but we can conjecture that as the tax *cut* seems to have had no effect on the gross private saving rate, so a personal tax *increase* would most likely leave it unchanged. If the corporate tax rate is left unchanged, it is possible, although quite conjectural, that a tax increase on consumers *alone* might help close the saving gap without greatly affecting the growth of capital investment. That is, a tax increase on consumers might contribute to lowering the federal deficit without changing the gross private saving rate. Such a change in tax policy would recognize the insensitivity of the gross private saving rate to changes in taxes and real interest rate and the sensitivity of capital investment to both.

Joseph Bisignano

171

53

Productivity and the Prospects for Outgrowing the Budget Deficit

*Richard McHugh**

INTRODUCTION

The federal government has been running budget deficits of unprecedented proportions, totaling $211 billion in fiscal year 1985 (FY85), and amounting to 5.5 percent of gross national product (GNP). By comparison, in the 1970s the federal government deficit averaged 1.8 percent of GNP, and in the 1960s only 0.3 percent of GNP. Moreover, official forecasts from Congress

---

*Richard McHugh, Associate Professor of Economics, University of Missouri, Columbia, prepared this article while he was a Visiting Scholar in the Research Department of the Federal Reserve Bank of Philadelphia.

and the Administration are for continued high deficits for at least the next five years, unless Congress cuts spending programs, raises taxes, or both.

The size of both the current and the projected federal deficits has heightened the pitch of the fiscal policy debate. Many analysts argue that deficits of this magnitude will be detrimental to the U.S. economy because the growing federal demands in the credit markets could keep real interest rates high and "crowd out" private investment. High real interest rates are likely to keep the value of the dollar high. A high dollar makes imports relatively less expensive, and it increases the demand for foreign-made goods at the expense of those produced at home. And this means slower growth for industries that rely heavily on export markets and for those that compete with imports.

Because the federal deficit is so large, these analysts argue that the economy would benefit from a deficit reduction.[1] They believe that the needed reductions in the deficit can be accomplished only with both expenditure cuts and tax increases. Indeed, legislators apparently take as given the need for fiscal initiatives, while debating the details of the various plans.

Other analysts, however, deny the need for such fiscal action. They claim instead that the economic climate is now much better for economic growth, and that robust productivity growth will be strong enough to reduce budget deficits automatically to acceptable levels.[2] The argument is that tax revenues rise more quickly than expenditures in response to real growth, and that real growth—particularly productivity growth—will be high enough to make the deficit shrink dramatically; in other words, the economy will outgrow the deficit. Indeed, substantial fiscal action is not only unnecessary, in their minds, it is also detrimental. According to their view, fiscal initiatives, especially tax increases, would actually aggravate the longer-term budgetary problem by dampening economic growth.

The claim that productivity growth will be high enough to reduce deficits to acceptable levels, if true, has obvious and important policy implications. But before policymakers can act on such claims, they need to form clear ideas of exactly what it means to outgrow the deficit, as well as the time frame in which this would occur. Unfortunately, those who deny the need for fiscal action do not always detail these goals. But, to help pin these down, we can propose a scenario that falls within the bounds of historical possibility. Suppose that the deficit goal is the average deficit-to-GNP ratio for the years 1954-1980—which is 1.3 percent—and that the time frame is ten years.[3] How likely is the economy to outgrow the deficit, in this sense, by 1995?

OUTPUT GROWTH AND DEFICIT PROSPECTS

Current consensus economic forecasts do not support the claim that the economy will outgrow the deficit any time soon. A typical forecast is that of Data Resources, Inc. (DRI), which recently published projections of the course of economic activity through 1995 (see Table 1).[4] Based on their assumptions of what fiscal initiatives Congress will probably enact, and on their judgement about other important economic variables, the deficit falls gradually as a fraction of GNP

[1]Some economists have argued that in an economy with a growing level of nominal GNP, deficits do not cause a problem unless the ratio of outstanding debt to GNP rises. Since 1981, the ratio of gross federal debt held by the public to GNP has grown from 27.5 percent to 39.1 percent, its highest level since 1965. For a discussion of alternative views on the appropriate goals for budget policy, see Congressional Budget Office, *The Economic and Budget Outlook: Fiscal Years 1986-1990*, Chapter III, (CBO, February 1985), and B. Horrigan, "Federal Budget Deficits: An Efficient Tax Perspective," this *Business Review* (May/June 1984) pp. 15-25.

[2]For example, Pierre Rinfret and Paul Craig Roberts, prominent supply-side economists, argue that real GNP could grow in excess of the President's Office of Management and Budget's optimistic forecast, and that it would be strong enough to balance the federal budget. (See *Business Week*, January 9, 1984 and *Business Week*, September 24, 1984.)

[3]Of course, this scenario is arbitrary to some degree, and it is open to debate; the assumptions used here are by no means the only reasonable interpretation of what it means to outgrow the deficit. Rather, these assumptions provide *one* reasonable interpretation. In any case, the goal of a 1.3 percent deficit-to-GNP ratio to be achieved in ten years can be regarded as a yardstick with which to evaluate the impact of alternative productivity growth scenarios.

[4]The DRI figures used in this article come from the DRI "U.S. Long-Term Review," Summer 1985. The forecast refers to the so-called "Trendlong" projection. There is no claim here that this forecast is in some sense better than others. Rather, the economic assumptions used broadly represent a consensus, and the econometric model used in the computations is state-of-the-art.

TABLE 1

THE LONG-TERM PROJECTION

	Average Annual Growth Rate for 1985-1995
Real GNP	2.9%
Labor Productivity	1.9%
Employment	1.0%

	Average Annual Level for 1985-1995
Inflation (GNP deflator)	5.0%
Unemployment	7.2%

SOURCE: DRI "U.S. Long-Term Review", Summer 1985.

over the coming decade. At present, the deficit represents about 5.5 percent of GNP. According to DRI, by 1995 that ratio will fall to 2.7 percent, which is more than twice the post-war average ratio of 1.3 percent.

Not surprisingly, those who believe that high deficits will disappear take issue with the consensus predictions. In particular, they argue that the real growth assumptions underlying these projections are unduly pessimistic, and that underestimating prospective real growth overestimates likely future deficits. DRI foresees average real growth of 2.9 percent each year from now until 1995. Does this forecast understate the economy's long-run growth potential, that is, its ability to increase output? And if so, where will faster growth come from? To answer these questions, it is necessary first to understand what determines the economy's long-run growth capability.

One way to analyze the economy's long-run growth potential is to focus on the amount of labor available to produce output and on the productivity of that labor. Total output in an economy can be expressed as the total hours of labor employed times output per man-hour of labor, or labor productivity. Hence, output growth is determined by the growth rate of the labor force and by the growth rate of labor productivity. The DRI forecast of 2.9 percent average annual real GNP growth, for instance, comes from a 1 percent average annual growth in employment and a 1.9 percent average annual growth in productivity.

Productivity Growth is the Key. While a surge in employment growth can permit faster real GNP growth, those who look for strong economic growth typically stress labor productivity growth. Basically, they believe that the consensus forecast of 1.9 percent annual growth in productivity is unduly pessimistic. They feel that it is reasonable to expect higher productivity growth and, hence, stronger real GNP growth and lower deficits.[5]

According to the DRI estimates, in order to reach our hypothetical deficit goal, productivity must grow at a 3.2 percent annual average rate over the next 10 years (Figure 1, p. 18). Such productivity growth not only exceeds the consensus forecast by more than a percentage point, but it also appears high by historical comparison. A review of our post-war economic experience reveals no extended period with productivity growth as high as 3.2 percent per year (Table 2, p. 19). During two periods, however, productivity growth did average 2.9 percent per year, quite close to the required rate. Thus, the needed productivity growth, while extreme, may not be out of the question.

[5]Although emphasis here is placed on higher productivity growth, higher employment growth also would raise long-run real GNP growth and lower the deficit. However, employment growth over any long period depends primarily on growth in the labor force, which in turn depends heavily on demographic factors, such as the existing population and its social attitudes. Thus, average employment growth is unlikely to deviate a great deal from the consensus projections.

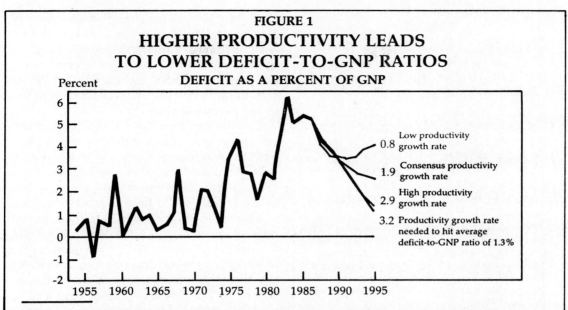

FIGURE 1
HIGHER PRODUCTIVITY LEADS
TO LOWER DEFICIT-TO-GNP RATIOS
DEFICIT AS A PERCENT OF GNP

0.8 Low productivity growth rate

1.9 Consensus productivity growth rate

2.9 High productivity growth rate

3.2 Productivity growth rate needed to hit average deficit-to-GNP ratio of 1.3%

NOTE: The deficit-GNP data shown in this figure were obtained by simulating the DRI model of the U.S. economy with the various productivity growth assumptions. For each assumed productivity growth, the simulation is performed so that the annual productivity growth is approximately the same as the average productivity growth.

But is this rate of productivity growth *likely*? This is an especially crucial question in light of the productivity growth the U.S. experienced during the two most recent business cycles. Table 2 reveals that labor productivity growth during the last two business cycles not only was far below the 2.9 percent post-war peak growth, but it also fell short of 1.9 percent annual growth, the consensus prediction for the coming decade. Therefore, the optimistic deficit reduction scenarios for the next ten years rely on a rapid acceleration of trend productivity growth relative to the 1970s and early 1980s.

WERE THE 1970s AN ANOMALY?

Analysts broadly agree on some of the economic forces that determine productivity trend growth, though there are important disagreements on the relative importance of these forces, and on how they interact with each other. Most everyone agrees that improvements in labor quality, that is, general education, skill levels, and so forth, increase productivity. Increases in the quantity or quality of capital equipment and in technological innovation also improve productivity. Finally, lower raw materials prices and less regulation are likely to improve productivity.

The analysts who feel confident that labor productivity growth will accelerate soon believe that the experience of the 1970s is an anomaly. They maintain that temporarily poor performances of the forces that determine productivity growth combined to slow productivity to a level far below its long-run trend growth rate. The forces that depressed labor productivity include a lack of growth in labor quality, large increases in energy prices, lack of technological innovation, and increased business regulation. The productivity optimists contend that the outlook for these forces has improved substantially in the 1980s, and that it will continue to improve in the coming years, making a return to the more rapid productivity growth rates of the 1960s likely.

Some Negative Forces Have Abated . . .

Declines in Labor Quality. In the late 1960s and

TABLE 2
PRODUCTIVITY GROWTH

Peak-to-Peak Period (year:quarter)	Growth Rate in Trend Productivity[a]
1948:4 - 1953:3	2.7%
1953:3 - 1957:3	2.1%
1957:3 - 1960:2	2.9%
1960:2 - 1969:4	2.9%
1969:4 - 1973:4	2.6%
1973:4 - 1980:1	0.8%
1980:1 - 1981:3	1.4%

[a]Measured as the annual rate of change from one business cycle peak to the next and excluding farm productivity. The technique of measuring labor productivity peak-to-peak is commonly used as a way of abstracting from cyclical variations in productivity growth when trying to measure trend productivity growth.

into the 1970s, the labor force contained a relatively large share of new entrants. The post-World War II baby-boom generation had reached working age and there was a large increase in women's participation rate in the labor force. This "double-barreled" influx of new entrants pulled down the average age and the experience level of the labor force. Because they lack experience, new workers generally are less productive than those who have held jobs. As a result, the average "quality" of the labor force stopped growing, and it may have even declined. In a recent study, Michael Darby calculates an index of labor quality growth and estimates that the quality of the labor force increased at a rate of 0.5 percent per year from 1948 to 1965, but remained essentially unchanged from 1965 through 1979.[6]

The outlook for labor quality growth has improved. The baby-boom generation has already made its debut in the workplace, and the disproportionate growth of women in the labor

[6]See Michael Darby, "The U.S. Productivity Slowdown: A Case of Statistical Myopia," *American Economic Review* (June 1984) pp. 301-321.

force is not likely to happen again. Over the next few years, as the proportion of the labor force made up of new entrants declines, the average age and experience level of the labor force will increase.[7] Everything else equal, the average growth rate of productivity attributable to this factor should increase.

Energy Price Increases. One of the most dramatic economic events of the past two decades was the extraordinary increase in the relative price of crude oil and other energy prices. From 1973 to the end of the decade, energy prices nearly tripled, while prices for all goods and services rose 85 percent. These huge energy price increases reduced labor productivity through two channels. First, as the relative price of energy increased, firms economized on the use of energy. The attempt to economize on energy pulled down the output produced by existing factories as energy usage declined. And this decline in output reduced labor productivity during that period. Second, the higher relative price of energy induced firms to invest in new plant and equipment that saved energy rather than labor. But this investment substituted energy-efficient capital for existing capital, without increasing the quantity of capital. As a result, this type of investment did not lead to any growth in labor productivity.

The odds of energy price increases in the 1980s even remotely approaching those of the 1970s are slim. In the last few years, the price of oil has fallen, in part as a result of the efforts of business and households to economize on en-

[7]In 1970, the labor force participation rate of women (43.3 percent) was just over half of that for men (79.7 percent). By 1982, the participation rate for women had risen to nearly 70 percent of that for men (52.6 percent to 76.6 percent). The Bureau of Labor Statistics (BLS) sees this ratio of participation rates of women to men rising to 76 percent by 1990—only a small increase. In the same labor force projections, the BLS forecasts that the percentage of the labor force made up of people between the ages of 16 and 24 will fall from 22.3 percent in 1982 to 17.7 percent by 1990. See Howard Fullerton and John Ischetter, "The 1995 Labor Force: A Second Look," *Monthly Labor Review*, (November 1983) pp. 3-10.

ergy use and in part because of the emergence of new suppliers of oil and of other sources of energy. Since it is likely that the adjustments to high energy prices made in the 1970s are mostly complete, and since oil prices have currently been weak, productivity growth is not likely to be as adversely affected by energy costs in the near future as it has been.

Lack of Innovation. Labor productivity can be affected favorably by technological innovations, such as inventions of new production processes, improvements in the operation of existing production processes, or enhancements in the quality (reliability, speed, and flexibility) of capital equipment. Many argue that the pace of pure technological innovation slowed considerably in the 1970s—that Americans simply ran out of ideas.

Ideas and innovations are hard to measure. However, some indication of the rate of change in this intangible "technology" can be gleaned from the Labor Department's measure of Multifactor Productivity (MFP) growth. MFP growth is defined as the growth rate of total output that cannot be accounted for by the growth rate of the inputs.[8] The magnitude of the MFP growth is attributed to the degree of technological innovation. The Labor Department's calculations confirm the view that growth of technological innovation slowed in the 1970s. The MFP grew

at an average annual rate of 1.7 percent during the period 1948 to 1973, but fell at a 0.1 percent annual rate from 1973 to 1981.[9] This evidence seems to support the view that the productivity decline may simply reflect a decline in technological innovation.

Causes of a slowdown in technological innovation are hard to identify, but some economists argue that the slowdown in technological innovation was presaged by an earlier slowdown in spending on research and development (R&D). The level of total R&D expenditures as a proportion of GNP fell from 3.0 percent in 1962, to only 2.2 percent of GNP by 1978.

To the extent that R&D spending determines technological innovation, the outlook for growth in technology is much improved. A 25 percent incremental R&D tax credit was authorized under the Economic Recovery Tax Act in 1981. Partly because of this, R&D expenditures have grown to 2.7 percent of GNP in 1984. The National Science Foundation, chief monitor of national R&D activity, anticipates that R&D spending once again will reach 3.0 percent of GNP by 1990.

Confidence that an increase in technological innovation is imminent does not come simply from the belief that if you rub more lanterns, the odds of finding a genie will increase. A genie is already on the loose—the microcomputer and robotics revolution. It is probably this, more than anything else, which accounts for the very favorable productivity outlook held by some analysts. As a wider share of industry adopts these fast, efficient, labor-saving robots and microcomputers, they should increase output per man-hour, which will increase real GNP as long as employment levels are maintained.

Increased Regulation of Business. In the 1960s and 1970s the perception grew that the physical environment had deteriorated and workplace health

[8]The concept and measurement of multifactor productivity (MFP) growth is similar to that of labor productivity growth in that they are both computed as the difference between the growth rate of output and the growth rate of one or more inputs. The general method to compute productivity growth is to find the difference between the growth rates of output and the growth rates of inputs. This difference is attributed to changes in the productivity of the inputs. In the calculation of labor productivity growth, total man-hours of labor is the measure of input. In calculating multifactor productivity growth, the input is measured as a weighted index of the capital and labor inputs, where the weights are set equal to the cost share of each factor in the total cost of production. The difference between output growth and the growth of this input index is attributed to technological innovation.

[9]See U.S. Department of Labor, Bureau of Labor Statistics, *Trends in Multifactor Productivity, 1948-1981,* Bulletin 2178, (September 1983).

hazards had increased in the process of achieving rapid economic growth. Congress enacted legislation, such as the Clean Air Act, the Clean Water Act, and the Occupational Safety and Health Act, which were intended to deal with these issues. The way these laws typically work is by "command and control," with the government specifying acceptable methods of production. This frequently required firms to change their methods of production and to invest in so-called "nonproductive" capital that improved the environment but did not increase the output of marketable goods. Because it diverted investment away from "productive" projects, this social regulation was unfavorable from the vantage point of labor productivity.

No major new pieces of regulatory legislation have been passed in recent years. Moreover, legislative debates over the renewal of the Clean Air Act and Clean Water Act concern mostly relaxation of their requirements versus the status quo, in contrast to the tightening versus status quo battles of the 1970s. It is unlikely that productivity will suffer for the sake of the environment in the next few years, as it may have in the past.

In sum, the case for an imminent productivity upsurge is built upon the belief that the factors causing low productivity growth in the 1970s have abated and are not likely to re-emerge. This observation suggests that productivity growth will return to its normal, higher level, making it more likely that the economy will outgrow the deficit without substantial fiscal policy action.

. . . But the Surge in Productivity Is Not Evident. Despite the likelihood that many negative forces have abated, the case for a resurgence in productivity growth is far from complete. Careful productivity growth studies, which take into consideration all of the forces mentioned and more, still find a disconcerting proportion of the productivity decline a mystery.[10] Because of

this, one must approach the qualitative forecasts of a productivity growth reversal from the 1970s with caution. This is especially true of forecasts of record-breaking gains in productivity growth.

The case for a surge in productivity growth based on the factors cited above would be greatly strengthened if there were evidence that productivity is growing rapidly now. Unfortunately, the behavior of labor productivity growth in the current recovery does not support the view that productivity growth is returning to previous highs.

Labor productivity growth behaves cyclically; generally it is high early in a recovery and it falls as the recovery matures. Therefore, it is misleading to look at any single quarterly—or even annual—growth rate, and to compare that number to the long-term average growth, which is itself difficult to measure (see PITFALLS IN MEASURING PRODUCTIVITY GROWTH p. 22). The growth rate of productivity depends not only on its long-term trend but also on the point in the business cycle at which it is being measured. One way of assessing relative productivity growth while controlling for cyclical influences is to compare the current productivity growth to past experience on a "quarter-after-trough" basis.

---

[10]Two important studies, E. Denison, *Accounting for Slower Growth: The United States in the 1970s*, (Washington, DC: Brookings Institution, 1979), and John W. Kendrick "Long Term Economic Projection: Stronger U.S. Growth Ahead," *Southern Economic Journal*, 50(4) April 1984, pp. 945-964, reach a similar conclusion. Kendrick finds that at least 40 percent of the productivity decline cannot be explained. That the decline has not been explained adequately by the factors mentioned in the text is not surprising to some. To illustrate, energy price increases may have adversely affected labor productivity, but energy costs are too a small a component of the total cost of production to have had a substantial impact on productivity growth, as many have claimed. Denison shows that, as a result, energy price increases explain no more than 5 percent of the productivity decline. Regulatory policy may have diverted investment funds toward "non-productive" capital, but the ratio of pollution abatement capital investment to total capital investment never exceeded 3 percent in any year. Total R&D spending may have fallen during the 1970s, but the bulk of the decline was in military R&D. Private R&D as a percentage of GNP actually rose in the 1970s.

Figure 2 compares the change in nonfarm labor productivity in the current recovery to the change during the average of all previous recoveries and to the best productivity growth episode, which started with the recovery that began in the first quarter of 1960. It is clear from Figure 2 that productivity in the current cycle is growing at below average rates, and certainly below the rates enjoyed during the productivity boom of the 1960s.[11]

The current behavior of productivity provides no indication that we are in the throes of a labor productivity boom. Several studies that look carefully at recent experience also find little support for an ongoing productivity surge. Peter Clark and Robert Gordon examine the behavior of labor productivity in the 1980s and, after accounting for the purely cyclical changes in productivity, find no evidence that trend productivity growth has accelerated at all from the rates experienced in the 1970s.[12] In a longer-term analysis of labor productivity growth trends, Darby finds that, once adequate account is taken

---

[11]One way to get a rough estimate of the underlying trend growth of productivity in this recovery is to assume that we are at a peak now, and to calculate the peak-to-peak growth rate using the last two peaks (1981:3) and (1980:1). This calculation makes sense only when the recovery is mature, since it is only in that case that the cyclical behavior of productivity will not distort seriously the result of such a calculation. It turns out that the average growth of productivity is 2.3 percent per year for 1981:3-1985:2, and it is 1.8 percent per year for 1980:1-1985:2.

The reason to use 1980:1 as a starting point is that the four-quarter recovery ending in 1981:3 was the shortest since 1919, and the second shortest in recorded American economic history. The rate of capacity utilization remained at only 80 percent during that peak. A measure of trend productivity growth, using as a reference point a quarter before the peak, will be biased upward since some of the purely cyclical productivity gains would be measured as trend productivity. Thus, it may make more sense to use the next-to-the-last peak as a basis for comparison.

[12]Peter Clark, "Productivity and Profits in the 1980s: Are They Really Improving?" *Brookings Papers on Economic Activity* (1), 1984, pp. 136-167; Robert Gordon, "Unemployment and Potential Output in the 1980s," *Brookings Papers on Economic Activity*, (2), 1984, pp. 537-564.

PITFALLS IN MEASURING PRODUCTIVITY GROWTH

One must be careful when trying to estimate the underlying trend growth of labor productivity based upon measured changes in output per manhour from one period to the next. The reason is that productivity tends to rise and fall with the business cycle. In times of economic slack, employers tend to delay laying off more employees than necessary, and during recoveries they delay hiring new workers. As a result, productivity falls below its trend during the early part of a recession, but once the recovery is underway, productivity rises because existing employees are utilized more fully. Therefore measured labor productivity grows faster—sometimes much faster—than its trend during the early stages of a recovery. As the recovery matures, measured labor productivity slows to its trend growth. To get good estimates of trend growth in labor productivity, it is important to account for its cyclical behavior. One way to measure the historic productivity growth is to measure its trend growth as the annual rate of change from one business cycle peak to the next. Another way is to compare the period-by-period behavior of productivity growth to the typical (and maybe the extreme) behavior of past productivity growth, taking as reference the beginning of the business cycle.

of changes in labor quality and of the measurement problems caused by the 1971-1974 price-controls period, there is little evidence of a dramatic downward shift in trend labor productivity during the 1970s.[13] If correct, Darby's analysis suggests that only the improvement in labor quality is likely to boost productivity growth, and that the abatement of all the other negative forces is unlikely to add to growth. The overall conclusion that emerges from careful evaluation of the recent evidence is that the behavior of productivity growth in the current recovery probably represents an improvement over the experience of the 1970s. But it does not warrant the

---

[13]Darby, "The U.S. Productivity Slowdown."

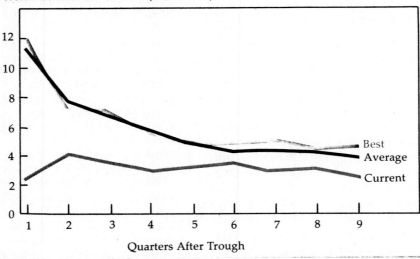

FIGURE 2

NONFARM PRODUCTIVITY GROWTH DURING RECOVERIES

Percent Cumulative Growth (annualized)

Quarters After Trough

presumption that labor productivity growth will be sufficiently high to allow the economy to outgrow the deficit.

CONCLUSION

In the world of economic policy, where consensus is one of the scarcest of commodities, most analysts argue that the federal government deficits, at their current and prospective levels, pose a risk to the health of the economy. Since 1981, the deficit figures have grown by leaps and bounds. In fiscal year 1985, after three years of economic growth, current tax receipts paid for only 78 percent of federal expenditures. The outlook for the immediate future is not much better.

There are two perspectives on what is to be done. One side views deficits as a chronic problem indicating the need for a shift in fiscal policy, namely, expenditure cuts and tax increases to control the deficit and to ensure future economic growth. The other side sees the deficits as a short-run problem that will be resolved not by government action but by healthy long-run economic growth that will result largely from strong productivity growth.

Whether the deficits will decline substantially as the economy grows depends very much upon whether productivity growth will resurge from its low rates of the 1970s to reach or even surpass its post-war highs. Research on the decline in labor productivity in the 1970s provides some information on future trends in labor productivity; and that literature does lead to expectations that productivity growth will not remain as low as it was during the 1970s. But the case made for a surge in labor productivity growth is speculative; there is little evidence to support it. Not only is the economics profession not satisfied that the experience of the 1970s has been adequately explained, but also the economy's recent productivity performance has been lackluster. So while a strong theoretical case for a snap-back in productivity growth can be made, more empirical meat must be put on that conceptual skeleton before such a scenario appears probable.

180

54

Awash in an Ocean of Oil

Overproduction sends petroleum prices into a harrowing free fall

Once again, a stunning shift in the price of oil sent tremors around the globe. Yet unlike the jolts that staggered the world economy in the 1970s, last week's quake caused prices to crash rather than climb. On Tuesday oil dropped below $20 per bbl. for the first time in seven years. Said Charles Maxwell, an analyst with the Cyrus J. Lawrence brokerage house near Wall Street: "This is one of the most important days in the oil markets in a decade." Since November, the price of petroleum contracts has plunged about 40%, including an 18% drop last week. Said Peter Beutel of Rudolf Wolff Futures, a New York City investment firm: "A whole new era has begun."

Indeed, as mild, springlike weather temporarily warmed much of the U.S. and Europe, an all-out price war seemed to be getting under way. To boost their shares of the energy market, hard-pressed members of the Organization of Petroleum Exporting Countries and rival suppliers Britain, Norway and Mexico have been flooding the world with an ocean of oil. The battle reflects the aggressive new tactics of Saudi Arabia, the largest OPEC producer, which has doubled its output in recent months. "The Saudis shocked the market," said one U.S. oil expert. "It was like being hit over the head with a baseball bat."

Last week Sheik Ahmed Zaki Yamani, the Saudi oil minister, issued a stern warning. Without a new agreement to curb production, Yamani said, "there will be no limitation to the downward spiral that may bring crude prices to less than $15 per bbl., with adverse and dangerous consequences for the whole world economy." The threatening words pushed prices into a free fall. North Sea oil dropped to $17.70 per bbl. before recovering a bit to finish the week at $18.50.

Plummeting oil prices can do both grievous harm and enormous good. Less expensive oil means lower energy costs for consumers and companies, which can give a substantial boost to U.S. and worldwide growth. At the same time, however, a further fall in oil prices could deal a crippling blow to U.S. energy firms and debt-ridden oil producers, including Mexico, Nigeria and Venezuela. Their woes might then threaten banks and rock the international financial system. Says Edward Yardeni, chief economist for Prudential-Bache Securities: "The oil-price collapse suddenly woke people up to the fact that the financial crisis is still out there. We'd become so jaded that it didn't

seem to worry anybody anymore."

Last week's declines stunned everyone, from commodities brokers to Texas oil barons. Panic swept the New York Mercantile Exchange, the nerve center of U.S. oil trading. "There was pure chaos on the floor," said Joel Faber, president of Faber's Futures and a governor of the exchange. As the price of crude fell, shipments of heating oil for February delivery plunged to 55.75¢ per gal., the lowest level since the late 1970s. Six blocks away, on the New York Stock Exchange, the Dow Jones industrial average dropped a total of 26 points on Tuesday and Wednesday before pulling out of its slump and finishing the week at 1529.93, down 6.77 points. Hardest hit were shares of energy firms, and banks with large loans to oil-producing countries. The stock of Chase Manhattan, for example, fell $7.125, a decline of nearly 10%, in two hectic days.

The fallout spread to foreign capitals and financial centers. Stocks traded on the Toronto Exchange last Wednesday lost about 2% of their value, to record the steepest slide in more than four years. "Even the bulls turned bearish," one moneyman said. As in the U.S., investors shunned shares of banks with substantial energy loans. In London, officials feared that the decline could sharply reduce tax revenues from Britain's North Sea wells. In Mexico, which desperately needs oil earnings to repay its $96.4 billion in foreign loans, the prospect of further price drops raised the specter of financial ruin. Elsewhere, leaders of oil-rich but otherwise poor nations, like Nigeria and Indonesia, were nervously eyeing prices.

In Washington, the Reagan Administration hailed the price slide as a victory. Said White House Spokesman Larry Speakes: "The effect of a drop in oil prices on the U.S. economy and particularly on U.S. consumers is favorable." Energy Secretary John Herrington was also ebullient. He called the tumble "good news for American consumers and outstanding news for American industries that are trying to compete worldwide." Still, President Reagan discussed the churning oil markets during the week in meetings with senior Administration officials. Said Herrington: "If there is to be price movement, we want it to be gradual."

Many economists stressed the positive aspects of the price collapse. Said Walter Heller, who served as chief economic adviser to Presidents Kennedy and Johnson: "This will be like a tonic for an economy, which, while it is not heading for a recession, has been showing only modest

growth." The Commerce Department reported last week that the gross national product grew at a 2.4% annual rate during last year's fourth quarter, down sharply from an estimate of 3.2%. The economy expanded 2.3% for all of 1985, marking the weakest gain since the recession year of 1982. Data Resources, an economic-research firm based in Lexington, Mass., estimates that a permanent cut in the price of crude oil to $20 per bbl. would add 2 percentage points to GNP growth by 1988 and create 900,000 new jobs.

Lower oil prices would of course also help restrain inflation, which rose at an annual rate of 5.3% in December and at a moderate 3.8% pace for 1985 as a whole. Since the U.S. and the rest of the developed world run on oil, any price cut would ripple through the economy to hold down the cost of everything from jet fuel to the raw materials used in plastics. For example, each 1¢ decline in the price of aviation fuel saves the highly competitive airline industry $110 million annually and provides an incentive for lower fares. Energy also accounts for 10% of total costs in the trucking industry. In addition, depressed oil prices would hold down the cost of such competing fuels as coal and natural gas, and thus bring savings to an even wider range of industries.

The benefits hardly end there. Chase Econometrics estimates that every $5-per-bbl. drop in oil prices will cut $9 billion off the U.S. trade deficit, which reached an estimated $145 billion last year. That record shortfall helped slow U.S. growth by siphoning dollars to other countries. As the gap closes, says Lawrence Chimerine, Chase Econometrics' chairman, "consumers and business can spend that money on other things."

Consumers will have to wait, however, before seeing lower prices at the gas pump and on heating bills. If they are sustained, drops in the price of crude oil normally take from 45 days to 90 days to work their way through refineries and distribution channels. An industry rule of thumb holds that every $1 decline in the price of crude cuts 2½¢ per gal. from the cost of heating oil and gasoline. Both now average about $1.15 per gal. If oil stays at about $20 per bbl., those product prices could fall as much as 25¢ per gal. within three months. A number of eager stations were unwilling to wait, and have already dropped the price of regular gas to below $1 per gal.

Some experts warn, though, that the cuts could prove smaller than expected.

"In this environment, gasoline and heating-oil prices are living an economic life of their own," says Dan Lundberg, a Los Angeles petroleum analyst. "They're influenced much more by the economics of the marketplace than by signals sent by speculators from the futures market."

Oil-company officers naturally share that view. "You can't expect to see a lock-step movement between products and crude oil," said William Hermann, chief economist for Chevron USA. "You'll see a pretty close relationship over a long period of time, but extenuating circumstances keep product prices up after crude falls." Such forces include rising marketing costs, and federal regulations that require refiners to use costly methods to remove most of the lead from gasoline.

Europeans, meanwhile, are already paying less for gasoline and heating oil. Thanks partly to the falling value of the U.S. dollar, the currency in which crude prices are set, Continental consumers are enjoying their biggest energy bargains in years. While European gasoline costs remain almost twice as high as those in the U.S., Swiss drivers last week saw their fifth price cut at the filling station since September, and their second of 1986. At $2.13 per gal., premium gasoline now costs less in Switzerland than at any other time since 1982. The price of Swiss heating oil, now $1.03 per gal., is at its lowest level since 1979.

Still, falling crude prices could have negative consequences that might rival or overwhelm the advantages they create. The greatest danger is the chance of a quake along the fault lines that run between banks on one side and oil producers and energy companies on the other. Said Alan Greenspan, a Manhattan-based economic consultant: "The situation is quite serious for Mexico. It will encounter considerable problems and may even create the impression that it could eventually walk away from its debt." Such a repudiation by the developing world's second largest debtor would be the realization of a nightmare that has haunted U.S. bankers for years.

Tumbling prices hurt Mexico because the Latin nation gets 70% of its export revenues from oil, which Mexicans have dubbed the economy's "fat cow." But that once ample creature is growing leaner by the day. So far, the drop in crude has cut $2.5 billion from Mexico's anticipated 1986 earnings, and the country may not be able to stand much more. "Falling oil prices will have an impact on a Mexican budget that is already stretched to the limit," says Economist Rogelio Ramírez de la O. He estimates that a sustained price of $20 per bbl. for oil would cause the Mexican economy, which is still suffering the financial effects of last year's earthquake, to show no growth in 1986.

Oil producers in the American Southwest face gusher-size troubles of their own. In Texas, the center of the U.S. oil industry, government analysts estimate that each $1-per-bbl. drop in prices will cost the state 25,000 jobs and $100 million in revenues. The declines make it less rewarding for companies to drill and develop wells. Local banks could suffer greatly if the fall continues. Says Frank Anderson, director of financial research for Weber, Hall, Sale & Associates, a Dallas brokerage: "The real problem will come if the contract price gets to $15 per bbl. and stays there for six months to a year. Then you'll see serious loan losses, a restructuring of bank portfolios and possibly even a reorganization of banks."

Experts in neighboring states issued similar warnings. In Oklahoma, officials said sliding prices could cut 10% from the state's already depressed oil production and could whack $50 million more out of a government budget that is now running a $197 million deficit. Oilmen fear that the declines could shut most of Oklahoma's 50,000 stripper wells, small units that individually produce no more than 10 bbl. per day but together account for the bulk of the state's petroleum output.

To forestall such developments, Congressmen from oil and gas states are seeking an oil import fee to raise the price of foreign crude and protect the U.S. energy industry. Says Democratic Senator David Boren of Oklahoma, who last week wrote Reagan urging him to support the plan: "If prices fall further, it will bring our exploration to a screeching halt." At Boren's request, Oregon Republican Bob Packwood, chairman of the Senate Finance Committee, agreed last week to hold hearings on the proposal.

Many economists support some form of energy tax as a conservation and revenue-raising measure. Heller called the drop in petroleum prices "a heaven-sent opportunity" to cut the federal budget deficit by taxing gasoline or oil. Martin Feldstein, who two years ago left his post as chairman of the Council of Economic Advisers to return to a teaching job at Harvard, has advocated a 20¢-per-gal. levy on gasoline.

The Administration, however, is squarely against anything of the kind. Reagan has rejected such ideas in the past, and is unlikely to abandon his well-known opposition to tax increases. Said Herrington: "I do not believe an import fee is called for. It's a tax." Instead of taxing oil, the Energy Secretary wants to spur exploration by giving oil and gas firms new tax breaks.

The idea of an energy tax would have seemed absurd just six years ago, when the U.S. was still reeling from the OPEC oil

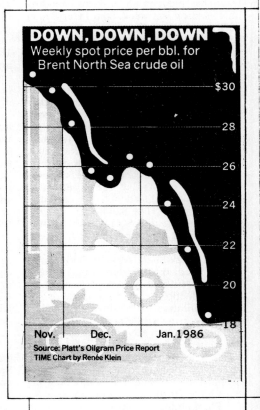

DOWN, DOWN, DOWN
Weekly spot price per bbl. for Brent North Sea crude oil

$30
28
26
24
22
20
18

Nov.   Dec.   Jan. 1986
Source: Platt's Oilgram Price Report
TIME Chart by Renée Klein

shocks of the 1970s. Those blows, which drove the price of crude from about $2 per bbl. at the start of the decade to $34 in 1982, marked an economic turning point. The huge increases pushed the U.S. into double-digit inflation and helped trigger severe recessions in 1974 and 1981. They drained billions of dollars from rich and poor nations alike and transferred the money to OPEC countries, which suddenly became lands of fabulous wealth. Perhaps most damaging of all, the price hikes created an era of economic stagnation from which much of the world is still recovering.

OPEC's very success proved its undoing. Faced with towering prices, the U.S. and other industrial countries learned to live with less oil. Americans traded in their gas guzzlers for smaller, fuel-efficient cars, insulated their homes and workplaces more effectively and switched to natural gas and other less expensive fuels. Industries installed modern equipment that conserved energy.

Meanwhile, nations found and developed vast new sources of oil. Petroleum from such locations as Alaska, Mexico and the North Sea poured onto the market. As a result, OPEC's share of the world oil market has shrunk drastically. The cartel that accounted for 63% of global output in 1979 can now claim only about 38%. That decline has left many OPEC members unable to pay for the grandiose development projects they began in better times. Saudi Arabia, for example, is running about $12 billion in the red on its $55 billion annual budget.

By 1983 the combination of conservation and new oil supplies turned oil prices around, and they began a slow descent. The sharp break started last December, when OPEC dropped all pretense of discipline and its members frantically tried to raise revenues by increasing their market shares.

The final blow came from Saudi Arabia, by far the largest oil producer, which has boosted its daily output from a low of 2.2 million bbl. last summer to a current rate of about 5 million bbl. That increase, more than any other single factor, pushed prices into a free fall.

Many experts believe that the Saudis are playing a dangerous game of chicken. Yamani clearly hopes to force Britain and other non-OPEC producers to the bargaining table for talks aimed at cutting output to support prices. While the British have so far shown little interest in such sessions, last week's plunge in North Sea oil prices could help change their minds. Yamani also wants his fellow OPEC ministers to consider production cutbacks when a five-member special committee meets next week in Vienna. Says William Quandt, a Middle East specialist at the Brookings Institution: "The Saudis want the price to go down, but they don't want it to collapse."

Speculation swirled last week about where prices would eventually settle. For every observer who thought the decline would quickly end, others expected it to continue. "Prices could fall so much more that it's scary," said Philip Verleger Jr., a Washington-based energy analyst. "If it's left up to the Saudis alone, prices could drop to $5 to $10 per bbl. if they make no effort to keep their production in check." For Yamani, the crunch could come in the spring, when demand traditionally slackens. If no production agreement is reached by then, $20 per bbl. could seem like a high price.

Some experts looked further ahead to consider the implications of last week's frenzy. They feared that cheap oil might lead to a return of wasteful ways that would make a new oil shortage inevitable at some point in the future. But the trend toward conservation will not easily be reversed. Says Economist Heller: "It would take a long, long time to go back to our old oil-guzzling habits. This could be a trap, but only if we are dumb enough to fall into it." —*By John Greenwald.*

Reported by Raji Samghabadi/New York and Gregory H. Wierzynski/Washington

55

Six Welfare Questions Still Searching for Answers

Henry J. Aaron

R EREADING THE declarations of war on poverty penned in the mid-1960s is a bit like contemplating baby pictures of now-grown children. There is a tendency to lapse into reverie, to recall fondly bygone emotions and events, and to muse on how innocent and full of hope the little ones — and their parents — once were. But then one realizes that those times are gone forever and cannot be retrieved.

And so it is to look back at the war on poverty. Two decades of frustration with imperfect policies and sluggish economic growth have left most of those present at the parturition with a sophistication and wary cynicism quite out of tune with the can-do optimism of the 1960s.

What is most striking about the emphasis on welfare in those early days of the anti-poverty campaign is that there wasn't any. The 1964 State of the Union Address did call for medical insurance under social security, an expanded food stamp program, and more public housing. But there was no mention — in the President's speech, in the famous chapter in the 1964 report of the Council of Economic Advisers, or in the formal announcement of the war on poverty — of any cash assistance program.

In fact, welfare developed into a prominent issue only after it became clear that millions of Americans would remain poor despite government's best efforts to add to their human capital, to lower the barriers of discrimination, and to cultivate a strong economy. Then, gradually, welfare — and welfare reform — emerged as a primary, if not the dominant, instrument for combatting poverty.

The story of this transformation has been told often, and I shall not repeat it here. Instead, I shall focus on six questions that go to the heart of the ongoing debate about welfare policy, six questions that deal with attitudes toward the poor and with the effects of welfare on their behavior. During the past two decades, these attitudes and assumptions have changed greatly. In these changes may be read the achievements and failures of the effort to reform welfare.

—— I ——

The first two questions must be taken together.

1. *Who should be eligible for aid?*
   a. *by income?*
   b. *by category?*

2. *What is the effect of welfare on pretransfer income (in other words, on earnings)?*

Henry J. Aaron is a senior fellow in the Economic Studies program at Brookings and a member of the economics faculty at the University of Maryland. He is a former assistant secretary of the Department of Health, Education, and Welfare. Among his publications are The Painful Prescription *(co-authored with William B. Schwartz) and* Why is Welfare So Hard to Reform? *An earlier version of this essay was prepared for a University of Colorado conference on the Great Society.*

President Johnson refused to mention welfare in connection with the war on poverty because he was convinced that any linkage with the former would damage the prospects of enacting the various programs to increase opportunities for the poor. His perception was that Congress would support programs to help people become self-supporting, but that it would not provide cash assistance to people *potentially* capable of self-support. Hence, the central tenets of the war on poverty were that those who might gain from training should be eligible for it; that everyone would benefit from removal of discrimination; and that a rising economy would raise all ships. Cash assistance was to remain limited to those who were not *expected* to work: the aged, the blind, the disabled, and single parents.

These expectations changed for two reasons. The first was an outgrowth of the premises of the war on poverty. If poverty could be substantially eliminated by education and training, by anti-discrimination laws, and by economic growth, then the causes of poverty were largely external to the poor. That in turn meant that cash assistance to those in poverty could be justified either as an act of compassion for the victims of exogenous forces or as a carrying cost until sound investments — in training programs, for example — began to pay out.

A second factor was that economists discovered the welfare system and found it inelegant, a complicated mishmash of rules and formulas. That the welfare system was complex is beyond question. But it was probably no more complex than many other federal programs — social security, for example — that were not found esthetically repugnant. Nevertheless, more united by a common revulsion against messiness than they were divided by ideology, academics of the political left and right joined together in calling for the provision of income assistance according to simple standards of economic need.[1]

Two assumptions lay behind the conviction that economic status alone should determine eligibility for cash assistance. The first, already noted, was that poverty was not the fault of the poor, that it was a condition imposed on them from without. The second was that cash assistance would not adversely change the behavior of its recipients. I have no hard data on the pervasiveness of these assumptions. I believe, however, that the perception that poverty among blacks was attributable to discrimination was far more widespread before the civil rights achievements of the 1960s and 1970s than it is today. The willingness to provide cash assistance to the poor without conditions seems to have been an early casualty of the slow economic growth in the United States since the first round of OPEC price increases.[2] If American workers were to be buffeted by events over which they had no control, they were less willing to provide aid to a few, with or without conditions.

The question of how cash aid affects the behavior of recipients has been the subject of intense study for the past two decades. More than $100 million and thousands of person-years have been lavished on research to measure the responses of those assisted.

The results of this analysis were not anticipated by the original sponsors of the cash assistance experiments. They believed that eligibility for aid should be based solely on income, not on marital status. They surmised that the general public expected recipients of cash assistance to reduce their work efforts sharply — and they were confident that the general public was wrong.[3]

The proponents of such assistance won this battle, but they lost the war. Their experiments found that few men who were offered cash assistance actually quit their jobs and that the reduction in the number of hours they worked was under 10 percent. But the tests also suggested that for every $100 provided to male-headed families, earnings would fall $25 to $50.[4] The effect of cash grants on the labor supply of female family heads was somewhat greater than the effect on males — and the impact on the behavior of wives and young single adults was greater still. This leakage could be reduced by imposing effective work requirements, but that strategy raised other questions to be addressed below.

The experiments established that the extension of welfare to two-parent families adversely changed their work patterns *enough to matter*. It was no longer possible to maintain that the behavior of the poor would not be adversely affected if cash assistance were provided until they could become self-supporting. It is doubtful that the reformers ever seriously threatened the dominance of the traditional American view that only certain groups among the poor deserve welfare. But it is clear that the idea that economic status alone should determine eligibility for aid flickered only briefly and guttered out.

—— II ——

The next two questions must be addressed concurrently.

3. *What obligations do the recipients of assistance owe to society?*

4. *Can large-scale work requirements be made to work? In other words, can they be made to do more than harass?*

Welfare recipients have rarely been given cash under neutral conditions. The workhouse was an early accompaniment of aid. More recently, the strings have included stigmatizing application procedures and the ministrations of social workers.

If poverty is believed to be the resultant of forces exogenous to the poor, then the attachment of unpleasant conditions to assistance is a gratuitous cruelty inflicted upon the already victimized. Indeed, this conception of poverty suggests that welfare should be regarded as a right—as a form of just compensation for a kind of casualty loss, the accident of poverty. This view, or something very much like it, lay behind the drive that began in the mid-1960s, and reached its apogee in the early 1970s, to deliver welfare payments in dignified settings, with rights of appeal and the assurance of due process, and without any coercion or requirements that the recipients of aid do anything in return for it.

There were at least three elements to this movement.

One was the simple insistence that normal legal procedures be followed and constitutional safeguards observed. A second was the effort to save applicants from being stigmatized by the processes of welfare and thereby compelled either to forego benefits to which they were entitled or suffer degradation in getting them. A third was the belief that the poor have a more or less unconditional right to cash assistance. Sometimes this right was asserted without qualification. On other occasions, it was acknowledged that conditions might be imposed, but only if they were surrounded with incentives and protections so generous that what began as conditions ended up resembling nothing so much as other rights. It was also suggested that work requirements were simply inoperable in practice.[5] But these contentions all came to the same thing: Cash should be provided on the basis of economic need and without strings.

This view had a remarkable effect on those served by welfare programs. Take-up rates increased. Procedures in welfare offices improved. But the position that cash assistance should be provided without conditions never appealed much to the general public or to Congress. As the courts prohibited "man-in-the-house" rules and state residency requirements, Congress mandated job-search by AFDC recipients. But for opposition from the Johnson and Nixon administrations, Congress might well have gone further than it did. On its brief journey to political oblivion, President Nixon's Family Assistance Plan became encrusted with conditions and mandatory "services." President Carter's stillborn welfare reform plan was predicated on the behavioral assumption that cash assistance without work requirements would produce unacceptable effects on labor supply and the political assumption that aid without conditions would not pass Congress.

The problem, of course, was how to make a work requirement real. The Carter program was the first to acknowledge that a work requirement without a job guarantee was unworkable. Although there was no precedent for promising to employ large numbers of actual or potential welfare recipients, the Carter administration committed itself to creating more than one million jobs for people who were demonstrably among the least employable members of American society. The logic was impeccable. But there was no credible evidence that the enterprise could be made to work. The administration's promise was never tested, however, because the cost of fulfilling it was so high — close to $10,000 per job per year, for an annual total of $10 billion — that Congress would have none of it.

Advocates of noncategorical cash assistance had reached an intellectual and political *cul de sac*. In an effort to gain acceptance of this approach to welfare, they had tried to persuade a skeptical public that poverty was visited upon the poor and that a change in the environment would drastically reduce it. Pending such a change, they argued, cash assistance should be provided without conditions and without regard for family status, on the basis of measurable economic need. This assistance would not reduce work effort enough to matter. The provision of aid was no more than a compassionate stopgap to tide the poor over until more fundamental improvements took effect.

But that argument did not take, and the facts did not support it. The behavioral effects of cash assistance were certainly not overwhelming, but they were large enough to matter. As a consequence, supporters of noncategorical cash assistance were forced to accept the proposition that conditions should be placed on the provision of assistance. Recipients of aid would have to accept jobs, if jobs were available.

The acknowledgement of the need for a work requirement created an insoluble dilemma, however. With a sufficiently coercive administrative system, potential welfare recipients could be required to accept existing low-quality, low-wage jobs in the private sector. If enough private sector jobs did not exist, public sector positions could be created at low cost. If a work requirement discouraged enough people from applying for welfare, costs might even be reduced. But the coercion that would be necessary to make such a requirement work violated notions of fairness and rights. Alternatively, the public sector could create jobs with sufficiently attractive working conditions and wages to reduce greatly the need for coercion. But the size of the program would be unprecedented, and its cost would be prohibitive, particularly since many workers in unattractive private sector jobs would find it expedient to switch to superior public sector jobs. Trapped on this political Moebius strip, welfare reform went nowhere.

—— III ——

5. *To what extent is the rising incidence of single-parent families traceable to increased assistance?*

The number of families consisting of a woman and her children rose from 4.1 million in 1960 to 6.7 million in 1982. The proportion of the poor residing in such families increased from 10.3 percent in 1960 to 19.5 percent in 1982. Only part of this trend can be explained by the coming of age of the baby boom generation. Another part, no doubt, is attributable to changes in sexual and social norms affecting the entire population. But the upturn in these statistics resembles the slowdown in economic growth since 1974, in the sense that there are many explanations of the phenomenon no one of which is wholly satisfactory, but few of which can be dismissed.

Among those that cannot be dismissed is the welfare explanation. Welfare, it is argued, contributes to the increase in the numbers of unmarried mothers in various ways. Girls with few economic or social prospects can achieve a measure of independence by having a child or, in some jurisdictions, simply by becoming pregnant, thereby qualifying in their own right for welfare payments. Welfare, it is alleged, not only discourages women from working (a claim to which the income maintenance experiments lend some support), but also discourages them from marrying (because married couples are generally ineligible for assistance). The same line of argument suggests that welfare encourages the breakup of two-parent families when unemployment occurs; by leaving a woman and her children, a man makes them eligible for cash assistance and, in most places, for health benefits as well. David Ellwood and Lawrence Summers have pointed out that the proportion of single-parent families kept increasing long after the number of people on welfare stopped growing and real benefits per person declined.

Whatever the effects of a categorical program like AFDC may have been, it was hoped and claimed that noncategorical assistance would reduce family instability. It would make payments to couples as well as single parents, so that the presence or absence of an unemployed spouse would not affect eligibility. Even under a negative income tax, however, there would still be incentives for a spouse eligible for unemployment insurance or with opportunities for sporadic market income to leave the family. Moreover, uncategorical assistance would do nothing to discourage young girls from seeking financial independence through pregnancy.

It was on this set of issues — the effects of cash assistance on family stability — that the income maintenance experiments dealt the campaign for noncategorical aid a second major blow.[6] According to the final report of the Seattle-Denver experiment, for example, the provision of unconditional cash assistance increased the rates of family dissolution by 53 percent for whites, 57 percent for blacks, and one percent for Chicanos.[7] This finding received some attention when it was released and further cemented opposition to noncategorical assistance.

There are grave doubts about its validity, however. For families that included children and that received cash assistance only, the rates of family dissolution appear to have dropped by 16 percent for whites, 4 percent for blacks, and 26 percent for Chicanos. This bizarre contrast seems to have stemmed from a sharp increase in family dissolution among childless couples and among families, with or without children, who received job counseling or education subsidies in addition to cash assistance.[8]

However this analytical debate is eventually resolved, the hypothesis that noncategorical welfare would increase family stability remains unsupported by empirical research. The contrary hypothesis has received official, if premature, support. Attention has shifted to measures designed to ensure that absent fathers shoulder financial responsibility for their offspring and their partners.

—— IV ——

6. *What reliance should be placed on in-kind assistance?*

Despite the attention lavished on attempts to reform the cash welfare system, only one lasting legislative change was made. The state-run programs of aid to the aged, blind, and disabled were consolidated into a single program: Supplemental Security Income.

However admirable this reform may have been, it was overshadowed by the transformation of in-kind assistance, much of which went to the poor. Medicare and medicaid vastly expanded the access of the aged, disabled, and poor to hospital and physician services. The number of publicly subsidized housing units increased by more than 100,000 units per year in the late 1960s and rapidly throughout much of the 1970s. The food stamp program was transformed from a small outgrowth of commodity distribution into the broadest federal program of economic assistance to the poor. Other initiatives — such as Head Start, nutrition support for women, infants, and children, and the earned income tax credit — took root and grew. The American people, it appeared, were prepared to provide much more assistance to the poor in the form of identifiable commodities than they would dream of making available in cash. And they were willing to do so without troubling themselves or their representatives about the possible effects of such munificence on labor supply or family stability.

Logic suggests that these programs should have the same types of effects on economic behavior that cash assistance has. Yet almost no one has tried to determine whether this is the case — even though the total amount of aid provided through in-kind programs dwarfs income-tested cash assistance. The mystery of why such an inquiry has not been made is heightened by the fact that social experiments to measure the effects of housing assistance and health insurance were begun at roughly the same time as the income maintenance experiments. The first set of these social experiments looked at the effects of housing assistance on housing expenditures and housing status, and the second set considered the impact of health insurance on health expenditures and health status, but neither examined the consequences of housing or health assistance for labor supply or family stability.[9]

The rapid growth of in-kind assistance and the sluggish growth of cash assistance contrast starkly with the proofs, well known to every survivor of at least two years of economics instruction, that the former is less valuable to recipients than the latter. On the basis of such proofs, economists have tried to persuade others that in-kind assistance is wasteful and that it should be converted to cash.

The unpersuasiveness of these arguments to everyone except economists is breathtaking. Politicians have long appreciated that support for aid to the poor increases if the aid appears to create jobs for the nonpoor — in the construction trades, for example, or on farms. For many years, the food stamp program has been bundled with agricultural programs to enable a coalition of rural and urban members of Congress to pass programs and approve expenditures that might be defeated if they were voted on separately.

"Politicians have long appreciated that support for aid to the poor increases if the aid appears to create jobs for the nonpoor...."

The American public has declared unmistakably that it is willing to provide to those in need of aid such commodities as basic housing, food, and health care, but it is unwilling to give poor people the cash to buy these items themselves. This attitude has persisted long enough to be taken as a constant on the welfare scene. Future efforts to modify the welfare system should treat it as a reality, rather than try to explain why it does not make sense.[10]

—— V ——

Ten years of weak economic growth and four years of tight budgets have shown that an ebbing tide lowers all ships (with the notable exception of military ships). Welfare programs of all kinds, along with other types of domestic spending, have been scaled back. The first cuts in cash assistance were passive, as the inflation of the 1970s eroded the value of fixed AFDC payments. States steadily tightened medicaid rules and eligibility in an effort to prevent increases in medical costs from showing up in state budgets. These reductions were offset in part by the growth of the food stamp program and the continued expansion of housing subsidies.

The election of Ronald Reagan brought general cuts in most cash and in-kind assistance programs. New AFDC rules rendered some recipients with low earnings ineligible for further aid. Food stamp benefits were lowered, and the implicit tax was increased. New subsidized housing starts were drastically curtailed. States were encouraged to apply for authority to administer experimental workfare programs.

Taken together, these measures reversed the direction in which welfare reformers in the Nixon, Ford, and Carter administrations had tried to go. Categorical distinctions were strengthened, rather than weakened. Benefit reduction rates were increased, rather than lowered. Workfare programs were promoted, rather than discouraged. And, perhaps most importantly, the traditional attitude that the welfare system is a seedbed of sloth and dependency reclaimed dominance from the upstart view that welfare is a right of the poor.

Probably the most significant explanation for these shifts of policies and attitudes is the difficulty of sustaining redistributional transfers when taxpayers themselves are living through hard times. But it is important to realize that the welfare reformers of the Johnson, Nixon, Ford, and Carter years were intellectually disarmed by the very experiments that they had initiated to prove the benignity of noncategorical assistance. Extrapolations of results from these experiments suggested that subjecting recipients to 100 percent tax rates would not seriously damage overall work incentives. The argument that making assistance noncategorical would improve family stability could no longer be made.

In short, the welfare reformer's ship is intellectually adrift in harsh economic weather. The climate is unlikely to improve unless and until economic growth resumes and the chronic budget deficits created by the 1981 tax cut are ended.

Even when conditions do improve, the prospects are dim for a resurgence of calls for noncategorical assistance. The intellectual predicate for that kind of reform has collapsed. An argument — or, more precisely, an appeal to compassion — can be made for raising the benefits paid by the least generous states. A case can also be made for linking cash to work or to training and education — although evidence is accumulating that training and jobs programs are rarely as beneficial as their proponents claim. A change in social attitudes toward poverty and the poor may occur with a change in the economic climate. But it is clear that the next generation of social policy-makers, unlike the last, will not have the luxury of relying on ideas from an inherited, unfinished agenda.

> "... the position that cash assistance should be provided without conditions never appealed much to the general public or to Congress."

1. I recall a debate in the mid-1960s during which Milton Friedman and James Tobin were allied in defending the negative income tax against two critics, one of the right and one of the left. At one point, Friedman noted the irony that he and Tobin were paired and commented that "disciplinary blood is thicker than ideological water."

2. Real AFDC benefits have declined steadily since 1974 because payments have not been adjusted to offset fully the effects of inflation. Richard A. Kasten and John E. Todd, "Transfer Recipients and the Poor During the 1970s," 1980, photocopied.

3. Robert A. Levine wrote: "Most proponents of the negative income tax believed, in the early days, that the greatest political problem that would arise in attempting to legislate an actual program would be the belief, among the public and in Congress, that any form of income maintenance for adult males would bring about a large increase in idleness among those who otherwise would have worked. The whole thrust of the negative income tax, of course, was precisely to avoid this outcome — to provide such men with financial incentives to work. But the advocates felt that, without evidence to the contrary, the conventional perception would prevail." "How and Why the Experiment Came About," in *Work Incentives and Income Guarantees: The New Jersey Negative Income Tax Experiment*, Joseph A. Pechman and P. Michael Timpane, editors, Brookings, 1975, pp. 16–17.

4. For a survey of the results of all four of the income maintenance experiments, see *Final Report of the Seattle-Denver Income Maintenance Experiment, Volume 1, Design and Results*, SRI International, May 1983. For a review of the results regarding labor supply, see part III, "Labor Supply Response," pp. 91–198. The estimates of the proportion of extra costs required to replace lost earnings were based on benefits payable under President Carter's Program for Better Jobs and Income and are reported in Henry J. Aaron and John Todd, "The Use of Income Maintenance Experiment Findings in Public Policy, 1977–78," *Industrial Relations Research Association Proceedings*, 1979, pp. 46–56.

5. "...[I]f work does not pay, a work requirement in most places and times would be ineffectual and inoperative, a costly and largely futile effort to compel the poor to behave in ways contrary to their own self-interest. It is unimaginable that a large bureaucracy would be capable of sifting millions of individual cases, each fraught with special problems, needs, and ambiguity, all requiring judgment if not wisdom. To inspire hard work is a laudable goal, but one not likely to be achieved through a work requirement without more authoritarian administration than most Americans are likely to accept." Henry J. Aaron, *Why is Welfare So Hard to Reform?* Brookings, 1972, pp. 49–50.

6. The first was the finding, noted above, that a sizeable proportion of the increased cost of noncategorical aid provided without an effective work requirement would go to replace reduced earnings.

7. *Final Report*, p. 291

8. These statistics are taken from an unpublished memorandum, dated September 2, 1981, by Glen Cain, who chaired a panel appointed by the Department of Health and Human Services to review the *Final Report*. Cain and his committee urged that the importance of the interaction between cash assistance and counselling be mentioned prominently in the *Final Report*. He maintained that this anomaly, as well as a number of others, made unjustifiable any firm statements about the effects of cash assistance itself on family stability. Among the other anomalies he cited were gross discrepancies in response across ethnic groups and the fact that *increases* in cash assistance seemed to *reduce* family dissolution.

The drafters of the *Final Report* ignored the entreaties of the Cain committee, and the Office of Planning and Evaluation, which sponsored the income maintenance experiments — on which more than $70 million was spent — refused to support further research on the effects of counselling and education subsidies.

9. In the course of the income maintenance experiments, a small amount of effort was spent examining the effects of cash assistance on health and housing; some modest impacts were found.

10. In fact, a strong analytical case can be made that assistance in kind, rather than in cash, is socially optimal, even if it is not favored by recipients. This argument proceeds from the assumption that taxpayers care how welfare recipients spend the assistance they are given; it does not deal with what may be the most important reason for the relative popularity of in-kind programs: logrolling.

56

From Welfare to Workfare

More than 20 states now require healthy aid recipients to earn their checks

For five years Maria Unzueta's sole source of income was a monthly welfare check. Separated from her husband, the San Diego mother of four made do on benefits totaling $7,920 a year. But now Unzueta, 39, is part of a local job-training program for welfare recipients in which she works 40 hours a week as a hospital file clerk and makes roughly the same amount of money she was getting on the dole. Under the workfare program, she still receives child-care benefits worth about $130 a month, but she hopes to be completely self-sufficient soon. "For me it's important to try and make it on my own," says Unzueta, "and provide an example for my children."

Requiring welfare recipients to work for their checks is not a new concept. Nor are the programs, which usually affect poor mothers with children to raise, as simple in practice as they are in theory. But workfare, which has slowly evolved from a somewhat cranky conservative notion to one with broad support, seems to be an idea whose time has come. Able-bodied welfare beneficiaries must accept occupational training and jobs in more than 20 states, and the number is growing.

In Washington, legislators are mired in trying to find ways to cut spending in accordance with the Gramm-Rudman deficit-reduction bill *(see Essay)*. Confronted with severe cutbacks in revenue sharing, states are searching for innovative ways to make their social programs more effective. Workfare could prove to be an important example for future experiments.

The idea has enjoyed an unusual bipartisan harmony: in statehouses around the country, Democrats and Republicans have joined forces to support legislation that combines the job programs traditionally favored by liberals with efforts to pare the welfare rolls advocated by conservatives. Jo Anne Ross, a Reagan appointee at the Social Security Administration, describes workfare as the "top priority of the Department of Health and Human Services." Says Joseph Califano, Secretary of the Department of Health, Education and Welfare during the Carter Administra-

tion: "If the kids are in school, then the mother can be working. Nearly everyone accepts that concept now."

Welfare has been a political battleground since federally financed public assistance was made law under the Social Security Act of 1935. Traditionally, conservatives have viewed welfare programs as handouts to the poor and an insult to the American work ethic. Liberals generally have considered it compassionate compensation for victims of economic and social circumstances beyond their control. But with the startling growth in the number of children being born to unwed mothers from the underclass, many of welfare's long-standing supporters have begun to question whether Aid to Families with Dependent Children programs may be exacerbating the problems they were designed to alleviate. Even some civil rights leaders and welfare recipients in the nation's inner cities are criticizing the system for helping perpetuate dependency from one disadvantaged generation to the next and for unintentionally encouraging the breakdown of the underclass's family structure.

California is embarking on the most sweeping statewide plan so far. Encouraged by the success of San Diego's local workfare system, the state legislature last September approved a program known as Greater Avenues for Independence, or GAIN. Approximately one-third of the state's 586,000 AFDC cases will be affected. As in most workfare plans, handicapped people and single parents with preschool children are exempt but may volunteer for the program. Welfare beneficiaries who do not register in GAIN stand to have their payments cut off.

After an evaluation of their skills, GAIN participants are given any necessary training, ranging from remedial math and language classes to high school equivalency courses. Once training is completed the welfare client has three months to find work in a job-search program. A trainee whose search is unsuccessful is enrolled in a one-year pre-employment preparation program to work off the welfare grant in

an assigned job, with time off for job hunting. Typical jobs include clerical positions or maintenance work in a parks department, day-care centers or programs for the elderly; the pay is the California starting wage, currently $5.07 an hour. If after a year the client still has not found a job, he must begin the evaluation and training program again.

The GAIN bill won in the state senate by a vote of 32 to 2 and in the assembly by 60 to 9. Republicans were all for a mandatory work requirement, while Democrats liked the education, child-care and job-creation provisions that were written into the legislation. GAIN is enrolling members gradually and will be fully operational in 1988. Though the program is expected to cost $304 million a year, GAIN supporters estimate that it will have saved the state $115 million by 1992.

While California's program is being touted as a model for the future, other ambitious workfare operations are in place around the country. New York hopes eventually to enroll more than 200,000 of its 1.1 million AFDC recipients in a revamped workfare program that went into effect last November with the support of Democratic Governor Mario Cuomo. "We're not letting them sit at home and get into the welfare syndrome," says Cesar Perales, New York State's commissioner of social services. "Exposing them to the workplace has real value." A program in Massachusetts instituted in 1983 led to employment for 19,000 former welfare clients and saved the state an estimated $54 million over two years. Other notable programs are operating in Pennsylvania, West Virginia and Michigan.

Workfare first became government policy, at least in theory, more than a decade ago. Congress strengthened a Work Incentive (WIN) program in 1971 during the Nixon Administration. But WIN suffered from inadequate funding, mismanagement and weak enforcement. In 1981, with the advent of the Reagan Administration, Congress passed legislation granting states more flexibility in administering WIN. For the first time, AFDC recipients could work in public agencies rather than in private-sector jobs. States were also allowed to use part of a recipient's welfare grant as a wage subsidy to his or her private employer. Given these new liberties, state governments began cooking up fresh workfare programs.

"Obligation" is a word that workfare supporters use frequently, arguing that welfare recipients have not fulfilled their responsibilities as citizens. Lawrence Mead, professor of politics at New York University, makes such a case in his new book, *Beyond Entitlement: The Social Obligations of Citizenship* (Free Press; $19.95). His most controversial theme: the poor need to have standards of behavior set for them. "We have to say, 'You have a real obligation we're not going to let you get away from,'" says Mead. Workfare, he maintains, can give poor people the discipline he feels they lack. Mead advocates expanding workfare programs to include mothers with children above age three rather than simply those whose children are old enough to be in school.

Workfare's philosophical opponents see it as a sort of punishment for being poor. They contend that the vast majority of welfare recipients are young unwed mothers with few if any marketable skills, who are often forced to take demeaning, low-paying jobs under workfare. Critics question whether there is even enough work to go around for the programs' undereducated participants. Says California Democratic Assemblyman Tom Bates: "When Ronald Reagan says, 'Go to the want ads and look for jobs,' he doesn't point out that they're for electrical engineers and highly skilled people."

There are other well-reasoned objections to workfare: that it displaces people in the regular labor force; that by exempting single parents with preschool-age children, it excludes 60% of all adult AFDC recipients; that, as Ohio has experienced, welfare savings can be less than program costs; that workfare places too much emphasis on getting clients into the job market quickly rather than enrolling them in education courses that could help them gain entry to more useful and lucrative lines of work.

A report released last month by the House Government Operations Committee criticizes programs that do not provide adequate child care for participants. Said the study: "The lack of safe and affordable child care can foreclose the possibility of employment, training, education and even opportunity to job hunt." Moreover, say critics, workfare does not address America's most serious unemployment problem: the jobless rate among black teenagers is currently 41.6%, compared with 6.9% for the U.S. as a whole.

Nevertheless, growing numbers of officials think that work-for-welfare programs are at least worth trying. And many workfare participants seem to agree. In Des Moines, Ruth Breitzke, 34, has been working since September as a volunteer at the juvenile court in return for her welfare check. "I enjoy what I'm doing here even though I don't get paid for it," says she. "It gives you the feeling that you can get back into the working world. It gives you that boost."

—*By Jacob V. Lamar Jr. Reported by Hays Gorey/Washington and Jon D. Hull/ Los Angeles*

57

Reagan's Record:
Welfare Statism Is Intact

Reagan's Record

Recent Budget Battles Leave the Basic Tenets Of Welfare State Intact

Paring Rather Than Ending Programs Will Let Them Flourish in Another Era

The Social Security Blunder

By PAUL BLUSTEIN
Staff Reporter of THE WALL STREET JOURNAL

WASHINGTON—On the night of May 9, 1985, David Stockman was huddled with Republican senators Robert Dole and Pete Domenici as the Senate neared a dramatic vote on a GOP plan to slash the federal budget by $56 billion. At 10:30 p.m., an aide brought some unwelcome news. Two Republican senators—Charles Grassley, an Iowa conservative, and Mark Hatfield, an Oregon liberal—were objecting to President Reagan's proposal to eliminate the Community Services Block Grant, a program that funds local organizations aiding the poor.

The vote was expected to be very close—in the end, at 3 a.m., Vice President Bush broke a 49-49 tie—so Messrs. Grassley and Hatfield got what they wanted. The block grant, a program descended from Lyndon Johnson's Great Society, lived to fight another day.

The incident exemplifies the history of Ronald Reagan's five-year campaign to shrink the federal government. Despite the declaration of Budget Director Stockman early in the Reagan presidency that "substantial parts" of the Great Society would have to be "heaved overboard," most of the programs that existed in 1981 remain in place today. Domestic spending growth has slowed sharply, but Congress has achieved savings largely by paring programs rather than pulling them out by the roots. That leaves open the possibility that the programs will grow back when the political climate changes, as some did following the historic budget cuts of 1981.

'Missed Opportunities'

Thus Mr. Reagan's legacy on domestic spending shapes up as more of a retrenchment than the revolution it is often called. "A lot has happened, but a lot less than I wish had happened," says Sen. William Armstrong, a conservative Colorado Republican. "The administration's record on the budget so far," he adds, "is one of missed opportunities."

Even Democrats who criticized many of the president's budget proposals as unwise and unfair agree that the federal role hasn't been radically reshaped. "We will have gone through eight years of the most conservative presidency we've ever had, and the basic structure of the American welfare state will be significantly intact," predicts Stuart Eizenstat, former President Carter's domestic policy adviser.

The president may defy the political odds and win sweeping budgetary changes during the rest of his term, particularly if Congress enacts a measure similar to the Gramm-Rudman bill. The Senate-passed proposal, which would set the government on a course to a balanced budget in fiscal 1991, would give the White House new fiscal powers and "unparalleled opportunities to avoid the normal checks and balances" that have buoyed domestic spending, Mr. Eizenstat says.

But many politicians and analysts doubt that the recent budget-balancing drive will lead to fundamental change in the nature of nondefense programs. The difficulties that Mr. Reagan has encountered to date,

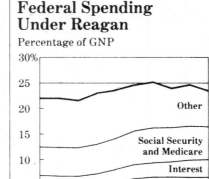

Federal Spending Under Reagan
Percentage of GNP

- Other
- Social Security and Medicare
- Interest
- Defense

'77 '78 '79 '80 '81 '82 '83 '84 '85 '86*
Fiscal year   *Estimate

they say, reflect the tough political and economic realities inherent in assaulting the federal establishment, and these realities will continue to constrain him or any future president.

A New Base

Mr. Reagan's imprint is most likely to resemble that which Dwight Eisenhower left on the New Deal, according to Hugh Heclo, professor of government at Harvard University. "The welfare state has been consolidated, in part by making it more viable and workable," Prof. Heclo says. "Some things they tried to kill and couldn't; that makes those programs less vulnerable to attack in future years. Some programs they've marginally adjusted, which establishes the base premise that it's OK to have them. Other things they didn't even try to adjust—they'd say, 'Honest to God, I won't touch this,' like Social Security. I call all of this establishing a new base."

In fiscal 1986, which started Oct. 1, this new base of government spending, including defense, will absorb an estimated 23.3% of the gross national product, far higher than the goal of 19% of GNP that Mr. Reagan set out to achieve and very close to the 23.5% when the president took office. Mr. Reagan blames Congress—especially Democrats—for the continued growth of spending because lawmakers rejected many of his proposed savings. But a look back at the budget battles of the past five years—and the president's role in them—suggests that resistance to cutting government runs deeper than Mr. Reagan cares to admit.

The president often backed away from pushing ambitious budget reductions, partly for partisan political reasons, partly because he embraced the basic aims of the programs or accepted a national mood of support for them. The huge middle-class entitlement programs posed the greatest political obstacles, so the smaller programs for the poor bore a disproportionate share of the cuts.

Moreover, the administration committed strategic errors, notably on the Social Security issue. And it often made the military buildup a higher priority than cutting domestic spending.

Changing Priorities

Still, Mr. Reagan's budgetary accomplishments are hardly trivial. Spending for domestic programs in fiscal 1986 is lower by an estimated $75 billion to $80 billion—

about 11%—than it would have been if pre-1981 policies had been followed. Some areas, notably housing and employment, have been cut deeply. Priorities have changed significantly: Non-defense programs other than Social Security and Medicare have declined as a share of the budget to 30% in the current fiscal year from 40% in fiscal 1981, while defense has risen to nearly 28% of the budget from 23%.

Perhaps most important is the fact that giant federal tax cuts and deficits have made it politically impossible for Congress to enact major, permanent new programs. Although big new programs stopped springing up several years before Mr. Reagan took office, the president "has changed the whole frame of reference within which the budget is debated," says Republican Sen. Slade Gorton of Washington.

But the deficit "starved" few programs to death, even in cases—such as the Small Business Administration and the Economic Development Administration—where many liberals questioned the programs' worth. And the deficit has sharply added to one spending category: Interest on the national debt has risen to about $140 billion in the current fiscal year from $69 billion in fiscal 1981.

"We didn't starve the beast," laments a White House official. "It's still eating quite well—by feeding off future generations."

The origins of the Reagan budget legacy can be found in the presidential campaigns of 1980 and 1984, when the president declared that "waste, fraud and abuse" were the main problem with federal spending. "He did not even suggest that the termination of some programs would be necessary," says William Niskanen, a former member of Mr. Reagan's Council of Economic Advisers.

In 1981, Mr. Niskanen continues, the president "put off limits some of the most important elements of the welfare state"—principally middle-class programs such as Social Security retirement and veterans' benefits. Because of the need to fund defense and debt service, that meant that more than 60% of the budget couldn't be touched.

The White House declared that the exempted programs were part of the "social safety net," which it described as "essential commitments" to the poor, elderly and disabled. But Murray Weidenbaum, Mr. Reagan's chief economic adviser at the time, says that the true, "unstated criterion" for the safety net was "which were the politically vulnerable programs and which weren't."

Among the politically vulnerable programs cut in 1981 were those providing benefits to low-income people. Congress substantially tightened eligibility for food stamps and Aid to Families with Dependent Children, principally by lowering the income that beneficiaries could earn.

The revisions didn't challenge the underlying theories of the low-income programs; rather, they were based on the president's oft-stated rationale that benefits should go only to the "truly needy." Liberals, however, attacked the proposals as cruel and self-defeating: They predicted that many poor working people would quit their jobs to remain on welfare.

The predictions proved wrong. Claiming vindication, conservatives say that working recipients weaned themselves from the system while those without jobs—the overwhelming bulk of the welfare population—remained unaffected by the legislation.

Ineligible for Medicaid

Liberals counter that many thousands of poor people suffered even though they held onto their jobs. There is evidence to support their claims. The congressional General Accounting Office found that about a fifth of those dropped from AFDC reported having to forgo medical care because they lost their Medicaid eligibility automatically upon losing their AFDC. And Jack Meyer, an economist with the American Enterprise Institute, says that a welfare mother of three earning $4 an hour has lost an average of nearly $2,000 in annual benefits.

"I can't believe this doesn't cause real pain for someone like that, and I think it's unfair in a world where we're hardly touching middle-class benefits," Mr. Meyer says.

Actually, programs with middle-class and corporate constituents didn't escape unscathed in the 1981 budget measure, which sliced $35.2 billion from projected fiscal 1982 spending of $740 billion.

For example, union members who lost their jobs to imports lost most of the extra benefits they were entitled to. College students, shipbuilders and small businessmen saw their subsidies reduced. One big program was eliminated—the public service jobs program, which was criticized for having provided jobs to laid-off city workers.

But many other programs found protective support in Congress. To win passage of its budget package, the White House made a number of concessions on lawmakers' pet programs, including the Clinch River breeder reactor, the Export-Import Bank and the Economic Development Administration, a Commerce Department program that purportedly aids distressed areas but has grown since its inception in 1965 to cover more than 80% of the country.

In 1981 the administration did make one stab at gaining savings from the most sacred cow of all—Social Security pensions. Its proposal was announced on May 12, 1981. By that time, Mr. Stockman had realized that because of the big pending tax cut, more savings would be needed—and fast—to keep the deficit from spinning out of control. His opportunity came when

Richard Schweiker, then Secretary of Health and Human Services, began seeking White House endorsement for a package to rescue the financially troubled Social Security retirement system.

Mr. Schweiker—along with some powerful members of Congress—hoped to forge a proposal that would gradually bring the system's outlays and revenue into line. "But Dave was looking for immediate savings," Mr. Schweiker says. Mr. Stockman inserted into the administration proposal a provision to reduce benefits for early retirees. This "would have created a real hardship for people who were just coming up on retirement and had made plans," says Mr. Schweiker, who nonetheless tried to sell the proposal publicly.

A Public Furor

The administration plan provoked a huge public furor, and the GOP-controlled Senate unanimously rejected it. President Reagan withdrew it in favor of establishing a bipartisan commission on the system's solvency. The commission, with economist Alan Greenspan as chairman, produced a compromise package of savings and payroll-tax increases that Congress adopted in 1983.

The commission won kudos for resolving Social Security's financial crisis, but President Reagan still lost control over the issue. Democrats hammered Republicans on Social Security during the 1982 elections, and GOP officials say that the reluctance of the White House and House Republicans to tackle the pension system in 1985 can be traced to the events of 1981.

The administration also made a "horrible error" in accepting the four-year farm bill passed by Congress in 1981, a Stockman aide says. "We artificially priced it (the bill) at a low level and talked ourselves into thinking it would be okay," he says. The administration also agreed to specific target prices for crops, believing that would be cheaper than indexing the target prices to inflation. With inflation and crop prices plummeting, the cost of farm programs soared to a staggering $22.9 billion by 1983, double the 1981 figure.

In the winter of 1981-82, the administration began preparing a new budget submission for fiscal 1983. But the rise in unemployment and the deficit had put the administration on the defensive. When Mr. Stockman presented the White House with a new list of spending cuts, Mr. Weidenbaum recalls, James Baker, then White House chief of staff, rejected many of them because he felt that they wouldn't pass Congress and would alienate the administration's constituencies. President Reagan himself decided against several Stockman proposals to kill programs.

Too Solicitous?

The president was too solicitous of his cabinet, Mr. Weidenbaum complains. "He would say—I'm paraphrasing—'Mac Bal-

Reagan's Impact on Federal Programs

A few programs were eliminated...

In millions of dollars	'81	'85
Public service jobs	$2,400	$ —
Postal Service general subsidy	486	—
Public Health Service hospitals	188	—
Regional development commissions	78	—
Youth Conservation Corps	71	—
National Consumer Co-op Bank	19	—
Revenue sharing[1]	5,140	4,617

...others survived attempts to eliminate them.

In millions of dollars	'81	'85
Ex-Im Bank direct-loan ceiling	$5,500	$3,900
Small Business Administration[2]	4,920	3,463
Amtrak	851	764
Urban Development Action Grants	371	500
Community Services Block Grant[3]	619	372
Economic Development Admin.	536	359
Legal Services Corp.[3]	324	302
Appalachian Regional Commission	348	196

Some programs were cut and stayed cut...

In billions of dollars

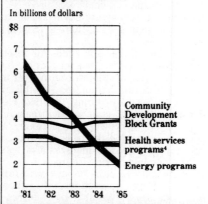

Community Development Block Grants

Health services programs[4]

Energy programs

...others were cut and grew back.

In billions of dollars

Elementary and secondary education programs

Social services programs[5]

Pell college-scholarship grants

Low-income programs were cut more deeply than middle-class entitlements.

Middle-Class Entitlements[6]

In billions of dollars	'82	'83	'84	'85
Spending path Reagan inherited	$263.7	$295.9	$306.9	$326.4
Actual outcome	258.2	286.7	286.6	305.3

Low-Income Benefit Programs[7]

In billions of dollars	'82	'83	'84	'85
Spending path Reagan inherited	$62.9	$70.5	$72.5	$76.9
Actual outcome	56.6	63.2	65.0	70.5

Percentage Cut From Inherited Spending Path

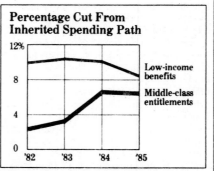

Low-income benefits

Middle-class entitlements

drige (the secretary of commerce) is a nice guy; I can't turn him down. Jim Watt (the interior secretary)—everyone's dumping on Jim Watt. We've got to be supportive.'"

The White House accepted many Stockman budget proposals, but not enough to come close to balancing the budget. The budget director and others lobbied hard for a tax increase to help plug the gap. After

agonizing, Mr. Reagan agreed, but then reversed himself when word of his "decision" leaked out. "We didn't come here to increase taxes," he angrily told a group of top officials. Mr. Weidenbaum recalls stunning the meeting into silence by retorting: "Mr. President, none of us wants to raise taxes. The problem is, we just haven't cut spending enough."

Later in 1982, after lengthy negotiations

and battles with Congress, the president agreed to support a tax increase projected to raise $100 billion over three years. Congress also enacted some spending cuts, though not as many as Mr. Reagan wanted.

The years 1983 and 1984 were characterized mostly by a stalemate in Congress and a holding action at the White House. Starting in late 1983, the administration adopted a strategy of waiting until after the election to deal with the deficit, save for a modest "down payment" package. Meanwhile, Congress quietly rescinded some of the cuts it had made in 1981.

Awaiting Change

Although most of the 1981 changes remain intact, "all of us have learned a lot" from the restorations, says John Cogan, a top official at the Office of Management and Budget. When a program is cut rather than killed, the bureaucracies and constituent groups supporting it can wait for the political environment to change, "and then they'll say, 'We haven't had a real increase in three or four years,'" Mr. Cogan says. "That's why if you're going to make a significant, permanent imprint on the level of government, you have to get rid of programs."

In some cases, the amounts of the 1981 cuts were eroded because the White House, eager to protect its military buildup, bought support by accepting domestic spending increases. Education, in particular, gained from this sort of bargaining. The administration also had to accept some backsliding from its 1981 housing cuts to persuade House Banking Committee Chairman Fernand St Germain, the Rhode Island Democrat, to push an $8.4 billion bill for the International Monetary Fund through his committee.

"Every time the administration wanted something from Congress, the price went up," Mr. Niskanen says.

In other cases, the White House simply yielded to political pressure for spending. In early 1983, for example, right at the end of the recession, it proposed a $4.3 billion anti-recession program. The bill that emerged financed a large number of classic, though temporary, "pork barrel" public-works items in the districts of congressional committee chairmen.

Resisting New Programs

Still, despite the recession, the administration succeeded in fending off proposals for popular new programs such as health insurance for the unemployed. The deficit helped block the proposals, administration officials acknowledge. But they deny charges that they actually planned the huge deficits as a way to force social spending down.

Sometimes the deficit undermined efforts to overhaul programs. "Everything we proposed had to show savings immediately," says an adviser. Take farm programs, he says: "You could probably persuade Congress to make some policy reforms that would have an effect over five or 10 years. The trouble is, we have to propose wholesale slaughter. They reject that out of hand. They're always able to argue the disruption is too costly. And they may be right."

This year was supposed to bring an attack on spending that would enshrine the Reagan revolution in history. The president had won a 49-state victory based in part on campaign promises to resist a tax increase, sustain the military buildup and keep hands off Social Security. Those promises helped focus pressure on the remainder of the budget, including the 20 domestic programs that Mr. Reagan proposed in February to eliminate. But they also made it difficult for him to negotiate flexibly.

The Senate produced a budget that would have sliced $56 billion from the projected 1986 deficit, curbing Social Security cost-of-living allowances and getting rid of 10 programs. Trades for votes protected many programs. Only one Democrat, Edward Zorinsky of Nebraska, was willing to vote for a plan that cut spending without raising any taxes. So Mr. Stockman and Senate GOP leaders had to bargain hard for every available Republican.

Praise From Mayor

Sen. Robert Kasten, a Wisconsin conservative, insisted on keeping funding for Urban Development Action Grants; he had drawn praise from the Democratic Mayor of Milwaukee for bringing federal grant money to Wisconsin. Others held out for saving rural housing and electrification programs. At a private meeting of GOP lawmakers, Sen. Lowell Weicker of Connecticut, who was fighting to restore money for education and health-research grants, blew up and called Mr. Stockman a "little twirp."

Aides say that Mr. Stockman privately voiced frustration that he couldn't throw a small tax increase into the package, thereby gaining 10 or 15 Democratic votes and avoiding much of the dickering with

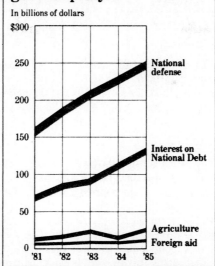

Some big budget items grew rapidly...

In billions of dollars

National defense

Interest on National Debt

Agriculture

Foreign aid

'81 '82 '83 '84 '85

...but only a few programs were created.

In millions of dollars	'84	'85
Child Health Assurance Program	$ —	$40
Rental development grants	—	20

Notes

[1]Congress resolved this year to terminate revenue sharing in 1987, but may change its mind.
[2]SBA direct-loan obligations and loan-guarantee commitments.
[3]Programs that the administration has tried to kill each year since 1981.
[4]Programs include Indian Health Services; Alcohol, Drug Abuse and Mental Health Block Grant; Maternal and Child Health Block Grant.
[5]Programs include Social Services Block Grant; Head Start; Older Americans Act.
[6]Programs like Social Security and Medicare that go to people of all income classes who qualify.
[7]Programs like Aid to Families with Dependent Children and Medicaid that go only to those below certain income levels.

Source: Office of Management and Budget

the marginal Republicans.

"What a difference that would have made to the politics!" agrees Senate Budget Committee Chairman Domenici. A bipartisan majority of the Senate would then have been voting for a package that included a cut in Social Security inflation adjustments.

Vulnerable on Social Security

Instead Senate Republicans found themselves vulnerable on Social Security as the House matched their spending-cut totals largely by slashing the newly unpopular military budget. Democrats began exploiting the Social Security issue, reminding voters of the president's 1984 campaign promise.

In the end, Mr. Reagan retreated from his reluctant endorsement of the Senate's Social Security cut; he and House Speaker Thomas P. O'Neill agreed that neither Social Security nor taxes would be part of any deficit solution this year. Angry Senate

Republicans negotiated a compromise with House Democrats on a package that makes a modest dent in the deficit and terminates only revenue sharing.

Despite conservative disappointment with the outcome of the 1985 budget battle, it's possible to look back at the Reagan years and find a number of programs that have been altered in ways that seemed unthinkable in the 1970s. For example, subsidies for new housing have been drastically reduced in favor of subsidies for existing units, which are much cheaper. Medicare outlays are subject to new cost controls that reimburse hospitals by specific ailment.

But for the most part, says the Carter administration's Mr. Eizenstat, the growth of government has undergone a "midcourse correction." Harvard's Prof. Heclo uses a football metaphor: "It's battling between the 45-yard lines," he says, adding: "That's typically American. It's a hell of a stable system."

58

BY WILLIAM S. WOODSIDE

HUNGER IN AMERICA IS REAL

Millions go hungry because the government has cut back too far on food programs.

■ Hunger in affluent America in the 1980s? "Not proved," we hear from official Washington. Stories of families going hungry are said to be exaggerated, and telecasts from soup kitchens are dismissed as anecdotal evidence, not facts and figures.

While the debate continues, millions of people in this country—many of them children—often go without food. I think that's a disgrace, and I am not alone. But for whatever reasons, there is a tendency to deny the problem rather than solve it.

Those who oppose federal food programs make four basic arguments against them: that the need is overstated, that the programs don't work, that they cost too much, and that the private sector should do more and the government less.

The first point is simply wrong. I was a member of a bipartisan study group, organized by the nonprofit Center for National Policy in Washington, that recently recommended changes in federal agricultural and food programs. We found abundant evidence of increased hunger in America, due partly to continuing unemployment and inflation and partly to reduced outlays for programs covering child nutrition, food stamps, and aid to families with dependent children.

The Harvard-based Physicians' Task Force on Hunger in America estimated early this year that up to 20 million Americans suffer from hunger several days a month. That was the latest in a series of studies that began in October 1982, when the U.S. Conference of Mayors brought the issue to public attention. This bipartisan group conducted a national survey and found hunger to represent "a most serious emergency."

Opponents of food assistance programs quibble over numbers and definitions. The President's Task Force on Food Assistance reported early in 1984 that it too found hunger in America but could not measure its extent. Later, a bill to set up a national nutrition-monitoring system that would provide such statistics was voted down in the House after Reagan Administration spokesmen declared it unnecessary.

Lacking an official hunger census, we look elsewhere for evidence. The Commerce Department estimates that the number of Americans living in poverty jumped from 24.5 million in 1978 to 35.3 million in 1983, more than at any time since 1960. Today a

family of four at the poverty line (an annual income of $10,200) has less than $10 a day to spend for food. Two out of five of the people living in poverty are children. The poverty rate for children under the age of 6 has reached 25% and is far higher among blacks and Hispanics.

The Reagan Administration argues that despite its spending cuts it has maintained a safety net for the poorest in society. Others contend that poverty statistics do not accurately reflect the total income of the poor because many receive in-kind benefits such as food stamps and free school meals, or that some people go hungry because federal programs are poorly managed, not underfunded.

However, it seems clear that many people are hungry today because the government is spending too little to help the needy. A recent Commerce Department survey indicated that 40% of the poor get no in-kind benefits whatever. Of the remaining 60%, many receive only one benefit (often medical care). Department of Agriculture figures show that the number of poor receiving food stamps dropped between 1980 and 1983, while the number of Americans in poverty was increasing.

Nationally, food stamp benefits average 47 cents a meal. What does 47 cents buy? Rice or beans, little or no meat, no fruit or fresh vegetables. Poor mothers say that as food benefits run out toward the end of the month, they often quell their children's hunger with the filling, but not particularly nutritious, combination of popcorn and water.

Waiting lists for federal food programs are now common. The Department of Agriculture says WIC (the Special Supplemental Food Program for High-Risk Women, Infants, and Children, which provides cereal, juices, and dairy products to needy families) currently serves about one-third of the mothers and infants eligible for assistance under the program. The other two-thirds are not mothers who choose to pass up benefits or do not know how to get them; some WIC clinics have long waiting lists and have to turn away eligible mothers and children because funding isn't adequate.

Anyone still undecided about the need for continued and effective food programs should visit a soup kitchen or a food pantry (volunteer groups that hand out canned

goods and staples) and talk to the workers and recipients. I did. I may not know the number of hungry Americans, but I know that a serious problem exists.

I also know that those who say nutritional programs don't work are mistaken. Despite horror stories about food stamp cheats (such examples can be dredged up about any large program) food assistance has been remarkably successful in the U.S.

LET'S LOOK at the record. A brief chronology of efforts to end hunger in America begins with the Great Depression and the first food stamp program, which helped both farmers and the unemployed. Hunger was largely forgotten during World War II. But in 1946 the U.S. Surgeon General testified that large numbers of wartime draftees had been rejected because of poor physical development due to malnutrition in childhood. The National School Lunch Act was passed as "a measure of national security."

The economy grew but hunger remained,

> **Government must do its share. Otherwise, hunger will exact terrible penalties in higher health care costs, a higher death rate, and millions of poorly nourished youngsters growing into poorly functioning adults.**

and in 1961 President Kennedy made more surplus agricultural commodities available and reestablished a pilot food stamp program. Under President Johnson the food stamp program continued, and a school breakfast program was begun. President Nixon called for an end to hunger in America at a White House conference in 1969, and Congress created WIC and a nutritional program for the elderly.

A comprehensive food assistance network, developed by both Republican and Democratic administrations, was in place to rescue those who slipped through the cracks of our economic structure. Health professionals began to find fewer malnourished people and credited food stamps, Head Start, school meals, and WIC.

Between the mid-1960s and the late 1970s the problem of hunger was identified, and millions of the hungry were fed as a result of humane and imaginative federal programs. Yet now, a few years later, this history has been forgotten and hunger has reemerged at a time of general prosperity.

Why slash programs that are needed and effective? Over the past four years, $12 billion was cut from nutrition programs, including food stamps and school breakfasts and lunches. Poverty grew, food costs rose, and hunger increased while assistance diminished. Nevertheless, the Administration and the Senate want to cut nutrition assistance by nearly $400 million in 1986. Some of the WIC money already appropriated to feed poor mothers and infants this year is being withheld by the Administration.

These actions arouse few cries of outrage. Washington assures us that poverty, hunger, and malnutrition are floating away on a tide of economic growth. We are also told that more urgent issues confront us, such as rising defense costs and the gigantic budget deficit. Hunger has been buried in an avalanche of other national problems.

I believe we've lost our perspective. As an economist and a businessman I know the dangers of deficit spending and I strongly favor deficit reduction. But the whole constellation of food programs came to $18.5 billion last year, or only about 2.2% of federal spending. Further cuts in this area will only increase suffering while making a token impact on the deficit.

Those who oppose the war on hunger have another argument. Instead of relying on government, they say, we should form partnerships between the public and private sectors to address massive social problems. The private sector *has* become much more active in the delivery of social services. But this concept is commendable only to the point at which private actions become a substitute for public sector responsibility.

AMERICAN CAN has studied food and nutrition for a long time and has identified areas in which the private sector can work effectively to supplement public sector programs. A company foundation is working with the Citizens' Committee for Children in New York City on a project to evaluate the local school meals program. We are helping the Conference of Mayors develop model municipal food policies. We are funding a program to improve the distribution systems of Second Harvest, a national organization that supplies soup kitchens and food pantries working to meet emergency needs.

Donations from the food industry to Second Harvest rose from ten million pounds of food in 1980 to 76 million pounds in 1984. Other private contributions to food banks, as well as a relatively modest government contribution of surplus food, brought total emergency supplies distributed last year to 140 million pounds.

But the success of volunteer programs does not lessen the responsibility of government. Today hunger is a social and public health problem, and government must do its share. Otherwise, hunger will exact terrible penalties in higher health care costs, a higher death rate, and millions of poorly nourished youngsters growing into poorly functioning adults.

Hunger in America is not the crime of the poor, it is the shame of the affluent. We must stop putting cost-consciousness first when the issue is hunger. Let's help our hungry neighbors by insisting on adequate government funding for programs that deliver food to those in desperate need. ∎

THE AMERICAN DREAM MAY BE COMING CLOSER FOR BLACKS

BY GARY S. BECKER

Blacks have made substantial gains in the past 40 years, and a surge of economic growth could erase today's high unemployment figures

GARY S. BECKER IS UNIVERSITY PROFESSOR OF ECONOMICS AND SOCIOLOGY AT THE UNIVERSITY OF CHICAGO

For more than a century, wave after wave of poor immigrants to the U. S. achieved rapid economic success. Germans and Irish in the middle of the 19th century, Italians and Jews in the late 19th and early 20th centuries—all reached economic parity with other Americans in three generations or less. Even Chinese and Japanese immigrants managed to climb out of poverty, in spite of powerful public and private discrimination.

Blacks originally came to the U. S. not as immigrants but as slaves. In *An American Dilemma*, published in 1944, Swedish economist Gunnar Myrdal focused on this unique experience of blacks to explain why they were the major exception to the American dream of up-the-ladder success. True, the earnings of blacks rose greatly from 1880 to 1940 as the economy developed. But my book *The Economics of Discrimination*, published in 1957, shows that during that long period their earnings did not rise much relative to those of whites.

JIM CROW LAWS. Prior to 1940, severe discrimination by state and local governments kept the level of education available to black children abysmally low. In the South, Jim Crow laws dating from the turn of the century repressed blacks in many other ways. Extensive government discrimination combined with widespread prejudice in the marketplace to retard the economic progress of blacks. Economists have been able to demonstrate that competition in product and labor markets raises the cost of discriminating against people for reasons of race, sex, religion, or other characteristics. However, the persistence of such discrimination against blacks shows that competition and free enterprise do not by themselves eliminate the effects of prejudice in the marketplace, especially when the prejudice is deep and widespread and when governmental and private discrimination are mutually reinforcing.

Yet the timing of Myrdal's study is noteworthy because the early 1940s turned out to be a watershed in the economic history of American blacks. In a recent Rand Corp. study, James P. Smith and Finis R. Welch documented that the earnings of black males increased from less than 45% of those of white males in 1940 to almost 60% in 1960 and to 70% in 1980. Other evidence shows that black women are now close to earnings parity with white women.

Smith and Welch attribute the rapid advance of black males after 1940 to several changes in their circumstances. Especially important was the sizable increase in both the number of years blacks were able to spend in school and the quality of education they received. In 1940 black males averaged only 4.7 years of schooling, compared with 8.4 years for white males. Today the difference in schooling for black and white males is less than 1.5 years. Moreover, general prosperity during most of these four decades induced large numbers of blacks to abandon Southern agriculture. At the same time, it promoted rapid economic progress of the South itself, particularly after 1970. In 1940 more than 70% of all blacks resided in the South, with about one-third working in Southern agriculture. Now almost all blacks live in cities or suburban communities, and more than half live outside the South.

Unfortunately, not all the news about blacks is good. Unemployment among black men has remained at about twice the rate for white men, and in 1985 the rate exceeded 40% for black men under the age of 20. At first, the incomes of black families rose rapidly, along with the incomes of black men and women. But after the mid-1960s, the growth in individual incomes diverged considerably from that of families. By 1984 unmarried women headed half of all black families with children, compared with less than 20% for white families. The sharp decline in the number of black families headed by married couples lowered the income received by the average black family, compared with that of the average white family.

PESSIMISTIC VIEW. Clearly, these trends in unemployment and family income give a more pessimistic view of black progress than do trends in individual incomes. Still, blacks have made substantial economic gains over the past 40 years. Moreover, the rise in the number of broken black families during the past 20 years is not mainly the result of discrimination by whites.

There is no reason to doubt that blacks can continue to make economic progress. A voucher system of financing education (BW—Mar. 24) would increase the quality of schooling available to inner-city blacks and other minorities. The instability of black families is partly related to the system of welfare payments and to the high unemployment of young black men. The welfare system can be changed to eliminate the penalty now imposed on intact families. Demand for the services of black men and women will continue to grow, and black unemployment will fall if economic growth becomes as rapid as it was in the period after 1940.

If all goes well, the beginning of the next century could see the end of this American dilemma—and the full participation by blacks in the American dream.

How to rescue the broken lives? While the black middle class progresses, millions fall behind in a leaderless, seemingly hopeless underclass. Are they slipping further back despite billions in federal aid or perhaps even because of these programs? Or is it because of basic shifts in the economy?

A NATION APART

It has been a long time building, but only now is the country paying attention to it: The alarming emergence within black America of a nation apart—a lost nation in a land of comfort.

The great majority of blacks are working out better lives for themselves. Over the past two decades, the percentage of blacks in the middle class has doubled. A young black man with a college education now earns just about as much as his white counterpart. Six of the 10 largest cities have black mayors. In living rooms across the U.S., the "Bill Cosby Show" is the most popular fare on television.

But a second nation has grown up within black America, and life is desperately different there. It is a nation outside the economic mainstream—a separate culture of have-nots drifting further apart from the basic values of the haves. Its growth is now the central issue in the country's urban centers.

A charged atmosphere of fear permeates the cities, heightening racial tension between blacks and whites. Though segregation is outlawed, subtle barriers are being solidified between races. Last year, violent protests broke out in Philadelphia when blacks moved into a white neighborhood.

The emergence of the black underclass, as it is now popularly known, is clothed in uncertainty and controversy. For one thing, no one is sure just how large the underclass is. About a third of all blacks live in poverty, but most of them—like most poor whites—hold jobs or use welfare temporarily before shifting back to the mainstream. The underclass, in contrast, is the seemingly irreducible core of poor inner-city blacks, those trapped in an unending cycle of joblessness, broken homes, welfare and, often, drugs and violence. That core is estimated at about 2 million to 3.5 million, or about one third of all poor blacks.

Statistics that are more reliable—and also more startling—relate what it is like for a black youngster growing up today:
• One in 2 lives in poverty.
• One in 2 grows up without a father.
• Nearly 1 in 2 teenagers is out of work.
• One out of 4 births is to a teenager.

• And 1 in every 21 young black men winds up murdered.

Such conditions, of course, are not limited to black neighborhoods. Some 23 million whites are poor in the United States today, and many of them have become mired, too. But the growth of an underclass in black urban centers, less than 20 years after the death of Martin Luther King, Jr., is a special agony for America.

Changing minds

The problems of the black underclass are baffling. Most immigrant groups in America—and indeed, many blacks—have moved up the economic ladder. As Prof. Glenn Loury of Harvard University puts it: "Every finding of a diminution in discrimination raises the terrifying question: Why then do blacks not succeed?"

Among civil-rights leaders, politicians and academics, a fierce debate is heating up about causes—and solutions, if any. Black leadership itself is fracturing. Those representing the Old Guard blame lingering racism and cramped economic opportunities. They see affirmative action, job training and expanded federal programs as the way out. Black intellectuals, such as William Julius Wilson of the University of Chicago, say that radical changes in the job market are swelling the underclass.

Disputing these views is a new breed of bootstrap conservatives, including some blacks, who say that race is no longer the critical factor. Political scientists Loury and James Q. Wilson of Harvard point to declining family values and ghetto culture as the central problems. They argue that far more self-help is needed among blacks themselves.

That view is gaining support among a growing number of blacks, too. *Washington Post* columnist William Raspberry wrote earlier this month about the rise of the black middle class and warned its members that a new message was needed for those left behind: "It would help enormously if the well-off would let the poor—especially the children—in on their vital secret: You can make it if you try."

Injecting even more emotion into the debate is the fact that within white America many influential minds are changing. Two decades ago, most white Americans readily supported federal assistance programs and new civil-rights laws. Some believe that such public support flowed from a guilty conscience about past injustices; others think it was part of a generous American spirit.

But clearly, the national mood has shifted. Popular political leaders from President Reagan to New York Mayor Ed Koch are publicly questioning how much good has come from hundreds of billions of federal funds spent on public assistance, education, income security and housing for the disadvantaged. Reagan asserts that federal assistance has only created a dependency on welfare and argues that employment-training programs of the past—such as the Comprehensive Employment and Training Act—were miserable flops. Implicit—and often explicit—in their argument is that the system is no longer to blame: Responsibility must rest more squarely on the poor themselves.

Perhaps as significant to the outcome of the national debate is that important black leaders also have shifted position. Two decades ago, when Senator Daniel Patrick Moynihan (D-N.Y.), working in the Johnson administration, produced his controversial report on the collapse of black family life, he was bitterly criticized by civil-rights leaders for even bringing the subject up.

That code of silence is now broken. Most civil-rights leaders are publicly discussing the problems of unwed mothers and fatherless families.

"There is a general cultural crisis where the basic moral standards of the society are dropping," says Jesse Jackson. "Somebody must say that babies making babies is morally wrong. . . . We shouldn't be equivocating and hee-hawing about that."

Joblessness as a norm

Even the term *underclass* is controversial, as it connotes a special subculture beyond hope and suffering, a lack of values as well as income.

It is a world where men are without jobs and women are without husbands. Some are career criminals; others broker numbers and hustle stolen goods.

Many are addicted to drugs and alcohol; in hospital emergency rooms, cocaine-related deaths tripled for blacks between 1982 and 1984.

Central to a swelling underclass is the quiet transformation of the urban job market during the past two decades.

Today, almost half of the 8.8 million working-age black men lack jobs, says a report from the Center for the Study of Social Policy. "They are either unemployed, out of the labor force, in correction facilities or unaccounted for."

Unlike ethnic groups in the century's first half, unskilled blacks have been unable to shed poverty by taking manufacturing jobs that offer decent wages. By 1970, the door to these jobs was virtually shut. In the last 15 years, only 1 percent of the 23 million jobs created in the private sector were in manufacturing—while more than 90 percent were in the service sector.

Many new jobs required relatively high education levels and were in the suburbs. As a result, members of other ethnic groups or white women took a significant proportion. Young black men, for whatever reason, took only 1 out of every 1,000 new jobs created between 1970 and 1983.

In New York, Philadelphia and Baltimore, entry-level jobs in both service and manufacturing industries dropped by more than 600,000 in the central city during the 1970s.

For most inner-city blacks, new service jobs—janitor, messenger, busboy—have not come near to compensating for the loss of manufacturing jobs.

Some conservative social scientists, such as Charles Murray, a research fellow at the Manhattan Institute for Policy Research, argue that inner-city blacks do indeed have opportunities in low-level jobs but are turning them down—in part because the fast life of the street makes it more attractive not to work. Others strongly disagree, pointing out that when decent-paying openings occur, employers are sometimes overwhelmed. In Washington, D.C., Marriott received 11,000 job applications for 363 openings in its new downtown hotel.

"Cyclical unemployment was the problem for black men in the past," says Eleanor Holmes Norton, head of the Equal Employment Opportunity Commission under President Carter. "Permanent unemployment is at the core of the black underclass today."

Flight of the middle class

Ironically, the collapse of inner-city communities has been accelerated by the success of middle-class blacks, who have been leaving the ghetto over the past decade. Gone with them are community role models: The doctor, the police officer, the straight-A student, the teacher. The vacuum they leave behind, says psychiatrist James Comer of Yale University, gets filled by "drug pushers, pimps and prostitutes. They're often the only successful people—the only ones with money—that the kids see."

As an alternative to working, many turn to the underground economy. A survey of 2,000 inner-city black teenage males found that about one fourth of their income was from crime.

Dominating underclass life is the continuous threat of violence. Homicide is the leading cause of death for young black men. High crime rates are accompanied by pervasive fear on the streets—between middle-class and poor blacks as well as between blacks and whites. To many community leaders, the underclass is increasingly outside the law.

"The issue is not poverty," says Harry Spence, former Boston Housing Authority administrator. "The real issue is social membership. People can live poor if they have some sense of participation and membership in the community."

The rise of matriarchy

All of this has a major impact on women and children in the inner city.

With so many men dropping out of the labor market, the pool of eligible males shrinks. Sociologist Wilson has calculated that for every 100 black women between the ages of 20 and 24, there are only 45 employed black men.

"This disparity," contends Norton, "has a lot to do with the change in mores in the poor-black community. Women grow up where they not only do not see people marry, they in fact don't see eligible men."

The decline of two-parent families is striking. In 1965, only 1 of 4 black families was headed by a woman. Now, almost half are headed by females. In contrast, 80 percent of black middle-class families have two parents present.

The ghetto is also reeling from the recent rise of black families headed by women who have never married, especially among teenagers. "Marriage," warns one report from the Children's Defense Fund, "is now an almost forgotten institution among black teens."

The prevalence of matriarchal families in the underclass has hastened what economists call the feminization of poverty. If present trends continue, 70 percent of black families will be headed by single women by the turn of the century. Says John Jacob, president of the National Urban League: "The absence of black males as heads of households has had a devastating effect on black America."

Economics and values

A large number of other minorities and whites also belong to an underclass culture of crumbling family structure, crime and poverty.

What's more, throughout U.S. history, different ethnic groups have experienced similar social disintegration and worked their way up from the slums. The Irish, for example, at the turn of the century, were among those plagued by domestic violence, broken families and alcohol problems.

Blacks, the largest and most visible minority, have met stiffer resistance compared with other immigrants.

Still, the collapse of the ghetto raises disturbing questions about the widening gap between poor blacks and those who have made it.

If part of the problem lies in the lack of opportunities for unskilled blacks, the upside-down value system of the underclass is also an obstacle. "We need to inculcate middle-class values," says the Rev. Charles Stith of Boston's Organization for a New Equality. "Children need to learn that hustling is very different from balancing a checkbook."

Politics of poverty

As Republicans and Democrats argue over budget cuts that affect the urban poor, a key issue is the role of welfare payments in fueling the underclass.

Concern that incentives are misdirected were stirred by Murray, author of the controversial book *Losing Ground*.

Yet the welfare-underclass link is complicated. In fact, welfare does not seem to be the key factor in forming female-headed families—since the number of black single mothers who are *not* on Aid to Families With Dependent Children grew just as rapidly during the 1970s as those who were.

The Reagan administration is attempting to force those on welfare to work. Some officials are also calling for a national family policy to curb high rates of illegitimate births and fatherless families—trends also soaring among whites. "The only way we're going to deal with some of these problems is by preventing future generations from growing into them," says Murray.

But with the budget deficit dominating the legislative agenda, no new federal initiatives are expected soon. In many cities, local programs to help students finish school and prevent out-of-wedlock births are trying to meet the growing needs of the underclass.

Yet to many political leaders, the existence of an underclass is a burgeoning problem for the whole nation and time is running out. "We're building social nitroglycerin that is going to explode," says Representative William Gray (D-Pa.), "and the country is going to pay for it one way or another." ∎

by David Whitman and Jeannye Thornton with Maureen Walsh of the Economic Unit and Ronald A. Taylor and the magazine's domestic bureaus

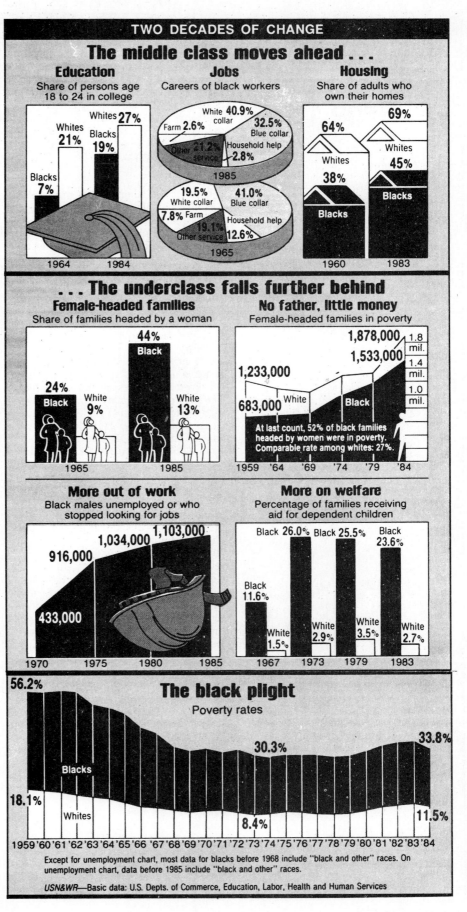

TWO DECADES OF CHANGE

The middle class moves ahead . . .

Education — Share of persons age 18 to 24 in college

Blacks 7%, Whites 21% (1964); Whites 27%, Blacks 19% (1984)

Jobs — Careers of black workers

1985: White collar 40.9%, Blue collar 32.5%, Household help 2.8%, Other service 21.2%, Farm 2.6%

1965: White collar 19.5%, Blue collar 41.0%, Farm 7.8%, Household help 19.1%, Other service 12.6%

Housing — Share of adults who own their homes

Whites 64%, Blacks 38% (1960); Whites 69%, Blacks 45% (1983)

. . . The underclass falls further behind

Female-headed families — Share of families headed by a woman

Black 24%, White 9% (1965); Black 44%, White 13% (1985)

No father, little money — Female-headed families in poverty

White 683,000 → 1,233,000; Black 1,533,000 → 1,878,000 (1959 '64 '69 '74 '79 '84)

At last count, 52% of black families headed by women were in poverty. Comparable rate among whites: 27%.

More out of work — Black males unemployed or who stopped looking for jobs

433,000 (1970), 916,000 (1975), 1,034,000 (1980), 1,103,000 (1985)

More on welfare — Percentage of families receiving aid for dependent children

Black 11.6%, White 1.5% (1967); Black 26.0%, White 2.9% (1973); Black 25.5%, White 3.5% (1979); Black 23.6%, White 2.7% (1983)

The black plight — Poverty rates

Blacks: 56.2% (1959) ... 30.3% ... 33.8% (1984)
Whites: 18.1% (1959) ... 8.4% ... 11.5% (1984)

1959 '60 '61 '62 '63 '64 '65 '66 '67 '68 '69 '70 '71 '72 '73 '74 '75 '76 '77 '78 '79 '80 '81 '82 '83 '84

Except for unemployment chart, most data for blacks before 1968 include "black and other" races. On unemployment chart, data before 1985 include "black and other" races.

USN&WR—Basic data: U.S. Depts. of Commerce, Education, Labor, Health and Human Services

A SHRINKING MIDDLE CLASS IS A CALL FOR ACTION

BY ROBERT KUTTNER

If incomes are becoming more and more skewed to the extremes, there is a good argument for interfering with market forces

During the past three years, a spirited debate has taken place over whether the rich are getting richer and the poor poorer. The casual signs of this trend are ubiquitous: luxury consumption, booming real estate, and affluent yuppies at one extreme of the economy—and intensification of poverty and economic isolation at the other.

The debate is complicated because this apparent polarization reflects multiple causes. Demographic shifts have played a major role. The enormous baby-boom cohort hit the labor market in the 1970s just as economic growth slowed and real wages fell. Women entered the job market in record numbers during the same decade. Both groups served to depress wages for new workers and produced a generational maldistribution of income.

Public policy exacerbated this maldistribution. Under the Reagan Administration, income transfers to the poor were sharply reduced. The income tax load was lightened, most notably for the rich, while the working poor faced higher Social Security taxes. Public-sector employment, a source of jobs paying better-than-average wages, began to decrease. The minimum wage, a major income protection for the lowest-paid workers, fell further and further behind the average wage. In the face of growing resistance from industry and a hostile National Labor Relations Board, unions organized few low-wage workers and concentrated on defending the gains of the relatively well-paid.

WORST OFF. The high unemployment of the 1970s and 1980s also played a part. High unemployment tends to impact most severely on young, inexperienced, relatively unskilled workers, who are the worst off to begin with. And the changing structure of employment apparently had an effect, too. As service jobs began replacing factory jobs, the economy generated more high-wage and low-wage jobs, and fewer in the middle.

All of this produced an increasing polarization in the national distribution of income, skewing it toward the extremes of poor and rich and eroding the middle-income group. Or did it?

Lately, a wave of revisionist criticism has pooh-poohed concern about a "declining middle." Economic writer Robert Samuelson cites Bureau of Labor Statistics data showing that the distribution of earnings along occupations is relatively stable. He also contends that any worsening in the income distribution was mainly the result of the 1982-83 recession. Economist Robert Z. Lawrence of the Brookings Institution suggests that the problem is mainly demographic—all those young and female workers. Once they become fully integrated into the labor force, the distribution problem will solve itself. And writer James M. Fallows reminds us that industrial transition, though it produces temporary dislocation, is really for the best in the long run because it reflects productivity gains that will eventually make the entire society richer.

IDEOLOGICAL NUMBERS. This debate, though partly technical, is also deeply ideological. If the optimistic revisionists are right and the distortions in income distribution are transient, then laissez-faire capitalism essentially works. That is, it produces a socially defensible distribution of income and wealth, and government's only role is to get out of the way and let the magnificent engine deliver the goods. But if the pessimists are right and the income distribution is truly becoming more skewed toward the extremes, then there is a good case for altering the distributive outcomes produced by the market, and perhaps a case that market capitalism, left alone, produces social instability. If so, we need nonmarket mechanisms to redistribute final income, even if the engine of production remains essentially capitalist.

A recent study by the Congressional Research Service and the Congressional Budget Office provides new evidence that the pessimists may be right after all. The study, *Children in Poverty*, compares the income distribution of households with children, over time. The distribution of family income is a key indicator, both because the family is the backbone of the middle class and because looking only at families holds the unit of analysis constant.

According to the study, which used Census data, there has been a widening gulf in the income distribution of American families. In 1968 the poorest one-fifth of families with children had 7.4% of the total family income. By 1983 this had dropped to just 4.8%, an incredible loss of more than one-third of their share. During the same period, the richest fifth increased its share to 38.1% from 33.8%.

Thus, it is not at all a foregone conclusion that the widening polarization of income will correct itself. One can, of course, dismiss the apparent erosion of a broad middle-income class as "merely" demographic or "merely" the result of high unemployment and industrial change. But for a young family looking for a middle-class way of life, that "merely" is small comfort. This may indeed be a period of explosive entrepreneurial growth and capitalist dynamism. But unless that growth produces an equitable distribution of benefits, something is deeply wrong with democratic capitalism. ∎

ROBERT KUTTNER IS ECONOMICS CORRESPONDENT FOR *THE NEW REPUBLIC* AND THE AUTHOR OF *THE ECONOMIC ILLUSION*

Are we *Losing Ground?*

Charles Murray's *Losing Ground: American Social Policy, 1950–1980*[1] has attracted much attention. Some find it the definitive analysis of what has happened to the poor in this country since the 1960s, when social programs were greatly expanded as a result of the War on Poverty and as part of the Great Society. Others consider the analysis a flawed attack on social programs to aid the poor. Among those who disagree with Murray, some quarrel with his choice of data and others take issue with his interpretations. All agree that the book, in calling to account government policies designed to help the poor, has focused attention on the many complicated interrelated factors—economic, demographic, and moral—that determine how poor people get by in this country.

Murray's position

Murray contends that in the face of increasing expenditures to aid the poor since 1965, their numbers have grown and their circumstances have worsened. His examination of data for the period from 1950 to 1980 leads him to believe that as spending upon the poor expanded, progress against poverty not only stopped, but unemployment rose, the quality of education declined, crime increased, and there was an acceleration in the breakdown of the family.

He argues that the programs of the Great Society arose from a changed outlook on the part of those who determine public policy ("the elite wisdom"). According to Murray, the intellectual consensus on the cause of poverty shifted in the 1960s from the view that an individual was responsible for his or her own well-being to the view that the system was at fault. This conviction was strengthened by the civil rights movement, which made many whites more fully aware that great inequities in opportunity existed. The new consensus, Murray maintains, had vast ramifications for poverty, race relations, education, crime, and the role of government. Public policy was extended beyond the provision of equality of opportunity in the direction of equality of outcome: handouts were offered instead of a hand up, as transfer programs for the poor expanded. In freeing the poor from responsibility for their own circumstances, this new consensus, embodied in government programs, altered their lives for the worse:

A government's social policy helps set the rules of the game—the stakes, the risks, the payoffs, the tradeoffs, and the strategies for making a living, raising a family, having fun, defining what "winning" and "success" mean. The more vulnerable a population and the fewer its independent resources, the more decisive is the effect of the rules imposed from above. The most compelling explanation for the marked shift in the fortunes of the poor is that they continued to respond, as they always had, to the world as they found it, but that we—meaning the not-poor and the un-disadvantaged—had changed the rules of their world. . . . The first effect of the new rules was to make it profitable for the poor to behave in the short term in ways that were destructive in the long term. Their second effect was to mask these long-term losses—to subsidize irretrievable mistakes (p. 9).

In what he calls a "thought experiment," to serve "as a device for thinking about policy, not as a blueprint for policy" (p. 220), Murray proposes that it would better the situation of poor people, and especially the minority poor, if we returned to the status quo ante (the 1950s):

The proposed program, our final and most ambitious thought experiment, consists of scrapping the entire federal welfare and income-support structure for working-aged persons, including AFDC, Medicaid, Food Stamps, Unemployment Insurance, Workers' Compensation, subsidized housing, disability insurance, and the rest. It would leave the working-aged person with no recourse whatsoever except the job market, family members, friends, and public or private locally funded services. It is the Alexandrian solution: cut the knot, for there is no way to untie it (pp. 227–28).

Having hypothesized this extreme position, Murray starts to tie the knot again: "Our first step is to re-install the Unemployment Insurance program in more or less its previous form" (p. 230). Next he pictures a woman "presenting the local or private service with this proposition: 'Help me find a job and day-care for my children, and I will take care of the rest.' " This suggests the need for programs that differ from existing ones in that they would be provided by either local governments or the private sector. He then states, "Hungry children should be fed; there is no argument about that" (p. 233). How, if food stamps and other transfers are eliminated, he doesn't say. But though Murray sees the necessity for some assistance to some of the poor, he maintains that their conditions deteriorated as the federal initiatives associated with the War on Poverty and Great Society gained momentum and that the culprits are the very programs put in place to aid the poor.

Many analysts have registered their differences with Murray's interpretations of recent trends and his policy recommendations.[2] This article highlights the critiques made by researchers at the Institute for Research on Poverty, who have assembled their arguments in an IRP Special Report, *Losing Ground: A Critique*

Reprinted with permission from *Focus*, Newsletter of the Institute for Research on Poverty: Fall and Winter, 1985.

Trends in poverty

Murray begins with the Institute's time series on pretransfer poverty—the number of poor persons with incomes below the official poverty line before receiving governmental transfers—which he relabels "latent poverty." He extends this series back to 1950. The percentage of persons who are classified as pretransfer poor dropped from 33 percent in the 1950s to about 21 percent in 1965, and was down to 18.2 percent in 1968, when Murray says the poverty programs began to take effect. After that date, even though more money was spent on social programs, the figure rose, reaching 19 percent by 1972, 21 percent by 1976, and 22 percent by 1980 (p. 65). Murray calls latent poverty the most "damning" of statistics because "economic independence—standing on one's own abilities and accomplishments—is of paramount importance in determining the quality of a family's life. . . . For this independence to have *decreased* would be an indictment of the American system whenever in our history it might have occurred" (p. 65).

Murray argues further that blacks (whom he uses throughout his book as a proxy for the poor) have gained not at all under the Great Society programs. In his Figure 4.4 (p. 62) he shows that whereas poverty (after transfers) among working-aged blacks dropped precipitously between 1959 and 1969, from 58 percent to 30 percent, a decade later—the very decade during which there was the high growth in social spending—progress stopped.

Sheldon Danziger and Peter Gottschalk of the Institute interpret the trend in pretransfer (latent) poverty differently. They find that the growth in pretransfer poverty coincides with rising unemployment as well as with the growth in social programs for the poor:

> As unemployment dropped between 1965 and 1969, pretransfer poverty declined. Since then, unemployment and pretransfer poverty have trended upward. Throughout the 1970s, the poverty-increasing impact of rising unemployment was offset by rising transfers. When transfers stopped growing and unemployment continued to rise, the official poverty rate rose by 1983 to the level of the late 1960s.[3]

Danziger and Gottschalk cite the growing gap between pretransfer poverty and poverty after transfers, especially if in-kind transfers are valued, as evidence of the increased importance of transfers in reducing poverty.

They argue that the importance of transfers in reducing poverty is unambiguous for the group with the largest increase in transfers—the aged poor. Poverty as officially measured among the aged has been reduced by between 30 and 50 percent since 1967 (see Table 1). Public spending on this group and the totally disabled, primarily through Social Security, Medicare, and Medicaid, accounted for over 75 percent of all 1980 expenditures for major income transfer programs. Another approximately 18 percent was spent on

---

Table 1

Official Incidence of Posttransfer Poverty for Persons Classified by Demographic Group of Their Household's Head, 1967–1980

| | All Persons | Aged Household Head | | Nonaged Household Head | | | |
		Whites	Nonwhites	White Men with Children	Nonwhite Men with Children	White Women with Children	Nonwhite Women with Children
1967	14.3%	27.0%	52.0%	7.5%	28.4%	38.2%	68.5%
1980	13.0	13.2	35.7	7.8	16.9	39.1	58.3
% Change 1967–80	−9.1	−51.1	−31.3	+4.0	−40.5	+2.4	−14.9

Source: Danziger and Gottschalk, *Losing Ground: A Critique*, p. 79. Computations by the authors from March Current Population Survey data tapes.

programs for those who were neither elderly nor totally disabled—chiefly Unemployment Insurance and Workers' Compensation. Thus, though the subtitle of Murray's book is broad: "American Social Policy, 1950-1980," he is in fact emphasizing only the 7.3 percent of the 1980 income transfers that go to nondisabled, nonelderly recipients of AFDC and food stamps.

Danziger and Gottschalk also reject Murray's conclusion that blacks lost ground relative to whites as a result of increased transfers. They argue that poor blacks did benefit from the changes in social policies. Though blacks remain poorer than whites after transfers, the poverty rate of nonwhite households with male heads and with children present declined in the period 1967–80 from 28.4 to 16.9 percent (see Table 1). At the same time poverty among comparable whites increased slightly, from 7.5 percent to 7.8. According to Danziger and Gottschalk, Murray's comparison of poverty rates of all blacks to those of all whites does not show these advances because nonwhites have become increasingly likely to live in households headed by women. Although the poverty rate for households headed by women remains consistently high, it did decline for blacks, but not

whites. Danziger and Gottschalk contend that unless the poverty programs caused this increase in families headed by women, a hypothesis they reject, the programs have improved the relative circumstances of the black poor.

All agree, however, that progress against poverty was disappointing in the 1970s. The official measure of the incidence of poverty showed a fairly steady decline from 22.4 percent in 1959 to 11.1 percent in 1973, at which time it began to rise, reaching 13 percent in 1980 and 15.2 percent in 1983, before falling to 14.4 percent in 1984. But why is poverty higher today than in the early 1970s?

Murray hypothesizes that the cause was the shift in social policy, not a lagging economy. He argues that the period from 1970 to 1979 was one of strong economic growth: "Even after holding both population change and inflation constant, per capita GNP increased only a little less rapidly in the seventies than it had in the booming sixties, and much faster than during the fifties. Growth did not stop. But, for some reason, the benefits of economic growth stopped trickling down to the poor" (p. 59).

Table 2

Median Money Incomes and Income Ratios for Black and White
Male Workers, 1948–1982, in Constant 1982 Dollars

Year	Median Income		Ratio B/W	Year	Median Income		Ratio B/W
	Whites	Blacks			Whites	Blacks	
1948	$ 10,064	$ 5,465	.54	1965	$ 16,185	$ 8,710	.54
1949	10,006	4,844	.48	1966	16,631	9,212	.55
1950	10,862	5,899	.54	1967	16,901	9,653	.57
1951	11,524	6,346	.55	1968	17,388	10,551	.61
1952	11,837	6,487	.55	1969	17,812	10,508	.59
1953	12,237	6,760	.55	1970	17,428	10,490	.60
1954	12,080	6,011	.50	1971	17,248	10,351	.60
1955	12,776	6,724	.53	1972	18,029	11,100	.62
1956	13,558	7,113	.52	1973	18,360	11,551	.63
1957	13,402	7,096	.53	1974	17,330	11,135	.64
1958	13,275	6,614	.50	1975	16,679	10,511	.63
1959	13,937	6,561	.47	1976	16,849	10,540	.63
1960	14,003	7,367	.53	1977	16,889	10,326	.61
1961	14,290	7,385	.52	1978	16,945	10,796	.64
1962	14,859	7,318	.49	1979	16,363	10,604	.65
1963	15,151	7,874	.52	1980	15,612	9,786	.63
1964	15,361	8,708	.57	1981	15,172	9,624	.63
				1982	14,748	9,493	.64

Source: Cain, *Losing Ground: A Critique*, p. 11, from U.S. Bureau of the Census, *Current Population Reports*, Series P-60, No. 142, "Money Income of Households, Families, and Persons in the United States: 1982" (Washington, D.C.: GPO, 1984), Table 40.

Glen Cain of the Institute blames the economy. He states that progress in fighting poverty stopped in 1973 because 1973 was the first year of a steady economy-wide decline in real earnings and family income, as measured by white median income.[4] (See Table 2.) He argues that "trends in earnings and incomes of workers and families are critically important, because poverty is a household or family concept. Median household income and earnings are logically and historically the principal correlates of poverty,"[5] whereas per capita GNP is only indirectly related to poverty. Per capita income may rise even though earnings are declining, simply because of a reduction in the proportion of children (or other dependents) in the population. From 1960 to 1980 the proportion of the population under age 15 did fall, from 33 percent to 24 percent. That GNP per capita can increase at the same time that poverty is increasing and family income is declining is demonstrated by Cain in Table 3. In this example, a decline in wage rates and an increase in the number of households cause poverty to increase, even though the number of workers and GNP per capita also increase.

A key factor supporting Murray's contention that the increase in government benefits contributed to increased poverty is his interpretation of the negative income tax (NIT) experiments.[6] Murray says that these experimental programs caused large reductions in work effort among participants. Yet Cain points out that the experiments provided much higher benefits than existing welfare programs, which means that the work disincentive effects Murray cites are much larger than those of current programs. In any case, Cain considers the work disincentives of the experimental programs to be small. In the New Jersey experiments husbands reduced their work effort by less than 5 percent. Wives reduced their work by about 25 percent, but because they ordinarily spent so little time in the work force, this reduction amounted to only about 63 hours a year. In the more generous Seattle-Denver Income Maintenance Experiment, husbands and wives reduced their work by 9 and 20 percent respectively. The 20 percent reduction in the work of wives, given their generally low wages, would make little difference in the family's poverty status, and could well improve their lives if the wife substituted work in the home for outside work.[7]

Danziger and Gottschalk make the point that transfers can only increase posttransfer poverty if recipients cut back on their work so much that their loss of earned income exceeds what they get from the program. These researchers find that the actual increase in AFDC and food stamps between 1960

Table 3

Illustrating How a Decrease in the Dependency Ratio Can Increase per Capita Income, Decrease Family (or Household) Income, and Increase Poverty

Assume the economy has six persons in time periods 1 and 2.

Demographic Unit	Family or Household Income	Poverty Level (By Size of Household)[a]
Period 1: (A high-fertility population.)		
One family: 2 adults, 3 children	$12,000	$11,884
One household of 1 adult	$6,000	$5,019

Per capita income = $3,000 (= $18,000/6)
Dependency ratio = 50 percent (= 3 children/6-person population)
Incidence of poverty = 0 percent

Period 2: (Twenty years later: It is assumed that marriage rates, birth rates, and wages for working adults have all declined.)

One family: 2 adults, 2 children	$9,000	$9,862
Two one-person households of adults	$5,000	$5,019
	$5,000	$5,019

Per capita income = $3,167 (= $19,000/6)
Dependency ratio = 33 percent (= 2 children/6-person population)
Incidence of poverty = 100 percent

Source: Cain, *Losing Ground: A Critique*, p. 14.
Note: Per capita income rose in period 2, yet every household has a lower income, which is now below the poverty line, and each family member in the multiple-person household has a lower income.
[a]These are the poverty-level incomes in 1982 for households of sizes 5, 4, and 1 (see *Statistical Abstract of the United States, 1984* [Washington, D.C.: GPO, 1983], p. 447).

and 1972 would have decreased weekly work effort by only 2.2 hours. They conclude that such an effect is not "sufficiently large to warrant eliminating AFDC and food stamps."[8]

Unemployment and labor force participation

Despite the high unemployment rates and stagnant incomes of the 1970s and whatever disincentives were created by government programs, the number of workers grew because of the entrance of the baby-boom population and women into the work force. Given the many labor market interventions of the Great Society period, why didn't the poor—specifically black youth in the ghettos—get more jobs, which provide the best route out of poverty? Murray writes:

If the 1950s were not good years for young blacks (and they were not), the 1970s were much worse. When the years from 1951 to 1980 are split into two parts, 1951–65 and 1966–80, and the mean unemployment rate is computed for each, one finds that black 20–24-year-olds experienced a 19 percent increase in unemployment. For 18–19-year-olds, the increase was 40 percent. For 16–17-year-olds, the increase was a remarkable 72 percent. . . . Something was happening to depress employment among young blacks. . . . For whatever reasons, older black males (35 years old and above) did well. Not only did they seem to be immune from the mysterious ailment that affected younger black males, they made significant gains (p. 73).

Not only were unemployment rates of black youth rising, their labor force participation rates (LFP) were declining. Furthermore, "the younger the age group, the greater the decline in black LFP, the greater the divergence with whites, and the sooner it began" (p. 78). In contrast with the figures for blacks, the LFP for white youth showed little change.

Though no one can take any comfort in the drop in the proportion of black employed youth, Glen Cain points out that Murray does not give due credit to the increased proportion of blacks enrolled in schools, which was a primary goal of many government programs. Cain shows that school enrollments rose for both white and black youth, that blacks gained relative to whites, and that over the period 1960–79, increased enrollments were a major source of the decline in the LFPs of black teenagers.[9] Furthermore, Cain points out that Murray uses civilian labor force statistics, at a time when military service had become an increasingly important source of employment for young black men. This focus on civilian statistics understates the proportion of employed black youth, and at the same time is a reason for the decline in the civilian labor force. Cain's adjustments reduce the gap in labor force participation rates between blacks and whites from the average of 14.5 percentage points emphasized by Murray to an average of 5.5 percentage points.[10] According to Cain, though the unemployment rate of black youth is a very serious problem, the total picture is not as grim as Murray claims.

The chief reason for the higher labor force participation rates of white youth than black youth is that white teenagers in school are more likely to be working than are black teenage students. Cain offers a demand-side explanation for the difference, rejecting Murray's contention that the Great Society reduced the work ethic of blacks. Cain suggests that the major source of jobs for young whites in recent years has been in the shopping centers, supermarkets, and fast-food restaurants that have been growing rapidly in the suburbs where most whites live. In those central cities populated by blacks, stores have been closing down.[11]

Some attribute black youth unemployment to discrimination. Murray rejects this explanation. He points out that those groups which in the past had suffered the greatest discrimination—the blacks competing for white-collar jobs—found their situation improved.

During the years between 1959 and 1980, blacks made extraordinary progress in entering white-collar jobs: from only 14 percent of employed blacks in 1959 to 39 percent in 1980. . . . In 1959, the ratio of whites to blacks in white-collar jobs was 3.2 to 1. In 1980 the ratio had fallen to 1.4 to 1 (p. 86). There is now a broad scholarly consensus that the gains in income parity are real and large among that subpopulation of blacks who obtained an education and stayed in the labor force. . . . It may be that, for all practical purposes, the racial difference has disappeared for this one subgroup (p. 89).

Education has been shown to pay off for blacks. According to Murray, "At some point between 1959 and 1962, blacks entering the labor force found a market in which their percentage increase in wages per unit of education was greater than that of whites. By 1965, the increase for blacks was more than half again as large as the increase for whites" (p. 90). Though this statement is controversial, Murray and his critics agree that black wage earners as a whole have made gains both absolutely and relative to whites since the War on Poverty began.[12] Black men's incomes relative to whites have increased (Table 2), and the incomes of black women have almost reached those of white women.

Is Murray right in stating that changes in social policies "radically altered the incentive structure" (pp. 167–68) and led to outcomes that were the opposite of what the planners of the War on Poverty and Great Society intended? What prevents black youth and other poor persons from getting an education or on-the-job training that will open up the possibility of escape from poverty? Have government-induced changes in family structure, schools, and the criminal justice system led to increases in poverty?

The family

Nothing has been more disquieting in recent years than changes in family structure. For many years AFDC has been blamed for the rise in illegitimate births and for the increased divorce rate. Indeed the common public perception of the AFDC mother is that of a woman who chooses to have children so that she can become eligible for welfare, or whose husband adandons her so that she can receive benefits.

Murray presents a description of the economic and family decisions of an imaginary couple, Phyllis and Harold, to bolster his argument that changes in social policies have been counterproductive. He argues that if Phyllis had become pregnant and had a child in 1960, this couple would have been better off financially if they had married and Harold had taken a low-paying job. But, owing to more generous welfare benefits and changed regulations, their rational choice in 1970 was not to marry but to live together (a choice made possible by the abolition of AFDC's man-in-the-house rule, which had held a man living with a woman responsible for her children's support). Phyllis could then draw benefits which totaled more than Harold could earn if he worked for the minimum wage. Furthermore, Phyllis could supplement her AFDC benefits by working. This arrangement would free Harold to work when and if he chose.

Many people have disputed Murray's presentation of Harold and Phyllis's choices. Robert Greenstein has pointed out that in Pennsylvania (the state Murray selected for his example) AFDC benefits are higher than in other states, and that Murray counts food stamps as part of the welfare package but not as part of the work package, though food stamps are available to all low-income families, two-parent or not, employed or not. Greenstein states that "taking a minimum-wage job was more profitable than going on welfare in most parts of the country in 1970. In some states with low welfare payments, such as southern states, minimum-wage jobs paid almost *twice* as much."[13] Murray, in his reply to Greenstein, says that *Losing Ground* underestimates the size of the 1970 package "by valuing Medicaid far below any of the commonly used figures. I left out the value of food supplements, school lunches, and other services. I did not include housing allowances."[14]

Certainly welfare benefits and rule changes did make welfare a more viable option in 1970 than it had been in 1960. But whether it led to changes in family structure is another matter. In a review of Murray's book, Christopher Jencks presents a wholly different picture of Harold's options:

In 1960, according to Murray, Harold marries Phyllis and takes a job paying the minimum wage because he "has no choice." But the Harolds of this world have always had a choice. Harold can announce that Phyllis is a slut and that

the baby is not his. . . . From an economic viewpoint . . . Harold's calculations are much the same in 1970 as in 1960. Marrying Phyllis will still lower his standard of living. The main thing that has changed since 1960 is that Harold's friends and relatives are less likely to think he "ought" to marry Phyllis. . . . Since Harold is unlikely to want to support Phyllis and their child, and since Phyllis is equally unlikely to want to support Harold, the usual outcome is that they go their separate ways.[15]

Murray does not base his contention that welfare destabilizes families on the assumption that women have babies simply to get welfare, which in any case, has been challenged by David Ellwood and Mary Jo Bane. They show that illegitimacy is no greater in states having generous AFDC benefits than in states having meager ones. They conclude that "differences in welfare do not appear to be the primary cause of variation in family structure across states, or over time. Largely unmeasurable differences in culture or attitudes or expectations seem to account for a large portion of differences in birth rates to unmarried women and in divorce and separation patterns among families with children."[16]

Murray counters that the relationship between AFDC and illegitimacy is discontinuous and that all states currently have benefits high enough to make it possible for an unmarried pregnant woman to have and keep her baby.

A break point exists at which the level of welfare benefits is sufficiently large that it permits an alternative to not having (or not keeping) the baby that would otherwise not exist. Once this break point is passed, welfare benefits become an enabling factor: they do not cause single women to decide to have a baby, but they enable women who are pregnant to make the decision to keep the baby. If in all states the package of benefits is already large enough to have passed the break point for a large proportion of the potential single mothers, then the effects on increases in the welfare package as measured by Ellwood and Bane will be very small.[17]

Sara McLanahan, an IRP researcher, presents an argument against Murray's claim that welfare benefits have been a major cause of the great growth in illegitimacy among blacks. She points out that while the illegitimacy ratio (the ratio of nonmarital births to all live births), which Murray uses to make his point, does take off in the mid-sixties, along with the growth in Great Society programs, the illegitimacy rate (the ratio of nonmarital births to the total number of women in the childbearing age range) does not. "For black women, the illegitimacy rate rose sharply between 1945 and 1960, leveled off between 1960 and 1965, and began to decline after 1965."[18] In other words the illegitimacy rate was declining during most of the time that welfare benefits were increasing, and when—according to Murray—the Phyllises of the world were choosing to use them. If pregnant women were choosing to have their children out of wedlock in response to rising welfare benefits, the illegitimacy rate should have been increasing, all else being equal.

Of course, all else was not equal, and the trend in the illegitimacy rate does not, in and of itself, disprove Murray's thesis. As a starting point, however, McLanahan argues that it is a better statistic than the illegitimacy ratio, which has all the limitations of the rate *and* is highly sensitive to trends in marriage and marital fertility. The reason the two trends (the rate versus the ratio) look so different for black women after 1965 is that marriage rates and marital fertility were declining even faster then nonmarital fertility.

Furthermore, the decline in marriage cannot be explained by increases in welfare, since this decline during the late sixties and early seventies was more pronounced for nonpregnant women than for pregnant women. Otherwise the illegitimacy rate would have gone up rather than down. McLanahan suggests that the decline in marriage, as well as the growth of female-headed families, may be "a response to improvements in the employment opportunities of women relative to men, and especially black men."[19] But this explanation raises the question once more of why so many fewer young black men are working.

Murray believes that the elimination of AFDC and other welfare programs "would drastically reduce births to single teenage girls. It would reverse the trendline in the breakup of poor families. It would measurably increase the upward socioeconomic mobility of poor families" (p. 227). The extent to which it would remedy these ills is disputed. Eliminating welfare will of course have a drastic impact upon women now on AFDC. In a study of the prospects for self-sufficiency of AFDC recipients, David Ellwood points out that the idea that welfare income can largely be replaced by earnings is without foundation. Although welfare mothers can become self-supporting if they work full time the full year, this is not the typical pattern of mothers of young children, whether heads of households or wives. The norm is still for mothers to spend considerable time with their children. Because few women on AFDC work full time, earnings alone seldom provide the solution to poverty among single-parent households. Furthermore, the two principal factors that enable women to work their way off of welfare are previous work experience and schooling. The prospects for young unmarried mothers without a high school degree are therefore not encouraging.[20]

Murray argues that single mothers who cannot support their children will have to marry or move in with relatives. His contention that AFDC enables them to live alone (or with their lovers) is supported by Ellwood and Bane, who have found that high AFDC benefits do have an effect on the living arrangements of one small group—young unmarried mothers—who are more likely to set up their own households in high-benefit states than to live with their parents.[21]

Education

As with the breakdown of the family, Murray links the growth of federal spending upon education to deterioration of the schools and a widening of the gap between the achievements of blacks and whites. He paints a picture in which blacks made gains before 1965, especially in enrollment. Black enrollment in high school rose from 76 percent of those between ages 14 and 17 in 1950 to virtual parity with whites, at 92 percent, by 1965 (p. 98). From 1960 to 1970, college enrollment of blacks aged 20–24 rose from 7 to 16 percent (p. 99). In 1977 24 percent of blacks aged 20–24 were enrolled in school, compared to 23 percent of whites in the same age group. But ironically, at the same time that blacks were reaching this parity, claims Murray, the value of a diploma in terms of achievement declined. He quotes from the National Commission on Excellence in Education:

> Each generation of Americans has outstripped its parents in education, in literacy, in economic attainment. For the first time in the history of our country, the educational skills of one generation will not surpass, will not equal, not even approach, those of their parents (Paul Copperman, quoted by the Commission, Murray's p. 101).

He concludes that whereas education for the disadvantaged was probably improving during the 1950s and early 1960s, nothing was accomplished by the subsequent federal investment in elementary and secondary education for the disadvantaged, and "after the mid 1960s, public education for the disadvantaged suffered as much as, and probably even more than, education for youth in general" (p. 101). He says that whereas the black-white gap in achievement appeared to be smaller in 1965 than it had been in 1960, "as of 1980 the gap in educational achievement between black and white students leaving high school was so great that it threatened to defeat any other attempts to narrow the economic differences separating blacks from whites" (p. 105).

He attributes this deterioration of achievement among blacks to the mind-set of the sixties—due process invaded the public schools, making adminstrators and teachers vulnerable to lawsuits if they suspended or otherwise disciplined students, and a general desire to help blacks get ahead meant lowering standards to avoid embarrassment when only whites received academic awards in mixed schools.

Murray terms the magnet schools an inherently good idea that failed because educators did not have the courage of their convictions. When enough gifted black students could not be found, they used quota systems, filling in with black students with lower potential, and giving whites the impression that even the brightest black students were not competitive with white students (pp. 183–84). He faults government programs for concentrating on the mentally retarded, the disturbed, and the learning-disabled, instead of helping the bright and motivated students.

Yet Michael Olneck, an IRP affiliate, disputes Murray's basic premise. According to Olneck, "blacks, on average, stood in no worse relation to whites in 1980 than they did in 1965, and may well have made gains."[22] He points out that high school enrollment in fact increased after 1965, because blacks who were enrolled in school were more likely to graduate than drop out. He maintains that high school graduation rates converged by race at least through 1978. Furthermore, because the poorer students are the ones most likely to drop out, the fact that they now remain in school will lower black average test scores in the higher grades. Nevertheless, Olneck says, blacks did not drop back in relation to whites in achievement. Olneck demonstrates that even though the achievement gap between blacks and whites has not closed, it also has not widened (see Table 4).[23] He writes: "That there was an enormous achievement gap between the races in 1980, that there was a catastrophic difference between blacks and whites in SATs, for example, are things I think

that I would be ready to join Murray in saying. To say, however, that there was a *worsening* trend since 1965 is simply not something for which I find evidence."[24]

Olneck does not, nor do other reviewers of social programs, point to much success from the many remedial education programs that have been attempted. Ten years after the first programs were implemented the general conclusion being drawn was that nothing worked.[25] Today there are grounds, if not for optimism, at least for hope. In a paper evaluating education and training programs in 1985, Nathan Glazer states:

A consensus has emerged on the educational changes of the 1970's and early 1980's which presents some modest encouragement for those who believe that "something can be done," but also raises some very serious questions when we consider what more can be done, particularly for those ages in which preparation for transition to work or college is being completed, and where we have done so badly.[26]

Table 4

White-Black Gap in Standardized Test Scores
(in terms of total standard deviation)

Year	Sample	Grade	Test	Gap (SD)	Source
1960	Project TALENT	9	Composite	1.28	Murray, Table 13, p. 253
1965	EEOR	6	Verbal	1.00	Smith in Mosteller
	(Coleman Report)	9	Verbal	1.00	and Moynihan[a]
		12	Verbal	1.01	
1972	NLS 1972	12	Composite	1.10	Direct calculation
1980	High School	10	Composite	0.96	Direct calculation
	and Beyond	12	Composite	0.82	Direct calculation
1980	SAT	11 & 12	Verbal	1.04	Murray, Table 16, p. 255[b]
			Math	1.05	
1980	U.S. Department	18–19 yrs.	Armed Forces Qualification Test	1.05	Murray, Table 15, p. 254[b]
	of Defense	20–21 yrs.	AFQT	1.14	
		22–23 yrs.	AFQT	1.20	
1982	High School	12	Composite	0.96	Direct calculation
	and Beyond	12 plus dropouts	Composite	0.93	Direct calculation

Source: Olneck, *Losing Ground: A Critique*, p. 46.

[a](White mean − black mean)/1.05 SD$_W$. These data indicate that the SD for the total population is approximately equal to 1.05 times the SD for whites. EEOR data are from Marshall S. Smith, "Equality of Educational Opportunity: The Basic Findings Reconsidered," in F. Mosteller and D. P. Moynihan, eds., *On Equality of Educational Opportunity* (New York: Random House, 1972).

[b]Age-specific SDs averaged, and used consistently.

Despite the limited results of most education programs, poverty rates clearly are lower for those with greater education; and it remains the common wisdom that one of the primary ways to overcome poverty is to invest more money in education. In this wisdom Murray evidently concurs. As part of his thought experiment for educational reform, Murray proposes free tuition up to and including graduate school.

Crime

"During the late 1960s and early 1970s, crime of all types did, in fact, soar" (p. 115). Murray further states that the rise among blacks was much greater than the rise among whites. He explains the increase in crime by pointing out that those who committed crimes were less likely to be arrested, and those who were arrested were less likely to go to prison. He mentions other Great Society changes that tipped the scales against the forces of law and order: Poor persons began to be accorded equal protection under the law, and access to the records of juvenile offenders was restricted. These changes were part of a larger picture: "The changes in welfare *and* changes in the risks attached to crime *and* changes in the educational environment reinforced each other" (p. 167). The results were that "the increase in arrests for violent crimes among blacks during the 1965–70 period was seven times that of whites" (p. 118). "The jump in black arrests for violent crimes (and, for that matter, for property crimes) was too sudden, too large, and lasted too long to be dismissed as just an anomaly of a turbulent decade" (p. 119).

Again, an Institute researcher disputes the attribution of causality from the Great Society programs to increases in crime. Irving Piliavin points out that the relative increase of nonwhite arrest rates was less than that of whites: "Overall, between 1960 and 1980 the relative increase in white arrest rates was 30 percent higher than that of nonwhites for property crimes and more than 300 percent higher than that of nonwhites for violent crimes."[27]

Murray argues that it is inappropriate to compare *rates* because "the black baseline rate was many times higher than the white baseline rate, decisively affecting the nature of the proportional change represented per unit change in the arrest rate" (p. 281, note 7). He maintains that there is a qualitative difference between the number of crimes committed by blacks before and after 1965.

Piliavin points out that the use of blacks as a proxy for the poor breaks down in the area of crime, because there has always been a strong relationship between poverty and crime. Therefore the whites with which Murray compares blacks are in fact poor whites, and the violent crime records for this subset of the poor (i.e., the white poor) do not coincide with the Great Society programs at all. White vio-

lent crime increased steadily from 1960 on. Furthermore, "poor nonwhites *and* poor whites experienced massive increases in property crime rates between 1965 and 1970, but both groups also had substantial increases (more so among whites) between 1960 and 1965, a period preceding the criminal justice changes that Murray believes led to the crime explosion of the late 1960s."[28]

Piliavin also points out that changes in the criminal justice system did not curtail the activities of the police. "At each five-year observation from 1960 through 1975, police arrested more individuals and at a higher rate per 100,000 population . . . than at previous observation points."[29] Despite increased efforts on the part of the police, crime rates rose. Nor was there any connection between a decline in the imprisonment of arrested offenders and increases in crime rates. "If the 1965–70 crime rate increases were due to changes in prison-sentencing practices during this period, the relationship is far from obvious."[30]

And yet, of course, something has changed. Life is much less safe than it used to be. Murray quotes a study that shows "at 1970 levels of homicide, a person who lived his life in a large American city ran a greater risk of being murdered than an American soldier in the Second World War ran of being killed in combat" (p. 117).

What does social science research suggest about the causes of the increase in crime, the decline in educational achievement, and changes in family structure, if Murray's critics are correct in concluding that these trends were not caused or exacerbated by the Great Society programs?

Social science research: What we know and what we don't know

The last section of Murray's book is titled "Escapism." In it he writes: "What should worry us . . . is a peculiar escapism that has gripped the consideration of social policy. It seems that those who legislate and administer and write about social policy can tolerate any increase in actual suffering as long as the system in place does not explicitly permit it" (p. 235). In a recent journal article he reiterates this point: "In many respects, the chief subject of *Losing Ground*'s indictment is not only the governmental reforms of the 1960s, but the inability, or reluctance, of modern social science to explore the questions it raises. *Losing Ground* examines the experience of the last thirty years of social policy and finds a variety of phenomena that demand explanation."[31]

While it is clear that the answers to numerous questions elude us, one has only to examine Murray's extensive citations to see how much has been learned in recent years. Indeed Gary Burtless and Robert Haveman argue that antipoverty programs have fallen into disfavor because they have been subjected to intense scrutiny and harsh evaluation.

> Society is not evenhanded in subjecting programs for the poor and nonpoor to experimental investigation. It has not examined transfers to the nonpoor with the same degree of intensity as it has examined those to the poor. We should therefore not be surprised that experimental scrutiny has been less kind to programs designed to benefit the poor.[32]

The social science community has regularly attempted to evaluate the effects of social programs. A recent example is Robert Lampman's *Social Welfare Spending: Accounting for Changes from 1950 to 1978.*[33] The papers presented in December 1984 at a conference, Poverty and Policy: Retrospect and Prospects, sponsored jointly by the Institute for Research on Poverty and the U.S. Department of Health and Human Services,[34] were another attempt to determine what has and has not worked, and why.

In fact, even though Murray's attack on Great Society programs has been vigorously challenged, there is little enthusiasm for merely expanding many of the existing programs he faults. Policy analysts, building on what has been learned, have suggested a variety of new antipoverty policies for the 1980s. Danziger and Gottschalk, for example, conclude that transfer programs are not an acceptable solution to the poverty of the working-aged poor, not because of their disincentives, which have been shown to be small, but because they do not provide work opportunities.[35]

They suggest, in addition to an expanded "workfare," special training programs for those who become long-term welfare recipients, and an increase in the incomes of those working for low wages through expansion of the Earned Income Tax Credit.[36] Again, existing research can be used to argue the strengths and weaknesses of this jobs strategy.

Irwin Garfinkel, an IRP affiliate, has proposed a Child Support Assurance program to require absent fathers to contribute to the support of their children. Whether or not the increased support payments can eventually reduce the number of households receiving AFDC is the subject of an ongoing research project at IRP.[37]

Even Murray's conclusion that more stress should be placed on the private sector and communities (pp. 229–31) can be evaluated on the basis of recent social science research. The fact that those communities with the greatest number of poor needing assistance are the poorest communities, with the fewest resources for the poor, raises some serious questions.[38] Furthermore, most philanthropy in the private sector is directed at the middle class (boy scouts, disaster relief)

rather than the poor.[39] It is therefore rather unlikely that a single mother going to a private agency with the proposal, "Find me a job and child care and I will do the rest," is likely to receive what she needs.

Conclusion

The Institute researchers who have critically reviewed *Losing Ground* reject its broad condemnation of the Great Society. They severally find that the programs that evolved from the War on Poverty and the Great Society have achieved at least some of their goals. They do agree with Murray that something different must be done in the 1980s if poverty and crime are to be reduced, if families are to be stabilized and educational achievement improved. And they concur that government policy must promote self-reliance for people capable of work.

Murray's thought experiments have had the desired effect. They have dramatized the difficulties inherent in devising strategies to combat poverty.■

---

[1]New York: Basic Books, 1984. Parenthetical page numbers in this article refer to Murray's book.

[2]Among the many reviews of Murray's book are Robert Greenstein, "Losing Faith in Losing Ground," *New Republic*, March 25, 1985, which continues in a debate between Greenstein and Murray in the April 8 issue; Christopher Jencks, "How Poor Are the Poor?" *New York Review of Books*, May 9, 1985; Richard D. Coe and Greg Duncan, "Welfare: Promoting Poverty or Progress?" *Wall Street Journal*, May 15, 1985. Several workshops and symposia have been held. A workshop at the Manhattan Institute was reported in *Manhattan Report*, 5:1, 1985. A symposium, "Alternatives to the *Losing Ground* Perspective," was part of the Conference of the American Public Welfare Association in Washington, D.C., May 7–8, 1985. Papers were presented by Joseph Goldberg, David Ellwood, Sar Levitan, Lee Teitelbaum, Vaughan Stapleton, Mary Jo Bane, Barbara Blum, and Eli Ginzberg. These papers will be published at a later date.

[3]Danziger and Gottschalk, "Social Programs—A Partial Solution to, but Not a Cause of Poverty: An Alternative to Charles Murray's View," in *Losing Ground: A Critique*, IRP Special Report no. 38, 1985, p. 78.

[4]Cain, "Comments on Murray's Analysis of the Impact of the War on Poverty on the Labor Market Behavior of the Poor," ibid., p. 10.

[5]Ibid.

[6]The two major negative income tax experiments were the New Jersey experiment and the Seattle and Denver experiment. The first is reported in three volumes in the IRP Monograph Series: *The New Jersey Income-Maintenance Experiment.* Volume 1, *Surveys and Administration*, is edited by David Kershaw and Jerilyn Fair (1976); volumes 2 and 3, *Labor-Supply Responses* and *Expenditures, Health, and Social Behavior*, are edited by Harold Watts and Albert Rees (1977). They are available from Academic Press, Orlando, Fla. The results of the second experiment are reported in U.S. Department of Health and Human Services, Office of Income Security Policy, *Overview of the Seattle-Denver Income Maintenance Experiment: Final Report* (Washington, D.C.: GPO, 1983).

[7]Cain, pp. 25–27, passim.

[8]Danziger and Gottschalk, "Social Programs," p. 85. Between 1972 and 1984 real benefits declined. That decline implies an increase in weekly work effort of 2 hours. Thus, the effect of the growth in AFDC and food stamps over the entire 1960–84 period is quite small.

[9]Cain, pp. 20–21.

[10]Cain, pp. 21–22.

[11]Cain, p. 23. Cain's explanation refers to the specific areas where white and black youth live, not suburbs and central cities in general. The central cities of the expanding Southwest and of the declining Northeast, for example, have quite different proportions of white and black populations. It should be noted that the use of an overall classification of central-city residence does not support Cain's explanation. David Ellwood and Lawrence Summers examine the employment status of youth who are not attending school, and they find that blacks living in central cities don't seem to fare much worse than those living outside the ghettos. They quote the 1980 census to show that 32 percent of those in central cities had jobs, whereas 38 percent of those living in the suburbs were working. This compares with 62 percent for white youth. (These are figures for both sexes, but Ellwood and Summers speculate that the differences for men alone between the central city and the suburbs would be smaller.) See Ellwood and Summers, "Poverty in America: Is Welfare the Answer or the Problem?" Paper presented at conference, Poverty and Policy: Retrospect and Prospects, Williamsburg, Va., December 6–8, 1984, revised March 1985, p. 39.

[12]Cain, p. 16.

[13]Greenstein, "Losing Faith in *Losing Ground*," New Republic, March 25, 1985, p. 13.

[14]Murray, "The Great Society: An Exchange," *New Republic*, April 8, 1985, pp. 21–22. As with food stamps, however, two-parent households are eligible for other food supplements, school lunches, public housing benefits, etc.

[15]Christopher Jencks, "How Poor Are the Poor?" *New York Review of Books*, May 9, 1985, p. 44.

[16]Ellwood and Bane, "The Impact of AFDC on Family Structure and Living Arrangements," *Journal of Labor Research*, forthcoming.

[17]Murray, "Have the Poor Been 'Losing Ground'?" *Political Science Quarterly*, Fall 1985, p. 93.

[18]McLanahan, "Charles Murray and the Family," in *Losing Ground: A Critique*, p. 3.

[19]Ibid., p. 5. See also William Julius Wilson and Kathryn M. Neckerman, "Poverty and Family Structure: The Widening Gap between Evidence and

Public Policy Issues." Paper presented at conference, Poverty and Policy: Retrospect and Prospects, Williamsburg, Va., December 6–8, 1984, revised February 1985.

[20]Ellwood, "Working Off Welfare: Policies and Prospects for Self-Sufficiency of Female Family Heads," IRP workshop paper, mimeo., 1985.

[21]Ellwood and Bane.

[22]Olneck, "Comments on Schooling," in *Losing Ground: A Critique*, p. 38.

[23]Olneck measures the gap using standard deviations (taken from Murray's Appendix). The standard deviation is a measure of dispersion or variation around the average in a distribution of values (e.g., years of education, test scores). It is calculated as the quotient of the square root of the sum of the squared deviations of individual values from the mean divided by the number of values or observations in the distribution. Expressing group differences as proportions of unit standard deviations allows one to measure changes in relative group differences over time.

[24]Olneck, p. 45.

[25]Nathan Glazer, "Education and Training Programs and Poverty; *or*, Opening the Black Box." Paper presented at conference, Poverty and Policy: Retrospect and Prospects, Williamsburg, Va., December 6–8, 1984, revised January 1985, p. 3.

[26]Ibid., p. 25.

[27]Piliavin, "The 1965–1970 Crime Increase as Seen by Charles Murray: A Critique," in *Losing Ground: A Critique*, pp. 60–62.

[28]Ibid., p. 64.

[29]Ibid., pp. 65–66. Murray counters that arrests per crime nonetheless declined.

[30]Ibid., p. 69.

[31]Murray, "Have the Poor Been 'Losing Ground'? " p. 95.

[32]Burtless and Haveman, "Policy Lessons from Three Labor Market Experiments," IRP Discussion Paper no. 746–84, March 1984.

[33]Orlando, Fla.: Academic Press, 1984.

[34]The edited proceedings will be published by Harvard University Press in spring 1986.

[35]Danziger and Gottschalk, "Social Programs," p. 88.

[36]Ibid., pp. 88–89.

[37]Ann Nichols-Casebolt, Irwin Garfinkel, and Pat Wong, "Reforming Wisconsin's Child Support System," IRP Discussion Paper no. 793–85, forthcoming.

[38]Michael Sosin, *Private Benefits: Material Assistance in the Private Sector* (Orlando, Fla.: Academic Press, forthcoming).

[39]Ibid.

63

Manpower Policies for the Disadvantaged: What Works?

Gary Burtless

WHEN AMERICA rediscovered its poor in the early 1960s, many policy-makers and academics viewed poverty as an essentially curable condition. They believed that people were poor for a variety of reasons, but that for each of these there existed a practical countermeasure. Enlightened and resolute social policies — including manpower policies—could eliminate the underlying sources of poverty.

An eloquent statement of this view can be found in the 1964 *Economic Report of the President*, written at the outset of the war on poverty. The 1964 *Economic Report* outlined a ten-point strategy to eradicate poverty, including an acceleration of economic growth, an end to racial discrimination, a more efficient labor market, an expansion of educational opportunity, additional job counseling and training for teenagers and poor adults, investments in the nation's health care system, and financial help for the aged and disabled. It may surprise present-day readers to learn that President Johnson and his economic advisers did not advocate cash aid to the nonaged, nondisabled poor. The 1964 *Report* noted that it would cost only $11 billion — less than 2 percent of GNP — to wipe out poverty using cash transfers. But this tactic was rejected: "Americans want to *earn* the American standard of living by their own efforts and contributions. It would be far better, even if more difficult, to equip and to permit the poor of the Nation to produce and to earn the additional $11 billion. . . . "

The war on poverty marked the real beginning of federal manpower policies designed to aid economically disadvantaged workers. Earlier manpower efforts had focused on alleviating skill shortages and helping workers who had been displaced by automation and structural change. These efforts were modest in scope and aimed primarily at experienced workers. Starting in 1964, the emphasis shifted; manpower initiatives became increasingly targeted on minorities, welfare recipients, and low-income youth. Programs have been funded under a long series of legislative acts and amendments, including the Manpower Development and Training Act (1962), the Economic Opportunity Act (1964), the Comprehensive Employment and Training Act (1973), and the Job Training Partnership Act (1982). Measured in constant 1983 dollars, annual spending on these programs rose from around $3 billion in the late 1960s to a peak of around $14 billion in the late 1970s. Since then, spending has declined to around $4 billion, and it is slated to fall even further in the next several years.

Federal manpower programs for the disadvantaged have used a variety of techniques intended to enable workers to earn their way out of poverty: classroom and other institutional training for specific occupations; more comprehensive instruction in basic skills; on-the-job training; targeted wage

Gary Burtless is a senior fellow in the Economic Studies program at Brookings. Before joining the Brookings staff, he worked as an economist with the Department of Labor and the Department of Health, Education, and Welfare. His most recent publication is Retirement and Economic Behavior, *which he edited with Henry J. Aaron.*

subsidies, meant to encourage employers to hire and train low-income job applicants; work experience and public service employment programs; and the development of job search capabilities. We have now had lengthy experience with these techniques. What seems to work best?

Classroom Training. Classroom instruction is the approach that comes to mind when most of us think of how to improve the job prospects of the poor. Disadvantaged workers are clearly lacking something vital to success, and it is often assumed that proper training can supply what is missing. The guiding tenet of training administrators everywhere is: "Give a man a fish and you will feed him for a day, but teach a man to fish and you will feed him for a lifetime." This maxim assumes that each man can be taught to fish — and that, once learned, fishing will prove to be a useful occupation. The alert trainee might reasonable ask, "Where's the fish?"

In theory, classroom training is given in occupations in which job opportunities for trainees are expected to be plentiful. In practice, however, job market predictions are imperfect, and it frequently turns out that trainees cannot find work in the occupations for which they were trained. Sometimes there are no jobs; sometimes the trainees cannot perform them. It is much easier to deplore this situation than to propose a workable remedy for it. Manpower agencies are constrained in their efforts by limited funding and by the resources of local training institutions. The people they serve are often extremely disadvantaged.

Has classroom training worked? The consensus of recent studies is that classroom training has significantly raised earnings among certain participants, particularly women and new entrants or reentrants to the labor market who have little recent work experience. It has worked less well or not at all for other groups, particularly men who have held steady but low-paying jobs. The main effect of classroom training is to raise the proportion of time that participants spend working. There is often only a small or negligible impact on the wage rate a participant can hope to earn. Classroom training thus appears to reduce spells of unemployment between jobs but not to change the type of job that participants hold. The precise amount of earnings improvement is a topic of debate. An analysis by the Congressional Budget Office and the National Commission on Employment Policy found that the earnings of female participants in classroom training programs increased by an average of $800 to $1,400 per year (in 1980 dollars), while those of male participants rose by only $300.[1]

These estimates, as well as previous ones, are subject to serious qualification. The ideal measure of a program's effect would be obtained by comparing the earnings of participants with what their earnings would have been in its absence. Since this is not feasible, analysts have used less reliable procedures. The usual method is to compare earnings trends in the participant group with trends in another group thought to be comparable. However, because the comparability of the two groups can never be established beyond a reasonable doubt, findings based on this technique are always subject to challenge. Analysts using different comparison groups often obtain markedly different results. Thus, some researchers have found that training programs reduce subsequent earnings, while others who have studied the same programs have reached just the opposite conclusion. It is unrealistic to expect that policymakers or the public can resolve the methodological disputes that divide statisticians and economists.

One way of reducing our uncertainty is to perform a controlled experiment. Under this strategy, a randomly selected group of disadvantaged workers is offered access to a manpower program. The subsequent earnings of these trainees are then compared to the earnings of an identically selected control group, which is not offered the service. Because the two groups are selected using identical criteria, the earnings difference between the groups is a reliable measure of the program's impact. Although the nation has spent over $100 billion (in constant 1983 dollars) on manpower programs and the value of these programs is hotly debated, the government has only rarely used controlled randomized trials to test the effectiveness of alternative programs.

One experimental test of institutional training was carried out in Seattle and Denver as part of a larger investigation of the consequences of a negative income tax. Most manpower training agencies assign clients to particular courses of study after deciding what type of training is appropriate for each trainee. The training voucher program tested in Seattle and Denver was less paternalistic; it permitted selected low-income enrollees to attend training programs of their choice and offered to pay half or all of their associated expenses, including the costs of tuition, books, transportation, and child care. (The fraction of expenses paid by the experiment depended on the plan to which a family was randomly assigned.) Participation in a highly structured job counseling process was mandatory for those who elected to use the training vouchers. The experiment included a control group, the members of which were not offered training vouchers.

> *"Although training vouchers were used by about 30 percent of the family heads eligible for them . . . the additional training did not lead to an increase in post-program earnings."*

The results of the experiment are extremely disappointing. Although training vouchers were used by about 30 percent of the family heads eligible for them and led some participants to take as many as three extra quarters of formal schooling, the additional training did not lead to an increase in post-program earnings. Participants experienced significant declines in earnings during their training periods, presumably because they reduced their work hours temporarily in order to take advantage of the instruction. The failure of their earnings to rise after the completion of training suggests that the instruction that they received may not have been worthwhile. Alternatively, some participants may have harmed their chances of obtaining employment or higher wages by missing out on valuable work experience during the months of training.

These findings are especially disquieting because they were obtained in a controlled experimental trial and hence are presumably reliable, and because they suggest that additional formal schooling is not by itself beneficial. However, the results are not directly applicable to many institutional training programs. Seattle-Denver enrollees were offered a degree of freedom in selecting courses of study that is not common in federal manpower programs. In addition, the counseling provided to the trainees might have been worse than the norm — although except for the unexpected outcome, there is no evidence of that. The study suggests that clients of manpower programs, left to their own devices, may not select optimal training courses. More

generally, it casts doubt on the utility of unrestricted classroom training for adult disadvantaged workers.

Comprehensive Training. The Job Corps represents an ambitious alternative to simple classroom training; it was designed to accomplish much more than simply remedy deficiencies of training. The program was established in 1964 under the Economic Opportunity Act and offers a comprehensive set of health, basic education, and vocational services to low-income youth. In contrast to other training efforts, it is essentially a boarding school aimed at removing young people from the supposedly undesirable influences of economically deprived neighborhoods. Careful studies of the program have usually concluded that its estimated benefits, in higher wages and lower crime, outweigh its costs. The Job Corps is very expensive, however. According to estimates in the 1984 U.S. budget, the cost of providing one year of service to a Corps member is above $14,000[2]— more than three times the cost of other types of training. But the comparative success of the Job Corps implies that expensive efforts may be required to offset the effects of a lifetime of disadvantage.

On-the-job Training. On-the-job training is another alternative to classroom training. Under this arrangement, private employers give entry-level positions to disadvantaged workers and in return receive subsidies covering a fraction of the wages paid to the trainees. The subsidy reimburses employers for the presumed extra costs of training disadvantaged workers. On-the-job training is more likely than classroom instruction to provide experience in occupations in which job openings exist. Indeed, many firms that offer on-the-job training provide permanent employment to participants at the end of their subsidized training.

During the late 1960s and 1970s, manpower officials believed that the payoff from on-the-job training was substantially higher than from classroom training. This view was reinforced by the fact that a larger fraction of on-the-job trainees ended up with permanent jobs. However, because of the reluctance of employers to hire disadvantaged workers, manpower agencies usually found it hard to locate enough suitable training positions, especially when the economy turned sour. Agencies had many more clients than positions in which to place them. Classroom training positions, by contrast, were reasonably easy to arrange.

The Congressional Budget Office study mentioned above casts doubt on the presumed superiority of on-the-job training to classroom training. The CBO found that on-the-job trainees were less disadvantaged than those who received classroom training. Their post-program earnings were higher than those of other trainees because they were more employable to begin with; in fact, many were probably assigned to on-the-job training positions rather than classroom programs precisely for that reason. This does not imply that on-the-job training has little value, though it does suggest that such training will be useful in only a minority of cases.

Wage Subsidies. A targeted wage subsidy is simply an offer by the government to pay employers part or all of the wage costs of hiring disadvantaged workers. It differs from on-the-job training in one respect: To qualify for the subsidy, employers are not required to pro-

216

vide training; they need only to provide jobs. Usually subsidies are limited in their duration, most often to one or two years. Several wage subsidy programs have been enacted, the most recent of which, the Targeted Jobs Tax Credit, offers companies tax credits on wages paid to certain classes of hard-to-employ workers, including welfare recipients and poor youths.

Employer participation in these programs, as in on-the-job training programs, has always been low. In fact, the number of workers whose wages are subsidized by the programs is far below the number of workers who are technically eligible to be covered. During the first two years of the Targeted Jobs credit program, fewer than 115,000 youths held subsidized jobs. Yet it is estimated that 2 million jobs per year are held by youths who are within the population that the Targeted Jobs provision is intended to benefit. Employers appear to be passing up opportunities to collect tax credits for employment decisions they are making anyway.

Policy-makers have speculated about why employers fail to take advantage of subsidy programs. One theory is that firms are ignorant of the advantages of such programs. Another is that employers are deterred from participating by their disinclination to take on an additional paperwork burden or by their fear of tax audits.

A recent wage subsidy experiment suggests a different explanation, however. A Dayton, Ohio, manpower agency was given responsibility for helping able-bodied welfare recipients find jobs. The agency randomly divided clients into three groups. Members of the first group were given tax credit vouchers that identified them to potential employers as being eligible for the Targeted Jobs Tax Credit. Those in the second group were given vouchers informing potential employers that the voucher holders were covered by a generous *cash* subsidy program. The value of the subsidy was set at a level identical to that of the tax credit—up to $4,500 over two years—but quarterly payments were made to employers directly rather than through the income tax system. Clients in the third group were given no vouchers and no information about the possibility of a wage subsidy. The recipients of vouchers were strongly encouraged to show them to prospective employers.

Only a small fraction of the vouchered clients succeeded in obtaining employment, and of those only a quarter worked for firms that bothered to apply for a tax credit or cash subsidy. But far more surprising was the finding that unvouchered job seekers were more successful in securing work than were applicants in the two vouchered groups. Twenty-one percent of the unvouchered clients, but only 13 percent of the vouchered ones, found jobs by the end of the five- to eight-week search period. A voucher apparently hurt, rather than helped, a job seeker's chances of employment because it identified the voucher holder as a member of an economically and socially disadvantaged group. The stigma arising from this identification is evidently a major handicap in job finding.

Work Experience as Training. If it is difficult to find work or training positions for disadvantaged workers in private firms, manpower officials have often found it much easier to place clients in government agencies and nonprofit institutions. The programs through which

this is done are of two kinds—work experience and public service employment—but their similarities are more important than their differences. In both, public or nonprofit employers create jobs for disadvantaged workers; manpower agencies then refer—and pay the wages of—clients to fill these positions. Wages are essentially subsidized at a 100-percent rate, a major reason why public and nonprofit employers find disadvantaged workers more attractive than do private employers.

The experience that clients receive in these programs is assumed to improve their employability, even if it trains them for only the most menial occupations. Time spent in the workplace may give new entrants and re-entrants to the labor market a clearer idea of what is expected on a job, and it may serve as a useful credential for later finding work.

The evidence is mixed regarding the impacts that work experience and public service employment efforts have on the subsequent earnings of participants. The Department of Labor (DOL) found that work experience programs actually reduce participants' subsequent earnings, while the CBO study cited above concluded that for female enrollees these programs raise earnings as much as classroom training does. As to public service employment projects, DOL analyses indicate that they are somewhat less effective than classroom training, and much less effective than on-the-job training, in

"Employers appear to be passing up opportunities to collect tax credits for employment decisions they are making anyway."

raising earnings. None of these findings was obtained using strictly experimental data; consequently, for the reasons discussed above, they should be viewed as suggestive, but not definitive. This explains the large discrepancies in the findings regarding the relative effectiveness of different training strategies.

The Supported Work Demonstration, conducted by the Manpower Development Research Corporation, tested the impact on especially disadvantaged workers of a carefully structured program of work experience. Only one of the four target groups involved in the study—welfare mothers—was found to have increased its earnings as a result of the program. The other three groups—high school dropouts, ex-convicts, and former drug addicts—showed either no earnings gains or slight losses. The Supported Work Demonstration was much better conceived and run than such programs typically are. Its failure to raise earnings for three out of four target groups suggests that work experience can aid only a subset of disadvantaged workers.

It may be unfair to judge work experience and public service employment programs by the criteria we apply to pure training programs, since they have objectives in addition to training. The Summer Youth Employment Program, for example, is primarily aimed at keeping city streets safe in the summer. (Its effectiveness on this score is unknown.) Public service employment is often justified as a mechanism to give jobs to the deserving needy when times are tough. If those who are placed in public jobs perform useful work and if their wages or stipends accurately reflect the value of that work, the true cost of helping the disadvantaged through this mechanism is small. But critics maintain that the tasks performed in work experience and public service projects have little value, which implies that the wages paid to job holders are merely a disguised form of income transfer. If this view is correct, these programs should be judged by their success as transfer programs and as efforts to equip workers for later competition in the unsubsidized job market. As transfer programs they may be perfectly serviceable, but as training programs they are frequently ineffective.

Job Search Training. A fairly new element in manpower programs for the disadvantaged is systematic training in job search techniques. Clients are encouraged to follow a rigorous and structured routine in looking for employment. Often the course includes an important element of motivation building and peer reinforcement. The idea is to motivate people to look for jobs for which they are already prepared rather than to train them for new jobs. Clients are not taught to fish, but to find existing jobs in the fishing industry. Obviously, this approach is far less expensive than the alternatives discussed above. There is evidence that it is modestly successful in helping clients find work earlier than they otherwise would. Workers' earnings are raised because they spend more time employed. If this approach were successful in the long run, it would improve the efficiency of the job market by speeding up the match between disadvantaged job seekers and available positions.

This limited degree of success would probably not satisfy the architects of the war on poverty. Many of the jobs that workers find are low-wage, dead-end situations that do not offer a way out of poverty, even if they do provide full-time, year-round employment. We should recall, however, that nearly *all* manpower strategies for the disadvantaged, including those that are far more expensive than job search training, share the same characteristic; they raise the amount of time that workers spend employed, but have little effect on their hourly wage rates. These gains in employment are valuable, however, and should not be lightly dismissed. They are simply too small to have a major effect on the poverty rate.

The Role of Manpower Policy. Manpower programs have delivered less than their proponents hoped, but more than their detractors acknowledge. They have not eliminated, or even substantially reduced, poverty among the working age population, but they have made a modest difference in the lives of many who participated in them. Our faith in manpower programs would be improved if policy-makers, analysts, and the public at large developed a more realistic view of what these initiatives can accomplish. Proper training can occasionally turn a welfare mother into a computer technician. (In fact, some welfare mothers will become computer technicians without any government aid.) But there is no magic training course that can guarantee *every* welfare mother self-sufficiency in a well-paid job. Where there are few jobs or a genuine incapacity to learn, a manpower program can accomplish little. Its main value may then be social, rather than economic; it offers evidence that society is at least trying to help those who seek to help themselves.

Manpower training programs for teenagers and adults can play a role, though a limited one, in reducing poverty. If past experience is a reliable guide, however, the impact on earnings will be small and in many cases expensive to obtain. Substantial poverty will remain among able-bodied adults with children. This residual poverty can be eliminated only if society is willing to change the distribution of economic rewards, either in the labor market or by reform of the tax and transfer system.

> *"Manpower programs have delivered less than their proponents hoped, but more than their detractors acknowledge."*

1. Congressional Budget Office, *CETA Training Programs: Do They Work for Adults?*, Washington, D.C., 1982, p. 19.

2. The actual cost per enrollee is lower than this because many Job Corps participants drop out of the program before completing a full year.

64

Social Security at 50 Faces New Crossroads

Among the old and the not-so-old, a crisis of confidence is a growing danger, as shown by a *USN&WR* survey.

Fifty years ago, Franklin Roosevelt signed into law the most ambitious legislation of the New Deal, the Social Security Act of 1935. Today, because of that stroke of the pen, workers look to the federal government to provide an adequate income for retirees, medical care for the aged, disability insurance and aid to families of deceased workers. Nearly 37 million people receive monthly checks.

Yet all is not well. As the government's actuaries set their sights on the next 50 years, Social Security faces a crisis that spans two generations—

A new tax revolt is brewing among many younger workers incensed at having to give up a bigger and bigger share of their paychecks to Social Security.

At the same time, protests by older Americans have, so far, stopped Congress from enacting a budget-cutting measure that would cap the 1986 cost-of-living adjustment for Social Security beneficiaries. But the proposal renewed the elderly's anxieties that benefits will be cut despite politicians' promises to the contrary.

These concerns and others emerged in an exclusive survey conducted for *U.S.News & World Report*. The results indicate that nearly two fifths of all adult Americans seriously doubt that they will see the benefits they have been promised. What's more, there is no consensus among the public—or the experts—about how to make Social Security secure for the 21st century.

Skeptics young and old. The fears about Social Security are most intensely felt by younger workers, who will not be eligible to collect a retirement check from the system until well into the next century. Half of the 18-to-44-year-olds who responded to the survey have no confidence in the government's ability to pay benefits promised under the Old Age, Survivors and Disability Insurance program. In addition, nearly 12 percent of elderly respondents who already have begun to collect Social Security are skeptical that their checks will continue to arrive each month.

The survey, conducted for *USN&WR* by Civic Service, Inc., of St. Louis and Washington, was based on 1,500 interviews. Among other findings, it reflects widespread disenchantment with the nation's retirement program. Millions share the worries expressed by Lionila Rios, a Houston bank employe: "By the time we get to retire, we won't receive any benefits."

Young Americans believe that they can't rely on Social Security to supply them with as much retirement income as it did for their parents. More than half of the individuals in both the 18-29 and 30-44 age groups saw Social Security as a minor income source, providing no more than 25 percent of their total postretirement earnings.

Moreover, many low-to-middle-income workers, who traditionally have been more dependent on the government's retirement program, also expect Social Security to furnish only a small fraction of their retirement income. More than 43 percent of the survey respondents earning $10,000 to $25,000 a year said that Social Security would account for a small proportion of their income upon retirement.

The New Tax Revolt

Younger workers gripe that they are paying too much in Social Security taxes. The *U.S.News* survey found that half of the under-45 generation thinks it is paying too much. Two fifths of their elders agree that the young are being unfairly taxed.

Today's tax rates are a far cry from those in effect when Social Security was enacted. In 1937, annual contributions were limited to 1 percent of a worker's first $3,000 in earnings. The most anyone could pay was $30 a year. In 1985, the tax rose to 7.05 percent of incomes up to $39,600, for a maximum levy of $2,792. By 1990, the tax will increase to 7.65 percent of income up to an estimated $51,600, for a maximum contribution of $3,947.40. As in the 1930s, employers pay a matching

---

A Young Urban Couple

Gregory and Ingrid Ochalek of Los Angeles pay more than $5,000 a year in Social Security taxes. Gregory, 33, is a tax-shelter specialist and vice president of a securities firm; Ingrid, 38, is vice president of a mortgage brokerage.

"The money withheld in our income bracket doesn't break us, but it's just not managed right. There's chaos, and that angers people like us," says Gregory. Eliminate Social Security? "Unconscionable," says Ingrid. "The other generation is depending on us."

"I won't feel guilty about cashing a Social Security check," adds Gregory. "I don't know whether I'll be getting everything I put into it, but there should be something back."

---

amount for each worker. For many employes, particularly younger members of the labor force and low-income workers, Social Security levies greatly exceed their federal-income-tax bite.

"An intergenerational conflict is brewing," warns Haeworth Robertson, managing director of Mercer-Meidinger, a pension consulting firm based in New York. "It's not at all far-fetched to think that young people will soon stand up and say: 'I don't think the system is fair, and I'm not going to pay the taxes.'"

The younger workers have good reason to protest. Critics such as Martin Feldstein, the Harvard professor who headed President Reagan's Council of Economic Advisers, believe "the Social Security program was a bonanza for those who got in on the ground floor."

Feldstein points out that those who retired in the past several decades and those about to retire will get back far more than they and their employers paid in taxes—benefits worth far more

than what they would have received had they used the money to purchase government bonds. But those days are over. Says Feldstein: "In the future, Social Security will no longer be a good deal for the vast majority of workers."

Expansion of Benefits

Indeed, over the past half-century, Social Security has been both a good deal and a godsend for millions. When the Social Security Act was signed on Aug. 14, 1935, a fifth of the nation's work force was jobless. Millions of elderly citizens had watched their life's savings vanish in a tidal wave of bank failures and the collapse of the stock market.

Before Social Security, observes Robert Ball, a former commissioner of the Social Security Administration, "the poorhouse toward the end of life—with all its horrors—was a very real part of America. Without Social Security, more than half the elderly would have had incomes below the government's rock-bottom definition of poverty." Now,

says Ball, only 14 percent of the elderly are below the poverty line.

During the past five decades, Social Security has expanded greatly, offering benefits well beyond its initial mandate. The original Social Security Act promised only modest relief. Benefits were limited to retirement payments. Social Security taxes were not collected until 1937, and only workers in industry and commerce were protected. Later, Congress extended coverage to include farmers, doctors and other self-employed individuals.

Today, 95 percent of the U.S. work force participates. In all, 123 million pay the taxes used to fund benefits in this pay-as-you-go program. Expenditures have grown dramatically. Social Security also pays benefits to disabled individuals and families of deceased workers. In 1965, Congress added medicare to the Social Security programs to help older people pay their medical bills. The total cost of Social Security now exceeds 240 billion dol-

---

How Americans View Social Security

☐ **How confident are you that you will receive your Social Security benefits?**

Very confident
█████████ 22.6%

Moderately confident
██████████████ 36.7%

Not confident at all
██████████████ 38.1%

No opinion
██ 2.7%

☐ **When you retire, what share of your income do you expect Social Security will provide?**

At least 75% of it
█████ 11.7%

About half of it
██████████ 32.1%

Less than 25% of it
██████████████ 46.2%

No opinion
█████ 10.0%

☐ **Some younger workers say they pay too much in Social Security taxes. Do you agree or disagree?**

Agree
██████████████ 45.8%

Disagree
█████████████ 41.7%

No opinion
█████ 12.5%

Results of a poll of 1,500 persons conducted for U.S. News & World Report by Civic Service, Inc.—

☐ **Would you support any of the following measures to strengthen the Social Security program's finances—**

Reduce benefits paid to current beneficiaries?

Yes	No	No Opinion
22.6%	69.2%	8.2%

Reduce benefits paid to future beneficiaries?

Yes	No	No Opinion
28.1%	63.0%	8.9%

Raise payroll taxes for workers and employers alike?

Yes	No	No Opinion
34.6%	57.7%	7.7%

Raise payroll taxes for employers only?

Yes	No	No Opinion
33.5%	58.9%	7.6%

Raise the minimum retirement age?

Yes	No	No Opinion
38.9%	56.3%	4.9%

☐ **The minimum retirement age for workers who collect full Social Security benefits is 65 and is scheduled to rise to 67 after the year 2000. At what age do you think workers should be able to retire and collect full benefits?**

65 years	52.8%
67 years	17.1%
68 years	6.3%
69 years	1.0%
70 years	9.8%
Other	9.5%
No opinion	3.6%

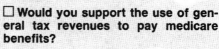
☐ **Would you support use of general tax revenues, rather than the Social Security tax alone, to pay retirement or disability benefits to Social Security beneficiaries?**

Yes
██████████████ 47.1%

No
███████████ 38.3%

No opinion
████ 14.7%

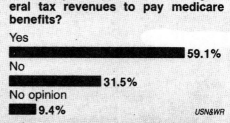
☐ **Would you support the use of general tax revenues to pay medicare benefits?**

Yes
██████████████ 59.1%

No
█████████ 31.5%

No opinion
███ 9.4%

USN&WR

220

A Longtime Pensioner

TUCKER, Ga.

At 101, Harvey Merrill, a retired Philadelphia stockbroker, is one of the country's oldest Social Security recipients. He firmly believes that people who haven't lived through the economic devastation of a depression cannot truly understand the peace of mind that Social Security brings to the elderly.

Experienced. Merrill is certainly in a position to know. He and his wife of 73 years, Helen, 95, began collecting benefits nearly 30 years ago. Their monthly stipend is $820.

Merrill began his working career at the turn of the century, when he traveled about the country selling axle grease. At the time of the stock-market crash of 1929, he was running a successful brokerage house. He vividly remembers the bleakness of the Depression. "They closed the stock exchange. There were no jobs. We lost our house and all the money we had in the bank. People were committing suicide right and left. One man killed himself in front of my office."

At one point, the couple and their two young sons had just 60 cents left, and the electric company was threatening to cut off service because of unpaid bills. "Mrs. Merrill sat on the porch and cried," he tearfully recalls a half-century later.

Timely aid. An anonymous donor sent the family a food basket with two chickens and fruit.

"The most wonderful thing President Roosevelt ever did," Merrill says, was to break the bond between old age and poverty. "You take an old fellow who doesn't have anything or anybody. At the least with Social Security, he has enough to rent a room and smoke a pipe if he wants."

Merrill sympathizes with young workers who face high taxes and uncertainty about Social Security's continued existence. Yet he insists there is no alternative. "They should never do away with Social Security," he declares.

By LINDA K. LANIER

---

lars annually.

Moreover, this expense is expected to go up sharply over the next three decades, mainly because people are living longer. By 2030, 22 percent of the population will be 65 or older. As advances in medical care lengthen lives, the federal tab for health care also rises.

Fears that the government might not be able to pay promised benefits first arose in the mid-1970s, when mushrooming payments began to outpace revenues. The annual deficits were covered by Social Security trust funds accumulated from surpluses in earlier years. When the retirement reserves were virtually exhausted in late 1982, Social Security faced insolvency. The White House and Congress were forced to act in order to keep the program afloat.

The rescue legislation included measures to boost revenues. For instance, scheduled increases in payroll-tax rates were accelerated. Self-employed individuals were required to pay rates comparable with the total amount paid by both an employed person and his or her employer. For the first time, Social Security recipients with high retirement incomes had to include in their taxable income up to half their government benefits.

The most important change, however, was a decision to raise from 65 to 67 the age at which workers may retire and qualify for full benefits, but its impact has yet to be felt. The age-limit increase will be gradually phased in between 2000 and 2027.

Saved or Not?

Government officials now insist that the 1983 reform package puts Social Security's retirement program—if not medicare—back in the black. "Benefits will be paid, on time, until well into the next century, even under pessimistic economic assumptions," declared Health and Human Services Secretary Margaret Heckler, whose department administers the Social Security program. To make her point, Heckler cites a report from the trustees of the Social Security funds, which concludes that the retirement program will be able to meet all of its obligations through the year 2020.

Others are optimistic further into the future. Says Alicia Munnell, an economist with the Federal Reserve Bank of Boston: "The system is adequately financed until 2050. Social Security will be there for today's young workers when it comes time for them to retire."

Many experts, however, are more skeptical about Social Security's long-term prospects. Rita Ricardo Campbell, an economist with the Hoover Institution at Stanford University, says the present benefit calculations do not fully recognize the impact of a rapidly aging population and a declining birth rate. To pay the level of benefits promised, she concludes, would require a doubling in Social Security taxes by the time baby boomers have retired. Adds Haeworth Robertson, who served as the Social Security Administration's chief actuary in the late 1970s: "The current Social Security program is not financially feasible in the long run."

What to Do Next?

Many solutions to Social Security's long-range problems have been proposed, but no plan has yet won broad support among the experts or with lawmakers. Robert Beck, chairman of Prudential Insurance Company and a member of the national commission appointed by Reagan to propose solutions to the Social Security funding crisis, dismisses fears that the program will go belly up. However, Beck believes Social Security payments should be subject to federal income taxes once retirees have received payments equal to their contributions.

Some business executives also are urging Congress to follow the lead of other industrial countries and limit the annual cost-of-living adjustments in Social Security benefits to 2 or 3 percentage points below the actual rate of inflation in consumer prices. Robertson reckons that the only practical solution is to raise the retirement age to as high as 70 or 72 early in the 21st century.

More-radical solutions are popping up, too. For example, Washington attorney Peter Ferrara advocates a plan that would enable workers to place part or all of their Social Security contributions in a savings plan akin to an individual retirement account. Upon retirement, participants would collect their contributions—plus interest.

A minority of Social Security experts say that future shortfalls should be offset by general tax revenues. Budget-conscious lawmakers are reluctant to enact a measure to achieve this because it would worsen the federal deficit. Congress is more likely to use regular income taxes to bail out medicare. That 72-billion-dollar-a-year program faces insolvency by 1998, according to official estimates. General revenues are already being used to pay for a good part of the medical expenses covered by the program.

Like the experts, the public is also deeply divided on how to bolster Social Security. The *U.S.News* poll found that none of the often suggested options met with approval from a majority of respondents. Fewer than one fourth of those sampled favored reducing benefits for current beneficiaries and just 28 percent supported benefit reductions for future retirees. Only one fourth would consent to tax increases.

Approximately 40 percent of Americans would be willing to work longer to get full pension rights, but a majority saw no need to change the current plan, which will raise the minimum retirement age to 67 by the year 2027.

Supplementing Social Security payroll taxes with general tax revenues to make up the shortfall received the strongest support. Nearly half—47 percent—of the respondents would earmark money from regular income taxes to help pay retirement and disability benefits. A larger percentage—59 percent—recommend the use of general tax revenues to help keep medicare going.

The debate about who should pay for Social Security now and 50 years hence is bound to continue to pit the young against the old. Experts worry that the longer any uncertainty persists, the greater the chances that an intergenerational conflict will prevent Congress from making the difficult decisions about how to keep the system financially sound.

"Social Security is very important to this country," stresses Beck of Prudential. "We must take the steps needed to increase the public's confidence that the system will pay off, so people do not have to live in fear." □

By PATRICIA M. SCHERSCHEL with RICHARD L. DeLOUISE of the Economic Unit and the magazine's domestic bureaus

A Widow

Ceola Foster, an Ypsilanti, Mich., mother of 15 whose husband Willie died nine years ago, receives $217 a month in Social Security benefits for each of five children under age 18.

"If he hadn't been working and paying in," she says, "I would have to be on welfare the rest of my life."

Her advice to young people who complain about paying Social Security taxes is not to be shortsighted. "You never know what you're going to come to in life. I never thought my husband would pass and leave me living on Social Security."

A Worker

Luis Mata is a 33-year-old Houston crane operator whose wife is a secretary.

"I can't base my future on Social Security," he says, "because I doubt that it will be here when I retire. I'd like to see the program continue, but I don't think it will." Why not? He expects economic conditions to force it out of existence.

Says Mata of the $22.56 in Social Security taxes deducted from his weekly paycheck: "I sure could use that money, but if it helps other people, it's O.K."

65

Reagan's Surprising Domestic Achievement

By Richard P. Nathan
And Fred C. Doolittle

Woodrow Wilson said that "the question of the relation of the states to the federal government is the cardinal question of our constitutional system." It cannot be settled, said Wilson, "by the opinion of any one generation, because it is a question of growth, and every new successive stage of our political and economic development gives it a new aspect, makes it a new question."

Wilson could not have been more right. Since Lyndon Johnson, every president has expressed a philosophy of federalism for his domestic program. Johnson called for a "creative federalism," Richard Nixon advanced what he called his "new federalism," and Jimmy Carter had a strong federalism concept imbedded in his "national urban program" of 1978.

But no modern president has had so clear and consistent a philosophy of federalism as Ronald Reagan. As a conservative spokesman, as a governor, and twice as a presidential candidate, he made much the same arguments, and urged much the same actions, that he has from the White House. He has argued for decentralization—for a reduction in the role of the federal government in domestic programs in general and in social programs in particular. More specifically, Mr. Reagan has sought to enhance the role of *states* as opposed to localities, which Messrs. Nixon and Ford favored in their efforts to decentralize.

Budget 'Blitzkrieg'

Many actions of the Reagan presidency express his federalism theory. These include the 1981 Stockman-led budget "blitzkrieg" to cut grants-in-aid programs.

In the 1982 State of the Union message, Mr. Reagan proposed a wide-ranging plan to "turn back" or "swap" federal functions with the states. The essence of this plan was that responsibility for welfare would be turned over to the states, with the federal government assuming responsibility for the Medicaid programs currently run by the states. All of this was to be combined with an elaborate restructuring of taxes and grants. This plan was not well received in Congress. As a result, the tendency has been to forget about Mr. Reagan's federalism agenda and concentrate instead on his budget cuts in assessing his impact on the domestic area.

Conventional wisdom holds that the Reagan administration was very successful in cutting domestic spending and shifting priorities to defense, but failed to obtain results in the name of its version of a "new federalism." In a word, we believe that this view is mistaken. In fact, the Reagan administration's domestic cuts, while significant in some areas, tend to be overrated in their importance. And his federalism reform efforts, which have nearly disappeared from the public consciousness, are turning out to have substantial impact.

The changes in federal-aid levels under Mr. Reagan are best understood if we divide them according to three main types of grant programs:

1. *Entitlement* programs, such as welfare and food stamps, where the payment of benefits is administered by states and localities.

2. *Operating* programs, under which the federal government provides grants to state and local governments for services such as education, public health and other social services.

3. *Capital* programs, where the federal government provides grants to states and localities for public facilities such as highways.

Looking across the three categories, we find that the biggest cuts were made in the first category, entitlement or welfare-type programs—cuts that hit immediately and stayed in place. These cuts fell most heavily on one group, the so-called working poor, made up primarily of female heads of household and their children living on a combination of earned income and welfare.

Cuts were also made in the second category, grants to states and localities for operating programs, including public-service employment. Under new block grants, federal funds went to state governments rather than cities or nonprofit organizations. The states gained new authority to set program priorities and distribute funds. Under some of the new block grants, funding cuts were partially cushioned by carry-overs from the previous categorical programs. States as well as localities also stepped in and replaced some of the federal-aid cuts.

Mr. Reagan's new Job Training Partnership Act, passed in 1982, also cut funding from the previous levels and in the process assigned the lead policy and management role to the states under this program.

Capital grants (the third category above) were initially slated for large cuts under Mr. Reagan, but even before the end of 1982, Congress increased funding for these programs. Moreover, there was an even bigger increase in 1982 in highway and mass-transit funding to combat the deep 1981-82 recession.

As it all turned out, the use of carry-over funding, emergency anti-recession appropriations in 1981-82, the replacement of some of the 1981 cuts by states and localities, and the unwillingness of Congress to continue to cut federal-aid spending after 1981 significantly dissipated the momentum of the Reagan domestic program in terms of its effects on state and local public finances and services.

The president, then, has made a palpable but not substantial impact on spending *levels*; the structure of domestic spending is another matter. If Mr. Reagan didn't get his "swap/turnback" plan through, just what did he end up with?

The changes made so far during Mr. Reagan's presidency add up to a significant increase in state influence. This can be seen in: (1) the discretion allowed under the new block-grant setup; (2) the new job-training role assigned to states; (3) the reduction in regulations and administrative oversight for many federal domestic programs; (4) changes in Medicaid that enhanced the power of the states to cut and control costs under this fast-growing program, and (5) the underlying shift in the behavior of the federal government in rejecting "laundry lists" of new programs to throw money at domestic problems.

Overall, we are impressed that the Reagan period has seen a resurgence in the role of state governments. The character and degree of this resurgence vary with the states, but in a large and well-established political system such as that of the U.S., such a shift is notable and important.

The basic response of state governments to the Reagan program consisted of actions taken to avoid or compensate for what otherwise would have been (or it was feared would have been) the effects of the Reagan cuts. These reactions have the appearance of stability, rather than change—but they do constitute change.

In addition to the enhanced state role vis-a-vis Washington, we detect a similar increase in the state role in relation to local governments. Local governments are increasingly turning to their state capitals as it becomes clear that the federal government is pulling back in domestic areas.

We also find major changes in the role and importance of nonprofit community groups, especially those that provide social services. With the exception of feeding programs for the hungry, these groups (many a throwback to Lyndon Johnson's "War on

Poverty'') are losing out under Mr. Reagan.

Sleeper Issue

Taken together, these structural changes in federal-state relations, in state-local relations, and in the role of nonprofit organizations affect a broad gamut of programs and agencies in the domestic public sector. It is unlikely that these changes will be temporary adjustments, easily reversible in subsequent years. This is where the big 1981 tax cuts enter the picture. Even if federal officials for domestic programs did attempt to reverse course and return to the "good old days," the federal deficits would cut them off at the pocketbook. Unless federal taxes are raised well above the level necessary to close the budget gap, which seems unlikely, the federal government does not have the fiscal flexibility to reverse this flow of influence and responsibility to the states.

Writing at the end of World War II, economist James A. Maxwell made a prediction about the relative roles of the federal and state governments in American federalism: "If the public demand for governmental services continues to grow, the state governments will soon appear to have more duties than they can handle effectively, and federal intervention will be indicated." Maxwell, of course, was right. We think that there has now been another basic shift. The federal government is pulling away from domestic and social programs, and state governments have taken on added duties and importance. Because of this, Ronald Reagan's version of a "new federalism" may turn out to be the major sleeper issue of his presidency.

————————

Messrs. Nathan and Doolittle are directing a study of Mr. Reagan's federalism reforms at the Woodrow Wilson School of Princeton University. This is based on a longer article to appear in the fall 1984 issue of The Public Interest.

66

High Cost of Keeping The Dollar Down

Business loves the lower dollar. But it may not like the tradeoffs necessary to hold it down.

by Marc Levinson

With the dollar down substantially from last year's stratospheric heights, hard-pressed American manufacturers are breathing sighs of relief. But betting that the dollar will remain at today's level is a risky proposition. Getting the dollar to drop was relatively easy. Keeping it down will be a far tougher challenge.

A stable exchange rate may be just the environment business needs to make long-term investment plans. But such a seemingly simple goal will require the use of all the government's economic tools, which would no longer be available to fight inflation, curb unemployment and spur economic growth. Because those other goals are more important than exchange rates, says Harvard University economist Martin Feldstein, "I just don't see how you can tell American business where the yen is going to be."

Two separate and very different challenges are involved in the dollar debate. One is the *level* of exchange rates, the number of pounds or marks required to buy one dollar. The second concerns *volatility*, the rapid fluctuation of currency prices. Volatility preoccupied economists in the 1970s, but now most agree that it is a far less serious matter than the level of rates. Moreover, companies can deal with volatility by buying and selling curren-

cy futures. "The level of the dollar is the major problem," asserts University of Chicago economist Jacob Frenkel. "Volatility is far less important."

While many economists believe the dollar should be stabilized, there is no consensus on the "correct" exchange rate against other currencies. Estimates of the "correct" rates for late 1984, for example, varied from $1.49 to $1.82 per British pound and 1.93 to 2.33 German marks to the dollar.

To make matters even more complicated, the "correct" rate may well change over time. If one currency rises more than another due to underlying factors such as lower inflation or higher productivity growth, the "correct" rate would change and attempts at stabilization would be wrong.

If speculation or the market's misperception of government intentions made the currency fluctuate, then intervention would be more appropriate.

Says Georgetown University economist Dale Henderson: "It's very important to know why exchange rates are changing. That's one of the biggest reasons why these ideas of fixing rates within a target range are off base."

One method of stabilizing exchange rates that has long been used is "intervention" by governments when one currency moves out of line. A bill reported out by the House Banking Com-

mittee in December by a wide bipartisan majority would mandate just that. Intervention in this sense means the purchase or sale of foreign currencies in coordination with other major nations.

Traders on the seventh floor of the Federal Reserve Bank of New York sell dollars for marks and yen on the open market, and invest that money in securities in Frankfurt and Tokyo. Meanwhile, foreign central banks sell dollar-denominated securities from their vaults and buy other currencies.

In this way, ten major central banks sold $10 billion between January 21 and March 1 of last year, helping trigger the fall in the dollar that began in early March. In September and October, after the five leading industrial powers agreed to try pushing down the dollar still further, intervention was their major tool. More than $10.2 billion was exchanged for other currencies.

On a day-to-day basis, irregular intervention can move currency prices by affecting market psychology. But over the long term, the amount central banks can spend on intervention is swamped by the hundreds of billions of dollars corporations can move around the globe at the push of a button. The Federal Reserve has estimated that U.S. banks alone trade more than $26 billion in currency *daily,* and estimates of the total world market are several times that figure. Because currency traders know that central banks' resources are limited, they often speculate against the same currencies the intervention is designed to prop up.

Most economists agree that intervention is a relatively ineffectual way of keeping a currency in line over the long haul and that monetary policy is by far the most powerful tool governments have to affect exchange rates. By tightening money supply growth, a central bank can force interest rates up and bring in foreign capital, increasing the relative price of the domestic currency. Looser monetary policy will generally drive interest rates down, and take the currency down as well.

But then monetary policy can't serve other ends, with consequences that could be far worse for business than a fluctuating dollar. "You can't use monetary policy purely to fix the exchange rate target because of other goals—you want to keep inflation under control and keep unemployment down," observes Harvard economist Jeffrey Sachs.

Fiscal policy can also affect the currency markets, but few Americans would be willing to tie national spending and taxation plans to exchange rates. If we did, goals dear to business, such as stimulating investment, would have to be abandoned; that stimulus draws in foreign capital, raising the value of the dollar. And fiscal policy, like monetary policy, can't be targeted towards changing the dollar's value against any specific currency. If the dollar is too low against the yen but not against the pound, U.S. fiscal and monetary policies won't help.

One proposal to stabilize the dollar, which has support across the ideological spectrum, is setting a target range for currency fluctuations. Within a narrow band—5% and 10% have been suggested—currencies would float freely, but if relative prices got out of line, governments would step in. The approach, one of whose chief proponents is economist John Williamson of the Washington-based Institute for International Economics, would force nations to make exchange rates the main objective of their economic policies. Bands have worked reasonably well in stabilizing the currencies in the European Monetary System. But the European economies, of course, are far more intertwined than those of the U.S., Germany and Japan.

Another idea, promoted by Columbia University economist Robert Mundell and many political conservatives, would return the world to a gold standard, with the U.S. Treasury agreeing to buy and sell gold at the current price of roughly $325 per ounce. This, too, would force nations to focus their policies on exchange rates.

The gold standard would also have the same shortcomings as the fixed-rate system used from 1946 to 1971, including frequent devaluations. And, because of the dollar's central role in the system, it would curb the U.S.'s ability to alter rates against other currencies.

A Stanford University economist, Ronald McKinnon, is pushing the idea of worldwide money supply limits. Under this approach, if the dollar were to rise sharply, the U.S. would have to increase its money supply while major trading partners cut theirs by the same amount, limiting inflation while keeping exchange rates from getting far out of line. While the proposal might work in theory, in practice it would require nations to hold to internationally-agreed limits on money supply growth—an event about as likely as obeying the rules that supposedly govern international trade.

The inherent weakness of all these proposals is that keeping the dollar down is not a unilateral game. Any system of regulating exchange rates requires close cooperation among the world's leading trading nations. If any one of them succumbs to other pressures—boosting money growth to stimulate a lagging economy in France, cutting spending to contain inflation in Germany—the game is over.

Given these formidable obstacles, the odds against exchange rate stability are—and must be—long. The world's central bankers will act from time to time to give exchange rates a nudge, but keeping the dollar on an even keel is far less important than controlling inflation and stimulating growth. In the complex world of economic policy, exchange rates can't be Number One. ∎

67

A time to dismantle the world economy

Professor Lester Thurow of the Massachusetts Institute of Technology argues that there is no magical free-market way in which the dollar is going to be devalued by the exact amount required to bring balance to the present international trading system. Such a fall would mean that Europe and Japan would lose the millions of jobs propped up by their exports to America. So the world will have to move to a new trading and financial system, preferably in an organised fashion but probably in a messy one

From 1962 to 1984 the world's exports rose from 12% to 22% of total output. Even in the United States, which has not traditionally been heavily dependent on international trade, exports rose from 6% of GNP in 1962 to 13% of GNP in 1981 before retreating in the face of an overvalued dollar. With exports rising as a fraction of GNP, the world was effectively becoming more and more economically integrated.

Will this postwar trend continue? I believe not. The world economy is in fact at a turning point, and the next ten years are likely to witness a lessening of economic integration.

The reasons for this belief are simple. First, the current degree of economic integration has outrun the world's collective political willingness to manage it. To make today's world economy work, the major industrial countries would have to be willing to co-ordinate their monetary and fiscal policies and to limit movements in exchange rates between major currencies. While both are within the realm of economic feasibility, neither seems within the realm of political feasibility. In the end the national instabilities produced by this collective management failure will force countries to reduce their involvement in the world economy.

Second, within the economies of each of the three major industrial actors—Japan, Europe and the United States—there are unsolved domestic economic problems that can most easily be solved by isolating oneself from world trade.

America faces a productivity problem. To be competitive on world markets at current wage rates it must accelerate its rate of productivity growth. If it cannot, it is likely to withdraw from international competition and retreat into protection.

Europe faces an employment problem. If it cannot begin to generate jobs in the framework of an open economy, it must retreat to a closed economy where it can generate jobs.

Japan faces a trade imbalance problem. Japan relies on exports to lead its domes-

tic growth; but, given the structure of the Japanese economy, the rate at which exports must grow to maintain prosperity far exceeds the rate at which imports will grow without major structural changes. If Japan cannot make the structural adjustments necessary to make imports grow as fast as exports, the rest of the world will gradually exclude Japan from their domestic markets and force Japan to reduce its dependency on world trade.

While each of these problems has a feasible local solution, the local solutions are politically difficult and unlikely to be put in place. To solve their local problems, all of the three major actors will find themselves forced partly to dismantle the current world economy.

The American problem

America faces a problem that is simply put. The huge technological edge enjoyed by Americans in the 1950s and 1960s has disappeared. Whereas America once had effortless economic superiority, it is now faced with competitors who have matched its economic achievements and may be in the process of moving ahead of it. What is worst, at precisely the moment when America's effortless superiority has vanished, the American economy has been absorbed into a world economy. For most goods there is now a world market, not just an American market. Competition is worldwide, not just American. As a result, America faces the difficult task of learning to compete in a new world economy just at the point when America's relative economic strength is weaker than it has been at any time since the second world war.

Productivity (output per hour of work) is the best general measure of a country's ability to generate a high and rising standard of living for each of its citizens. It is also a measure of America's ability to compete as a high-wage country on world markets. To fall behind on productivity is to fall behind on introducing the new products and the new production technologies that give American products an

edge in world markets. If American productivity is not equal to that of the best, America can compete only on the basis of wages that are lower than those of the world's productivity leaders. While it is certainly possible to compete based on low relative wage rates (most of the world does so), I know of no American who wants to do so. Americans want to compete from a position of equality or superiority—not from one of inferiority.

MANUFACTURING PRODUCTIVITY 1983

Country	Output per hour of work (1983 prices) $	Annual rate of growth 1977-83 %
Germany	20.22	2.5
United States	18.21	1.2
France	19.80	3.5
Italy	17.72	3.1
Japan	17.61	3.9
Canada	17.03	0.9
United Kingdom	11.34	3.3

Manufacturing is probably the best place to look at America's productivity performances vis-à-vis the rest of the world. All manufactured goods are potentially tradeable (they account for 70% of America's exports) and essentially homogeneous from country to country.

The table above sets out estimates of the level of manufacturing productivity for seven leading industrial countries in 1983. As these statistics from Data Resources show, the United States has already been surpassed by West Germany and France. Since most of the small northern European countries have productivity rates similar to those of Germany and France, all of northern Europe with the exception of Ireland and the United Kingdom may now have moved slightly ahead of the United States in manufacturing productivity, with Italy and Japan not far behind.

While America's previous position of economic superiority has clearly ended, its current position is probably not one of inferiority. West Germany, the most advanced country, has a 10% statistical edge but, given the vagaries inherent in any such measurements, a 10% edge is not an unambiguous lead. A correct interpretation of the data is, I believe, that the rest of the world has caught up with the United States but is not yet ahead. America's competitive position is one of "an equal among equals".

There is a real danger, however, that America is falling from parity to inferiority if one examines comparative rates of growth of productivity. American productivity growth rates have been below those of Europe and Japan ever since the war, but more importantly they are still below those of Europe and Japan even though these countries have now essentially caught up. In the years from 1977 to 1983, productivity grew at the rate of

1.2% per year in American manufacturing: one-half Germany's growth rate (2.5%), one-third the French rate (3.5%), and less than one-third the Japanese rate (3.9%). Manufacturing is also a relatively bright spot in the American productivity picture. Since the war, productivity growth in the private economy has steadily fallen from 3.3% (1947-65) to 1% (1977-84). And in the past 12 months (the second quarter of 1984 through the second quarter of 1985), there has been no productivity growth in the United States.

If such differences in growth rates continue to exist for very long, substantial inferiority cannot be far away.

To outsiders there are simple solutions for America's productivity problems. Nobody can build a high-quality economy out of low-quality inputs just as nobody can build a high-quality product out of low-quality components. Yet whenever the basic inputs—capital, labour, management, labour-management relations—going into the American economy are compared with those of the competition they just don't seem to measure up.

In America's large cities 8% of those entering the workforce test out as functionally illiterate (ie, they cannot read at a fifth-grade level). The average American 17-year-old knows half as much mathematics as the average Japanese 17-year-old. Given such science and maths scores it should come as no surprise that Japan produces twice as many engineers per capita as the United States and that with twice as many engineers on the payroll Japanese products seem to be a little better engineered. In America, test scores both for those leaving high school and going on to college and for those leaving college and going on to graduate school have fallen 10% in the past 15 years. Where America once had a labour force with educational abilities equal to that of the best, it no longer does.

In 1984, America's gross fixed investment (a measure that includes investment in housing) was 16% of GNP. At the same time the Germans were investing 20% and the Japanese 28%. If America were to have kept up with the Japanese in terms of plant and equipment investment per worker (and in the long run it must), it would have had to have essentially doubled its investment to 30% of GNP because of its more rapidly growing labour force. In any one year such gaps make little difference, but compounded over a few decades they spell the difference between success and failure.

America's personal savings rate, 5% in 1983, was the lowest in the industrial world by a factor of almost three. Our neighbours the Canadians saved 13%, the West Germans 14%, the Japanese 21%

and the Italians 23%. It does not take a genius to know that Americans cannot compete on world markets saving less than their competitors.

America invests less in civilian research and development than any of its major industrial competitors. American civilian R&D spending runs at about 1.5% of GNP while our competitors are spending 2%. Americans aren't smarter than the Germans or French. German scientists with money will beat American scientists without money most of the time. In the 1950s and 1960s America spent more, not less, on civilian research and development than its competitors.

While it is harder to quantify, American management cannot escape its share of the blame. American firms have undeniable problems with quality control. When asked to rate the quality of their cars, buyers listed only two American-built cars among the top ten. Management is responsible for quality control. If American products are shoddily built, then American management is shoddy.

On that famous bottom line, each major input into the economy will have to be as good as those of the competition if America is to be competitive. A world-class economy demands world-class inputs. Converting existing American inputs into world-class inputs is not technically hard. But doing so is politically difficult. It is not easy to tighten up a school system or reduce consumption.

A far easier solution will be to extend protection to non-competitive industries and gradually reduce America's involvement in international trade. The social changes necessary to meet foreign competition with superior products and productivity are difficult to accomplish while the laws necessary to keep the rest of the world out of the American market are easy to pass.

The European problem

In Europe the problem is a lack of jobs. Unemployment has risen every year for more than a decade and is now well into the double-digit range. In some countries unemployment exceeds the levels seen in the Great Depression. No set of democracies can tolerate such a situation for long. Europe's current slow withdrawal from the world economy will eventually become a flight into protection to create jobs unless the employment problem can be turned around.

While on a net basis there have been no new jobs generated in Europe since 1970, the American economy has in the same period of time generated more than 30m; more than 4m in 1984 alone. If one looks at the reasons for the differences between the United States and Europe, it is a good illustration of how it is easy to solve the

problems of others while remaining unable to solve one's own problems.

The European problem begins with macro-economic co-ordination. President Reagan proved that Keynesian economics still works, but President Mitterrand also proved that no country in Europe is big enough to practise it alone. If demand is to be expanded, all will have to expand simultaneously. If such co-ordination cannot be arranged, the European common market simply isn't viable.

While America and Europe are often seen as similar, their labour markets are in fact very different. Relative to the price of capital, American wages were 37% lower in 1983 than they were in 1972. This has not happened in Europe. Wages have risen relative to the price of capital until very recently.

The relative price of capital and labour provides a key signal for capitalists making investment decisions. In Europe, where labour costs were rising relative to the cost of capital, firms were told to substitute capital equipment for workers wherever possible. Workers were becoming more expensive relative to machinery. Firms responded as they should to these signals, and the European capital-labour ratio rose 3% per year in the decade ending in 1983. Firms, however, only add employees if their sales growth exceeds their productivity growth. Combine high-productivity growth with governments generally unwilling to pump aggregate demand into the system and European firms could meet their markets with the same or smaller labour forces. The net result was good productivity growth but bad employment growth.

In the United States the capitalists got a very different signal. With labour costs falling relative to the cost of capital, firms were told to substitute workers for capital equipment wherever possible.

The relative movements in average wages also underestimate the real differences between the two economies. Legally-mandated and socially-expected fringe benefits are much larger in Europe than in America. By law, workers in Belgium get a six-week vacation. By law, nobody gets any vacation in the United States and two weeks is the accepted social norm.

There is also less variance in wages in Europe than in America. Minimum wages are much closer to average wages in Europe than they are in America where the legal minimum wage is just 40% of the average hourly wage and largely unenforced (8% of the American workforce works at less than the legally mandated minimum wage). In the recession of 1982 only 43% of those unemployed received any unemployment insurance payments whatsoever and among those who did receive payments it replaced 40% of what they had previously earned. As a result, industries can thrive in the United States paying low wages whereas they could not pay low wages and survive in Europe. Much of America's employment gain has in fact been in low-wage jobs which the average European worker would reject as unacceptable.

It is easy for an American to tell Europeans to lower their wages, reduce fringe benefits, and relax legal minimum wages, but it is politically hard to do so. No one wants to give up those long vacations and generous fringe benefits.

Europeans are often envious of the rapid growth of new firms in Silicon Valley in California. Their response has tended to focus on subsidies for research and development and the need for a European venture capital industry to help new start-ups. Such activities are unlikely to solve the European jobs problems. What is needed is different forms of social organisation.

New start-ups have one great advantage in America. Firms can easily fire unneeded workers. Advance notice need not be given; severance pay need not be paid. Firms simply do not need to carry unneeded workers if demand is not what was expected. Workers can be hired with the knowledge that if they are not needed they can be quickly fired.

In Europe firings range from difficult and expensive to impossible. This makes it much riskier and more expensive to go into business. What is a reasonable risk in America where labour is a variable cost becomes an unreasonable risk in Europe where labour is an overhead fixed cost.

I am not recommending the American solution to the European job problem. It would be far better to create labour market flexibility with a variable bonus such as that of the Japanese, but if Europe is not able to adopt some solution to its labour market rigidities it will have to close its economy and reflate to create jobs. If one looks at what has happened to unemployment rates in the past decade (up from 2% to more than 11%) under the current system it is difficult to imagine that the current system can continue.

The Japanese problem

Japan relies on exports to keep its economy running. When the multiplier effects are included, exports accounted for all of Japan's growth in 1983 and two-thirds of its growth in 1984. In 1981 and 1982 there were quarters when domestic Japanese sales were falling but the economy was still growing. Exports were providing more than 100% of the net growth in Japan. When these exports hit the American and European economies, however, they cut local sales and produce unemployment. The unemployment that would

normally flow from a stagnant Japanese domestic economy was essentially being exported.

America's trading deficit with Japan, $37 billion in 1984 and likely to be much higher in 1985, is economically and politically unacceptable. Within the United States, the trade imbalance leads to irresistible political pressures to retreat into ever-widening circles of protection.

Americans have to take some of the blame for the trade deficit with Japan. American firms have refused to design products explicitly for the Japanese market, have refused to learn the Japanese language and customs, have demanded instant success, and have often acted as if it is the duty of Japan to run its economy precisely as the American economy is run. The American government has contributed to the problem by letting the dollar-yen exchange rate rise until it is simply impossible for any American manufacturer to compete.

The origins of Japan's trade surplus are easy to find. Both after the Meiji restoration and the second world war Japan was a poor country desperately anxious to catch up. Its limited foreign exchange earnings had to be devoted to buying foreign technology and machinery that Japan could not produce for itself. To meet this need the whole economy was organised to minimise imports of non-essential goods. If a firm wanted to expand, for example, it had to find ways to expand that did not require foreign goods.

In a western country, that legitimate national need would have taken the form of (easily dismantlable?) legal rules and regulations. In Japan's non-legal consensus society they took the form of social norms and social organisation. How does a foreign firm break in as a new supplier of industrial components, for example, when Japanese firms place a premium on maintaining long-term intimate supply relationships with nearby suppliers in the just-in-time inventory system?

Japan now has an industrial structure that does not absorb imports just when it needs to buy imports to hold markets open for its exports. To change that internal structure, however, involves major industrial shifts that are politically no easier to accomplish in Japan than they would be in the United States or Europe.

There are essentially two options. Japan could practise domestic Keynesian economics to keep demand growing and change the structures of its economy and culture so that imports grow in pace with exports, or Japan could find itself systematically kept out of foreign markets to hold its exports down. From the point of view of a world economy the first option is far better since it leads to an expansion

rather than a contraction of world trade and economic integration. But the second option is by far the more likely.

Macro-economic co-operation

In the recovery from the 1981-82 recession the Reagan administration proved that Keynesian aggregate demand policies still work and that the United States is still strong enough to use Keynesian policies to restart the world's economic engines. What is not clear, however, is how long the United States can pull the resultant load.

Of the 3m jobs lost in the 1984 trade deficit of $123 billion, Japan, Europe plus Canada, and the rest of the world each received the gift of about 1m American jobs if bilateral deficits are examined. The OECD estimates that one-third of the growth in Western Europe in 1984 could be traced to the American recovery and the high value dollar. Despite this external impetus to their economic growth, most of the rest of the world was still caught up in slow growth in 1985. Most industrial countries had positive growth rates, but few countries outside of the United States had growth rates strong enough to reduce unemployment. And without those millions of jobs from America most of the rest of the world would still have been buried in the recession that began in 1981.

There is a real question as to how long the United States can continue to provide such a Keynesian stimulus to the rest of the world. America, like France earlier, is being inundated with rising imports and falling exports. Between 1981 and 1984 imports captured 42% of the growth in domestic American spending. Even such a historically-strong exporting industry as agriculture lost half its foreign markets between 1981 and 1984.

The difference between France and the United States was that the value of the dollar did not fall. In 1983 and 1984 foreigners were willing to finance America's trade deficits, and the inflows of capital paid for the outflows of funds necessary to buy all of those foreign-made products. This was possible since the United States was running a monetary policy where real short-term interest rates were being held at levels twice those in Japan or West Germany. America was a very attractive place to park money.

Such a combination of policies presents a number of short-run and long-run problems. While a large budget deficit can keep a recovery going in the face of high real interest rates, the high real interest rates discourage the economy from making the long-term investments it ultimately needs to be competitive. The recovery is oriented to consumption (demand) rather than to investment (supply). What works in the short run (pump consumption into the systems) hurts in the long run (there is too little investment).

While a large budget deficit can offset high interest rates and prevent a recession, a rising trade deficit requires a large and *rising* budget deficit. If the trade deficit were to be larger than the federal budget deficit, the two would represent a net subtraction of demand from the American system and in conjunction with high interest rates lead to a recession. As a result, ever higher federal deficits are required to offset ever higher trade deficits.

In the United States this requires a willingness on the part of both the federal government and the country to go ever deeper into debt. While ever larger federal debts are undesirable, they are probably manageable; Americans hold both the assets (bonds) and the liabilities (taxes owed). But an ever larger international debt is not manageable. Foreigners own the assets; Americans hold the liabilities. In a few years the sums get so large that foreigners have neither the willingness nor the ability to lend what must be lent even if interest rates remain high.

A trade deficit financed by foreign borrowings represents a debt like any other debt and nobody can forever accumulate debts that grow faster than one's income. At some point the rest of the world will decide that it has lent America enough, just as America decided that it had lent Mexico enough, and the lending will stop. When this happens the value of the dollar will fall.

The United States will regain the 3m jobs it is now losing but be hit by an inflationary shock in the form of much higher prices for imports. The rest of the world will lose 3m jobs but be helped on the inflationary front with cheaper imports. America, as France did earlier, is apt to apply a dose of austerity and a retreat from the goal of full employment and economic recovery. The rest of the world essentially becomes a train which the American locomotive can no longer pull uphill. As the American locomotive starts to slide backwards under the weight of its load, however, the rest of the train slides backwards with it.

The current situation comes about for a simple reason. While the United States has been pursuing an expansionary fiscal policy of large and rising federal deficits, the rest of the industrial world has been pursuing exactly the opposite policy. America expanded its structural budget deficit from 1980 to 1984, but the rest of the industrial world contracted theirs. Conversely the rest of the world has run a low-interest-rate policy while the United States was running a high-interest-rate policy. The net result has been a rapid

recovery in the United States which fuelled a weak recovery in the rest of the industrial world. Abroad, the positive demand effects from the American trade deficit more than offset the negative demand effects from falling foreign government deficits. But unless one believes that the United States can forever run a large trade deficit the macro-economic underpinnings of the current recovery are unsustainable. Whenever the dollar falls and the American trade deficit unwinds, the recovery in the rest of the world stops.

Given the current degree of world integration, it is no longer possible to have unco-ordinated national economic policies where countries attempt to go it alone. Yet co-ordination has repeatedly proven to be beyond reach at the annual economic summits of the industrial powers. This leaves those powers with no option but to sharply reduce the current degree of economic integration and return to the era when it was possible to have viable national economic policies.

At the moment, the world is on this track—moving towards less economic integration and more viable national economic policies. The process is already under way as industry after industry—steel, shipbuilding, cars, consumer electronics—is withdrawn from real international trade and becomes a "managed" industry with formal or informal quotas or other government marketing arrangements. Protection will provide the vehicle for disintegrating the world economy and making national economic policies once again viable, but at an enormous economic and political price.

Co-ordinating exchange rates
Co-ordinating monetary and fiscal policies would remove some of the violent swings in exchange rates, but not all. Flexible exchange rates are an area where the economics profession was simply wrong. Back in 1971, when the world went on to the current system of flexible exchange rates, economists were sure that it would be impossible to have large fluctuations in exchange rates between major countries over short periods of time or to have currencies that were fundamentally over or undervalued. Yet in the past decade both have occurred.

If changes in productivity, inflation and nominal exchange rates are added together, the real dollar-yen exchange rate rose an amazing 70% over a few months in the early 1980s.

With such violent swings in exchange rates, it simply isn't possible to run efficient economies. Nobody knows where economic activity should be located; nobody knows the cheapest source of supplies; wherever economic activities are located they will be located in the wrong

place much of the time. The result is a needless increase in risk and uncertainty, rising instability from protectionism, a shortening of time horizons as firms seek to limit risk and uncertainty by avoiding making long-term commitments, reductions in major new long-term investments, large adjustment costs as production is moved back and forth to the cheapest locations, the expectation of future inflationary shocks, with consequent instability in interest rates.

Left alone, the dollar will eventually fall. The German multinational treasurer who has moved his marks into the United States at three marks to the dollar knows that he will only get DM200m and not DM300m back when he tries to move his $100m out after the dollar has fallen to two marks to the dollar. He also knows that foreigners will not forever be willing to add to the dollar bank accounts at a rate high enough to finance the American trade deficit. At some point they will have too many of their assets tied up in dollar investments and will stop investing more. As a result the treasurer and every other investor would like to be the first person out of the door when the dollar starts to fall. As a consequence, the dollar is likely to fall very fast when it starts to fall. And given the history of the past decade, the dollar is apt to plunge right through its equilibrium point, shifting from being overvalued to being undervalued. If the dollar is 40% overvalued, a fall of 60% would not be surprising.

When this happens, the world rapidly moves from a situation where it is coping with an overvalued dollar to a situation where it is coping with an undervalued dollar. Economies are disrupted both here and abroad. Production that has moved offshore moves back. This is good for recovery in the United States but bad for recovery elsewhere. And if the dollar-yen exchange rate is going to move rapidly back and forth between 277 and 177 every few years, neither side knows where it is most efficient to locate production. As a consequence nobody is willing to build major new facilities in either America or Japan.

Anyone who believes in gravity and watches water run uphill has a fundamental problem. Facts are difficult to deal with when they conflict with theory. Before changing theories, most human beings will spend long periods of time pretending that the facts don't exist.

For believers in the virtues of free unregulated markets, such as the Reagan administration, it is simply impossible to have a persistently overvalued dollar. Free markets can't produce bad results. Yet there the dollar sits grossly overvalued, destroying American industry and agriculture. Water is running uphill.

It is true that no country has an unlimited ability to hold up the value of its currency. For America to hold up the value of its currency it must buy dollars, and this can only be done to the extent that it has previously acquired the foreign currencies necessary to buy dollars in international currency markets. When foreign exchange reserves are spent, America has no further ability to hold up the value of its own currency.

Countries have, however, an unlimited ability to hold down the value of their currencies, and fortunately this is what the United States needs to do. To hold down the value of the dollar, America must sell dollars; and there is no limit on the number of dollars that can be sold. America prints dollars. The only limit has to do with how fast a country wants its money supply to grow, and even here it is possible to offset adverse money supply effects with what is called a sterilised intervention. There is a fundamental difference between government interventions designed to hold a currency above levels consistent with its productivity and inflation and interventions designed to prick a speculative bubble and force a currency down to its appropriate level.

In little more than a decade the prevailing intellectual fashions have gone from "governments can stop any and all movements in foreign exchange rates" (that is the belief required to operate a fixed exchange rate system) to a belief that "governments can do nothing about foreign exchange rates" Neither is true.

To correct the situation one need not go back to fixed exchange rates—that is neither possible nor desirable—but it does mean an international agreement to dampen wild fluctuations. The obvious answer is some system of crawling pegs where an attempt is made to isolate the changes needed in foreign exchange rates to accommodate changes in countries' long-term competitiveness—their relative rates of inflation and productivity—from the temporary factors that cause capital flows from one country to another. Nobody can make these judgments perfectly but, as the European monetary system demonstrates, it is possible to dampen wild fluctuations.

This is unlikely to occur, however Intellectual fashions often dominate current events and the present intellectual fashion favours non-intervention. But with non-intervention and wild currency fluctuations in what is in fact the world's reserve currency, the current world economic system cannot work. Eventually nations will revert to more workable. even if less desirable, national solutions.

On the surface the events of the past six weeks (the currency interventions of the Group of Five and the American willingness to think about something other than austerity as a cure for third-world indebtedness) are hopeful signs that policy makers now know they cannot go on as before. Below the surface, however, there is little sign of change. To lower the value of the dollar by the amounts needed the Japanese and Germans would have gone home to develop new domestic policies for stimulating their economies and the Americans would have gone home to develop new policies for quickly narrowing their budget deficit. Upon arriving home from the meeting of the Group of Five, all three finance ministers announced that there would be no change in domestic monetary and fiscal policies.

In such a context it is not surprising that it was possible to get an agreement to lower the value of the dollar by about 10%. Such an agreement does not threaten the European or Japanese jobs gained in their export surpluses with America. The hard, and yet to be seen, part is the rest of the 40% fall in the value of the dollar that would be necessary to bring America's exports and imports back into balance. That part would bring those millions of jobs back to America and they then would have to be replaced by jobs generated in the domestic European or Japanese economies.

Needed: an international manager

As it is now structured the international trading system is not working. Most of the world is still experiencing stagnation with rising unemployment. That can only continue with the current pattern of monetary and fiscal policies. America's productivity, Europe's employment, and Japan's export surpluses all threaten the system. Every year the number of products subject to formal or informal restrictions gets larger.

Structural changes will be required to make the world trading system work. This, in turn, requires management. For unless there is a manager actively concerned about the future of the international trading system, the system will simply disappear in a sea of protection.

While the United States is no longer strong enough to dictate economically to the rest of the world, as it did immediately after the war, it is still the strongest country in the industrial world. In the next 20 years the manager's job is going to be one of seeking consensus and making compromises—not giving orders. Only the United States is capable of filling this frustrating role. Unfortunately America has abdicated this responsibility. It needs to take it up again.

Forgive some debt, forget protectionism, and trust the IMF.

HOW TO SAVE THE THIRD WORLD

BY JEFFREY SACHS

NOBODY IS HAPPY with the International Monetary Fund these days. As the IMF's annual meetings convened October 8 to 11 in Seoul, South Korea, the Fund found itself under fierce attack from left and right. Most Latin American governments see the IMF as an agent of American commercial banks. Supply-siders in the Reagan administration and in Congress complain that the IMF's heavy emphasis on austerity in the debtor countries is an obstacle to world growth. In recent weeks, administration officials have stated their intention of enlarging the World Bank's role, in the belief that the bank will be more growth-oriented than the Fund.

This crescendo of complaint reflects growing anxiety about the debt crisis in developing countries. When financial chaos in mid-1982 in Mexico and several other debtor nations first threatened world economic stability, there was hope for a quick fix. The Reagan administration believed that the debtor countries would be rescued by financial retrenchment under IMF supervision, a decline in U.S. interest rates, and an economic recovery in the advanced industrial economies that would expand markets for their products.

Ironically, the worry today isn't that optimistic projections about interest rates and growth were wrong, but that they were right! The favorable trends in the world economy have simply not been enough to defuse the crisis, and the debt structure is as shaky today as it was in 1982. Even before the recent earthquakes threw Mexico's debt repayments into doubt, Latin American debtor countries were talking tough about paying off their loans. Peru's President Alan Garcia said at the U.N. last month, "We are faced with a dramatic choice: it is either debt or democracy." He threatened to withdraw Peru from the IMF unless it offered some relief.

That tough talk is being echoed throughout Latin America. The IMF is bearing the brunt of global disappointment, though most of the specific criticism is unfair and illogical. More than any government or other international institution, the Fund has held the world financial system together in the past three years. In many ways its performance has been innovative and even brilliant in successfully avoiding the global defaults and economic disarray that similar economic circumstances brought about in the

1930s. We continue to live under the shadow of the debt crisis, not because of the nefarious plans or ineptitude of the IMF, but rather because the "quick fix" so ardently desired is simply not available.

Who is to blame for the debt crisis? Politicians and intellectuals in debtor countries like to blame the developed world, particularly the United States. They point to rising U.S. interest rates, which have forced up the costs of debt repayments and depressed the prices of commodities that poor countries sell in world markets. Creditors, on the other hand, emphasize ineptitude and corruption in the debtor countries. Both views have some merit.

To summarize a complex history, the rise in world interest rates following the Federal Reserve Board's shift to tight money in 1979 was the decisive common element in bringing on the crisis in dozens of developing countries. Like American farmers, the foreign governments borrowed big in the 1970s with the expectation of continued low interest rates and continued rapid inflation. They thought they could pay off their debts with cheap dollars. Paul Volcker tripped them up.

But the effects of the "Volcker shock" differed widely in different nations. As with farmers, prudent and relatively well-managed borrowers escaped with limited damage. Countries that used their loans for productive investments in exporting industries were able to keep up their interest payments, even at higher rates. The East Asian countries—especially Indonesia, Korea, Malaysia, Taiwan, and Thailand—used foreign loans to finance a large expansion in export capacity. These countries all have avoided a debt crisis.

Less satisfactory were cases where the money was used to finance investment in high-cost domestic industries, heavily protected from foreign competition and unable to compete on world markets. Many Latin American countries fall in this category. Worse off are countries like Argentina, which used foreign borrowing to finance extravagant consumption expenditures or military adventures. Finally, there are the cases like Mexico, Venezuela, and again Argentina, where many of the dollars that the government borrowed from abroad found their way, legally or illegally, into the U.S. bank accounts of private citizens and public officials.

Consider two of the IMF's most important crisis clients, Mexico and Venezuela. Both countries are major oil exporters, and yet they squandered the advantage of high oil

Jeffrey Sachs is professor of economics at Harvard University.

prices between 1978 and 1982. In both cases, overvalued exchange rates depressed the non-oil export industries, channeled investments into the wrong sectors, and encouraged private citizens to speculate against the exchange rate by trading domestic assets for U.S. dollars. The Mexican and Venezuelan governments borrowed billions of dollars from U.S. banks, in order to stabilize an unrealistic exchange rate, at the same time that their citizens were legally taking billions of dollars outside of the country to invest abroad! According to some analysts, Venezuelan citizens have as much money invested abroad as the Venezuelan government owes to U.S. banks: about $25 billion. But this doesn't help the government pay its debts, since Venezuelan citizens will not willingly trade their dollar assets to the government in return for Venezuelan bolivares, a currency they do not trust.

Many debtor governments believe that explicit debt forgiveness is now a moral imperative. But the moral case for wholesale debt relief is unconvincing, except with respect to the world's poorest countries, as in sub-Saharan Africa. Should Venezuela's debts be forgiven when Venezuelan citizens have used those dollars to buy extensive real estate and financial holdings in the U.S.? Should Argentina's, when much of the money was used to finance a wasteful yet popularly supported war in the Falklands? Why should Venezuela, which had oil and wasted it, get debt relief and not energy-starved Korea, which also borrowed heavily but used its loans far more wisely? Korea paid for its heavy borrowings with several years of consumer austerity as resources were moved from domestic to export industries. Should that austerity be ignored while profligacy elsewhere is rewarded?

THE International Monetary Fund took center stage in the debt crisis in the summer of 1982, when the Mexican government announced that it couldn't meet the interest payments on its debts. Bank lending to debtor countries dried up, and suddenly many announced that they, too, couldn't make their payments. The IMF's main role in the debt crisis has been to make loans to debtor countries in return for the promise of policy reforms. This approach, known as "conditionality," has long been a fundamental precept of IMF lending. Borrowing from the Fund is voluntary. Despite the vitriol about Fund policies, no country has to submit if it doesn't want to.

The strategy worked out in 1982 by the IMF, the United States, and the other major creditor governments had three key elements. First, new loans would be made on a case-by-case basis, with conditionality, rather than attempting any grand global bailout. Second, existing debts would be "rescheduled" rather than forgiven. Missed interest payments would be tacked on to the total amount due. Third, the commercial banks would be obligated to come up with some new money as part of the IMF program, so that they wouldn't be seen as getting off scot-free.

This last element was crucial and ingenious. It helped to guarantee an adequate supply of new money for the debtor countries. In the circumstances of 1982-83, no individ-

ual bank wanted to make new loans to the crisis countries, even though collectively such lending was the only feasible way to avoid outright defaults on the debt. Developing countries acceded to conditionality not only to get IMF money, but also to get the new money from the banks that an IMF program brought along. With the short-term crisis avoided, debtors and creditors alike were urged to hang on until a U.S.-led world recovery would allow the debtor countries to expand their exports and thereby pay off their debts.

Three years later, the major Latin American debtor countries all have tightened their belts, sharply reduced their imports, and continued to meet their interest payments. But their economies have not grown. Austerity in the debtor countries has not been followed by economic expansion. Real living standards, down sharply from the 1970s, have not yet begun to improve.

ONCE AGAIN, the debtor countries' problems are both external and internal. World prices of commodity exports have continued to fall in the past two years, despite the growth of world trade. Many debtor countries have gotten a lousy bargain: they are selling more but earning less. Also, despite IMF prodding, the banks have continued to pull out of Latin America, further squeezing countries that have been depending on at least small amounts of new loans. Meanwhile, many of the counterproductive policies in the debtor countries that helped bring on the debt crisis have remained in place, despite IMF supervision. Entrenched political interests in the debtor countries have blocked many needed reforms.

IMF programs often are accused of hurting the poor to the benefit of the rich within the debtor countries. Yet IMF programs may well do more for the poor, in restoring sound economic management, than anything that the debtor governments would do themselves. Consider one of the most loathed elements of IMF conditionality: devaluation of the currency. Devaluation is essential to spur exports. But it raises the domestic price of food, and usually lowers the real wages of urban workers. On the other hand, rural agricultural workers typically benefit, since their products sell at a higher price. Devaluation often leads to more egalitarian income distribution, since it transfers income from the urban sector to the poorer rural sector. But it is almost always resisted in Latin America, since urban workers have far more political muscle than rural peasants.

This political reality helps to explain the debt crisis itself. Export industries—needed to produce foreign currency to pay off the debt—have been underdeveloped because most governments since the 1940s, whether military or civilian, have drawn their support from a clientele of capitalists and unions in non-export sectors, whose interest is for government protection rather than export promotion. The restoration of growth requires a complete reorientation of these economies toward exports. Even when the leaders of these troubled nations know this, they are politically unable to act.

The supply-side attack on the IMF is more bizarre, since the IMF, like the supply-siders, has long been accused of an excessive reverence for the free market. But these natural allies have become foes, partly because the supply-siders misunderstand IMF policies and partly because of their fanciful ideas about the economics of development.

Supply-siders carry their insouciance in the face of high budget deficits to ludicrous extremes in the case of the developing countries. They frequently have attacked the IMF for stressing government cuts and tax increases. Unfortunately, the notion that growth alone can restore fiscal balance is even sillier in Latin America than it is in the U.S., where it also has proved to be an empty hope. Throughout Latin America, budget deficits have been on the order of eight to 15 percent of GNP in recent years, compared to five percent in the U.S. Unlike the United States, Latin American governments no longer have the luxury of borrowing from abroad to finance those deficits. So they have taken to money printing and rapid inflation as a way to finance their overspending. History teaches that high inflation (well over 100 percent per year in Brazil and Peru; and recently up to 1,000 percent per year in Argentina, and about 40,000 percent per year in Bolivia) must be stopped before any sensible long-term reforms of an economy can be instituted. Reducing inflation means reducing budget deficits; and unfortunately, reducing budget deficits generally means austerity in the short run.

DESPITE some success for the Fund's approach, the debt situation looks increasingly bleak. The major debtor countries seem unable to grow out of the debt crisis. With their restive citizens chafing under continued austerity, the debtor governments are talking tougher. The pessimism is apparently shared in the U.S. financial markets. The stock prices of major commercial banks are far below their book values, partly in recognition of the fact that the true value of their claims on Argentina, Brazil, or Mexico are worth less than their value on paper. The implicit market value of debts held by American banks seems to be about 75 cents on the dollar for the major debtor countries, and as little as 20 cents on the dollar for claims on Bolivia.

To pay off their debts, the developing countries need to grow. To grow, they need a major increase in exports. In an ideal adjustment, the Latin American debtors would shift production toward labor-intensive exports to the U.S. and Europe. New export earnings could be used both to make debt service payments and to pay for the increased imports needed for faster growth. The advanced economies, meanwhile, would shift resources away from their labor-intensive sectors, and toward the capital goods industries that would find growing markets in the debtor countries.

There are two obstacles to such a textbook adjustment. One is the political power of currently favored industries within the debtor countries. The other is the rise of protectionism in the developed world, which makes a strategy of export-led growth look foolhardy to debtor nations. Protectionist pressures are strongest in just those industries

where the debtors could make a significant export push, such as basic steel and textiles.

Breaking this logjam will require skillful political leadership in the United States, Europe, and Japan. Potentially, though, there is a natural coalition of forces against protectionism, including the commercial banks whose claims are at risk; capital goods exporters whose markets have been decimated by the debt crisis; exporters generally, who will be hurt by rising tariffs; and organized consumer groups, since it is consumers who ultimately bear the costs of protectionism in the form of higher prices.

Like it or not, however, political leaders in the creditor countries must also explore ways to cancel some of the debt repayment, rather than merely postponing it. A partial debt cancellation is not necessarily a moral imperative, but it may be a pragmatic one. For the debtor governments, the political and economic costs of default no longer clearly outweigh the burdens of austerity.

IN A SENSE, the Reagan administration's new focus on the World Bank is an acknowledgment of this reality. The administration has been looking around for a way to ease the Latin debt burden (without debt cancellation), and sees the World Bank as a source of credits. The administration also hopes to encourage new commercial bank loans in tandem with World Bank lending, though the private banks are understandably balking at further increases. The World Bank's focus on "structural adjustment" has made it seem like an attractive vehicle for reforming the debtor economies. Unfortunately, the conditionality the World Bank attaches to its structural adjustment loans is notoriously lax, so that a sharp increase in World Bank lending to the Latin American debtors might just pile up the debt burden and make the problems all the worse in the future.

A better alternative might be to cut some of the losses on the debt today, rather than dragging out a process that will ultimately end at the same place. A program of debt relief should preserve the key elements of the current strategy. The IMF should continue to oversee conditionality, with relief negotiated on a case-by-case and year-to-year basis. Debt relief must be a spur to beneficial reform, rather than a substitute for reform. The burden of the debt write-offs should be borne both by the banks that made the loans and, inevitably, by the taxpayers of the creditor countries. This is not completely unjust: as depositors in the banks, average citizens have been the ultimate beneficiaries— more than the shareholders—of the high interest rates paid by the debtor countries.

Partial debt relief is especially appealing now because the financial markets already have discounted the value of bank claims on the debtor countries. Shareholders already have "eaten" these losses (though larger losses might come later). But we haven't enjoyed the benefit that would come from acknowledging those losses. The carrot of partial debt forgiveness could be used to induce needed economic reforms in the debtor countries, while the governments in those countries could hold out the debt relief as a sign to their citizens of a more hopeful economic future. □

BAKER'S PLAN HAS A PECK OF PRACTICAL PROBLEMS

■ Treasury Secretary James Baker envisions a three-pronged attack on the problems of 15 debt-laden developing countries. On one front he wants the debtor countries to make structural changes in their economies that will increase growth, produce sound balance-of-payments positions, and cut inflation. The countries are supposed to strengthen their private sectors and reduce budget deficits, put in supply-side programs such as tax reductions, liberalize trade, and promote foreign investment. Such policies, Baker says, will build confidence, encouraging domestic savings and stopping the flight of capital.

If the debtors buckle down to those prescribed changes, lenders open Fronts 2 and 3: commercial banks around the world grant the countries about $20 billion of new loans over the next three years; and the so-called multilateral development banks—the World Bank, the Inter-American Development Bank, and others—supply another $20 billion. Lending would continue case by case, with each country's loans negotiated separately.

Baker wants to see the World Bank play a major role in making good things happen. In recent years it has begun making what it calls "policy-based loans," which aim at Baker-like structural changes. For example, the Bank finances certain imports for countries willing to knock down trade barriers that would have kept those imports out. In almost all its loans it operates with carrot and stick, doling out money only as borrowers make headway. Baker wants the Bank to prod the 15 countries.

But behind the facade of this plan are endless complications that may scuttle it:

▶ Baker's structural changes add up to political dynamite and are impossible to put into effect quickly, if at all. The Reagan Administration has campaigned for such changes before and has got so little that Baker is making another pass at the well.

▶ Lining up the banks will be an organizational nightmare. For the plan even to get started, some 700 banks in 50 nations have to commit to lend $20 billion, providing those structural changes get made. In percentage terms the money asked is not big, amounting to only 7.3% of the banks' outstanding loans to the 15 countries, or an annual increase of about 2.4%. The U.S. money center banks can see a compelling reason to put that up: the investment promises to keep interest payments on existing loans flowing in. Also, as Baker has said, the big banks "have an ox in the ditch." They are looking for any way to get that fellow out.

But U.S. regional banks have reason to balk. Many have written down their foreign loans by a lot or sold loans to eliminate their exposure to a given country. Suppose a regional has largely written down its Brazilian loans and is out of Argentina entirely. Is it now to get back into Argentina by joining in the $20-billion commitment? Whoa. As a banker bitingly says, "This is not a new-business effort." Yet the cooperation of the regionals is essential to Baker's plan because the money center banks aren't ready to sign on by themselves. Were they to do that and be called on for new loans, part of the money would flow back to the regionals as interest on old loans.

▶ The World Bank is an imponderable: conservative, methodical, bureaucratic, a big borrower in the financial markets and therefore superprotective of its credit rating (AAA). In its 1985 fiscal year, a period of desperate need for many countries, it did not commit all the money it had expected to, partly because so few countries met its standards of creditworthiness.

In recent congressional hearings, Baker has conceded that his plan will be difficult to execute and uncertain in results. But, he says, "we do not see any alternative to an approach of this nature." In other words, count this as a last-ditch effort.

A Baker's Dozen Plus Two

For U.S. banks Latin America is the zone of pain. But Baker wanted support for his plan from foreign banks with problem loans concentrated elsewhere, so his list of troubled debtors has geographical spread. Variable interest rates apply to more than half the debt, which means the interest burden can swing sharply. Interest figures show what the countries owed in 1985—but some, such as Peru and Bolivia, didn't pay in full.

COUNTRY	FOREIGN DEBT in billions	1985 INTEREST in billions	estimated % of 1985 GNP	DEBT OWED TO U.S. BANKS in billions
Brazil	$103.5	$11.8	5.8%	$23.8
Mexico	$97.7	$10.0	6.3%	$25.8
Argentina	$50.8	$5.1	7.9%	$8.1
Venezuela	$32.6	$4.1	8.1%	$10.6
Philippines	$27.4	$2.1	6.2%	$5.5
Chile	$21.9	$2.1	12.9%	$6.6
Yugoslavia	$20.0	$1.7	3.6%	$2.4
Nigeria	$18.0	$1.8	1.9%	$1.5
Morocco	$14.4	$1.0	8.2%	$0.9
Peru	$13.9	$1.3	10.8%	$2.1
Colombia	$13.9	$1.3	3.3%	$2.6
Ecuador	$7.9	$0.7	6.0%	$2.2
Ivory Coast	$6.3	$0.6	8.7%	$0.5
Uruguay	$4.9	$0.5	9.8%	$1.0
Bolivia	$4.2	$0.4	10.0%	$0.2
TOTAL	$437.4	$44.5	Average 7.3%	$93.8

Baker Would Make U.S. Poorer

By Allan H. Meltzer

Nearly universal acclaim has been given to this season's new look in Treasury policy. Secretary James Baker's proposals to lower the value of the dollar, in concert with other governments, and to lend to the Latin American debtor countries are usually described as "bold initiatives." This is not surprising. The Treasury's program is the type of activism often praised by those who are more concerned about the need to do something than about what is done. To see what is being done, we must look below the surface.

Mr. Baker's Treasury seeks to lower the U.S. standard of living. Of course, he does not announce that intention. Governments never do. But that is what he is after, and that is what he will achieve if he is successful for a time in his efforts to lower the dollar and raise the U.S. price level without, at the same time, raising the wage level.

The September agreement with the finance ministers and central bankers of other lending countries is, so far, a monetary agreement. The U.S. works to push its interest rates down relative to other countries. Lower interest rates reduce foreign investment in the U.S., reduce foreigners' demand for dollars and make the dollar cheaper for foreigners. A cheaper dollar raises the cost of foreign goods imported into the U.S., the cost of foreign travel by Americans and lowers the cost of U.S. products purchased by foreigners.

A Return to Phillips Curve

Higher prices for foreign goods reduce the real purchasing power of American consumers but increase jobs for those who produce exports. These are the initial effects. They do not last. When people find that, at higher prices, their incomes buy less, they will demand higher wages. As wages rise, so does the cost of exports, and the initial stimulus to exports vanishes. Abroad, prices and wages are reduced, removing the cost disadvantage that follows the appreciation of foreign currencies. The lasting effect is a lower after-tax real return to capital in the U.S. resulting from the failure to index depreciation expense.

All this may sound familiar—a repeat of the Phillips-curve games of the 1970s—and it is just that, a return to policies that traded short-term benefits for persistent, longer-term costs. Then, we talked about boosting employment by pushing prices higher. The policy worked only as long as wages did not rise as fast as prices. Now, we talk about increasing exports and reducing imports by pushing down the dollar.

This, too, works only as long as wages rise more slowly than the prices that consumers pay.

Some praise the policy but do not expect prices to rise. They expect foreigners to fight for market share by reducing their profits instead of raising prices. Their praise is misplaced. If their predictions prove correct, Mr. Baker's policy will fail. For the policy can only achieve its short-term increase in net exports by reducing standards of living to lower the cost of exports and by raising import prices to lower the demand for imports.

The public has, perhaps, been lulled into believing that the only choice is between different methods of reducing living standards: the protectionist policies advocated by many in Congress or Mr. Baker's policy of forcing the dollar down. The alternative to cutting our standard of living is to increase productivity. This cannot be achieved instantly, but it is within our ability if we are wise.

The government's greatest contribution to higher productivity would be a program to stimulate investment through the marketplace by shifting resources from consumption. To achieve this shift requires two bold moves. First is a reduction in

> *One solution to our trade problem raises productivity and rewards our efforts with higher incomes. The other lowers our standards of living until we are able to compete.*

government spending; since government spending is mainly for consumption, lower government spending would free resources for investment. Second is a policy that increases incentives for investment. In place of the tax bill produced in the House and supported by Mr. Baker that disregards the effect of taxation on our international competitive position, I propose the reduction, and gradual elimination, of the corporate income tax. This tax falls most heavily on investment and capital in place. Eliminating it would encourage firms to invest more by raising their after-tax returns. Higher rates of investment would raise capital per employed worker. With more and better quality of capital, produc-

tivity rises. Higher productivity would permit U.S. producers to export more, to compete more effectively at current, or even higher, wages and standards of living.

The initial effects of lower corporate taxes and reduced government spending would be a stronger dollar. Capital would flow in to earn the higher after-tax returns on investment. But with government spending reduced, investment would rise. Increased productive investment would later provide the income to service the foreign debt and pay higher wages to the, then, more productive workers.

There are two types of solution to our trade problem. One encourages us to compete by raising productivity and rewards our efforts with higher incomes and standards of living. The other lowers our standards of living until we are able to compete. Mr. Baker believes, mistakenly, that the budget deficit is the main cause of the trade deficit and current interest rates. He sees no way to reduce the trade deficit other than by debasing the currency. Most of us will learn to regret his decision.

Mr. Baker's second major initiative, announced to an indebted world in November, is to increase our lending to Latin America. This proposal deserves scrutiny also. The U.S. is currently the world's largest borrower. How is it able to lend to the world's largest debtors?

Of course, the U.S. cannot lend. It can only relend what it has borrowed from others. Mr. Baker's proposal is for U.S. bankers and the government in one way or another to act as intermediaries, borrowing on the strength of their own less risky balance sheets and relending to the more risky countries to the south. And, the Treasury hints, there may be direct loans from the government in addition to the loans that the Treasury squeezes out of the reluctant bankers.

These are the first steps. What follows? The Latin Americans must either export more to us and others to service their increased debt, or the banks—the World Bank, the government, someone—must lend even more later to service the larger debt and to renew the promise that Mr. Baker now holds out. To export more, the Latin Americans must produce more at lower cost, and, contrary to our policy of reducing imports, we must import more.

Much-Needed Steps

Mr. Baker thinks this can be accomplished by strengthening the private sector in Latin America, and by reducing bureau-

Reprinted by permission of Allan H. Meltzer, Olin Professor of Political Economy and Public Policy, Carnegie-Mellon University.

cratic restrictions. Anyone with experience in Latin America will recognize these are desirable and much-needed steps. They do not require more dollars as much as they require decisions by the governments involved to shift from policies that redistribute income to policies that increase productivity and income. Latin American governments have not welcomed these opportunities in the past, even in recent years when the alternative was to lower their standards of living decisively.

The likely outcome of Mr. Baker's proposal is that experienced Latin Americans will relend many of the dollars in the U.S., or in other safe havens, until they see evidence that permanent reforms have been made. Such skepticism is warranted. The debtor countries are not likely to boost net exports permanently to a level that will service their increased debt. The U.S. banks and government will face a choice of either taking the loss or lending more.

Despite the lavish praise of IMF adjustment programs, more than three years of experience with those programs has brought us no closer to a resolution of the debt problem. Mr. Baker's proposal is not likely to do better. Like its predecessor, it will waste our resources.

Mr. Baker's second initiative, like his first, will leave us poorer.

Mr. Meltzer is Olin professor of political economy and public policy at Carnegie-Mellon University.

71

International Trade and Investment

America's trade problems have reached crisis proportions. The decline of the U.S. international economic position has caused untold hardship for millions of American workers and scores of communities and threatens the economic health and security of our nation. Despite some improvement in the domestic economy from the depths of the 1982 recession, U.S. trade deficits have continued to increase dramatically, setting new records each year.

While other nations are maintaining or increasing their barriers to imports, subsidizing their exports, and directing investment flows to benefit their own economies, the Reagan Administration clings to a belief in "free trade" and mythical market forces. At a time when positive governmental action is desperately needed to reverse the erosion of America's industrial base, this rejection of reality has had disastrous consequences for the U.S. economy.

In 1984, the United States merchandise trade deficit reached a record $123 billion, more than 75 percent greater than the previous high of $69 billion set in 1983. The deficit for 1985 is projected to exceed $138 billion.

For manufactured goods alone, the U.S. deficit increased from $38 billion in 1983 to $89 billion in 1984 and will grow to over $105 billion this year. All manufacturing categories contributed to this sharp deterioration in trade with major declines seen in telecommunications and electronic equipment, industrial machinery, transport equipment, clothing and footwear.

Manufacturing employment, while somewhat improved from the 1982 recession, remains at a level far below what existed when President Reagan took office. The first six months of 1985 saw a further reduction of 220,000 jobs in this most important sector. Overall, it is estimated that more than 3 million jobs have been lost or not created due to America's continuing trade decline.

The Reagan Administration's response to this tragedy can best be described as studied indifference; it centers more on what the U.S. government should not do than what it is able to do. The Administration's continued emphasis on free trade and market forces has served basically to disguise its unwillingness to take action in support of American industry and American workers. The United States is virtually alone in its belief in open markets and free competition. Other countries see trade as a means to achieve their own domestic economic development and employment of their people. Practices such as quotas, stringent inspection requirements, discriminatory standards, buy national policies, export subsidies, industrial targeting programs, coproduction requirements, are practically universal. Continued attempts by the United States to reduce the use of these measures have not been successful and our own market has remained open to an increasing volume of imports.

This trade policy framework, together with the ill-conceived monetary and fiscal policies of the Administration, has contributed significantly to the massive trade deficits the United States faces today.

The fiscal policies of the Administration created huge budget deficits which together with the tight money, high interest rate policies of the Federal Reserve Board have contributed to the massive increase in the dollar's exchange value. During the last two years, the dollar has risen in value more than 30 percent against the currencies of other industrial countries. This appreciation is no different than a 30 percent tax on exports and a 30 percent cost advantage for imports. It comes on top of an appreciation of equal magnitude in the previous three-year period. These same policies have encouraged massive capital inflows to the United States from other countries and have to some degree slowed those countries' economic growth and their ability to buy U.S. goods. In ad-

Reprinted by permission of Murray Seeger, AFL-CIO
Department of Information, Washington, D.C.

dition, high interest rates in the United States have significantly increased the cost of debt service in a number of developing countries, further reducing their ability to purchase U.S. goods and increasing their need to acquire dollars through exports to the United States. The Administration policies which helped create this situation remain unchanged.

Existing trade statutes that are supposed to provide remedies for injury and "unfair trade practices" have not worked. The "escape clause" (Section 201 of the Trade Act of 1974) was supposed to provide a safety valve for those industries threatened with or experiencing serious injury from imports. During its 20-year existence, the escape clause has failed to fulfill its promise to injured industries and workers.

Of the 55 cases filed since the Trade Act of 1974 became law, only 12 have resulted in any relief. Even in these cases the relief has never been enough to allow the injured industry to fully recover from the import assault. During the last two years import-impacted industries such as steel, copper, and shoes have all been denied relief under the escape clause.

For unfair trade practices similar problems exist. Practices such as dumping, subsidies, and disruptive imports from non-market economies have cost thousands of jobs. Existing relief mechanisms have been ineffective as filing procedures are costly and complicated, the required documentation too extensive, and the burden of proof falls entirely on the injured party. In addition, many injurious practices developed in recent years such as natural resource subsidies are not even covered under current law.

Efforts to improve trade law and policy during the past two years were, with few exceptions, unsuccessful. The Reagan Administration's policy objectives centered largely on further trade liberalization and increasing the openness of the U.S. market to imported products.

The 98th Congress, just prior to adjournment, enacted legislation known as the Trade and Tariff Act of 1984 that included a number of measures sought by the Administration.

The Generalized System of Preferences (GSP), a program that provides duty-free access for a wide range of products from some 130 developing nations was extended for 8.5 years. Originally adopted as part of the Trade Act of 1974, GSP was designed as a "temporary, unilateral, non-reciprocal system of tariff preferences." Import-sensitive articles were not to be granted duty free-status. Nevertheless, the extension continues eligibility for products competing with import-injured U.S. industries, including electronic equipment, auto parts, and metal products. Newly industrialized nations which no longer need preferential treatment, as well as some communist countries, are still included in the program. Congress did, however, direct the President to exclude countries from GSP that were not taking steps to afford internationally recognized labor rights to workers in those countries. Based on this provision, the AFL-CIO and affiliated unions requested the removal of a number of countries from the GSP. The Administration has yet to act.

The 1984 Act authorized the President to negotiate and enter into a bilateral "free trade" agreement with Israel. The agreement was concluded and implemented this year. Following consultation and agreement by the appropriate congressional committees, "free trade" agreements with other countries may be negotiated.

This legislation also allowed the President to eliminate tariffs on a variety of semiconductor and related products. Despite the continued deterioration of the U.S. trade position in this sector and growing offshore production, tariffs were eliminated in 1985.

In addition, the 1984 Act made changes in the anti-dumping and countervailing duty statutes, included provisions designed to encourage the elimination of foreign barriers to U.S. wine exports, and mandated annual reports on foreign trade practices that impede U.S. exports. Of perhaps greater significance, the Act, for the first time, gives the President specific negotiating authority regarding international trade in services and barriers to direct U.S. foreign investment.

Finally, the 1984 Act provided authority to the President to negotiate bilateral voluntary restraint agreements on steel. Over the last two years, the American steel industry has been besieged by unfairly priced and subsidized imports, with market penetration exceeding 26 percent in 1984. In his announcement denying Section 201 import relief in September 1984, the President directed the negotiation of agreements that would reduce imports (excluding semi-finished steel) to 18.5 percent of the domestic market, a level determined to be normal if steel was traded fairly. The Congress, in providing the necessary authority, made the restraints contingent upon the steel companies reinvesting their earnings. While agreements have been reached with a majority of steel-producing countries, imports continue to take 25 percent of the domestic market.

In other trade policy developments, the Voluntary Restraint Agreement (VRA) with Japan on autos, restricting imports to 1.68 million units a year, expired in 1984. The agreement was extended for one year with import levels increased to 1.85 million units. In March of this year, despite a U.S. trade deficit of more than $37 billion with Japan, of which $20 billion was motor vehicles alone, the Reagan Administration announced that it would not seek any further extension of the VRA. With this decision, the United States became the only major auto producing nation with no limits on imports of Japanese cars and trucks. The Japanese government subsequently announced it would administratively limit exports to 2.3 million units in 1985, an increase of almost 25 percent over 1984. This surge will create increased unemployment in the auto industry and accelerate plans of domestic producers to produce offshore.

The bilateral telecommunications agreement with Japan that theoretically guaranteed access to the Japanese market for U.S. exports expired in 1984. Despite insignificant sales to Japan by U.S. producers and a rapidly declining trade balance in this sector, the Reagan Administration extended the agreement.

For textile and apparel trade, the last two years showed unprecedented surges in imports and harm to the domestic industry. Despite the existence of the Multi-Fiber Arrangement (MFA) which contemplated a 6 percent annual growth rate for imports, imports grew 25 percent in 1983 and 32 percent in 1984. Import penetration reached 42 percent last year. Legislation is before Congress to require the effective enforcement of the MFA thereby limiting the disruptive impact of imports on the domestic economy. The Reagan Administration is currently opposed to this crucial legislation.

Trade in services is also an area of rapidly growing significance to the U.S. economy. The problems encountered by specific service industries in international trade are quite diverse. Banking, insurance, broadcasting, health care, shipping, construction, entertainment, air transport and many other industries have little in common except that they all provide ''service,'' and questions of definition, foreign practices, and the domestic employment impact of trade in services must be resolved. Further, what some view as barriers to trade in services, are in fact proper and even essential social and economic policies of the United States and foreign countries.

Unfortunately, the Reagan Administration's major trade policy initiative, a new round of multilateral trade negotiations, continues to have liberalizing trade in services as a major goal. Negotiations alone are incapable of solving America's trade problems in either services or goods.

Despite the fact that only a small portion of the volume of shipping is generated by U.S.-owned flagships, the Reagan Administration has resisted positive action and has even failed to properly enforce provisions of the Cargo Preference Act and the Jones Act, further weakening the nation's maritime industry.

Trade Adjustment Assistance has been targeted for extinction by the Reagan Administration, further harming workers unemployed because of imports. The current program provides some benefits for training, job search, or relocation assistance, though at an inadequate level.

International trade is strongly affected by international investment flows. While the United States continues to have larger holdings in plant and equipment overseas than foreign interests have in America, other forms of capital, attracted by relatively high interest rates, have been flooding into this country. The United States became a debtor nation in 1985. Unlike most other countries, the United States does not adequately regulate and monitor these flows.

The Reagan Administration has encouraged direct U.S. investment abroad by negotiating a number of bilateral investment treaties that provide greater protection for U.S. firms overseas; supporting the extension of OPIC, the government agency that insures U.S. corporations abroad; and participating in discussions to establish a Multilateral Investment Guarantee Agency that would internationalize insurance for private investment.

The federation, in an effort to address labor relations problems relating to direct foreign investment in the United States, has brought charges against Kawasaki, BASF and Norsk-Hydro under the Guidelines for Multinational Enterprises of the Organization for Economic Cooperation and Development at both the national and international levels.

To address the problems of international trade and investment, AFL-CIO President Lane Kirkland has testified before Congress and the International Trade Commission and met with officials of private groups as well as with U.S. and foreign government representatives. AFL-CIO Vice President John Lyons has served as chairman of the Labor Advisory Committee on Trade Negotiations whose membership consists of union officers and staff.

* * *

Excerpt from The National Economy and Trade, the Report of the Executive Council of the AFL-CIO to the Sixteenth Convention, Anaheim, California, October 1985.

Foreign Trade and the U.S. Economy: Dispelling the Myths

by Murray L. Weidenbaum

Every day we read and hear about companies and their employees who are so hard hit by the flood of imports. What is the evidence? The truth is far less dramatic than the overblown charges. Let me cite six key examples.

The Myths

Myth #1. Japan is the problem. If only they opened their markets to our products . . . It is surely true that Japan maintains an intricate variety of obstacles to imports that compete with its own products and that its government reduces those obstacles only in response to our constant pressure. Furthermore, our trade deficit with Japan—$33 billion in 1984—is far greater than our trade deficit with any other country. Yet, even if Japan did no foreign trade at all, the United States would still be experiencing a historically high excess of imports over exports. Without Japan, our total current account or trade deficit in 1984 would have been $69 billion—$11 billion more than the previous year's record breaker.

Meanwhile, our traditional export surplus with Western Europe has turned into a trade deficit, standing at $13 billion in 1984. Our trade accounts with Canada and Mexico are likewise in the red—$20 billion and $6 billion respectively last year. In fact, the United States has a trade deficit with almost every nation in the non-communist world. Hence, it is silly to say in effect that everyone is out of step except us. We in the United States must be doing something basically wrong.

Myth #2. The United States is an island of free trade in a world of protectionism. It would help to clear the air if we would acknowledge that not all of our actions are angelic. We have created many obstacles to inhibit imports into the United States. "Buy Amer-

Murray L. Weidenbaum, former chairman of the president's Council of Economic Advisers, is director of the Center for the Study of American Business at Washington University of St. Louis. This article is based on remarks delivered at a Cato Institute Policy Forum in December.

Reprinted with permission of Murray L. Weidenbaum and Cato Policy Report, January/February, 1986.

ican statutes give preference to domestic producers in government procurement. American flag vessels must be used to ship at least one-half of all the commodities financed with U.S. foreign aid. Agricultural laws limit imports of sugar, beef, dairy products, and mandarin oranges.

Despite all the talk about being the only country that practices free trade, only 30 percent of our imports are now allowed in without paying a tariff—down from 54 percent in 1950. Numerous non-tariff barriers are imposed by federal, state, county, and

> **"Protectionism is a politician's delight because it delivers visible benefits to the protected parties while imposing the costs as a hidden tax on the public."**

municipal governments. For example, local construction codes are a popular device to keep out foreign-produced building supplies.

Myth #3. Imports are dragging down the American economy, depressing employment especially in manufacturing. In reality, the rapid rise in employment in the United States in recent years is the envy of the rest of the world. Total U.S. civilian employment has increased from 98.8 million in 1978 to 107.2 million today. That 8.4 million rise far exceeds the increase in Japan and Western Europe combined.

Then again, we hear so much about the decline in U.S. manufacturing. But I'll let you in on a well-kept secret. Industrial production reached an all-time peak in 1984, when the Federal Reserve's index averaged 122. 1985 is on a high plateau, averaging 124 since

January. Moreover, manufacturing's share of the real gross domestic product has held steady for the last 30 years—at about 25 percent. Indeed, services have loomed larger than goods production in the United States at least since 1929, which is as far back as the national income accounts go.

In addition, the total number of manufacturing jobs has fluctuated in the vicinity of 19 million since 1970. This is not booming growth, but it is certainly a far cry from the supposed decline and fall of U.S. manufacturing that we hear so much about. My colleague at the Center for the Study of American Business, Richard McKenzie, is doing research that shows that the total employment of production workers in the United States is continuing to rise. The fastest growing opportunities for production workers are occurring in the service industry. Manufacturers are performing fewer activities in-house and are contracting out more to suppliers, many of whom are classified as part of the service sector. The total employment of production workers rose from 47 million in 1975 to 62 million in July 1985.

The Myth of Protecting Jobs

Myth #5. Protection is the way to save jobs. Wrong again. Protectionist actions increase the cost of producing goods and services in the United States, reducing the competitiveness of American products. A recent study by Arthur Denzau at the Center for the Study of American Business shows that if the United States had imposed a 15 percent import quota on steel in 1984, as the steel industry sought, 26,000 steelworker jobs could have been saved—but at the cost of 93,000 jobs in the steel-using industries. Higher prices for protected domestic steel would have made American automobile and durable-goods producers less competitive.

Protectionism is the most inefficient welfare program ever designed. A government spending program in which the benefits delivered to recipients amounted to only 50 or 60 percent of the costs would be criticized as shamefully wasteful. But in the case of protectionism, the typical increase in prices paid by American consumers far exceeds the total wages of the jobs that are "saved." In the case of footwear quotas, the ratio of costs to benefits was 9 to 1; in the case of steel and autos, 4 to 1. Protectionism is a politician's delight because it delivers visible benefits to the protected parties while imposing the costs as a hidden tax on the public.

Myth #6. Workers in import-affected industries deserve to be treated more generously than other employees. I know of no reason why workers in industries facing serious international competition should be viewed as more meritorious than, say, defense workers who lose their jobs when government contracts are completed or cancelled. After all, the line of causation from the government's budget deficits to the high-priced dollar to rising imports to reduced employment is far more indirect than the link between a government decision to close a military facility and the resultant economic hardship.

Recommendations

The most effective way of dealing with the rising tide of imports is not to try to dam up foreign trade. It is to increase the competitiveness of American industry. I would like to suggest five positive approaches to foreign trade policy that would help American business compete.

1. Reduce the budget deficit. Although the linkages are complex and indirect, financing a string of $200 billion deficits has raised real interest rates substantially, and that, in turn, has attracted large amounts of foreign capital. The substantial inflow of foreign money has increased the demand for dollars and has resulted in a major appreciation of the dollar. The high relative value of the dollar has made it easier for foreign companies to compete against American companies.

2. Gear tax reform to enhance productivity and competitiveness. Most tax reform proposals to date ignore the repercussions on international trade.

"Protectionist actions increase the cost of producing goods and services in the United States, reducing the competitiveness of American products."

The industries hardest hit by imports are those whose tax burdens would rise the most under the various tax proposals submitted by Messrs. Bradley, Gephardt, Kemp, Kasten, Regan, Reagan and Rostenkowski.

This is not the time to elevate the development of an ideal tax system to the top of the roster of public issues. Tax policy must continue emphasizing incentives for the items important to enhancing our international competitiveness: saving, investment, and research and development.

3. Renew the regulatory reform effort. The costs of producing goods and services in the United States can be decreased by launching another effort to reduce government regulation of business. Studies of U.S. and Western European regulation show that we impose much higher economic costs in achieving similar social benefits. Closer attention to the tremendous burdens imposed by EPA, OSHA, and other regulatory agencies would help restore industrial competitiveness.

4. Reduce U.S. barriers to U.S. exports. About one-half of our trade deficit with Japan could be eliminated if

Congress rescinded the bans on the export of timber and oil. Also, restraints on the export of strategic goods should be administered with common sense. It does not contribute to national security to prevent American companies from selling items overseas that are readily available from foreign competitors.

5. American business and labor must face the challenge of increasing their productivity. We cannot blame our poor production practices on foreigners. The answer is not to prop up industries with import restrictions or government subsidies or to try to prevent businesses by law from closing or "running away." Labor and management in each company need to face the challenge of enhancing their competitive-

---

"Protectionism is the most inefficient welfare program ever designed."

---

ness. Protectionism is counterproductive because it lessens the pressure on management and labor to lower costs and improve quality. The painful fact is that foreign competition is a most effective spur to greater productivity.

Fundamentally, free trade is a consumer issue because the consumer bears the burden of protectionism. Why are consumer organizations mute on the subject of protectionism?

I'll conclude by quoting my favorite advocate of free trade, Lee Iacocca. In defending new joint-production arrangements with foreign companies, Iacocca bluntly observes: "If you don't go to the lowest-cost source, you're an idiot." But supposedly that is true only for business. When consumers follow Lee's advice, they are attacked for being unpatriotic.   ∎

Chart 1

GROSS NATIONAL PRODUCT

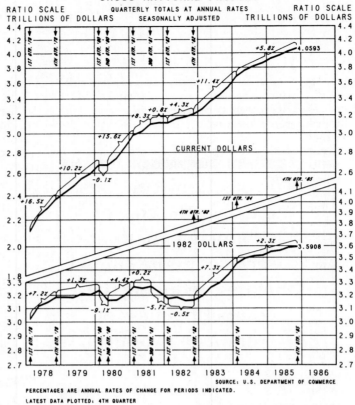

RATIO SCALE QUARTERLY TOTALS AT ANNUAL RATES RATIO SCALE
TRILLIONS OF DOLLARS SEASONALLY ADJUSTED TRILLIONS OF DOLLARS

CURRENT DOLLARS

1982 DOLLARS

SOURCE: U.S. DEPARTMENT OF COMMERCE

PERCENTAGES ARE ANNUAL RATES OF CHANGE FOR PERIODS INDICATED.

LATEST DATA PLOTTED: 4TH QUARTER

PREPARED BY FEDERAL RESERVE BANK OF ST. LOUIS

Chart 2

PRODUCTIVITY, COMPENSATION, AND LABOR COSTS

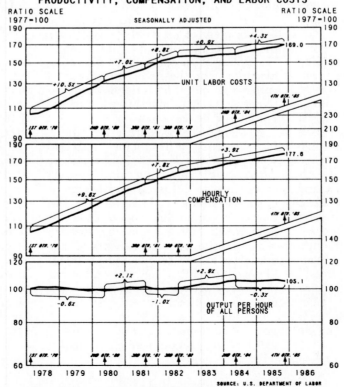

RATIO SCALE SEASONALLY ADJUSTED RATIO SCALE
1977=100 1977=100

UNIT LABOR COSTS

HOURLY COMPENSATION

OUTPUT PER HOUR OF ALL PERSONS

SOURCE: U.S. DEPARTMENT OF LABOR

PERCENTAGES ARE ANNUAL RATES OF CHANGE FOR PERIODS INDICATED.

LATEST DATA PLOTTED: 4TH QUARTER PRELIMINARY

PREPARED BY FEDERAL RESERVE BANK OF ST. LOUIS

Chart 3

EMPLOYMENT

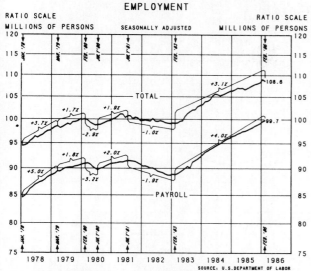

RATIO SCALE
MILLIONS OF PERSONS   SEASONALLY ADJUSTED   RATIO SCALE
MILLIONS OF PERSONS

TOTAL

+3.1%   108.6

PAYROLL

99.7

1978 1979 1980 1981 1982 1983 1984 1985 1986

SOURCE: U.S. DEPARTMENT OF LABOR

BEGINNING JANUARY 1986, TOTAL EMPLOYMENT DATA INCORPORATE NEW PROCEDURES FOR ESTIMATING
MEASURES OF IMMIGRATION AND EMIGRATION INCREASING TOTAL EMPLOYMENT BY ABOUT 0.3%.

PERCENTAGES ARE ANNUAL RATES OF CHANGE FOR PERIODS INDICATED.

LATEST DATA PLOTTED: FEBRUARY PRELIMINARY

PREPARED BY FEDERAL RESERVE BANK OF ST. LOUIS

Chart 4

UNEMPLOYMENT RATE

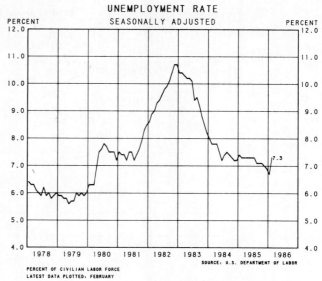

PERCENT   SEASONALLY ADJUSTED   PERCENT

7.3

1978 1979 1980 1981 1982 1983 1984 1985 1986

SOURCE: U.S. DEPARTMENT OF LABOR

PERCENT OF CIVILIAN LABOR FORCE
LATEST DATA PLOTTED: FEBRUARY

PREPARED BY FEDERAL RESERVE BANK OF ST. LOUIS

Chart 5

PRICES

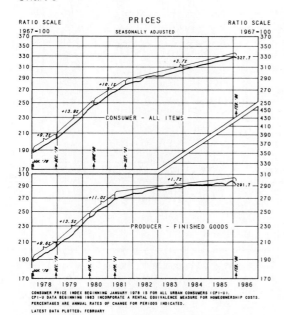

RATIO SCALE
1967=100   SEASONALLY ADJUSTED   RATIO SCALE
1967=100

+3.7%   327.7

CONSUMER - ALL ITEMS

+1.7%   291.7

PRODUCER - FINISHED GOODS

1978 1979 1980 1981 1982 1983 1984 1985 1986

CONSUMER PRICE INDEX BEGINNING JANUARY 1978 IS FOR ALL URBAN CONSUMERS (CPI-U).
CPI-U DATA BEGINNING 1983 INCORPORATE A RENTAL EQUIVALENCE MEASURE FOR HOMEOWNERSHIP COSTS.
PERCENTAGES ARE ANNUAL RATES OF CHANGE FOR PERIODS INDICATED.

LATEST DATA PLOTTED: FEBRUARY

PREPARED BY FEDERAL RESERVE BANK OF ST. LOUIS

Chart 6

Inflation (growth rate of the GNP deflator)

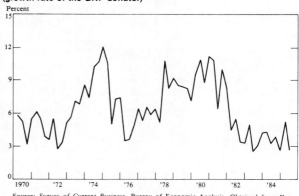

Percent

1970 '72 '74 '76 '78 '80 '82 '84

Source: *Survey of Current Business*, Bureau of Economic Analysis. Obtained from Data
Resources, Inc.

Prepared by Federal Reserve Bank of Kansas City

Chart 7

Composition of Total Budget Outlays
Percent of GNP

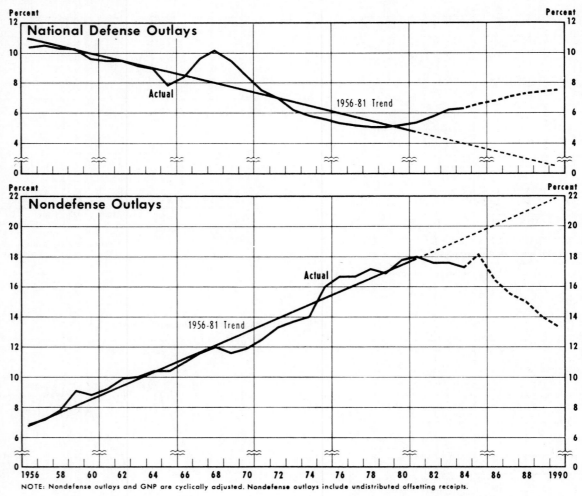

National Defense Outlays

Actual

1956-81 Trend

Nondefense Outlays

Actual

1956-81 Trend

1956 58 60 62 64 66 68 70 72 74 76 78 80 82 84 86 88 1990

NOTE: Nondefense outlays and GNP are cyclically adjusted. Nondefense outlays include undistributed offsetting receipts.

Prepared by Federal Reserve Bank of St. Louis

Chart 8

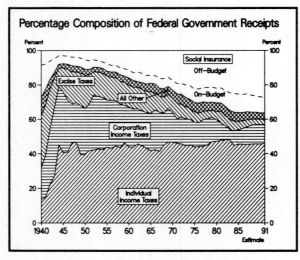

Percentage Composition of Federal Government Receipts

Social Insurance

Off—Budget

Excise Taxes

All Other

On—Budget

Corporation Income Taxes

Individual Income Taxes

1940 45 50 55 60 65 70 75 80 85 91
Estimate

Prepared by the Office of Management and Budget

Chart 9

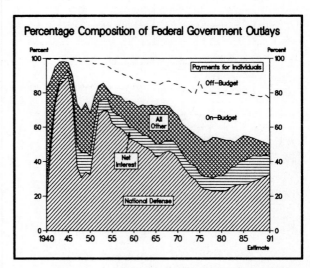

Percentage Composition of Federal Government Outlays

Payments for Individuals

Off—Budget

On—Budget

All Other

Net Interest

National Defense

1940 45 50 55 60 65 70 75 80 85 91
Estimate

Prepared by the Office of Management and Budget

Chart 10   M₁ Target Ranges

Billions of dollars

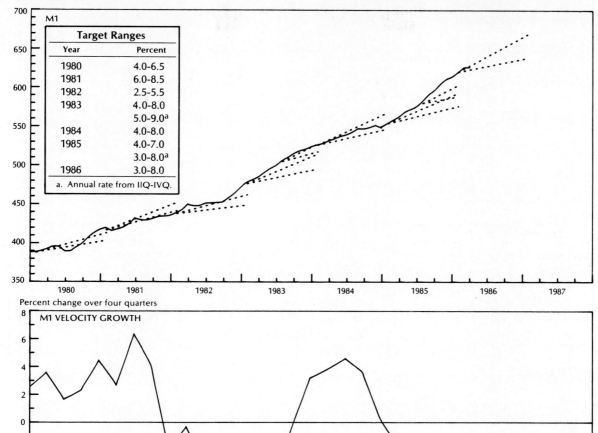

Target Ranges	
Year	**Percent**
1980	4.0-6.5
1981	6.0-8.5
1982	2.5-5.5
1983	4.0-8.0
	5.0-9.0ᵃ
1984	4.0-8.0
1985	4.0-7.0
	3.0-8.0ᵃ
1986	3.0-8.0
a. Annual rate from IIQ-IVQ.	

Percent change over four quarters

M1 VELOCITY GROWTH

NOTE: Dotted lines represent long-run target ranges.
SOURCES: Board of Governors of the Federal Reserve System; and U.S. Department of Commerce.

Prepared by Federal Reserve Bank of Cleveland

Chart 11

MONEY MARKET RATES

MONTHLY AVERAGES OF DAILY FIGURES

FEDERAL FUNDS

3-MONTH TREASURY BILL

7.48

6.56

LATEST DATA PLOTTED: MARCH

PREPARED BY FEDERAL RESERVE BANK OF ST.LOUIS

Chart 12

Real interest rate

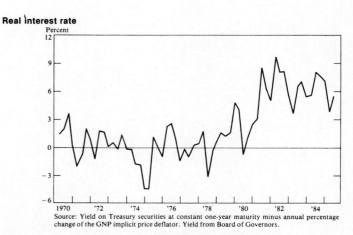

Source: Yield on Treasury securities at constant one-year maturity minus annual percentage change of the GNP implicit price deflator. Yield from Board of Governors.

Prepared by Federal Reserve Bank of Kansas City

247

Chart 13   Federal Borrowing and Private Savings

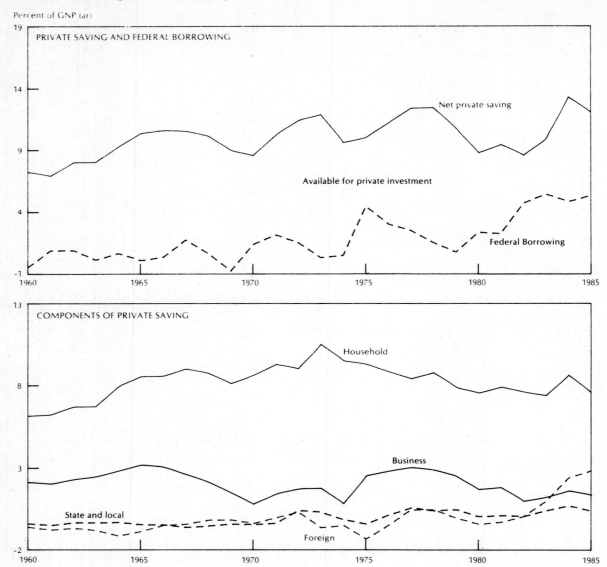

Percent of GNP (ar)

PRIVATE SAVING AND FEDERAL BORROWING

Net private saving

Available for private investment

Federal Borrowing

COMPONENTS OF PRIVATE SAVING

Household

Business

State and local

Foreign

NOTE: Private saving includes state and local government surpluses.
SOURCE: Board of Governors of the Federal Reserve System.

Prepared by Federal Reserve Bank of Cleveland